# India's Water Futures



When it comes to water, we flush and forget. We use, abuse and almost never recycle.

The water sector in India, since the 1990s, has seen some new ideas formalized legally and institutionally, while others are still emerging and evolving. Confronting the reality of current water management strategies, this volume discusses the state of the Indian water sector to uncover solutions that can address the imminent water crises.

This book:

- analyses the growing water insecurity, increase in demand, inefficiency in water use and growing inequalities in accessing clean water;
- sheds light on water footprint in agricultural, industrial and urban use, pressures on river basin management, depleting groundwater resources, patterns of droughts and floods, watershed-based development and wastewater and sanitation management;
- examines water conflicts, lack of participatory governance mechanisms and suggests an alternative framework for water regulation and conflict transformation;
- highlights the relationship between gender discourse and water governance;
- presents an alternative agenda for water sector reforms.

This volume, with hopes for a more water secure future, will interest scholars and researchers of development studies, environment studies, public policy, political studies, political sociology, and, NGOs, media and think tanks working in this area.

**K. J. Joy** is Senior Fellow with Society for Promoting Participative Ecosystem Management (SOPPECOM), Pune, India, and is the Convener of Forum for Policy Dialogue on Water Conflicts in India.

**S. Janakarajan** is a professorial consultant at Madras Institute of Development Studies, Chennai, India and is the President of South Asia Consortium for Interdisciplinary Water Resources Studies, Hyderabad, India.

"While the escalating demand for water to fuel industrial growth and urbanisation puts a question mark on the future of the water sector in India, this volume, covering a wide range of issues from science to policies, law, governance, and institutions, presents emergent thinking, ideas and pathways for a paradigm shift that offers hope for sustainable development."

—***Brij Gopal, Founder-Coordinator***, *Centre for Inland Waters in South Asia, Khajuraho and Jaipur, India*

"Ramaswamy Iyer was a distinguished civil servant who, after the mid-1980s, emerged as one of India's leading thinkers, scholars and informed commentators on the country's water resources and their efficient, equitable and sustainable use. For almost three decades, his writings had a profound influence on the public discourse on water issues. This volume, by a number of water experts, is a fine and enduring tribute to his intellectual contributions."

—***Jairam Ramesh***, *Member of Parliament and former Union Minister, Government of India*

"The contribution of Ramaswamy R. Iyer in promoting new and necessary ideas on water management in India is immense. This book, published in his honour, is a suitable tribute to that contribution. It is a record of the task ahead for attaining equity and environmental security in water governance in India."

—***Jayanta Bandyopadhyay***, *Distinguished Fellow, Observer Research Foundation, India*

"This volume is unprecedented in its sweep and depth. It addresses the entire gamut of water-related issues in India and examines each very deeply. And this is accomplished without losing sight of the interlinkages between different aspects of the water crisis that India faces. Expectedly then, governance by antiquated institutions emerges as the most significant roadblock in moving towards viable and necessary solutions. Though it introduces an optimistic note by claiming that the direction of change in water policy has survived changing governments, the tasks ahead seem daunting nevertheless. My felicitations to the editors and authors for putting together a volume that is sure to become a 'must-read' for researchers and policy-makers alike, much as Ramaswamy Iyer would have wanted it to."

—***Kanchan Chopra***, *Former Director and Professor, Institute of Economic Growth, New Delhi, India; and Co-Editor, Ecology, Economy and Society, the Journal of INSEE*

"Changing the way we think about water was Ramaswamy Iyer's project. This volume pays tribute to that endeavour and elaborates it, on the premise that discourse and practice co-evolve. The book is an important document in that it consolidates for a wider audience the thinking that went into water resources policy reform through the preparation of the 12th Plan. The book can be read as a manifesto for necessary structural change; it is a searchlight in an era of mostly depressing news on the state of India's water resources."

***—Peter Mollinga,*** *Professor, SOAS University of London, UK*

"Ramaswamy Iyer was a mentor to Arghyam from its initial days. His work and contribution to the water sector inspire nothing short of a societal transformation with regard to this key resource. I hope this book will add to a vigorous discourse."

***—Rohini Nilekani****, Chairperson, Arghyam*

# India's Water Futures

## Emergent Ideas and Pathways

**Edited by K. J. Joy and S. Janakarajan**

Routledge
Taylor & Francis Group
LONDON AND NEW YORK

First published 2019
by Routledge
2 Park Square, Milton Park, Abingdon, Oxon OX14 4RN

and by Routledge
605 Third Avenue, New York, NY 10017

First issued in paperback 2020

*Routledge is an imprint of the Taylor & Francis Group, an informa business*



*British Library Cataloguing-in-Publication Data*
A catalogue record for this book is available from the British Library

*Library of Congress Cataloging-in-Publication Data*
A catalog record has been requested for this book

ISBN 13: 978-0-367-73276-9 (pbk)
ISBN 13: 978-0-8153-8404-5 (hbk)

Typeset in Sabon
by Apex CoVantage, LLC

## Essays in Honour of Ramaswamy R. Iyer

Ramaswamy R. Iyer: 1929–2015

Photo credit: Sohail Akbar

The ideas, viewpoints and approaches that Prof. Ramaswamy R. Iyer – an eminent scholar, activist and policy-maker and former Secretary of Water Resources, Government of India – propounded for about 30 years or so, ever since he, as the Secretary of Water Resources, drafted the first National Water Policy (NWP) in 1987, could form the core of the alternative paradigm for water. This volume, though it could not come out when Prof. Iyer was alive, is a humble attempt to keep alive his legacy as well as an attempt to take it forward.

# Contents

# Figures

# Tables

# Foreword

## Water crisis is ours to change

*Sunita Narain*

In the summer of 2018, the Himalayan town of Shimla literally ran out of water. But this is not the only town to have been confronted with this crisis. According to the 2018 Composite Water Index of the Niti Aayog, 600 million people – roughly half of Indians – face high to extreme water crisis; worse, 70 per cent of the available water is contaminated. And by 2020, Delhi, Bengaluru, Chennai and Hyderabad will run out of groundwater, and, by 2030, as much as 40 per cent of India will have no drinking water.

But this is one future we can change. Water is a replenishable resource – it snows and rains each year. More importantly, other than in the case of agriculture, we don't consume water. We use and discharge. Therefore, it can be treated and then reused and recycled. The agenda is also clear. First, to augment available water by capturing every drop and doing this everywhere. In a climate-risked India, when rainfall is extreme and variable, it means doing more to capture rain and to recharge groundwater. The second and most important agenda is to combine water augmentation with efficiency. Each drop must bring more crop and more of everything. This means designing deliberately to reduce water usage. In agriculture, it means changing cropping patterns so that we stop growing water guzzling crops like rice, wheat and sugarcane in areas where water is scarce. It means redesigning policies to incentivize farmers to diversify crops; promoting diets that value water-prudent crops.

If water efficiency is the agenda for agriculture, then water-recycling has to be the agenda for cities and industries. Remember, we have no data on how much water is used today in urban and industrial India.

The last estimation was done in the mid-1990s, which had reported that agriculture uses some 75–80 per cent of the available water. This is completely out of date. As cities grow, they will require water. Increasingly, this water will have to be brought from farther locations, which would increase cost and losses in transmission. Whatever water cities have is therefore expensive and is supplied inequitably to residents. Where people get little or no water, they dig into the ground, which in turn depletes groundwater.

Worse, and criminally so, cities do not discharge clean water back into the environment – 80 per cent is discharged as waste. The question is how much of it is cleaned and made available for reuse. We can do this. But we don't. Instead we flush, we forget, use and abuse. Whatever is there, is contaminated.

The fact is that toilets are mere receptacles to receive waste: when we flush or pour water, the waste flows into a piped drain, which could be either connected, or not, to a sewage treatment plant (STP). This STP could be working, or not. The key is to build toilets that work and toilets that are connected to systems that will safely dispose of human excreta so that it does not become another source of pollution and another source of bad health. So, building toilets, however essential, must not be confused with sanitation.

But if we reinvent the way we treat our sewage, we can save water – first, by not allowing it to be polluted and, second, by turning waste back into a resource. This is a potential game-changer.

Till now, the paradigm for urban sanitation has been costly. It requires first the supply of water, which, if it is transported over longer and longer distances, increases cost of supply. The more the water that is supplied, the more the sewage that is generated. So, the next part is to build underground conveyance systems to connect each household and also to transport the wastewater over longer and longer distances to sewage treatment plants so that it is cleaned before discharge. But even this is not enough. The fact is that our rivers have little clean water to assimilate even treated effluents. This means sewage treatment plants have to clean waste to near-bathing water quality before release into rivers. This never happens. Pollution grows even as governments chase pipe-dreams of building more sewage treatment plants, underground drains and toilets. It never adds up.

This approach also misses the opportunity. My colleagues at the Centre for Science and Environment have worked on what we call 'shit-flow' diagrams of cities – maps of the journey of sewage. This brings out two realities. One, nearly all Indian cities do not treat or safely dispose of the bulk of human excreta. Two, most toilets in almost all cities are not connected to underground pipes but to individual septic tanks. This is on-site treatment, which needs to be recognized and worked with.

This on-site system would work if the septic tank is built to specification, if the system for collection of human excreta is regulated and if the sludge so collected is taken to treatment points so that it can be made safe for reuse.

The fact is that sludge is nutrient rich. Today, the global nitrogen cycle is being destroyed because we take human excreta, which is rich in nutrients and dispose it in water. In this case, we can return human excreta back to land, use it as fertilizer and reverse the sanitation cycle. The faecal sludge, after treatment, can be given to farmers and used as organic compost or it can be treated and mixed with other organic waste – like kitchen waste – and used for biogas or used for manufacturing fuel pellets or ethanol.

The bottom-line is that unless our system of waste management is affordable, it cannot be sustainable. We need solutions that can reach water to all, take back the waste of all and do this in ways that can reinvent the business of sewage so that it works with the current on-site technologies and will not only provide employment but also provide sustainable solutions so that waste is not waste, it is a resource. This is even more important in today's climate-risked world.

Each year, without fail, we have a vicious cycle of crippling and backbreaking droughts and then devastating floods. But the fact is that this cycle is finding a new 'normal'. First, floods and droughts come together. Today, even as 40 per cent of the country's districts face prospects of drought, close to 25 per cent districts have had heavy rainfall of more than 100 mm in just a matter of hours. Rainfall has become more variable and extreme.

In 2017, Chandigarh, a city of open parks, was submerged under water. It had deficient rains till 21 August of that year, and then it got 115 mm of rain in just 12 hours. It drowned. In other words, it got roughly 15 per cent of its annual monsoon rain in just these hours. Also in 2017, Bengaluru had hardly any rain and then it poured. It got 150 mm of rain in just about a day, which is close to 30 per cent of its annual monsoon rain. It is no wonder that the city drowned.

This is a double-whammy. The fact is that on the one hand we are getting our water management wrong – we are building in floodplains, destroying our water bodies and filling up our water channels. On the other hand, climate change is beginning to show its impact on the monsoons. It is leading to what scientists predicted would happen, more rain in a fewer number of rainy days. Thus, more rain and more extreme rain events.

It is time we woke up to this reality. This means learning to cope with twin scenarios all at once. This means being obsessive about how to mitigate floods and how to live with scarcity of water. But the good news is, doing one can help the other. But we need to stop debating, dithering or dawdling. We know what to do. And we have no time to lose – climate change will only increase with time as weather and rainfall will only get more variable, more extreme and more catastrophic.

The answer to floods is what has been discussed for long; in fact, was practised in flood-prone regions of India many decades ago. It requires planning systems that can divert and channelize water so that it does not flood land and destroy life. It means linking rivers to ponds, lakes and ditches so that water is free to flow. This will distribute the water across the region and bring other benefits. It will recharge groundwater so that in the subsequent months of low rainfall, there is water for drinking and irrigation. It will also ensure that there is food during the flood period, as wetlands are highly productive in terms of fish and plant food.

Mitigating floods and droughts has only one answer – obsessive attention to building millions and millions of connected and living water structures that will capture rain, be a sponge for flood and a storehouse for drought.

Our water future is about our water wisdom. We need to learn from the fascinating case of ancient Roma (Rome) and Edo (the city out of which grew Tokyo). Romans used to build huge aqueducts that ran for tens of miles to bring water to their settlements. These aqueducts are the most omnipresent symbols of that society's water management even today. And many experts have praised the Romans for the meticulousness with which they planned their water supply.

But no, these aqueducts represent not the intelligence but the utter environmental mismanagement of the great Romans. Rome was built on the river Tiber. The city did not need any aqueduct. But as the waste of Rome was discharged directly into the Tiber, the river got polluted, and water had to be brought from afar. Water outlets were few as a result, and the elite appropriated these using a system of slaves. On the contrary, the traditional Japanese never discharged their waste into the rivers. Instead they composted the waste and then used it in the fields. Using the rivers, Edo had numerous water outlets and a much more egalitarian water supply.

Water and culture go together. Water shortage is not about the mere failure of rain. It is about the failure of society to live and share its water endowment.

This is why this volume, *India's Water Futures: Emergent Ideas and Pathways*, is so critical in our water-stressed times. This is also why we must remember and acknowledge the contribution of late Professor Ramaswamy R. Iyer. The challenge is to confront the reality of current water management strategies and have the courage to stand for a different and more water secure future. The problem is in our mind – and in our inability to think and do things differently.

Professor Iyer was a rare bureaucrat who had the ability to engage with contesting ideas. His most important contribution, in my view, is that he was prepared to stand with the challengers of the dominant water paradigm. In the 1990s, India's only method of water management was to build infrastructure of a particular kind – dams, canals and pipelines to supply this water – the bigger the better. The problem was not the method but the mindset of its practitioners who did not allow for any other idea to be placed on the table. The rigidity of the water management paradigm was the root of the problem. Nothing was possible. Not even a discussion.

This is where Professor Iyer made a difference. He was part of the establishment, but he was willing to allow new ideas to propagate and blossom. This was critical then as it is now.

We are at a new juncture where livelihoods are threatened because of water mismanagement. We are also at a juncture when urban-industrial growth will demand more water for its development. The question is how will India balance the needs of the old – agriculture and drinking of its rural populations – with the needs of the new – urban and industrial sectors? How will water productivity be enhanced so that it remains affordable and also sustainable?

This volume presents a water paradigm that is no longer the alternative fringe. It must be at the core of decision-making. So, read it because you must. This is about making us water secure, because we are water-wise.

# Acknowledgements

We would like to thank the following persons and institutions without whom this book would not have seen the light of day.

All the authors for their contributions and, even more than that, for their perseverance. This was a long, drawn-out journey for them – from the first draft of their chapters to the final versions – outliving moments of uncertainties about the future of the book itself.

Sunita Narain for writing the Foreword at a very short notice.

The Centre for Policy Research (CPR), New Delhi and the Arghyam Trust, Bengaluru for providing the resources to organize the three-day conference, 'Water Sector in India: A Critical Engagement – Felicitation Conference in Honour of Prof. Ramaswamy R. Iyer' held in November 2013 that brought together academics and activists engaged in the water sector from across the country. It was during this conference that the idea about the book took shape. Pratap Bhanu Mehta, the then President of the CPR, fully backed the proposal to hold this conference and took personal interest in it, right from its planning to its successful completion.

The paper presenters and participants of the conference for making the conference an intellectually stimulating experience.

Prof. Ramaswamy R. Iyer for agreeing, albeit reluctantly, to the idea of the Felicitation Conference and for his handholding during the whole process. Our only regret is that this book could not come out during his lifetime.

Prof. Ramaswamy Iyer's wife, Suhasini Ramaswamy and his two sons, Sriram and Mahadevan, for their continued support during the Felicitation Conference and after.

Sugeeta Roy Choudhury for a thorough copyediting job.

The Routledge reviewer for constructive suggestions on each of the chapter.

Routledge for agreeing to publish this book under its banner and bringing it out in such an elegant manner. Shoma Choudhury, the Commissioning Manager, and her colleagues Aakash Chakrabarty, Commissioning Editor, and Brinda Sen, Editorial Assistant, have been a great source of support and encouragement.

The Society for Promoting Participative Ecosystem Management (SOPPECOM), Pune for its continued support, including financial support, from the time of the Felicitation Conference till the present. Neha Bhadbhade of SOPPECOM for her support, especially in the final stages of the book project.

None of the above are, of course, responsible for any errors that may still be there in the book and for which we take complete responsibility.

K. J. Joy and S. Janakarajan

# 1 Introduction India's water futures

## Emergent ideas and pathways

*K. J. Joy and S. Janakarajan*

## Introduction

A lot has been written about the multi-faceted crisis in the water sector in India. This book is not primarily about the crisis; nor does it offer a comprehensive critique of the water sector by analysing its various problems.[1] Instead, the book posits that, along with the crisis, there is a wide range of changes taking place – changes in mindsets and worldviews, practices, polices, legal regimes and institutions around water that need engagement. Some of these changes are formalized legally and institutionally; some others are still fluid, discussed and debated, experimented with and yet to find political commitment. In a sense, they are still 'work-in-progress' or 'emergent' ideas and pathways of change. They are 'emergent' because they are still flexible and fluid, have not found political commitment, are not formalized legally or otherwise and, at the same time, offer freedom to make changes as part of the process itself. This book is primarily about these ideas and pathways. The various chapters in the book dealing with different aspects of water offer pointers on how to move forward in each of these aspects. The book is also an effort to recognize and appreciate the contribution made by late Prof. Ramaswamy R. Iyer (Prof. Iyer henceforth) to the changing water sector discourse in India.

This introductory chapter starts with a brief discussion on the globally increased political sensitivity around water, as this could be seen as a first step in the changes taking place in the water sector. Then it moves to a discussion about the broad changes taking place in the Indian water sector. The third section is a brief note on Prof. Iyer and his contribution in changing the water sector discourse in India. The fourth and the final (and more substantial) section discusses the overall coverage of the book by talking about the issues the various chapters in the book engage with and the critical insights emanating from each of them.

## Increased global sensitivity

Water has become one of the most important items of agenda for discussion across governments the world over. The subject has become even more critical ever since the debate over global warming induced climate change turned into a hot subject, cutting across national and disciplinary boundaries. There are serious deliberations on issues relating to glacier melting, extreme weather events, water security, food security, ecological and environmental security, rapid urbanization, commercialization of water utilities, contestations and conflicts and so on. In all these debates, water security takes centre stage. Global events such as the World Water Forum and the Stockholm World Water Week have been emphasizing the need for putting water on a high political agenda. These international forums have been striving to elicit a political commitment from the governments across the world for better water governance, conservation, civil society participation, building partnerships and, most of all, for global mutual collaboration to address all water-related concerns.

The Ministerial Statements from the different World Water Forums reflect, at least on paper, the political commitments of various governments in relation to water.

> We . . . are determined to address the global challenges related to water within the context of sustainable development. We, therefore: Reaffirm the prior commitments made by national governments to achieve the internationally agreed upon goals on water and sanitation, including those in Agenda 21 and the Johannesburg Plan of implementation, and acknowledge the decisions of the United Nations Commission on Sustainable Development (UNCSD), the multilateral agreements relevant to water, water use, sanitation and health.[2]
>
> We reaffirm that water is at the core of sustainable development and support the inclusion of one dedicated water goal and water-related targets in the Post-2015 Development Agenda. We note that Integrated Water Resources Management (IWRM) and its balanced relation with food and energy is important to effectively cope with increasing food and energy requirements towards sustainable development. . . . We reaffirm our commitment to the human right to safe drinking water and sanitation and ensuring progressive access to water and sanitation for all. . . . We stress that water is one of the major issues in tackling climate change.[3]

Though there is a big gap between the international commitments and actual practice, they do serve as pegs to affix our own concerns in the water sector and hold the respective governments accountable to honour the commitments they have made in international forums.

## Water sector in India: issues, concerns and changes

### *Issues and concerns*

Many of these issues, as reflected in the global discourse discussed earlier, are highly relevant to India. Of course, India has its own specific issues too. Indeed, the biggest concerns of the Indian economy, polity and society include these: falling or stagnant agricultural growth and the emerging food security complications, rapid industrialization and urbanization, rural – urban migration, ecological and environmental insecurity and growing inequities. The direct impact of these changes is the escalating demand for water for non-agricultural uses, especially industrial and urban uses. As a consequence, millions of gallons of potable water are transferred from rural to urban areas every day and water is getting increasingly (re)allocated from agriculture to industries and urban areas (Joy *et al.* 2014). For example, in Maharashtra, over six to seven years, starting from 2003, nearly 1500 $mm^3$ of water has been re-allocated from agriculture to urban and industrial uses (Prayas 2010). This is just one example. This type of water (re)allocation is leading to increased inter-sectoral conflicts (Joy *et al.* 2008; Joy and Paranjape 2009). The preoccupation with 8–10 per cent growth through the industrial route is going to put enormous pressures on freshwater. The biggest challenge for India in the days to come is how it is going to manage the growing competing demands for water from different sectors.

Rising urban and industrial water needs also contribute to enormous pollution load. The Indian hydrocracy at best engages in freshwater management (read, water supply augmentation measures) but never ever engages seriously with issues concerning wastewater or in what form and shape the 'return flows' come back into the system. Indeed, in many developed countries equal, if not more, importance is given to wastewater management strategies. As a result of neglect of such an important issue, water pollution in India has become the most serious concern. The wastewater generated through urban sewage and industrial effluents have been conveniently discharged into the sea, freshwater bodies, low-lying lands, rivers and streams, impacting both surface and groundwater (CSE 2012).

The other important issues include inefficient use of water, dying of rivers due to pollution load as well as damming and diversions, depleting groundwater conditions and lack of groundwater regulation, lack of protected drinking water supply and sanitation facility for a vast majority, and unsustainable and unprofitable agriculture.

It is also important that these challenges are not discussed in isolation. The complexities of Indian socio-economic, political and cultural issues make things shoddier. What we see today in India is persisting poverty, growing inequality and deprivation, widespread farmers' suicides, lack of access to basic needs such as food, water, housing and health care, fractured institutions, competitive populism, myopic and sectoral approach for growth and development, lack of transparency, lack of information flow, lack of scientific data generation and dissemination, inadequate and unscientific planning, rapid, uncontrolled and unplanned urbanization, conversion of rural poverty into urban poverty and so forth.

The climate change threat is looming large and needs to be handled in this overall vulnerable situation in the country. The rural economy (and the Indian economy is predominantly rural) contributes to livelihoods of a vast majority. The Indian rural poor who depend upon subsistence farming are more vulnerable due to climatological factors. As a result of climate change, freshwater availability is expected to be more seasonal since roughly 75 per cent of the annual water supply is realized through the monsoon across India. It is feared that due to the fast melting of the Himalayan glaciers, the present perennial rivers of India such as the Indus, the Ganges and the Brahmaputra are quite likely to become seasonal rivers. Salt water intrusion and increasing salinity in coastal water bodies, such as backwater canals and estuaries, are going to be a serious problem in the near future. It is also anticipated that all deltas are going to become more vulnerable due to a lack of sediment flow, sea-water intrusion and the overall sea-level rise. This is going to result in a huge food security problem as well as a livelihood security problem across India.

## *Changing water sector discourse in India*[4]

The water sector discourse has been drastically changing in India, or, for that matter, the world over, since the early 1990s. One could say that the first round of changes took place roughly between 1990 and 2005.[5] Many new concepts, terminologies and governance structures have entered the discourse. Integrated Water Resource Management (IWRM) finds a mention in all policy documents. Participatory

Irrigation Management (PIM) through Water Users' Associations (WUAs) is legally mandatory in any state in India. River basin organizations, multi-stakeholder platforms and processes, and independent regulatory bodies are part of the larger institutional design for water governance in India.

As for the state, it has moved from the earlier largely techno-centric model to approaching the crisis from an economic and institutional perspective. After the Dublin Principles of 1992 (ICWE 1992), the discourse around water has changed. Water is increasingly seen as an economic good. Clearly, the thrust, for a certain period, moved away from investing in infrastructure to managing the resource through smart governance. Institutions and pricing thereby became the keywords with the state, changing its role from one of service provider to one of regulator.[6] The state has proactively focused on taking steps, at least in some cases at the instance of multilateral donors,[7] to put forth policies, laws and rules and for the supposedly better management of 'scarce' water. Formulation of new laws and policies, institutional reforms, creation of water entitlements and building partnerships between users, private interests and the state have been some of the important aspects of the water sector reform package of the state.

Earlier, water provisioning was in the hands of state agencies/organizations. This has been changing since the 1990s. Now the emphasis is on public-private partnerships. There is an increasing role for private service providers in both drinking water and irrigation water management. There is also a move to make water rights tradable, the state of Maharashtra being an example of this. The policy push towards economic pricing of water stems from a shift in the worldview around water – a shift from water being primarily a 'social good' to an 'economic good'.

Water transfers – both real and virtual – are taking different shapes and forms. For example, water is getting transferred from low value food crops (in economic terms) to higher value commercial crops, or other higher priority sectors (industries, cities). From the supermarkets of developed countries, one can buy grapes cultivated in the water-scarce regions of Maharashtra (Larrington-Spencer 2014, as quoted in Zwarteveen 2015) and bananas grown on the desert coast of Peru.[8] Water has already been brought under the purview of global trade by its inclusion in the General Agreement on Trade and Services (GATS). All these and many other developments in the water sector (and also those outside it) seem to indicate that the water sector has been impacted significantly by the Liberalization, Privatization and Globalization (LPG) regime unleashed in the country since the early 1990s.

Within India, Maharashtra seems to be leading the pack in ushering in most of these reforms. The policy initiatives in Maharashtra in the early 2000s – the Maharashtra State Water Policy (2003), the Maharashtra Management of Irrigation System by Farmers Act (2005) and the Maharashtra Water Resources Regulatory Authority Act (2005) – all reflect this. In fact, the timing of these reforms makes the motivation of these policy initiatives suspect. The reforms have coincided with the huge loan that the government of Maharashtra has taken from the World Bank as part of its irrigation sector reforms – a loan of US$325 million to assist the implementation of the Maharashtra Water Sector Improvement Project. The World Bank has hailed the reforms that have been unleashed in Maharashtra as exemplary, especially fixing entitlements, appointing independent water regulatory authorities and so on (Brisco and Malik 2006).[9]

Over the last 20–30 years, efforts have also emerged from within civil society (including the academia), challenging the dominant water paradigm and creatively engaging with and responding to the challenges posed by both the crisis and the changes that are taking place (as part of the reform process). Alternative strategies are being put forward that focus more on the sustainable and equitable use and democratic governance of water. The innumerable struggles against dams (against displacement and submergence), mass mobilizations around equitable water distribution, innovative experiences in Participatory Irrigation Management (PIM) that go beyond efficiency and address concerns of equity, sustainability and democratization, struggles against water privatization of various types, multi-stakeholder platforms and processes to resolve conflicts around water pollution, large number of successful watershed development experiences throughout the country, struggles by the farmers against water being increasingly taken over by industries and cities, and many such positive experiences are all part of the efforts by non-state actors to find answers to the multi-faceted and multi-tiered water crisis.

One could say that the insights and lessons from these innovative experiences and experiments found an institutional space to consolidate when Dr Mihir Shah, the then member of the Planning Commission, constituted eight Working Groups (and also a few sub-groups within them) dealing with different aspects of water as part of the 12th Five Year Plan preparations in 2011–2012. This was a path breaking effort because, unlike the usual practice of bureaucrats heading these Working Groups, for the first time all of them were headed by experts from either academia or civil society organizations. In fact, we would call this as the beginning of the second 'wind of change' which continues till date. Wider consultations were organized on the draft reports of the Working Groups. Most of the contributors of this volume either chaired these Working Groups or were members or were part of the consultative meetings. Though the new political regime that assumed office at the centre in 2014 abolished the Planning Commission, some of the important new initiatives started as part of the 12th Five Year Plan have been taken forward. The new government that assumed office in 2014 set up three committees: one to finalize the draft National Water Framework Law, the second one to draft the Model Groundwater Bill and the third one to look at the restructuring of the two most important water institutions in the country, namely, the Central Water Commission (CWC) that primarily deals with surface water and the Central Ground Water Board (CGWB), dealing with groundwater in the country, and suggest a new institutional design for the water sector. The draft reports were presented for wider consultation; serious efforts were made to get critical inputs from the academia and civil society organizations and, most importantly, suggestions were taken on-board while finalizing the reports, which does not happen very often in India. While these three reports – *Draft National Water Framework Bill, 2016,*[10] *Model Bill for the Conservation, Protection, Regulation and Management of Groundwater, 2016,*[11] and *A 21st Century Institutional Architecture for India's Water Reforms*[12,13] – have not been accepted by the government, together they constitute the second wave of water governance reform package. Interestingly, all these efforts were led by Shah, irrespective of a change in the government, ensuring continuity of ideas as well as approach (Joy 2016). Shah has brought together all the important elements of all these three reports in his chapter, 'Reforming India's water sector: which way forward?', the last chapter of the book.

The motivation for the first round of reforms and the second round of reforms seems to be quite different. The first round of reforms was primarily pushed in the direction of water privatization, economic pricing of water and so on by the LPG regime and the bilateral lending agencies, whereas the second round of reforms was driven primarily by internal conviction, civil society experience and normative concerns like sustainability, equity and democratization.

## Changing water sector discourse: contributions of Prof. Ramaswamy R. Iyer[14]

It is in this context of setting an alternative agenda for the water sector in India that the late Prof. Ramaswamy R. Iyer (1929–2015), an eminent scholar, activist and policy-maker and former Secretary of Water Resources, Government of India, becomes all the more relevant. The ideas, viewpoints and approaches that Prof. Iyer propounded for about 30 years or so, ever since he, as the Secretary of Water Resources, drafted the first National Water Policy (NWP) in 1987, could form the core of the alternative paradigm for water.

Prof. Iyer was a true, public spirited activist-intellectual. He was exceptional among the policy analysts and academics in the country as he was never afraid to take positions, be it on the controversial Sardar Sarovar Project on the Narmada river, the Cauvery inter-state water dispute, the Mullaperiyar dam conflict between Kerala and Tamil Nadu or the issue of interlinking of rivers (ILR). He also contributed to the water-environment-development discourse through the various government committees that he was part of especially after his retirement.[15]

Prof. Iyer's writings on water-environment-development cover a wide range.[16] He published extensively on water policy, inter-state water disputes, linking of rivers, water conflicts, trans-boundary water treaties concerning India and its neighbours like Nepal, Pakistan, Bangladesh and China. His recent writings on Water Framework Law, Alternative Water Policy, proposed amendment to the Land Acquisition, Rehabilitation and Resettlement Act 2013, environmental clearances report of the High-Level Committee for reviewing environmental laws and so on, have contributed significantly to making the debate more informed.

Healthy and living rivers have been a passion for Prof. Iyer and that is what prompted him to anchor the lecture series on India's rivers – an initiative of the India International Centre, Delhi – and later converting that into an edited book, *Living Rivers, Dying Rivers*.[17] He writes:

> rivers are treated as if they were pipelines to be cut, turned and joined; waste, pollutants and contaminants are inflicted on them far beyond their coping capacity; the floodplains of rivers are occupied, leaving no space for the accommodation of floods; sand is mined from their beds; borewells are sunk into their beds for extracting the water flow reducing base flows; and so on. . . . The engineer (or some engineers) would like to control and manipulate rivers; the economist (or the economist of a certain persuasion) regards rivers, and water in general, as a 'resource' to be fully exploited for human use, and also as a commodity subject to market force. Neither view leaves room for thinking of rivers as living things, as ecological systems, as having roles to play beyond

> serving human economic activity, and as having an existential and not merely an instrument value.
>
> (Iyer 2015: 436–437)

It is fascinating that some of his latest articles critically assess recent government policies on environment, social justice and development. His articles – 'Environment and Development: Some Thoughts for the New Government',[18] 'A Development Manifesto',[19] 'Against Developmental Fundamentalism'[20] and 'A Hasty, Half-baked Report on Environment'[21] – have attempted to critically evaluate some of the initiatives of the new Bharatiya Janata Party (BJP) led National Democratic Front (NDA) government at the Centre, which were seen by many as 'setting the clock back'. Indeed, his cryptic comment, '*Dramatically faster environmental approvals is bad news, not good news*' in a way sums up his overall take on the current government's efforts to speed up environmental clearances for various infrastructure projects. Furthermore, Prof. Iyer's work has come to symbolize an alternative worldview of the water sector. His writings have been a sort of dissenting voice against the mainstream policies and perspectives on water. The alternative water policy that he wrote (Iyer 2011) brings together all such dissenting concerns. Prof. Iyer also tried to give a legal framework to the alternative water policy through the sub-group (part of the 12th Five Year Plan Working Group on water governance) he headed for the Planning Commission to draft a Water Framework Law for the country.

Though his contribution to the water sector discourse in India over the last three decades or so has been decisive and unmatched, it did not go down well with the water establishment of the country, perhaps because his clear-cut views and unambiguous statements, buttressed with facts, did not toe the line of the water establishment.[22] It is in this background that a felicitation conference 'to honour, acknowledge and celebrate' his contributions to the water sector was organized in 2013.[23] The idea of this book originated in this conference that tried to engage critically with the various issues in the water sector.[24]

## The book: coverage, emergent ideas and pathways

The book contains 15 chapters, including this introductory one, dealing with most of the important sectors and themes in the Indian water sector. They cover river basins and climate change, watershed development, groundwater, public irrigation systems, urban domestic water, waste management, environmental flow, irrigated agriculture, gender and water, dams and environmental governance, water conflicts and independent water regulatory institutions. We have not categorized or organized the chapters under different themes as they are not easily amenable to such categorization. They are more like standalone pieces representing different sectors/themes. The book does not have a 'typical' concluding chapter by the editors. Instead, Shah's essay, 'Reforming India's water sector: which way forward?' does the function of a concluding chapter as it captures very well the emergent thinking, ideas and pathways to restructure the Indian water sector in a more sustainable, equitable, efficient and democratic manner.

### *Indian water sector: an overview*

The first chapter after this introductory one is A. Vaidyanathan's 'Water resource development in India: achievements, shortcomings and remedial measures', providing a critical overview of the water sector in India. Vaidyanathan very incisively shows that the water sector in India is inefficient, inequitable and unsustainable. According to him, 'the deficiencies of water resource planning and management cannot be addressed through piecemeal changes in existing policies and institutions but call for radical systemic reforms that recognize and tackle their root causes'. As a first step towards this restructuring he calls for a comprehensive programme for improvement of data on all aspects, pro-active effort to encourage and support research and engagement with civil society organizations involved in micro-level data collection.[25] Other important suggestions he puts forth includes a shift from supply augmentation to efficiency measures, handing over water management to participatory institutions at different levels and a rational pricing system overseen by an independent regulatory authority.

### *Bio-physical factors, human interventions and basin management*

One of the important initial steps for scientific and socially and environmentally sensitive river basin management is to know how much water the basin has for various uses. The relationship between flows, bio-physical factors and different types of human interventions in the context of river basin management has not received much attention in India. Human interventions in the form of land use and cropping changes, large-scale watershed developments and upstream groundwater pumping, along with climatic factors, are changing the rainfall – runoff relationship drastically. Veena Srinivasan and Sharachchandra Lele engage with this important gap in 'Managing river basins: re-examining the biophysical basis'. They argue that the conventional understanding of river basin planning and river basin management has serious misconceptions, especially in the context of urbanizing watersheds. And they suggest that integrated water management in a river basin, especially in the Indian context, will require a more rigorous understanding of hydrology and the impact of human interventions, particularly on issues such as 'dependable yield', conjunctive use of surface and groundwater, inter-basin transfers and inter-state water sharing.

### *Watershed development in a changing agrarian context*

Over the last two decades, watershed development has received serious attention from planners, funders, practitioners and researchers. However, there does not seem to have been much of an attempt to problematize the watershed development approach in the context of the large-scale changes sweeping the rural landscape of our country. Abraham Samuel and K. J. Joy in their chapter, 'Changing land use, agrarian context and rural transformation: implications for watershed development', engage with the new set of issues coming up in the context of watershed development in the country. Watershed-based development is a flagship programme in the country to take care of ecological degradation as well as to stabilize rural livelihoods, especially in drought-prone regions. If watershed development has to continue to deliver these twin goals then, the chapter argues, the programme needs to be re-oriented as the agrarian context has been fast changing since the 1990s, mainly as a result of neo-liberal developmental policies and programmes. This is reflected in large-scale changes in land use, livelihood patterns, agrarian relations (especially increasing proletarianization and also feminization of agriculture workforce) and rural aspirations. The chapter calls for a biomass-based planning approach to watershed development as it can tie together both the sustainability and livelihood needs together, opening up avenues for non-farm incomes to people.

### *Environmental flow and river basin management*

Environmental flow (e-flow) as an important element of basin management is a rather late entrant in the water sector discourse in India. The 2012 National Water Policy does talk about it. However, it has not really percolated to actual basin planning; not only political will but also the wherewithal of how this can be actually done is largely missing. In 'Environmental flows in the Indian context: prospects and challenges', Latha Anantha[26] and Neha Bhadbhade make the case for making e-flows mandatory for long-term sustainability of rivers. India being the third largest dam builder in the world, the timing, frequency, duration and magnitude of water flows to the downstream are conditioned by the whims and fancies of large dam-based projects. This seriously affects the river ecology. The chapter contests the conventional engineering wisdom that water going to the sea is a waste and therefore every drop of it should be harnessed and utilized. The most important contribution of this chapter is to engage with the debate on what constitutes environmental flow. It also makes a very important observation that in the Indian context, environmental flow in a river is seemingly a political choice rather than a hydrological need.

### *Urban domestic water*

Urban waterscape is an important, emerging area of water scholarship as well as civil society action. Kuntala Lahiri-Dutt's chapter, 'Water use practices of the urban middle class in India: insights from metropolitan Calcutta', discusses the middle-class practices of use of water for household consumption and argues that a part of the rise in consumerism has been changes in middle-class perceptions of clean and pure water, leading to changes in water use practices. Material consumption (and in this case water) is both a status and a means to get into a particular 'class' and new tools and technologies that mediate the relationship of the individual to water (and sanitation) at the household level 'also represent new ways of being that recreate the middle-class subject as one who embraces change in the aspiration to join the conventional global consumer model of over-consumption'. Also, 'new consumptions, and new ways of consuming things like water, allow the middle classes to become global citizens, and the radical transformation is not only expressed in behaviour in public spaces but in the intimate space of one's home'. This chapter also brings home the need to go beyond big pictures and broad-brush assessments and critiques of neoliberal policy reforms in the context of urban service provision and 'understand changes at the household as part of scaling down in thinking about water' which 'can have far-reaching policy implications'.

### *Urban wastewater management*

Urban waste – both solid and liquid – management is an important challenge facing the country. Neelam Rana and N. C. Narayanan in their chapter, 'The centralized approach to wastewater management and implications for sanitation governance: an analysis of the intent and practice of the national urban sanitation policy in India', discuss the critical issue of urban wastewater treatment and management. According to this chapter, the state's centralized approach is the root cause for the state's failure in wastewater management and pollution abatement in urban areas. The chapter cautions that the state's wrong approach contemplates privatizing sewage management and treatment through Public-Private Partnership (PPP) models, a euphemism for privatization. The authors say that the National Urban Sanitation Policy 2008 made some radical departures and is intended to make sanitation services provision more inclusive through decentralized and participatory processes. However, their study of the city sanitation plans shows that the policy recommendations on contextual appropriateness of technology options were largely ignored, and cities chose to follow the centralized imagination of service provision. Also, there has been centralization of decision-making which greatly limited the decision-making powers of urban local bodies to plan sanitation interventions in accordance with their capacity and demands. According to the authors, this 'led to concentration of infrastructure in bigger cities, with side-lining of the concerns of smaller cities and poorer households in most parts of urban India'.

### *Reforming public irrigation*

Irrespective of massive public investments, performance of public irrigation in the country in the form of canal irrigation continues to be a serious concern. Tushaar Shah's chapter, 'Canal irrigation performance and impacts: applying contingency theory to irrigation management in India', tries to find an answer to this issue. Making a comparative analysis of the socio-political environment in which irrigation systems functioned in the past in different regions, Shah suggests that the performance of irrigation systems is contingent on their external task environment. According to him, the external task environment has never been taken into account seriously; instead, all efforts to improve canal irrigation performance have focused on changing the agency-farmer-system interaction. Drawing from organization theory, he advocates the use of contingency theory, which essentially says that there is no 'silver bullet' to improve the working of any organization; instead, the optimal course of action is contingent upon its internal and external situation. Thus, any initiative to improve irrigation performance needs to engage with both the external and internal factors.

He also suggests that performance benchmarking, a major driver of performance improvements in public systems, can be the first step to improve performance management in irrigation in India.

### *Groundwater, agriculture growth and poverty alleviation*

Groundwater is being seen as the lifeline of India as the bulk of domestic and agriculture water needs are being met through groundwater. However, extensive use of groundwater has resulted in competitive pumping resulting in the depletion of groundwater, contamination, increased costs of groundwater irrigation, debt accumulation and also farmers' suicides (Janakarajan and Moench 2006). P. S. Vijayshankar and Himanshu Kulkarni in their chapter, 'Out of balance: agricultural growth and groundwater depletion in two backward states of India', problematize the relationship between environmental quality and poverty alleviation in the context of groundwater. The two states of Rajasthan and Madhya Pradesh that the authors use to examine this relationship seem to have adopted a growth path to move out of poverty through intensification of groundwater use, which seems to be pushing them in the direction of an environmental disaster. Such a strategy is being used by many other states too. The authors emphatically argue that the way forward is to operate within a framework of groundwater management and governance that combine poverty alleviation with protection of the environment as against a framework of trade-off between the two. The authors also suggest certain crucial design elements of such a strategy that include participatory groundwater management, balanced use of surface and groundwater to correct the 'Hydrological Disequilibrium', enhanced groundwater recharge, demand management of agricultural water use, power sector reform and legal and institutional arrangements.

### *Agriculture water footprint*

Increasing water footprint in agriculture is an important issue that needs urgent engagement as freshwater is finite and the bulk of it goes into agriculture. With increasing urbanization and industrialization, more water would move out of agriculture over time. And this is already taking place (Joy *et al.* 2011). Agriculture is being depicted as the most 'inefficient' user of water – in terms of water use efficiency as well as the value (in terms of monetary income) it generates. In short, agriculture may have to do with much less water than what it is using presently. The chapter by Biksham Gujja and Hajara Shaik, 'Reducing water for agriculture for improving productivity: adapting and up-scaling innovative approaches', emphasizes the need for improved water use efficiency and conservation through appropriate technology and water governance. By examining the experiences of System of Rice Intensification (SRI) and Sustainable Sugar Initiative (SSI), the authors argue that adoption of such agronomical practices can substantially reduce the water footprint in agriculture. The strategic direction and interventions that they suggest include the following: (1) investment in innovations which reduce water use for agriculture while improving the yield, (2) a shift in government's role from being a water provider and builder of extensive infrastructure projects to being a facilitator of innovation and supporter of practical solutions initiated by the public and private sector and (3) the government's approach needs to shift from 'creating and increasing the irrigation potential' to 'improving the productivity and profitability of irrigated areas'. The authors also call for a radical transformation of water management, both as a concept and as a practice. For that to happen, the farmers, the government agencies, the private sector and the civil society need to have a major dialogue.

### *Gender and water*

Over the last two decades or so, 'gender' has entered the water lexicon quite forcefully. It finds place in almost all water-related policy documents. Institutions crafted around watershed development, participatory irrigation management and drinking water have explicit provisions for the participation of women. There are also movements – not too many – that demand women's access to water. Funding agencies over the years have become more sensitive to the gender question in water governance and have been providing resources to push the 'gender-water' question. There is also an emerging scholarship around the question of gender and patriarchy in water. However, no substantial changes seem to have taken place on the ground in terms of the gender equitable water management and governance system. Sumi Krishna and Seema Kulkarni's chapter, 'Gender and water: why we need alternatives to alternative discourses', examines why the progressive terms of discourse and recent policy reforms have not led to a more gender equitable and sustainable system of water governance, particularly in relation to women in India. The authors suggest that the gender and social aspects of natural resource management have to be integrated into the planning process. This could be achieved if, on the one hand, the gender and water discourse is embedded in an interdisciplinary and multi-sector approach to natural resources and, on the other hand, the broader political struggles for resources integrate feminist perspectives and engage with women's collective actions around water.

### *Inter-state water conflict: need to go beyond hydrology*

Water conflicts in general and inter-state conflicts in particular have been on the rise in India in recent times. Inter-state water sharing issues have been cropping up time and again: Andhra Pradesh and Telangana over the Krishna and the Godavari; Punjab, Haryana and Delhi over the Sutlej-Ravi-Beas waters; Karnataka and Goa over the Mahadayi; Odisha and Chhattisgarh over the Mahanadi and Karnataka and Tamil Nadu over the Cauvery are all examples of this. Stepping out of the mainstream narration of inter-state conflicts, Narendar Pani in his chapter, 'Inter-state water conflicts and linguistic identity in India: the case of Cauvery', argues that the current approach in resolving inter-state water disputes is inadequate because inter-state disputes are viewed purely on hydrological grounds and give no place to other issues such as linguistic identities and social issues. Using a Gandhian interpretation of Oberschall's theory of conflict, Pani demonstrates how the Cauvery dispute is part of a larger social conflict. Inter-state water disputes are not always about water alone: linguistic and cultural identities, worldviews and sub-nationalism are all part of it. He argues that 'by treating the dispute as one essentially between the states, it reinforces the linguistic identities, particularly those of Karnataka and Tamil Nadu'. The Tribunal 'could have gone a step further and determined the shares of individual districts in the basin. By localizing the sharing of the river's waters, it would have once again raised issues that would not necessarily become weapons in the linguistic battle'. He also says that a legally mandated institutional space needs to be created for negotiations among various stakeholders in the Cauvery basin.

### *Dams and environmental governance*

Environmental governance around dams has been a contested arena in India. Many of the agitations against large dams in India are a result of the failure of the state to implement its own polices properly. Himanshu Thakkar, in his chapter, 'Dams and environmental clearances: learnings and way forward', engages with the issue of decision-making in the context of dams. Though the need for environment clearances for dams has been felt in some form or the other since the mid-1970s, and the process formally started after the passage of the Environment Protection Act of 1986, he says that 'we continue to remain on a rather steep learning curve'. The chapter brings out forcefully the pathetic track record of the Environmental Appraisal Committee (EAC) as it has not rejected a single project. Looking at the judicial system involved in environmental governance of dams – the National Environmental Appellate Authority (NEAA), the National Green Tribunal (NGT), the High Courts and the Supreme Court – the author says, 'we [have] yet to see [a] really effective judicial activism on environmental clearances related to dams'. The chapter also outlines some of the emerging issues (like environment flows, impact of climate change on dams and contribution of dams to climate change, increased glacier melting and its impact on rivers and dams, biodiversity protection, dams and disasters, muck disposal, impact of dams on sediment regimes of rivers, carrying capacity and so on) that need to become part of the environmental governance around dams. The author cautions that unless we bring in fundamental changes and makes the environmental decisions and governance more transparent, accountable and participatory, people would soon lose faith in the whole system. Thus, the way forward is 'to bring in real faith in our democracy and people in environmental governance'.

## *Independent regulatory authority for water*

Bringing in independent regulatory authority (IRA) into the water sector, as in the case of other services like electricity, telecom, etc., is being posited as an important institutional reform to take care of the ills plaguing the water sector in India. The primary rationale is to take out the regulatory function from the legislative and the executive, though there are many in the water sector who believe that setting up IRAs is an essential step towards water privatization. In his essay in this volume, Vaidyanathan too recommends setting up an independent regulatory body to oversee water tariff. Maharashtra was the first Indian state to usher in an IRA for water when it enacted the Maharashtra Water Resources Regulatory Authority (MWRRA) Act 2005.[27] In fact, the 10th Finance Commission and the various water policy documents also talk about the need for such an authority in each state. Following Maharashtra, a couple of other states (like Uttar Pradesh) have already passed such an Act. However, the effort seems to be to transplant IRA models from the north (Dubash and Morgan 2013) – primarily a privatization-centric conventional IRA model – which may not work in India. Sachin Warghade and Subodh Wagle's chapter, 'Rationale for independent regulatory agency for water in India: reconceptualizing credible commitment', discusses the relevance and role of IRA in a parliamentary democratic governance system. They do this with a critical analysis of the experience of the MWRRA and conclude that privatization-centric conventional IRA model would not work for water. They call for an IRA based on the core commitment of achieving social objectives and an institutional design based on procedural accountability through effective provisions for transparency, accountability, participation and capacity building (TAP-C).

## *Winds of change*

As mentioned earlier, the book concludes with Mihir Shah's chapter, 'Reforming India's water sector: which way forward?', in which he highlights the need for a much-needed paradigm shift in the approach to water management as envisaged in the 12th Five Year Plan. This involves a shift to a multi-disciplinary, participatory management perspective, with particular focus on command area development, improving water use efficiency, breaking energy – groundwater nexus, watershed restoration and groundwater recharge and water use regulation, recycling and reuse of urban water and, most importantly, to have a completely new outlook on institutional framework and water law enactments and enforcements. Interestingly, though the political regime changed after the 12th Five Year Plan was formulated[28] and also the Planning Commission itself got wound up, many of the ideas contained in this chapter have formed the core of the three important initiatives of the Ministry of Water Resources and Ganga Rejuvenation, namely, *Draft National Water Framework Bill, 2016; Model Bill for the Conservation, Protection, Regulation and Management of Groundwater, 2016*, and *21st Century Institutional Architecture for India's Water Reforms, 2016*. All these three initiatives together could be, in a way, called as the water sector reform package. Interestingly, all these three initiatives had been led by Shah.

If Prof. Iyer were alive, perhaps he would have been quite happy to see that many of his ideas are actually forming the core of the emergent ideas and pathways that this book engages with. This volume, though it could not come out when Prof. Iyer was alive, is a humble attempt to keep alive his legacy as well as an attempt to take it forward.

## Notes

1 This is not to say that a rigorous critique is not important. It is very important as the critique is the first step towards looking for alternatives.
2 5th World Water Forum, Ministerial Statement, www.worldwatercouncil.org/fileadmin/wwc/World_Water_Forum/WWF5/Ministerial_Statement_22_3_09.pdf (accessed on June 2018).
3 7th World Water Forum Ministerial statement, www.worldwatercouncil.org/fileadmin/world_water_council/documents/publications/forum_documents/Ministerial%20Declaration%20%207th%20World%20Water%20Forum%20Final.pdf (accessed on June 2018).
4 This section is based on a similar section from Joy *et al.* (2011: 11–16).
5 The year 1990 denotes the beginning of the restructuring of Indian economy and 2005 is the year where Maharashtra goes for big ticket reforms as discussed later in the chapter.
6 The National Water Policy 2012 does hint at this change in roles, http://mowr.gov.in/sites/default/files/NWP2012Eng6495132651_1.pdf (accessed on 20 June 2018).
7 The state of Maharashtra enacted the Maharashtra Water Resource Regulatory Authority (MWRRA) Act 2005 to fulfil a condition set by the World Bank when it gave a loan of $325 million to the government of Maharashtra for the Water Sector Improvement Project (WSIP) in 2005.
8 Caroline Dominguez-Guzmán, a PhD student Margreet Zwarteveen is collaborating with, is currently studying this (cited in Zwarteveen 2015).
9 For a detailed critique of water sector reforms in Maharashtra, see Joy and Kulkarni 2010.
10 Ministry of Water Resources, River Development & Ganga Rejuvenation, "Draft National Water Framework Bill, 2016", http://mowr.gov.in/policies-guideline/policies/draft-national-water-framework-bill-2016 (accessed on 23 June 2018).
11 Ministry of Water Resources, River Development & Ganga Rejuvenation, "Model Bill for the Conservation, Protection, Regulation and Management of Groundwater, 2016", http://mowr.gov.in/sites/default/files/Model_Bill_Groundwater_May_2016_0.pdf (accessed on 23 June 2018).
12 Ministry of Water Resources, River Development & Ganga Rejuvenation, "A 21st Century Institutional Architecture for India's Water Reforms", www.indiaenvironmentportal.org.in/files/file/Report_on_Restructuring_CWC_CGWB.pdf (accessed on 23 June 2018).
13 The *Economic and Political Weekly* (Vol. 51, Issue no. 52, 24 December 2016) carried a set of 13 articles which commented on the report along with a response from the Chair of the Committee, Dr Mihir Shah, www.epw.in/water-governance (accessed on 23 June 2018).
14 This section of Prof. Ramaswamy Iyer's contribution to the water sector discourse is an adapted version of Joy and Janakarajan (2015). After his death many tributes and commentaries appeared in various journals, newspapers and websites which capture him as a person as well as his contributions. They include the following: www.indiawaterportal.org/articles/tribute-prof-ramaswamy-iyer; www.business-standard.com/article/current-affairs/ramaswamy-r-iyer-not-your-typical-bureaucrat-115091400029_1.html; www.countercurrents.org/iyer130915.htm;

https://thewire.in/environment/watering-the-arid-fields-of-administration-with-intellectual-rigour-and-honesty (all accessed on 22 June 2018) and the Special Issue of *SAWAS* (South Asian Water Studies), 'In Memoriam Ramaswamy R. Iyer (1929–2015)', Volume 1, Issue 2, November 2015 (Contributors include: Kuntala Lahiri-Dutt, S. Janakarajan, Dipinder Kapur, Ranjan K. Panda, Nitya Jacob, K. J. Joy, and Safa Fanaian).

15 A few important ones are these: Member of the Committee on the Pricing of Irrigation Water set up by the Planning Commission (report submitted in 1992); Chairman of the Working Group on Participatory Irrigation Management set up by the Planning Commission for the formulation of the 9th Five Year Plan in 1996-1997; Member of a Committee ('Five Member Group') which studied the controversial Sardar Sarovar Project; Member of a High-level Expert Committee to review the environmental and resettlement aspects of the Tehri Hydroelectric Project (1996–1997); Chairman of a Task Force on Natural Resources, Environment, Land, Water and Agriculture, set up by the Commission on Centre – State Relations in 2008–2009; and Chairman of a Sub-group on a Draft National Water Framework Law set up by the Planning Commission as part of the formulation of 12th Five Year Plan in 2012–2013.

16 On water alone, he has published five books (including those edited by him) and 197 articles. He has also written innumerable other articles on a wide range of subjects like social justice, politics, literature, culture, public enterprises, public administration, economic policy, governance and music.

17 Oxford University Press, 2015.

18 *Economic and Political Weekly*, 21 June 2014, XLIX(25): 19–21.

19 *Economic and Political Weekly*, 1 November 2014, XLIX(43 & 44): 25–26.

20 *The Hindu*, 30 May 2014.

21 *The Hindu*, 13 February 2015.

22 According to Prof. Iyer, the relationship between him and the Ministry of Water Resources and the Central Water Commission (CWC) underwent a change as he became a critic of big dams (Iyer 2013).

23 The three-day conference, 'Water Sector in India: A Critical Engagement – Felicitation Conference in Honour of Prof. Ramaswamy R. Iyer', was held on 25–27 November 2013 held at India International Centre, Delhi with support from the Centre for Policy Research and the Arghyam Trust that brought together academics and activists engaged in the water sector all across the country.

24 The issues included climate change, surface water management, groundwater, gender and water, privatization, drinking water and sanitation, agricultural water use, environmental flows, industrialization and water, watershed development, droughts and floods, water conflicts, transboundary water disputes, water quality, water and laws water institutions (including independent regulatory institutions and so on).

25 Vaidyanathan headed the 12th Five Year Plan Working Group on Water Database Development and Management. The report is available at http://planningcommission.gov.in/aboutus/committee/wrkgrp12/wr/wg_data.pdf (accessed on 21 June 2018).

26 Latha passed away in November 2017 and we deeply regret that she is not with us to see her essay on environmental flows, a theme that was very close to her heart.

27 It is available at www.mwrra.org/Document%207.pdf (accessed on 22 December 2016); also see SOPPECOM 2012 for a critical assessment of the MWRRA

28 The 12th Five Year Plan was formulated during the United Progressive (UPA) government and it was replaced by the National Democratic Alliance (NDA) government in 2014.

## References

Brisco, John and R. P. S. Malik. 2006. *India's Water Economy: Bracing for a Turbulent Future*. New Delhi: Oxford University Press. © World Bank, https://openknowledge.worldbank.org/handle/10986/7238 (accessed on 20 June 2018).

CSE. 2012. *Excreta Matters: How Urban India Is Soaking Up Water, Polluting Rivers and Drowning in Its Own Waste*, Volume 1 & 2. New Delhi: Centre for Science and Environment (CSE).

Dubash, K. Navroz and Bronwen Morgan (eds.). 2013. *The Rise of the Regulatory State of the South: Infrastructure and Development in Emerging Economies*. London: Oxford University Press.

ICWE. 1992. 'The Dublin Statement on Water and Sustainable Development', International Conference on Water and the Environment (ICWE) in Dublin, Ireland, 26–31 January, www.un-documents.net/h2o-dub.htm (accessed on 20 June 2018).

Iyer, Ramaswamy. 2011. 'National Water Policy: An Alternative Draft for Consideration', *Economic and Political Weekly*, XLVI(26 & 27): 201–214, 25 June.

Iyer, Ramaswamy. 2013. 'The Story of a Troubled Relationship', *Water Alternatives*, 6(2): 168–176.

Iyer, Ramaswamy. (ed.). 2015. *Living Rivers, Dying Rivers*. New Delhi: Oxford University Press.

Janakarajan, S. and Marcus Moench. 2006. 'Are Wells a Potential Threat to Farmers' Well-Being? The Case of Deteriorating Groundwater Irrigation in Tamil Nadu', *Economic and Political Weekly*, XLI(37), 16–22 September.

Joy, K. J. 2016. 'An Important Step in Reforming Water Governance', *Economic and Political Weekly*, LI(52), 24 December, www.indiawaterportal.org/sites/indiawaterportal.org/files/an_important_step_in_reforming_water_governance_joy_economic_and_political_weekly_2016.pdf (accessed on 23 June 2018).

Joy, K. J., Biksham Gujja, Suhas Paranjape, Vinod Goud, and Shruti Vispute (eds.). 2008. *Water Conflicts in India: A Million Revolts in the Making*. New Delhi: Routledge.

Joy, K. J. and S. Janakarajan. 2015. 'A Tribute: Ramaswamy R. Iyer', *Economic and Political Weekly*, 50(39), 26 September.

Joy, K. J. and Seema Kulkarni. 2010. 'Engaging with the Changing Water Policy Discourse on Maharashtra', Globalisation Governance Grassroots Series No. 12. Pune: National Centre for Advocacy Studies.

Joy, K. J., Seema Kulkarni, Dik Roth, and Margreet Zwarteveen. 2014. 'Re-Politicising Water Governance: Exploring Water Re-Allocations in Terms of Justice', *Local Environment: The International Journal of Justice and Sustainability*, 19(9): 954–973, doi:10.1080/13549839.2013.870542.

Joy, K. J. and Suhas Paranjape. 2009. 'Water Use: Legal and Institutional Framework', in Ramaswamy Iyer (ed.), *Water and the Laws in India*. New Delhi: Sage.

Joy, K. J., Priya Sangameswaran, Latha Anantha, Shripad Dharmadhikary, M. K. Prasad, and K. P. Soma. 2011. 'Life, Livelihoods, Ecosystems, Culture: Entitlements and Allocation of Water for Competing Uses', A Position Paper by the Thematic Subgroup on Water Entitlements and Allocations for Livelihood Needs and Ecosystem Needs, Forum for Policy Dialogue on Water Conflicts in India, Pune, http://waterconflictforum.org/lib_docs/MinimumEntitlementsReportwithcover.pdf (accessed on 20 June 2018).

Prayas. 2010. 'Sinchananche Pani Udyogana Va Shaharana Valavinyachya Maharashtra Rajyatil Dhoranancha Va Amalbajavanicha Abhyas', A Marathi Document for Private Circulation. Pune: Resources and Livelihood Group, Prayas.

SOPPECOM. 2012. 'Maharashtra Water Resources Regulatory Authority: An Assessment', www.iwmi.cgiar.org/iwmi-tata/PDFs/2012_Highlight-33.pdf?galog=no (accessed on 20 June 2018).

Zwarteveen, Margreet. 2015. 'Regulating Water, Ordering Society: Practices and Politics of Water Governance', Inaugural Lecture 529, www.un-ihe.org/sites/default/files/oratie_margreet_zwarteveen.pdf (accessed on 20 June 2018).

# 2 Water resource development in India

## Achievements, shortcomings and remedial measures

*A. Vaidyanathan*

### Achievements and shortcomings of the Indian water sector

In sheer quantitative terms, the achievements of the last six decades in developing the country's water resources are both unprecedented and unquestionably impressive. The main features of this development – in terms of the magnitude of investments, the expansion in controlled water supply for agriculture and non-agricultural uses, its contribution to increasing agricultural production – are too well known to need any elaboration. There is good reason to believe that almost the entire increase in crop output has come from expansion of irrigation which facilitated more intensive use of land, shifts to higher value crop patterns and increasing yields of most major crops.

However, the manner in which the programmes have been conceived, implemented and managed leave a lot to be desired. The list of complaints is long and well known but not acted upon. These include the following:

- Projects to be implemented are chosen without adequate preparatory investigation.
- Technical soundness and economic viability of the projects are not put to rigorous professional scrutiny before being approved.
- Large upward revisions of scope and design of projects are approved without critical scrutiny.
- Combined with lax contracting and monitoring procedures, the above results in enormous delays and cost escalations before completion.
- Shortfalls exist in realizing the design potential in terms of volume of water delivered and area irrigated.
- Substantial, avoidable losses occur in conveyance and distribution of water from source to field in the case of surface projects.

- Significant deviations of actual crop patterns from those envisaged in design have occurred towards more water intensive crops.
- Widespread unauthorized use of water exists outside designated commands and crops.
- Groundwater extraction is practically unregulated.
- Water system managers are focused on delivering water without much concern for efficient use of the resource in terms of output per unit of water.
- Crop yield per unit of land is several times higher with irrigation compared to rainfed areas, but the difference varies greatly across regions and is also everywhere considerably less than the potential attainable with proper management of known and proven technology.
- More important are the indications that contrary to the expectation of synergetic effects of the combination of irrigation, fertilizers and improved seeds, yields per unit of consumptive water under irrigation are not significantly higher and may in fact be less than that of rainfed crops.

### *Unequal distribution of benefits*

The water resource development programme in the country is not only inefficient, but its benefits are also unequally distributed in some of the following ways:

- Inter-regional inequality in the proportion of crop area that is irrigated has been reduced to some extent but remains high, as does the impact in terms of increased yields per hectare.
- At the national level, and in many regions, the distribution of the increases in irrigated area is skewed in favour of larger farms.
- The expansion of area irrigated by groundwater has come about due to a phenomenal expansion in the number of wells/tubewells along with their progressive deepening.
- Expansion in the number of wells/tubewells and their energization has not been accompanied by a proportionate increase in the volume of water supplied or area irrigated by them.
- While the proportion of households having wells has increased, larger farmers are better placed to chase falling water tables by deepening the wells.
- Even within surface project commands, those with larger holdings have an advantage in exploiting conjunctive use possibilities, in influencing the timing and quantum of available system supplies and in getting away with violations by way of unauthorized extraction of water and crop pattern regulation.

- Incidence and intensity of water-related conflicts – between uses and users within individual systems, across systems and regions – is increasing. Conflict resolution mechanisms are neither functional nor effective.
- Perhaps the greatest inequity of the way water resource development is planned is the callous indifference to displacement and loss of livelihood of large numbers of people occasioned by construction of dams and large-scale canal networks, and adverse effects on the environment and livelihood sources of downstream communities.

### *An unsustainable system*

The system is not just inefficient and inequitable, but the way it has been and continues to be managed also poses threats to sustainability. Dangers to sustainability arise mainly from the following factors:

- Land degradation from water logging and salinity due to imprudent use of irrigation, failure to check and reverse growing pollution of water sources by agricultural chemicals, industrial and urban wastes.
- An obsession with construction of new large-scale projects for augmentation of surface water supplies unmindful of the fact that in most parts of the country the utilizable potential is already more or less exploited and that what remains is concentrated in areas where costs and risks of exploitation are much higher and also requires international agreements.
- The hype about interlinking of rivers as the panacea to solve the country's water problem is fundamentally flawed, in terms of technical feasibility and costs, conflict potential as well as being fraught with horrendous environmental consequences.
- There is compelling evidence that the groundwater table has been falling progressively in more and more areas as is the area irrigated per well, suggesting that the present rates of exploitation are unsustainable.

## The problem is with water management and governance

The deficiencies outlined above are the result of serious systemic flaws in the way water resources development is organized. Water is designated as a state subject under the Constitution. States are therefore empowered to determine the strategy for water resource development in their territories, choose where, when and what projects are to be taken up, and determine rules of allocation and use of water for various purposes, subject to certain restrictions in the case of inter-state rivers. The centre is empowered by the Constitution and attendant legislation to determine the total availability of water in such basins and its distribution between riparian states. This task has been done in the 1950s and 1960s by a series of tribunals whose awards are accepted as binding. The centre also has the authority to intervene in and facilitate resolution of inter-state disputes over sharing of water and to set up organizations for integrated management of inter-state rivers. However, these statutory powers have been used sparingly and hesitantly.

That the size and content of the development plans and the specific water resource projects of the states to be taken up are subject to review and approval by the Planning Commission has made little difference. The Commission's review of sector-wise plans is perfunctory. The process of appraisal of specific project proposals by an expert committee at the centre leaves much to be desired in terms of rigour and professional objectivity. Few state proposals have been rejected. On the contrary, the states have asserted their autonomy by taking up a large number of them (over 300 at last count) without the Planning Commission's approval. The audit of project implementation by the CAG is mostly confined to financial aspects; critical assessments of the deviation of realizations in terms of outcomes and impact relative to expectations and mandatory recommendations for corrective action, are rare. Water policy statements of the states and the centre shy away from these problems, without addressing the basis of and mechanisms for balancing competing claims and objectives and ensuring accountability for performance.

We have a situation in which all functions relating to development and management of surface water resources and regulation of groundwater resources are effectively vested with the state governments. They decide what surface projects are to be taken up and where. They have assumed the responsibility for the design, construction and management of all major and medium surface water projects, making and enforcing rules for allocation, scheduling and pricing of water for various uses, and resolving conflicts that arise in these matters. They have as a matter of policy also decided to bear all the costs of development and management in their budgets and to charge users of water much lower rates than even the costs of operation and maintenance (O&M). Groundwater development is left to the private sector, subject to government approval of location and spacing of wells and sanction of power connections. In all these matters, the government follows an extremely liberal policy of providing cheap credit and cheap energy to encourage the exploitation of this resource. This conflation of authority to deal with all aspects of water resource development with hardly any checks and balance mechanisms has had profound adverse consequences for the manner in which this resource has been managed.

Expansion of irrigation is essential for increasing agricultural production in the country. The demand for water for non-agricultural uses, though still relatively small compared to what is used for irrigation, is also growing, but at a much faster rate. The ground level pressures for expansion of supplies for all uses are very strong. Politicians respond positively to this pressure, both for objective reasons and also as a means for cultivating electoral support. It also happens that water resource projects involve lucrative construction contracts known to be open to kickbacks. This conjunction of factors has led to serious erosion in the care with which projects are prepared and evaluated. Political expediency of responding to ground-level demands has become the decisive factor in deciding what projects are taken up and at what scale. The huge number of unapproved projects in the pipeline, enormous upward revisions in scope and costs of projects and inordinate delays in project completion are a direct result of this phenomenon. The central government and the Planning Commission have become mute spectators, unwilling and unable to address the problem.

There was a time when it was recognized that, while the government funds the entire capital cost, beneficiaries should bear a part of this cost through betterment levies and that water charges should be adequate to cover operation and maintenance (O&M) costs. This position has since been abandoned on the specious grounds that water is essential for agriculture and that farmers are too poor to afford charges on this basis. The provision for collection of betterment levies from beneficiaries, as well as the proposition that at least 1 per cent of capital costs should be recovered from users, was given up. Even the attenuated recommendations of the Planning Commission and the Finance Commission that user charge recoveries should cover at least O&M costs, were not followed.

Rates are neither adjusted (despite soaring O&M costs) nor are dues at prevailing rates assessed and collected correctly. Some ten states have since revised the rates to varying degrees but another five have not made any changes for over 25 years. A Planning Commission committee report (Planning Commission 1992) estimated that the actual assessment was much lower than the amount due at the prescribed rates and the actual collection was only a fraction of assessment. Currently, actual revenues are estimated to be less than one-eighth of the reported O&M expenditure for the country as a whole, with the proportion being much lower in a majority of states. This has resulted in a massive and continuing increase in the volume of unrecovered costs on account of irrigation to be borne by the budget.

At the same time, the budgetary allocations for O&M have been increasingly short of levels needed to ensure that the systems are kept in good operating condition. Many of the old systems are in disrepair, and several of the newer ones are incomplete in varying degrees thereby impairing their capacity to realize their full designed potential. They are designed primarily to deliver water to different sections of the command and not to ensure optimum use of available water to areas serving numerous users, growing a wide variety of crops. The distribution systems have not been designed to regulate quantum and timing of water deliveries at the field level; and are not equipped with control structures for flexible regulation of supplies according to the condition of crops being grown in the area.

The entitlement of users is to get water for their land and not for crops. Most systems have restrictions on the kinds of crops that can be grown. But actual crop patterns invariably turn out to be very different from design assumptions. These are the outcome of decisions of individual cultivators depending on their calculations of relative returns to crops and ability to access supply to meet their requirements, invariably in violation of rules. The situation in this respect, being variable, depending on seasonal and market conditions, is unpredictable and certainly beyond the ability of system managers even to monitor much less to control at the field level. In general, their scheduling decisions, based on the reservoir levels and seasonal rainfall, are limited to timing and sequence of water releases to different branch canals and tertiary distributaries. These decisions are based on rules of thumb to deal with different contingencies. Once water is released, the competition among users (including those who are without entitlements) for access to water and the attendant widespread conflicts get articulated. These are resolved, not on the basis of clearly defined rules applied through transparent institutional mechanisms, but by the relative power of different claimants, vis-à-vis each other, to access surface or groundwater and in their ability to persuade, pressure and bribe system functionaries.

In predominantly groundwater irrigated areas, competition and conflict arise in the need to deepen wells and install more powerful pumps to extract water from a falling groundwater table. Though the government is empowered by law to regulate the process, it has chosen not to do so. Instead, it has followed policies – through providing cheap energy and increased supplies of cheap credit – to encourage it. In this respect, smaller holdings are at a distinct disadvantage compared to larger farmers who can better afford to incur the cost involved from their own resources or through borrowing. As a result, the expansion of groundwater irrigated area is, on the average, much slower than the increase in the number of wells. Moreover, the proportion of the increase in area irrigated is getting increasingly skewed in favour of larger farms.

Over time, the scope, nature and intensity of problems in ensuring equitable, efficient and sustainable management of water are increasing for several reasons including: (1) the emergence of sizable groups who have managed to establish unauthorized access to waters of individual systems or rivers feeding them, with the connivance or consent of the government; (2) the growing pressure of demand from non-agricultural uses for surface and groundwater being used for agriculture; (3) deterioration in water quality of both surface and groundwater sources due to pollution from untreated industrial effluents and urban wastewater; (4) the damage caused to natural groundwater recharge regimes of riverbeds by indiscriminate sand mining and the adverse impact of excessive diversion of surface flows on downstream and coastal ecology; and (5) pent up frustration of the millions who have suffered from displacement caused by the construction of large-scale surface water systems and the callous disregard for fulfilling commitments for their rehabilitation.

That these problems are becoming more widespread and intense is evident from numerous government reports, research studies, press reports, and court cases. But they tend to be viewed and dealt with as separate, localized problems from different disciplinary and interest group perspectives. The responsibility for monitoring these phenomena and dealing with them are mostly in the domain of state governments. Few states have shown the willingness and ability to tackle the problems seriously. Many have passed legislations indicating dos and don'ts, and penalties for violations. But these are widely known to be far too weak and loophole-ridden to be effective. Ground level agencies which are supposed to generate objective and validated data are far too under-funded and under-staffed. Such data as are collected are often not available in the public domain or even to those directly affected. Establishing cases against violators in courts of law using available data as evidence is difficult enough. But the difficulties are compounded by the complexity of the issues involved, enormous delays and uncertain outcomes of litigation, exacerbated by the lack of the necessary expertise and knowledge of the adjudicating bodies, and the fact that enforcement of even such corrective measures/penalties they impose is effectively thwarted by the political clout of violators.

Altogether, the current state of water resource development and management in the country is at best a functioning anarchy, obsessed with investments for expansion of the overall water supply. Concerns about the mounting crisis in the efficiency and sustainability of water use are widely voiced in the public domain by experts and activists as well as in the rhetoric of plan documents and official policy statements. But there are hardly any significant changes in institutional arrangements, management and policies that would be conducive to promoting these objectives. Initiatives like command area development and accelerated irrigation development programmes focus on physical investments for fuller, speedier utilization of the potential created. They are believed to have had some effect, but no objective in-depth assessments are available.

User participation in management of surface systems has gained some currency. Several states have encouraged the creation of Water Users' Associations (WUAs) at the tertiary levels. The role assigned to them varies widely; they have created an institutional axis for interaction between local user communities and system managers. Some have been entrusted with the task of managing maintenance of distribution networks with funds provided by the government; very few have been given the responsibility to collect water rates as well. This is the case even in states which have gone farthest to have elected user representatives on management committees at different levels. The results by all accounts are mixed but remain to be systematically and objectively documented. In no case has the government devolved to them the authority to make and enforce rules of allocation use, much less determine rates in the system as a whole. In a few states, which have raised water rates to meet rising costs and rationalize their structure, collections have improved and cover the major part of O&M costs. But none of these have a made a significant change to the status of water management which continues to be a functioning anarchy, incurring huge and continuing losses, and is marked by inefficient and inequitable use of available supplies. The seriousness of the situation has not sunk into the consciousness of those served by existing systems, the general public or the political class and bureaucracy.

## Way forward: tinkering with the system is not enough

That deficiencies of water resource planning and management cannot be addressed through piecemeal changes in existing policies and institutions but call for radical systemic reform that recognize and tackle their root causes, has been recognized by several expert committees and scholarly studies. This has been reiterated by detailed reviews of problems of this sector commissioned by the Planning Commission as part of the preparation for the 12th plan. The following are the key elements of a long-term reform strategy for tackling them that emerge from these deliberations:

*(1)* ***Shift focus from the present near-exclusive preoccupation with augmentation of supplies, giving primacy to measures to improve efficiency of water use***: The utilizable potential of all rivers, except in the lower Ganges and the Brahmaputra basins, has been more or less exploited. The potential additions to supply from ongoing projects of central Indian and peninsular rivers, many of which are unapproved, are relatively small and are proving to be inordinately expensive and taking far too long to complete. The proposed outlays on these need to be substantially reduced by stopping further outlays on projects, work on which has not started yet or is in the very early stages. Developing the potential in the Ganges-Brahmaputra basin, and bringing the water to regions which need it, is not only likely to be far more expensive but also likely to pose formidable technical challenges and cause unacceptably large and serious adverse environmental impacts.

In case of groundwater, there is widespread, large and continuing decline in water tables and decline in the area irrigated per well. The effective increase in the availability of water, and extent of area irrigated is likely to be far from commensurate with the huge amount of private investments that have gone into the process. Policies which help or encourage private investments in agriculture need a thorough review based on a careful reassessment of this aspect from available data; this would also be useful in identifying areas with significant unexploited potential.

*(2)* ***Programmes and policies for augmenting effective supply of water from sources already in operation by reducing avoidable conveyance and distribution losses and increasing the output per unit of effective on-field supply should be given much higher priority over those seeking to augment existing supplies.*** Many of the existing surface systems (major, medium as well as minor ones) are in a poor state of repair due to a lack of proper maintenance. It is necessary to conduct a concerted programme of intensive surveys to assess the incidence of losses due to seepage, leakages and non-consumptive evaporation and the kinds of improvements by way of rationalization and modernization of the distribution works appropriate to reducing them. This preparatory effort itself would call for large outlays. Much larger amounts will be needed to implement the modernization works.

In the case of groundwater, the programme for aquifer mapping, being initiated during the current plan, will give a better idea of storage capacity of aquifers already in use and the extent of extraction and recharge. This will also identify scope for reducing avoidable waste and for increasing the rate of recharge.

The integrated watershed development, which has the potential to significantly augment water available for rainfed areas, must be given far greater attention than at present. Increasing the proportion of local rainfall for local use is necessary to arrest the widening disparities in water supply for domestic and agricultural productivity between rainfed and irrigated tracts. It will require significant increase in the scale of allocation of funds but on a much smaller scale than is being spent on new works and deepening of wells/tubewells.

*(3)* ***A shift in priorities may well result in a reduction in the scale of investments being spent in the name of water resource development.*** But more importantly, it requires a sea change in the current scope and content of tasks that water resource departments of the government, and indeed water professionals generally, have to perform, as also in the organizational and managerial structures appropriate for that purpose. The planning and project design/implementation functions for different aspects of water resource planning, within a unified organization at the state level. At the same time, their primary role should not be, as is currently the case, limited to the design and construction of projects for delivering water to their end uses. They should be responsible for ensuring that techno-economic issues involved in making certain that delivered water can be used efficiently, are explicitly dealt with before finalizing the design. The expertise needed for this purpose does not exist in the design offices that are staffed entirely by civil engineers.

It also calls for changes in the existing arrangements for independent critical appraisal of project proposals before approving their implementation and for revisions in scope and cost estimates thereafter. The existing arrangement in which all these functions, as well the task of ensuring timely completion of projects within approved budgets, are currently handled in the Central Ministry of Water Resources and the erstwhile Planning Commission[1] is unsatisfactory. Besides being inimical to objectivity, the procedures are opaque, the scrutiny is perfunctory and the veracity of techno-economic data underlying the proposals is without critical inspection. All too often, what is proposed is approved without any significant change. Institutional arrangements for monitoring deviations from approved scope, schedules, costs and outcome either do not exist or are at best dysfunctional. They are allowed to go unchecked, leave alone being penalized. At a minimum, the project appraisal function and the authority to monitor implementation and enforce sanctions against major violations must vest with the Planning Commission.

*(4) **Vest the authority and responsibility for continuing operations of surface systems at all levels (from small-scale local works to large systems, up to and including the basin level) to organizations managed by elected representatives of users, with the professional managerial personnel being seconded and answerable to them.*** They should be left free to decide all aspects of management – water allocation, scheduling, internal conflict resolution and pricing. The role of the government should be limited to laying down the basic framework in which these organizations are to function, the scope and content of water rights of members, the mechanisms for periodic audit of their performance, and the resolution of conflicts at different levels. These organizations must be required to be financially self-reliant, with powers to decide the internal tariff and scheduling of available water between uses and users, and to levy and collect rates to be charged and collected from users, subject to review and approval of the basis for these decisions by independent regulatory authorities.

In dealing with these matters, it is important to recognize that given the extensive area covered by systems and the enormous number of users, it is impossible and far too expensive to rely on the bureaucracy to carry out maintenance and repair, to monitor and enforce observance of rules regarding entitlements and responsibilities and to also determine and collect dues, right down to the individual user. These tasks can be made more manageable, and less expensive, by dividing these responsibilities between the decision-making bodies and the bureaucracy at the system level on the one hand and those of WUAs at the ground level on the other hand.

The idea is for the system management to specify the entitlements of individual tertiary level user associations, and to frame contracts to deliver the specified volume and duration to each of them at a specified charge per unit volume, subject to the association undertaking responsibility for maintenance of facilities within its command, leaving it free to decide how the use of water by members is to be regulated and to assess and collect user fees from them. The contract must specify not only the penalties imposed on the associations for violations but also on the system management if it fails to deliver the agreed amounts and the timing of the water supply to the associations.

To be effective, these institutional changes must be accompanied by a system of pricing that ensures the recovery of the full operating and capital costs of managing these tasks at a reasonable level of efficiency, subject to review by an independent regulatory body. This is essential to ensure that each system is financially self-reliant and that users have a strong incentive to make efficient use of the water they get. A proposal along these lines, advocated by a committee of the Planning Commission some 20 years back, has again been recommended in the report of a Working Group on surface irrigation for the 12th Plan. However, the Plan document does not even refer to the need for these reforms.

In the case of groundwater, which is entirely in the private sector, the present system of heavy subsidies on energy for pumping has a two-fold adverse effect on efficient and sustainable use of this depleting resource. Lower cost of energy, in so far as it means higher net returns, stimulates larger demand for groundwater. The deepening of wells and tubewells to get water from falling water tables increases the costs. But the fact that it is proceeding apace suggests that it is still profitable at current levels of energy prices. Raising the cost of energy would therefore not only slow down the growth of demand for groundwater but also at the same time save a large part of investment that goes into deepening which in any case doesn't contribute to increase in the total water availability.

A restructuring of institutions and policies along the aforementioned lines is essential to correct the current chaotic state of water resource management and reverse its unchecked drift towards disaster. This is not to suggest that this can or will be done: the mindsets and entrenched interests of all concerned – the political class, the bureaucracy, water users and indeed the public at large – are not interested in it and are in fact inimical to such reform. Activists are naturally preoccupied with pleading and agitating to check the continuing tendency to launch projects without proper preparation, unmindful of their adverse environmental impact, and to find solutions to numerous and growing conflicts, particularly water-related ones, that are festering in different parts of the country. The focus in many cases tends to be on particular aspects of localized conflicts and the inability of existing arrangements for adjudication to come up with enforceable solutions. It is evident that conflicts in a particular facet of water management are related to and affected by technical and institutional problems in related facets and how they are handled. Deficiencies in the way different facets of programmes are designed, implemented and managed, and how they can be solved, needs to be addressed in a broader systemic perspective.

That there is no constituency for systemic reform is obvious. Such a constituency has to be created and nurtured. Lack of adequate, reliable data on the contribution of different sources to the country's overall water resources, the utilizable and utilized volumes from different sources for different end uses, the efficiency of their use and their environmental impact, is a serious problem. A Planning Commission Report (Planning Commission 2011) has drawn attention to the fact that validated data on most of these aspects are not even compiled and put into the public domain. The need for a comprehensive programme for improvement of data on all these aspects and the need for a pro-active effort to encourage and support research has been recognized and incorporated as part of the 12th Plan. Besides endorsing these recommendations and urging the government to implement the proposed programme, much can be gained from the voluminous literature that describes the condition of and problems faced by specific systems spread all over the country. Activist organizations' archives can provide far more detailed information on these aspects. A systematic and organized collation of this material in a comprehensive State of Water Resources in India report could be a powerful means to sensitize the public about the nature, magnitude and spatial spread of problems and the inability of existing arrangements to solve them. This needs to be supplemented by research studies to better understand the difficulties – conflicting interests of different stakeholders, legal, economic, political and institutional impediments – in finding and implementing solutions for different kinds of problems.

## Note

1 The Planning Commission no longer exists; it has been substituted by the Niti Aayog which is more like a 'think tank'.

## References

Planning Commission. 1992. *Report of the Committee on Pricing of Irrigation Water*. New Delhi: Government of India (GoI), http://planningcommission.gov.in/reports/publications/pub92_pricwtr.pdf (accessed on 8 March 2018).

Planning Commission. 2011. *Report of the Working Group on Water Database Development and Management for the 12th Five Year Plan (2012–2017)*. New Delhi: Government of India (GoI), http://planningcommission.gov.in/aboutus/committee/wrkgrp12/wr/wg_data.pdf (accessed on 8 March 2018).

# 3 Managing river basins

## Re-examining the biophysical basis

*Veena Srinivasan and Sharachchandra Lele*

### Introduction

There is widespread acceptance of the idea that water should be managed using river basins as a unit. The argument is that the surface catchment of a river forms the physical boundaries within which the water moves. This movement of water connects all the water users within that river basin and hence the basin is the unit at which coordination between water users should occur. As society's technological capacity to modify the movement of water has increased, the interconnectedness has become more manifest across larger distances, amplifying the call for basin-scale water management (Iyer 2007; Molle 2009).

In India, the National Water Policy of 1987 stated that river basin planning is necessary and recommended the setting up of River Basin Organisations (RBOs). In fact, the first such organization was the Damodar Valley Corporation, set up by special legislation back in 1948 (SANDRP 1999). The River Boards Act was passed in 1956. However, despite this path breaking law of 1956, not a single River Basin Organisation has been constituted under this Act (Iyer 1994). In parallel, the Inter-State Water Disputes Act was passed in 1956, for setting up Tribunals to govern the sharing of inter-state rivers. In practice, the functioning of River Boards has been far from the ideal of river basin management institutions (SANDRP 1999; Raju and Taron 2008; Shah and van Koppen 2006). They have been rightly criticized for focusing too narrowly on the operations of specific dam projects. Similarly, Tribunals have not functioned smoothly (Iyer 2002), and some analysts have argued that Tribunals and Boards can undermine each other (Raju and Taron 2008). Critics of the idea of basin-scale management draw attention to social processes and actors that operate from beyond basin boundaries; but even they do not deny that the intra-basin biophysical processes tie such actors together.

The question is whether the biophysical basis is fully understood and integrated into the actual planning, management or adjudication of water use in river basins. In our observation, at least in the Indian context, basin-scale management has been interpreted narrowly as the management, apportioning or adjudication of *surface water in the major river channel* and regulating the construction and operation of *major surface water utilization structures* as the means of such management. Thus, 'Water Disputes Tribunals' (WDTs) have *de facto* become '*river* water disputes tribunals'. For instance, the Cauvery Water Disputes Tribunal (CWDT) describes its goal as 'apportioning waters of the River Cauvery' (CWDT 2007).

Similarly, the RBOs have focused on the construction and operation of major dams, barrages and diversions of surface water, rather than on the integrated management of all the water in the basin. For instance, the Damodar Valley Corporation states its goal as fostering

> integrated development of the Damodar Valley command area and achieve excellence in its multifaceted activities of control of floods, provision of irrigation, generation, transmission and distribution of electrical energy and also soil conservation, unified tourism, fisheries, socio-economic & health development of villages *within a radius of 10 km of its projects*.
>
> (emphasis added)

In contrast, the much lauded Murray-Darling Basin Authority in Australia 'has been planning the integrated management of water resources of the Murray-Darling Basin' (Gaur and Amerasinghe 2011).

This focus on surface water and major structures appears to be premised upon and reinforced by certain assumptions about the nature of hydrological processes and the ability of human beings to modify them. For instance, the guidelines for river basin planning put forth by the Central Water Commission mention conjunctive use of surface and groundwater as if they were different sources, with groundwater augmenting surface water availability (Basin Planning and Management Organization 2007: Sec.14.5). Further, the focus on big dams suggests, again implicitly, that smaller structures do not affect river flow significantly. Finally, the design and operation of large dams as well as the apportionment of river waters is done on the basis of 'dependable yield', a concept in which a historical series of measured streamflows at a gauge is taken as the basis for estimating the 75th or 90th percentile flow in the river. The core assumption is that the historical pattern of rainfall and flows will (on an average) continue in the future. But this so-called dependable yield may not be dependable at all. In this chapter, we explore all these assumptions critically, and suggest that integrated water management in a river basin, especially in the Indian context, will require a more rigorous understanding of hydrology and the impact of human interventions.

## The hydrological cycle

As discussed in the previous section, the choice of 'river basins' as the appropriate unit of management is rooted in the cyclical movement of water that connects different parts of the river basin. Water evaporates, travels into the air and becomes part of a cloud, falls on earth as precipitation, and then flows back to the oceans, evaporating on the way or at the end. This sequence of processes repeats itself again and again and is called the water cycle (see Figure 3.1a).

In a 'pristine' catchment (shown in Figure 3.1A), as rain falls on the ground, a part of it enters the soil (infiltration) and a part of it runs off and travels over the ground surface into lakes and rivers (surface runoff). The portion that infiltrates moves downward through openings in the soil. As the water moves through the soil, the vast majority of it is taken up by the roots of vegetation and goes back to the atmosphere through the leaves (evapo-transpiration). The water that

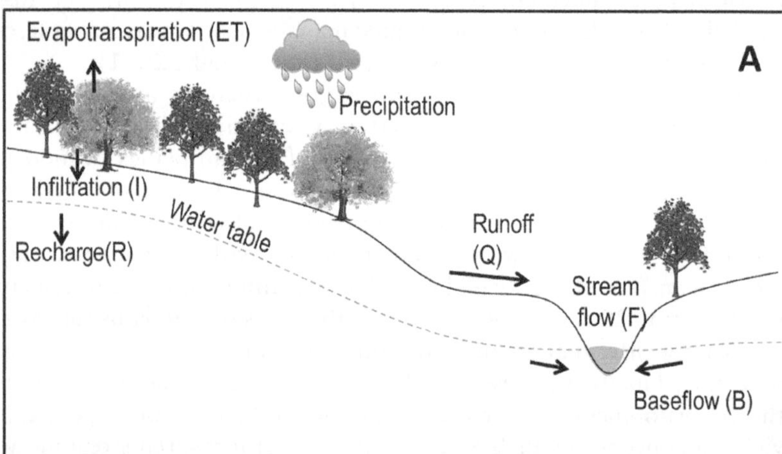


*Figure 3.1A* The Water Cycle in a Pristine Catchment

Source: Authors

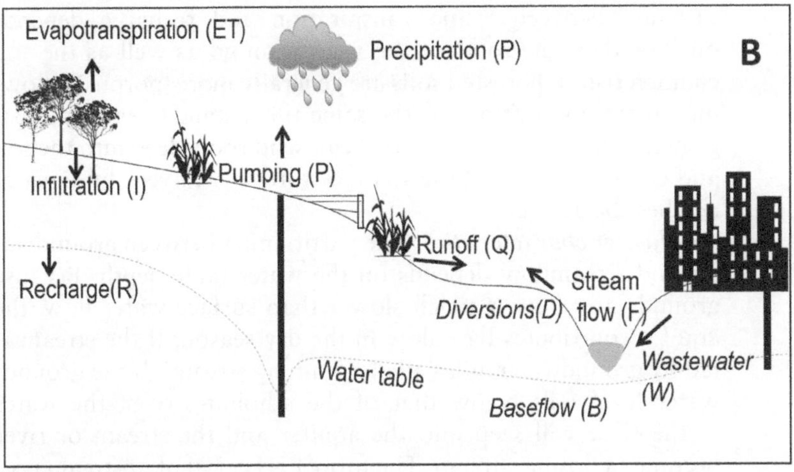


*Figure 3.1B* Modification of the Water Cycle in a Human-Dominated Catchment

Note: Italics indicate components whose presence or change is usually ignored or oversimplified by basin planners.

Source: Authors

makes it past the root zone goes into the aquifer (recharge). The surface below which the aquifer is completely saturated (holds as much water as it can) is called the water table. Groundwater within the aquifer also moves albeit much more slowly than surface runoff. If the water table intersects a stream surface or land surface, it contributes to the stream as 'base flow'. The total water flowing in the river is called 'streamflow'.

How much streamflow occurs in a pristine river basin depends on the magnitude and intensity of rainfall, the topography and soils, vegetation characteristics (rooting depth), groundwater levels and aquifer characteristics. Their role is briefly described here.

***Rainfall intensity:*** The partitioning between infiltration and runoff depends on two things – how intense the rainfall is and how shallow the water table is. If the soil is completely saturated, the rain will runoff. Even if the soil is not saturated, there is an upper limit to water absorption into the soil, which depends on the soil characteristics and topography. Thus, a greater fraction of the rain runs off during more intense rain events.

***Vegetation characteristics:*** Of the water that infiltrates, the partitioning between evapo-transpiration and recharge depends on how deep the roots of the vegetation go as well as the soil characteristics. Forested soils are generally more 'porous', allowing greater infiltration. At the same time, some trees (e.g., fast-growing species like eucalyptus) can send roots deep into the soil and capture almost all the soil moisture so that very little water reaches the aquifer.

***Groundwater characteristics***: The partitioning between groundwater and streamflow depends on the water table depth. Because groundwater flow is much slower than surface water flow, the aquifer contributes base flow in the dry season. If the stream is fed by groundwater, it is called a 'gaining stream'. If the groundwater level falls below that of the adjoining river, the water in the river will seep into the aquifer and the stream or river becomes a 'losing' stream. The former is typical of upstream portions of the catchment, while the latter may occur in the deltas or floodplains.[1] This two-way relationship between groundwater and surface water implies that they must be treated as a single resource, rather than separate buckets or pools or flows.

In pristine river basins, these processes tend to be stable (or changing very slowly). Over time, about the same fractions of rainfall end up as runoff, evapo-transpiration and recharge, and these fractions can be assumed to be constant in planning and allocating water resources, such as the building of the first dam in such a basin.

## Overlooked human interventions

Most WDTs and RBOs implicitly assume either a pristine hydrological cycle[2] (Figure 3.1A) or at least that the flows in the anthropogenically altered hydrological cycle (Figure 3.1B) are stable and known to the river basin agency. They measure the flows at different gauging stations, accounting for the withdrawals from the river upstream of the gauging station via major schemes for different uses. The computation of total annual streamflow at the downstream control point (such as a dam), including upstream withdrawals/diversions, is termed as 'the yield of the river system' and used as the basis for planning and allocation of water to different uses/users.

This approach, however, does not work well in human-dominated basins, where direct and indirect human interventions alter almost every link in the hydrological cycle (Figure 3.1B) and constantly evolve. New large dam and inter-basin projects, which greatly modify flows, continue to be commissioned. Groundwater extraction by lakhs of users changes water levels in the aquifer, altering base flows. Grazing, cultivation, paving or replacing forests with agriculture changes evapo-transpiration and infiltration rates. Streamflow is impeded by the construction of dams and diversion weirs. Diversion of water for domestic and industrial uses of water may then generate wastewater or 'return flows' that come back to the river. This may occur at a different location, with a time lag and at a diminished quality. Finally, the cumulative effects of human actions are beginning to modify climatic patterns themselves.

However, of all these interventions, only the construction of multiple major or medium-sized dams and diversions has been factored into river basin planning methodologies in India. This may have been acceptable during the first decades after independence. The river basin-scape at that time was characterized by agriculture that was still primarily rainfed, with a few small-sized traditional surface irrigation structures and very little groundwater use. The overall land-use pattern (forests, grasslands and agriculture) also seemed relatively stagnant, and the fraction of area under human settlements and the amount of water diverted for domestic use was small. Over the last three to four decades, the picture has changed dramatically: micro-level human interventions in the hydrological cycle have become ubiquitous, and their cumulative impact can no longer be ignored. The major forms of these interventions and their effects are discussed later.

### *Direct human interventions: groundwater extraction*

As discussed in the section on the hydrological cycle, groundwater abstraction and use affect surface water directly and indirectly in many ways. We summarize here the evidence that suggests that streamflows in many Indian rivers, especially in peninsular India, might be declining due to this phenomenon.

The magnitude and growth of groundwater exploitation in India is greater than that of any other country in the world as documented by Shah *et al.* (2007). According to their estimates, India has the largest land area under groundwater irrigation in the world, with 53 per cent of its irrigated area being groundwater irrigated. The estimated groundwater withdrawal in India (at 250 $km^3$ per year) is more than twice that of the United States, which has the second highest quantity of withdrawal in the world. Equally important, the rate of growth in groundwater extraction has been nothing short of phenomenal, as it was only 10–20 $km^3$ per year in 1960. Consequently, 16 per cent of the districts in India are already classified as 'over-exploited' or 'critical' (Central Ground Water Board 2011). This trend is sharper in peninsular India, partly because the hard rock geology of that region results in low recharge rates for deeper aquifers.

A number of studies in the last decade or so have examined the impacts of groundwater pumping outside canal command areas.[3] Ranade (2005) was perhaps the first to estimate that the amount of upstream groundwater use in the part of the Narmada river basin was as high as 15 per cent of Madhya Pradesh's share of river waters. He argued that groundwater abstraction should be included in the Narmada Water Disputes Tribunal's decisions. Subsequently, a study of the Malaprabha basin found that sugarcane cultivation had dramatically expanded in the Malaprabha dam catchment (Heller *et al.* 2012). This cultivation was being carried out using a combination of groundwater pumping and direct lift from the river and could explain the decline in the inflows into the dam (Reshmidevi and Badiger 2009).[4]

Our recent work in the Arkavathy basin provides further evidence of this phenomenon (Srinivasan *et al.* 2015). We found flows reaching the Thippagondanahalli reservoir near Bangalore had declined by more than 75 per cent over a 40-year period. We then systematically tested and eliminated alternative explanations for this decline, including changes in rainfall patterns, rise in temperature leading to increased evapo-transpiration, and an increase in stream channel blockages. Groundwater extraction and its application to agriculture, leading to increased consumptive use of water, was estimated to have increased four-fold during the same period, and it is the single largest possible explanation of streamflow decline, with possibly a small contribution from water consumption by eucalyptus plantations. While the growth in groundwater extraction and consequent decline in groundwater levels have been widely acknowledged, there is little explicit inclusion[5] of the impact that this might be causing on river flows.

It is interesting to note that right from the early days of Water Dispute Tribunals (WDTs), the link between groundwater and surface water has been acknowledged. However, either the link has been assumed to be too difficult to understand or the direction of flow is treated as uni-directional, i.e., from surface to groundwater, as in the recharge of groundwater in canal commands (cf. endnote 5). In the deliberations of the Krishna Water Disputes Tribunal (KWDT) in 1962, it was acknowledged that groundwater should be part of the water resource to be allocated. However, the KWDT eventually decided that

> having regard to the fact that there is no available data relating to the underground water which the parties can place before the Honourable Tribunal . . . the underground water resources of the States concerned will not be regarded as alternative means of satisfying their needs and will not be taken into account for purposes of equitable apportionment of the waters of the river Krishna and the physical basin (river-valley) thereof.
>
> (D'souza 2006)

Both the Narmada and Godavari Water Disputes Tribunals took similar positions: because groundwater flow cannot be accurately estimated from the technical point of view, groundwater flows are therefore not fully cognizable from the legal point of view. Both tribunals decided that groundwater should be omitted altogether in the consideration of allocation of inter-state rivers (GWDT 1979; NWDT 1978 as quoted in CWDT 2007).

Almost three decades later, there was considerable evolution in the scientific understanding as well as the importance accorded to groundwater. The Cauvery Water Disputes Tribunal Award of 2007, in fact, devotes almost 60 pages to groundwater. However, it does so in a lopsided manner. Groundwater is only taken into account in the context of recharge in command canal areas and the extent to which existing groundwater use should be counted as part of Tamil Nadu's allocation. With Tamil Nadu and Karnataka agreeing early on to consider only groundwater in the Cauvery delta area for assessment and allocation, groundwater in the non-deltaic parts of Tamil Nadu and Karnataka, lying within the Cauvery basin, was not considered. Instead, the discussion centred on the extent to which groundwater use in the Cauvery delta is dependent on recharge from the canals and (by extension) on releases from the Mettur dam (CWDT 2007: Vol. III, 112–171). The idea that excessive groundwater depletion outside of the delta region could reduce streamflow is not acknowledged anywhere. Indeed, in allocating Bangalore's share, the tribunal assumes that 50 per cent of Bangalore's domestic water needs can be met from groundwater (CWDT 2007: Vol. III, 103), as if it is a separate unconnected resource.

Recent policies and legal frameworks such as the Draft National Water Framework Bill (2016) and the Model Groundwater Bill (2016) pay lip service to the idea of integration but don't specify how the integration should be achieved.

### *Direct human interventions: check dams and other SWC structures*

Watershed development has been the centrepiece of rural development projects in India since the 1990s (Joy *et al.* 2004). Most of these projects involve the construction of soil and water conservation (SWC) structures on drainage lines, such as check-dams, gully plugs and *nala* bunds. Some also use area treatments such as field bunds and continuous contour trenches. These structures are designed to 'slow' the flow of water and encourage infiltration. Starting in the early 2000s, a debate began on the likely impacts of large-scale watershed development on downstream flows (Batchelor, Rama Manohar Rao and Manohar Rao 2003).

Studies which carefully evaluate the impact of watershed development on downstream flows at different scales remain few and far between. The earliest effort, by Batchelor, Rama Mohan Rao and James (2000), was based on simple water balance calculations in one milli-watershed in Karnataka. Subsequently, they expanded their study to two milli-watersheds and showed that watershed development reduced the amount of water exiting the milli-watershed (in the form of streamflow) by ~50 per cent (Bishop *et al.* 2009). Similarly, a detailed empirical study of the impacts of *johads* (structures larger than check dams) in the well-known Aravari River basin in Rajasthan showed that these structures did increase groundwater recharge and thereby benefitted agriculture, but they also did decrease downstream flows. Specifically, larger rainfall events were required to generate similar flows downstream after the construction of the *johads* (Glendenning and Vervoort 2010; Glendenning and Vervoort 2011).[6]

It is important to note that the downstream impacts are not caused by the construction of upstream SWC structures per se. The check dams do increase infiltration (although some water will evaporate). In the absence of any change in water extraction, this infiltrated water would eventually contribute to increasing the base flow from the groundwater table to the river. The problem is that SWC structures are built in order to increase water available for farming or other human uses in surrounding areas. Typically, the recharged water is immediately pumped out from existing and new wells by the farmers and applied in agriculture. That is precisely what makes watershed development attractive to people in those micro-watersheds. But water made available for farming in upstream watersheds is then water made *un*available downstream.

How widespread is this impact? Since the 1990s, millions of hectares have been brought under watershed development in the country (Joy *et al.* 2004). Because multiple agencies are involved, there is no comprehensive and up-to-date database that would indicate what structures have been constructed where, and how many are still intact.[7] There is anecdotal evidence to suggest that multiple programmes are adding up to a phenomenal density of structures: a census of check dams in two milli-watersheds in the upper Arkavathy basin showed a high density of 1.35/sq km of watershed area. The impacts of watershed wide interventions such as field bunding, laser levelling etc. are expected to be even more severe. The complete absence of small-scale 'minor irrigation' structures in all river sharing agreements is striking and has been eloquently noted by several authors previously (Kumar *et al.* 2006).

### *Land cover and land use*

That land cover in the catchment will influence the rainfall-runoff relationship, and therefore the pattern of flow in a river, has long been recognized and has been the subject of a large fraction of the hydrological literature internationally. Land use is important because evapotranspiration from natural vegetation and rainfed crops/grazing land or 'green water' accounts for almost two-thirds of the precipitation. This has been shown globally (Oki and Kanae 2006) as well as in Indian river basins (Venot 2008). Therefore, changes in land cover and land use could have tremendous impacts on streamflow and by extension dependable yield.

Different types of land cover transitions may have different impacts in different biophysical contexts. Broadly, the following transitions seem relevant to the Indian context:

- Degradation in the quality of natural forest cover in upper catchments.
- Conversion of natural forests to plantations in upper catchments.
- Conversion of forests to rainfed agriculture.
- Conversion of rainfed agriculture or barren land to unirrigated plantations.[8]
- Conversion of agriculture to built-up areas.

The consequences of the first transition have been the subject matter of much debate in the forest hydrology literature, with one school arguing that decline in tree densities should lead to decreased evapo-transpirative losses and therefore increased streamflows overall and another school arguing that forest degradation also leads to reduced infiltration and therefore to high monsoon but low summer flows (Bonell and Bruijnzeel 2004). In the Himalayan context, there was a raging debate about the impact of forest loss and degradation on floods in the Gangetic plains, but the consensus now seems to be that the flooding impacts have been over-stated (Ives and Messerli 1989; CSE 1992). This is complicated by the fact that forests play a key role in atmospheric moisture cycling and may alter rainfall patterns themselves.

The second transition (forests to plantations of fast-growing species) has, however, been universally acknowledged to have negative consequences for streamflow due to increase in evapo-transpiration by fast-growing trees. At the same time, it has been shown that conversion of degraded forests to fast-growing plantations may have mixed impacts, since it also improves infiltration rates (Krishnaswamy *et al.* 2012).

The consequences of the conversion of forests to agriculture seem to be less studied in the Indian context.[9] Much of course depends on the nature of agriculture that replaces forests. Rainfed single-crop cultivation (settled or shifting) may change streamflow only slightly, whereas terraced paddy cultivation may reduce downstream flows significantly. But there is little clarity about the magnitude of these effects.

The conversion of rainfed agriculture back to unirrigated tree cover has again been a subject of much debate but limited research. The debate was sparked by the promotion of eucalyptus, pine and other such fast-growing tree plantations under the so-called Social Forestry projects across India in the 1980s. Eucalyptus in particular was heavily criticized for being a highly water-consumptive species (among other negative attributes). The research on eucalyptus plantations in the Kolar district of Karnataka seems to broadly confirm that the evapo-transpirative losses due to eucalyptus could be as high as 100 per cent of the rainfall in the region (Calder *et al.* 1997; Calder, Hall and Prasanna 1993). But the exact consequences of particular extents of conversion at the watershed scale on streamflows have been studied only in the context of the Nilgiris (Sikka *et al.* 2003), where a long-term monitoring study has shown that conversion of Shola grasslands to eucalyptus plantations has systematically reduced streamflows. Overall, therefore, it is clear such conversions will contribute to reduction in streamflows.

Finally, it is obvious that conversion of agriculture to built-up areas through the expansion of cities will reduce infiltration and increase surface runoff (by increasing impervious areas) during the monsoon while decreasing dry season base flows (as infiltration will have decreased). However, till recently, these effects were considered to be significant only in the context of urban flooding, and not at the scale of river basins because the fraction of built-up area in a typical river basin in India is hardly significant. This, however, may change as the Indian landscape gets increasingly urbanized. Overall, the impacts of land-cover changes on streamflow may go in opposite directions depending on the type of change. But it is clear that all the transitions mentioned previously are happening in India at a significant scale, and, largely, the effects of these transitions are yet to be factored in.

### *Irrigation return and urban wastewater flows*

Although many basin institutions acknowledge the existence of return flows, in most cases these are assumed to be fixed. Thus, a specified per cent of urban (80 per cent) and industrial (97.5 per cent) withdrawals are assumed to return to the system (CWDT 2007) in allocating flows. Although this represents the percentage of wastewater that *should* return to the basin as return flows, it is unenforceable as the actual flow of wastewater is not tracked. No one knows if the return flow assumptions hold true in specific instances. In fact, there are several ways in which wastewater 'leaks' out of the system.

*Technology can alter how much wastewater is returned to the basin.* As technologies change and become more efficient, the quantity of wastewater returned could decrease. Because river water could cycle multiple times through human systems before it finally reaches the sea, water available downstream is often simply wastewater generated by upstream users. For instance, wastewater recycling is becoming a viable alternative for urban and industrial water users. This would have no impact on the watershed if the users simply abstracted less. But urban wastewater recycling is not often accompanied by a decrease in urban withdrawals; rather it is justified as the best way to meet growing urban demand. Similarly, drip irrigation technology has made agricultural water use much more efficient. However, many studies have pointed out that what it does may actually worsen water stress at the catchment scale – the so called irrigation efficiency paradox (Sivapalan *et al.* 2014; Scott *et al.* 2013). In other words, drip irrigation technology often simply induces an increase in the irrigated area; water withdrawals stay the same but return flows decrease, so that overall water availability downstream declines.

*New uses may emerge for the return wastewater flows that previously did not exist.* As technologies and societies evolve, new (inadvertent) uses for water and wastewater may emerge which were not originally foreseen. For instance, the CWDT assumes that 80 per cent of urban water allocations will return to the basin. In practice, because Bangalore's sewerage system lags far behind its piped supply system, much of the untreated wastewater ends up in urban lakes and streams. Some of these urban lakes, which were once seasonal, now hold water through the year because of the continuous trickle of sewage. They have become habitats for waterfowl. If lakes hold water throughout the year, they also evaporate more. Environmental amenities were never envisaged as a legitimate use of the Cauvery water supplied to urban areas; yet this use has spontaneously emerged. Much of the water in urban lakes recharges groundwater and is reused by the surrounding communities. Similarly, wastewater is now increasingly consumed by peri-urban farmers to grow irrigated crops such as baby corn and mulberry round the year. Because the water is contaminated with sewage (and sometimes industrial effluent), it is not recognized as 'Cauvery water irrigation' by any of the interested parties and yet must be significant in terms of the water balance.

*Third, new sources of water may generate additional wastewater.* Inter-basin imports of water into cities and unsustainable groundwater extraction introduce 'new sources of water' into river basins. Since most urban water use is non-consumptive, much of the imported water ends up as wastewater. For instance, the ephemeral Noyyal river in Coimbatore is a perennial river today, largely because of sewage generated by Coimbatore city. Almost all of the water supplied to Coimbatore is sourced from local groundwater or inter-basin imports (Srinivasan *et al.* 2014) from the Siruvani and Bhavani basins. Since much of the imported water ends up in the river as wastewater, a new source of water suddenly becomes available downstream of the city.

*Fourth, piped supply and sewerage infrastructure may carry the wastewater outside the basin altogether.* The issue of where return flows will end up is addressed in an inconsistent manner in the various tribunals and RBOs. For instance, the CWDT acknowledges that urban and industrial water use at the tail end of the delta (e.g., Karaikal region of Pondicherry) will not return to the system (CWDT 2007: Vol. V, p. 103). However, this is ignored in the case of upstream cities like Bangalore. A sizeable percentage of the Cauvery supply is transferred 'out of the Cauvery basin' to eastern Bangalore; the wastewater from these areas ends up in the Pennar and Ponnaiyar river basins (Harsha 2012).

### *Climate patterns changes (global and local)*

That global climate change will influence regional and local rainfall and temperature regimes is well recognized and estimating the nature and magnitude of these changes is the subject matter of much research. Several studies have analysed long-term trends all over India (Jain and Kumar 2012; Ghosh *et al.* 2012). Overall, these studies show that there are no discernible trends in average rainfall, although the spatial and temporal frequency of high and moderate rainfall events may be changing. Several recent studies (Jain and Kumar 2012; Kothawale and Rupa Kumar 2005) report an increase in the annual mean, maximum as well as minimum temperatures, with an accelerated warming during the last decades of the 20th century, especially in the post-monsoon and winter seasons. However, studies also show that trends observed at larger scales are not always observable at finer scales, possibly because of the spatial variability of local changes such as rapid urbanization, industrialization and deforestation (Ghosh 2009).

To a large extent, one may see these effects as 'exogenous' to the basin itself, as the contribution of greenhouse gas emissions from India to global climate change is still very small. Recent studies, however, point to some evidence that rainfall and temperature patterns are also affected by what are being termed as 'tele-connections', from local and regional land use/land cover changes to the regional climatic (Mahmood *et al.* 2014). It appears that these local changes may be equally important, at least in determining water availability in specific watersheds. For example, large-scale urbanization may be altering the time and spatial distribution of precipitation and urban heat island effects may be changing potential evapo-transpiration. Other studies have found evidence linking the delayed onset of the monsoon to winter and spring season irrigation in basins in India (Guimberteau *et al.* 2012; Wei *et al.* 2013). Links between forest cover and climate have also been established but are more complex (Bonan 2008) because forests affect climate through multiple pathways – carbon, water and energy.

## Discussion and way forward

The gaps described in the previous sections suggest that we need a new approach to river basin management in human-dominated basins, which includes most river basins in India. What might be the contours of such human-intervention sensitive and biophysically integrated river basin management?

To begin with, both RBOs and WDTs must allocate and manage all the water available in the basin, not just the flow in the rivers. This includes both the so called blue water (groundwater and surface water) and green water (soil moisture or evapo-transpiration) components (Falkenmark and Rockström 2006). This in turn will necessitate much greater coordination between the monitoring agencies (the Central Water Commission and the Central Groundwater Board, but also between state agencies responsible for surface and groundwater monitoring and the forest departments). Unfortunately, currently there is no communication between these agencies, and there are little systematically peer-reviewed efforts to analyse the data they collect to check for quality and then to estimate and explain the trends. At the same time, this will also require groundwater agencies focusing on 'aquifer based management' (Kulkarni and Shankar 2009) to also include exchanges between ground and surface water more explicitly. Recent efforts to integrate the ground and surface water agencies (Shah 2016) have been met with stiff resistance.

Second, managing water resources without understanding how much water is available, how much is being used and by whom, is going to be a non-starter. We need comprehensive water budgeting, simultaneously in each watershed and the river basin as a whole, to ensure that water resources are allocated within and between communities fairly and transparently. The problem is that the variables are being monitored by different state agencies and the quality of the data is often inconsistent (i.e., different sources are not internally consistent) and the spatial resolution at which these datasets are made available is often inadequate (i.e., typically taluka or district-scale, which is too coarse). Improving this will require the active cooperation of action agencies such as irrigation and watershed departments, water and electricity boards, and municipalities, so that what is actually happening on the ground can be estimated. Some of this is now being undertaken by the National Water Mission (nwm.gov.in) under the State-Specific Action Plans.

Finally, a more fundamental challenge is to change the paradigm altogether – from that of a one-time estimation of dependable yield to continuous adaptive management. To achieve this, the focus of monitoring must expand from just the 'outcome variables' (flow in the main river channel and the groundwater level) to include the 'influencing variables' (for example) and to incorporate them into the analysis. All the changes mentioned previously – groundwater pumping, check dam construction, shifts in vegetation cover, urbanization etc. are ongoing and intensifying. Compounding the problem is that decisions made by many independent users cannot be controlled or tracked by a single river basin agency. When coupled with the uncertainty in climate system, the idea of fixing allocations at a particular point in time seems absurd.

None of the inter-state tribunals and RBOs are equipped to addresses this. Many of the tribunals acknowledge these factors in their deliberations but ultimately adopt a pragmatic approach. However, many of the institutions were put in place in the 1970s. Today, we are surely in a better position in terms of both data and models to generate improved estimates of resource use (surface and ground) and to incorporate the aforementioned linkages. New data sources, including low-cost sensors, remote sensing and participatory approaches, are making it possible to track water use, flows and generate new insights that were hitherto not possible. What we need, which is increasingly becoming possible, is a shift towards 'adaptive management' (Holling 1978).

Adaptive management has been described as 'learning to manage while managing to learn' (Bormann *et al.* 1994). The idea of adaptive management is based on the insight that the ability to predict future key drivers influencing an ecosystem, as well as system behaviour and responses, is limited because of the inherent complexity of social-ecological systems. In the context of water, river basin management must be adaptive and allow managers to change management practices based on changes in system behaviour or new information (Pahl-Wostl *et al.* 2007). An integral component of adaptive management is social learning – developing and sustaining the capacity of different authorities, experts, interest groups and the public to constantly learn and better manage their river basins effectively. This will require a broad-based effort to enhance hydrological literacy in the country.

## Notes

1 Floods themselves may recharge the groundwater in floodplains.

2 We are focusing on the hydrological impacts of human interventions alone. It is true that human interventions also influence soil erosion and the movement of silt through rivers. But this is outside the scope of this chapter, as are the impacts of industrial and domestic effluents on water quality.

3 In canal command areas, the seepage from unlined canals recharges the shallow aquifer and that water becomes available for well-based irrigation. This phenomenon is recognized in river basin planning in India. Here, pumping may be beneficial to an extent as it keeps the land from getting water-logged.

4 This also draws attention to the possible role that direct lift irrigation might play in reducing river flows. A study of west-flowing rivers in the Karnataka

Western Ghats also points to this possibility in the case of the Polali River in the Dakshina Kannada district (Lélé *et al.* 2007).

5 Internationally, the influence of groundwater pumping on streamflows has been recognized for some time and has been gaining prominence in the recent literature (Madsen 1988; Zeng and Cai 2014). However, there are very few such hydrological studies in the Indian context.

6 So, it was not surprising to see officials of the Minor Irrigation Department in Karnataka getting into confrontations with officials of the Watershed Development Department, saying 'please don't do your watershed development in the catchments of our irrigation tanks', as we observed in a workshop in Bangalore in 2007.

7 This is partly because watershed development is carried out by many different agencies (departments of watershed development, agriculture, command area development, rural development etc.) obtaining funds from many different programmes (employment guarantee, rural development, drought proofing and many projects funded by foreign aid agencies). And partly because there is no incentive for these agencies to maintain such databases: funds can be spent repeatedly in the same micro-watersheds if their SWC treatment history is obscured.

8 We do not consider conversion of rainfed agriculture to irrigated crops here, because in most cases they are accompanied by surface irrigation systems (tanks or large dams with canals) or groundwater irrigation systems, which have already been discussed earlier in the chapter).

9 This may be surprising, considering that the last century or so has witnessed a huge expansion in the cultivated area at the cost of forests in the Indian sub-continent. For instance, the Kerala portion of the Western Ghats saw 25 per cent of its forest cover shifting to cultivation between 1973 and 1993 (Jha, Dutt and Bawa 2000). However, it may be partly explained by the fact that, since the passing of the Forest Conservation Act 1980, the conversions have slowed down dramatically, and the scale of conversion is now much more at the micro-level for development projects rather than large swathes for agriculture.

## References

Basin Planning and Management Organization. 2007. *Guidelines for Preparation of River Basin Master Plan*. New Delhi: Central Water Commission.

Batchelor, C. H., M. S. Rama Mohan Rao and A. J. James. 2000. *Karnataka Watershed Development Project: Water Resources Audit*. KAWAD Report 17. Bangalore: Karnataka Watershed Development Society.

Batchelor, C. H., M. S. Rama Mohan Rao and S. Manohar Rao. 2003. 'Watershed Development: A Solution to Water Shortages in Semi-Arid India or Part of the Problem', *Land Use and Water Resources Research*, 3(1): 1–10.

Bishop, E., I. Calder, C. H. Batchelor, J. Garratt, and A. Gosain. 2009. *Development and Application of the HYLUC-Cascade Model for Investigating the Water Resource Impacts of Rainwater Harvesting Structures in India*. Newcastle University, Newcastle: The Centre for Land Use and Water Resources Research, pp. 11.

Bonan, G. B. 2008. 'Forests and Climate Change: Forcings, Feedbacks, and the Climate Benefits of Forests', *Science*, 320(5882): 1444–1449.

Bonell, M. J. and L. A. Bruijnzeel. 2004. *Forests, Water and People in the Humid Tropics: Past, Present and Future Hydrological Research for Integrated Land and Water Management*. Cambridge: Cambridge University Press.

Bormann, B., P. G. Cunningham, M. Brookes, Van W. Manning, and M. Collopy. 1994. *Adaptive Ecosystem Management in the Pacific Northwest*. General Technical Report PNW-GTR-341. Portland, OR: U.S. Department of Agriculture, Forest Service, Pacific Northwest Research Station.

Calder, I., R. Hall and K. T. Prasanna. 1993. 'Hydrological Impact of Eucalyptus Plantation in India', *Journal of Hydrology*, 150(2–4): 635–648.

Calder, I., P. Rosier, K. T. Prasanna, and S. Parameswarappa. 1997. 'Eucalyptus Water Use Greater than Rainfall Input-Possible Explanation from Southern India', *Hydrology and Earth System Sciences Discussions*, 1(2): 249–256.

Central Ground Water Board. 2011. *Dynamic Groundwater Resources of India*. Faridabad: Central Ground Water Board, http://cgwb.gov.in/Documents/Dynamic-GW-Resources-2009.pdf (accessed on 28 May 2018).

CSE (Centre for Science and Environment). 1992. *Floods, Flood Plains and Environmental Myths. State of India's Environment: Third Citizen's Report*. New Delhi: Centre for Science and Environment.

CWDT (Cauvery Water Disputes Tribunal). 2007. *The Report of the Cauvery Water Disputes Tribunal: Volumes I to V*. New Delhi: Cauvery Water Disputes Tribunal, Ministry of Water Resources, Government of India (GoI).

D'souza, R. 2006. *Interstate Disputes over Krishna Waters: Law, Science and Imperialism*. New Delhi: Orient Longman.

Falkenmark, M. and J. Rockström. 2006. 'The New Blue and Green Water Paradigm: Breaking New Ground for Water Resources Planning and Management', *Journal of Water Resources Planning and Management*, 132(3): 129–132.

Gaur, A. and P. Amerasinghe. 2011. 'A River Basin Perspective of Water Resources and Challenges', in P. Tiwari and A. Pandey (eds.), *Water: Policy and Performance for Sustainable Development, India Infrastructure Report, 2011*, Volume 3–17. New Delhi: Oxford University Press.

Ghosh, Subimal, Vishal Luniya, and Anant Gupta. 2009. "Trend Analysis of Indian Summer Monsoon Rainfall at Different Spatial Scales." Atmospheric Science Letters 10 (4): 285–90.

Ghosh, S., D. Das, S. C. Kao, and A. R. Ganguly. 2012. 'Lack of Uniform Trends but Increasing Spatial Variability in Observed Indian Rainfall Extremes', *Nature Climate Change*, 2(2): 86–91.

Glendenning, C. J. and R. W. Vervoort. 2010. 'Hydrological Impacts of Rainwater Harvesting (RWH) in a Case Study Catchment: The Arvari River, Rajasthan, India. Part 1: Field-Scale Impacts', *Agricultural Water Management*, 98(2): 331–342.

Glendenning, C. J. and R. W. Vervoort. 2011. 'Hydrological Impacts of Rainwater Harvesting (RWH) in a Case Study Catchment: The Arvari River,

Rajasthan, India: Part 2. Catchment-Scale Impacts', *Agricultural Water Management*, 98(4): 715–730.

Guimberteau, M., K. Laval, A. Perrier, and J. Polcher. 2012. 'Global Effect of Irrigation and Its Impact on the Onset of the Indian Summer Monsoon', *Climate Dynamics*, 39(6): 1329–1348.

GWDT (Godavari Water Dispute Tribunal). 1979. *The Report of the Godavari Water Disputes Tribunal (With the Decision)*, Volumes, I and II. New Delhi: Godavari Water Disputes Tribunal, Ministry of Water Resources, Government of India (GoI).

Harsha, J. 2012. 'River Diversion Schemes Versus Waste Water Recycling for Bangalore City', *Current Science*, 103(2): 144–146.

Heller, E., J. Rhemtulla, S. Lele, M. Kalacska, S. Badiger, R. Sengupta, and N. Ramankutty. 2012. 'Mapping Crop Types, Irrigated Areas, and Cropping Intensities in Heterogeneous Landscapes of Southern India Using Multi-Temporal Medium-Resolution Imagery: Implications for Assessing Water Use in Agriculture', *Photogrammetric Engineering and Remote Sensing*, 78: 815–827.

Holling, C. S. (ed.). 1978. *Adaptive Environmental Assessment and Management*. International Institute for Applied System Analysis: xviii + 377. New York: John Wiley and Sons.

Ives, J. and B. Messerli. 1989. *The Himalayan Dilemma: Reconciling Development and Conservation*. New York: Routledge.

Iyer, R. R. 1994. 'Indian Federalism and Water Resources', *International Journal of Water Resources Development*, 10(2): 191–202.

Iyer, R. R. 2002. 'Inter-State Water Disputes Act 1956: Difficulties and Solutions', *Economic and Political Weekly*, 37(28): 2907–2910.

Iyer, R. R. 2007. *Towards Water Wisdom: Limits, Justice, Harmony*. Los Angeles: Sage Publications.

Jain, S. K. and V. Kumar. 2012. 'Trend Analysis of Rainfall and Temperature Data for India', *Current Science (Bangalore)*, 102(1): 37–49.

Jha, C. S., C. B. S. Dutt and K. S. Bawa. 2000 'Deforestation and Land Use Changes in Western Ghats, India', *Current Science*, 79(2): 231–238.

Joy, K. J., S. Paranjape, A. K. Kiran Kumar, R. Lele, and R. Adagale. 2004. *Watershed Development Review: Issues and Prospects*. CISED Technical Report. Bangalore: Centre for Interdisciplinary Studies in Environment and Development, www.indiawaterportal.org/sites/indiawaterportal.org/files/WatershedDevelopment_FullReport.pdf (accessed on 28 May 2018).

Kothawale, D. R. and K. Rupa Kumar. 2005. 'On the Recent Changes in Surface Temperature Trends over India', *Geophysical Research Letters*, 32(18).

Krishnaswamy, J., M. Bonell, B. Venkatesh, B. K. Purandara, S. Lele, M. C. Kiran, V. Reddy, S. Badiger, and K. N. Rakesh. 2012. 'The Rain – Runoff Response of Tropical Humid Forest Ecosystems to Use and Reforestation in the Western Ghats of India', *Journal of Hydrology*, 472: 216–237.

Kulkarni, H. and P. S. Shankar. 2009. 'Groundwater: Towards an Aquifer Management Framework', *Economic and Political Weekly*, 44(6): 13–17.

Kumar, M. D., S. Ghosh, A. Patel, O. P. Singh, and R. Ravindranath. 2006. 'Rainwater Harvesting in India: Some Critical Issues for Basin Planning and Research', *Land Use and Water Resources Research*, 6(1): 1.

Lélé, S., J. Vaidyanathan, S. Hegde, B. Venkatesh, and J. Krishnaswamy. 2007. *Influence of Forest Cover Change on Watershed Functions in the Western Ghats: A Coarse-Scale Analysis*. Project Report Submitted to UNESCO Man and Biosphere Programme. Bangalore: Centre for Interdisciplinary Studies in Environment and Development.

Madsen, H. 1988. 'Irrigation, Groundwater Abstraction and Stream Flow Depletion', *Agricultural Water Management, Agrohydrology – Recent Developments*, 14(1–4): 345–354, doi:10.1016/0378-3774(88)90088-1.

Mahmood, R., R. A. Pielke, K. G. Hubbard, D. Niyogi, P. A. Dirmeyer, C. McAlpine, A. Carleton, R. Hale, S. Gameda, and A. Beltrán-Przekurat. 2014. 'Land Cover Changes and Their Biogeophysical Effects on Climate', *International Journal of Climatology*, 34(4): 929–953.

Molle, F. 2009. 'River-Basin Planning and Management: The Social Life of a Concept', *Geoforum*, 40(3): 484–494, doi:10.1016/j.geoforum.2009.03.004.

NWDT (Narmada Water Dispute Tribunal). 1978. *Report of the Narmada Water Disputes Tribunal*. New Delhi: Narmada Water Disputes, Ministry of Water Resources, Government of India (GoI).

Oki, T. and S. Kanae. 2006. 'Global Hydrological Cycles and World Water Resources', *Science*, 313(5790): 1068–1072.

Pahl-Wostl, C., J. Sendzimir, P. Jeffrey, J. Aerts, G. Berkamp, and K. Cross. 2007. 'Managing Change Toward Adaptive Water Management through Social Learning', *Ecology and Society*, 12(2): 30.

Raju, K. V., and Avinandan Taron. 2008. "River Basin Organisations in India: An Overview." In Anonymous (Ed.), Managing Water in the Face of Growing Scarcity, Inequity and Declinging Returns: Exploring Fresh Approaches: Proceedings of the 7th Annual Partners Meet, 2: 612–45. Hyderabad: IWMI-TATA Water Policy Research Program, International Water Management Institute.

Ranade, R. 2005. 'Out of Sight, Out of Mind: Absence of Groundwater in Water Allocation of Narmada Basin', *Economic and Political Weekly*, 40(21): 2172–2175.

Reshmidevi, T. V. and S. Badiger. 2009. 'Impact of Irrigation Intensification on Inter-Sectoral Water Allocation in a Deficit Catchment in India', Proceedings of Symposium JS.3 at the Joint IAHS and IAH Convention, Hyderabad, September. Wallingford, UK: IAHS Press.

SANDRP. 1999. *River Basins Organisations in India: Institutional Frameworks and Management Options. A Case for Fundamental Review*. Thematic Reviews: Institutional and Governance Issues. New Delhi: South Asia Network in Dams, Rivers and People (SANDRP), www.zef.de/uploads/tx_zefportal/Publications/75c0_0f22_Saravanan-RiverBasin_wcd.pdf (accessed on 28 May 2018).

Scott, C. A., S. Vicuña, I. Blanco-Gutiérrez, F. Meza, and C. Varela-Ortega. 2013. 'Irrigation Efficiency and Water-Policy Implications for River-Basin Resilience', *Hydrological Earth System Science Discuss*, 10: 9943–9965.

Shah, M. 2016. 'A 21st Century Institutional Architecture for India's Water Reforms: Report Submitted by the Committee on Restructuring the CWC and CGWB', July, http://cgwb.gov.in/INTRA-CGWB/Circulars/Report_on_Restructuring_CWC_CGWB.pdf (accessed on 28 May 2018).

Shah, T., J. Burke, K. Villholth, M. Angelica, E. Custodio, F. Daibes, J. Hoogesteger, M. Giordano, J. Girman, and J. Van Der Gun. 2007. 'Groundwater: A Global Assessment of Scale and Significance', in D. Molden (ed.), *Water for Food, Water for Life: A Comprehensive Assessment of Water Management in Agriculture*, pp. 395–423. London: Earthscan.

Shah, T. and B. van Koppen. 2006. 'Is India Ripe for Integrated Water Resources Management? Fitting Water Policy to National Development Context', *Economic and Political Weekly*, 41(31): 3413–3421, 5–11 August.

Sikka, A. K., J. S. Samra, V. N. Sharda, P. Samraj, and V. Lakshmanan. 2003. 'Low Flow and High Flow Responses to Converting Natural Grassland into Bluegum (Eucalyptus Globulus) in Nilgiris Watersheds of South India', *Journal of Hydrology*, 270(1–2): 12–26.

Sivapalan, M., M. Konar, V. Srinivasan, A. Chhatre, A. Wutich, C. A. Scott, J. L. Wescoat, and I. Rodríguez-Iturbe. 2014. 'Socio-Hydrology: Use-Inspired Water Sustainability Science for the Anthropocene', *Earth's Future*, 2(4): 225–230.

Srinivasan, V., S. Kumar, P. Chinnasamy, S. Sulagna, D. Sakthivel, P. Paramasivam, and S. Lele. 2014. 'Water Management in the Noyyal River Basin: A Situation Analysis', Environment and Development, Discussion Paper 2, Banglore: Ashoka Trust for Research in Ecology and the Environment (ATREE).

Srinivasan, V., S. Thompson, K. Madhyastha, G. Penny, K. Jeremiah, and S. Lele. 2015. 'Why Is the Arkavathy River Drying? A Multiple Hypothesis Approach in a Data Scarce Region', *Hydrology and Earth System Sciences*, 12(1): 25–66.

Venot, J. P. 2008. 'Why and Where Are the Krishna Waters Disappearing?' *Economic and Political Weekly*, 43(6): 15–17.

Wei, J., P. A. Dirmeyer, D. Wisser, M. G. Bosilovich, and D. M. Mocko. 2013. 'Where Does the Irrigation Water Go? An Estimate of the Contribution of Irrigation to Precipitation Using MERRA', *Journal of Hydrometeorology*, 14(1): 275–289.

Zeng, R. and X. Cai. 2014. 'Analyzing Streamflow Changes: Irrigation-Enhanced Interaction Between Aquifer and Streamflow in the Republican River Basin', *Hydrology and Earth, System Sciences*,18(2): 493–502, doi:10.5194/hess-18-493-2014.

# 4 Changing land use, agrarian context and rural transformation

## Implications for watershed development

*Abraham Samuel and K. J. Joy*

### Introduction

Rural India has been undergoing a slow but profound transformation, especially since the last three decades, impacted by local and global factors and drivers. There are significant changes in land use, livelihood patterns, employment, agricultural systems, consumption patterns, asset ownership and composition, cultural and social ways of living and levels of aspiration.[1] While there is a consensus around the need for growth and development at a dominant level, there are also critical voices around the type of growth, its social and environmental sustainability and the extent of inclusiveness in the growth paradigm. In order to address the spatial, geographical and social inequality and distribution of growth benefits, there are a large number of programmes being implemented within the welfare framework in the country. An estimate shows that by the end of the 11th plan, there were 147 centrally sponsored schemes operational in the country (Chaturvedi 2011). This is apart from the innumerable other programmes by state governments. A large number of programmes are meant for the rural areas. A significant issue that emerges in this context is how these programmes are placed in relation to the transformation that is taking place and whether they are working as shock absorbers or facilitating changes in a positive and sustainable way. It is also important to address how new strategies and approaches are incorporated in the operationalization to enable them to be in tune with the emerging demands. In this context, the chapter would try to look into the watershed development programme in the country, which has a fairly consistent history in terms of policy and programmes.

## Agro-ecologies and watershed development

It is estimated that 78 Million ha (Mha) out of 140 Mha of net sown area is rainfed/dry land and 65 Mha[2] of the total geographical area of 328 Mha is classified as degraded land. Given these figures, the importance of watershed development for resource conservation and livelihood promotion cannot be underscored sufficiently. Out of the 127 Agro-Climatic Zones (ACZs) in India, 73 are predominantly rainfed. Rainfed agro-ecologies cover about 87 per cent area of coarse cereals and pulses, 77 per cent of oilseeds, 66 per cent of cotton and 50 per cent of cereals. Rainfed areas are home to a majority of rural poor and marginal farmers and, at the same time, are also risk and distress prone. Dry land agriculture currently constitutes 55 per cent of the net sown area of the country, and drylands are home to two-thirds of livestock and 40 per cent of India's population (NRAA 2012). These areas, historically characterized by under investment and policy neglect, are slowly emerging as the thrust areas for accelerating agriculture production in the country.

Watershed development is one of the major policy initiatives in this direction, seen as having the potential to address the development needs of socio-economically and agriculturally marginalized communities that inhabit these areas. In that sense, the watershed development initiative is an important move in the direction of promoting equity across regions, farming situations and different agro-climatic conditions in the country.

There is considerable emphasis on watershed development based agricultural development and livelihood promotion in the rainfed areas.[3] This received further impetus with the introduction of the new programme – Integrated Watershed Management Programme (IWMP) – midway during the 11th plan. With increased unit cost, enabling institutional arrangements, introduction of production and livelihood components and so on, IWMP marks a fundamental shift from the way watershed development was so far implemented. Thus, it aims to address environmental sustainability, production enhancement and livelihood security in the dry land areas of the country.[4]

Compared to other flagship programmes, the allocation for watershed development is not very significant, but that does not undermine its importance as a major strategy for rural development, agricultural production, livelihood promotion, and environmental stabilization. Estimates show that till the end of the 10th plan, an estimated 508.99 lakh ha of area was treated under various schemes of the central government at a cost of Rs 19251.22 crores (GoI 2007: 42). The new programme, known as the Integrated Watershed Development Programme (IWMP) under the new guidelines, was introduced in the 11th plan (in the year 2009), which undertook 24.21 Mha in the last three years of the plan, with a central allocation of Rs 3864.23 crores to various states. An additional 5 Mha of area was undertaken during 2012–2013, the first year of the 12th plan. However, the progress of the projects has been very poor due to various reasons as observed in the field and also highlighted by the data available in the public domain.

We argue that while the potential of watershed development for production and livelihood enhancement is widely accepted, it needs to reformulate its strategy if it has to remain relevant for rural development in the face of changes that are taking place in rural India. These areas where changes are occurring have considerable relevance for watershed policies and strategies. Acknowledging and addressing these changes would influence the way watershed development can be seen as a rural development strategy, with the potential of addressing the development needs of the rainfed areas.

## Changing land use

The geographical and social focus of watershed development, as the various state level perspective plans[5] show, are the rainfed areas, while the prioritized watersheds are in the socially and environmentally poor areas. However, these areas are undergoing a silent transformation unleashed by changing land use based on the ever-increasing demand for non-agricultural uses – for industries, settlements, other infrastructural needs, mines, sub-urbanization and urban outgrowths, special economic zones and so on. Most policy documents give tacit support for conversion of 'non-productive lands' for non-agricultural purposes, thus putting the drylands at risk of increasing land use changes and challenges. For example, the policy statement in the Draft National Land Utilisation Policy 2013 states that 'reasonable restrictions on acquisition of at least certain types of agricultural land should be introduced. The prime farmlands, which may include the command areas of irrigation projects, double cropped land etc. as relevant in each state/region/local area, should be protected'. In other words, non-prime lands could be considered for meeting the demands for lands for the non-agricultural sector. The available data on land use changes also points to these aspects. With demand for such lands on an increase, these areas would witness drastic changes in the years to come. While these changes have their impact on food and livelihood security of the poor, they may also have long lasting environmental implications and sustainability risks.

The available evidence on land use (Directorate of Economic and Statistics 2013) shows that there is a significant reduction in the cultivable area. Over the years, there has been a significant increase in the area under non-agricultural use. During the last six decades (1950–1951 to 2012–2013), cultivable land has reduced by 7,691,000 ha, while the area utilized for non-agricultural use has increased by 17,156,000 ha. The increase of non-agricultural land use is mainly contributed by barren and uncultivable land, lands under miscellaneous tree crops and groves, culturable waste and permanent fallow, and, to some extent, by cultivable agricultural land. In the first four decades after independence, one could observe an increase in cultivable land as well as in the net area sown, while that figure gets contracted by the late 1980s. However, since the early 1990s, there has been a significant reduction in both cultivable land and net area sown. This shows that agricultural lands have been getting converted to non-agricultural lands since the advent of economic liberalization in the late 1980s. These changes have implications for food production and livelihood of the rural marginal farmers, as these are the focus of watershed development programmes.

Table 4.1 provides the changes in land use from 1980 to 2014. It shows that between 1980–1981 and 2014–2015, while the cultivable land has shrunk by 3,270,000 ha, the increase in non-agricultural land use has been significant (by 6,925,000 ha). During the same time, there

*Table 4.1* Changes in Major Land Use in India 1980–1981 to 2014–2015

| *Broad land use category* | *1980–1981 (000'Ha)* | *2014–2015 (000'Ha)* |
|---|---|---|
| Total cultivable/agricultural land | 185,156 | 181,886 |
| Net area sown | 140,288 | 140,130 |
| Land under non-agricultural use | 19,958 | 26,883 |
| Barren and unculturable land | 30,209 | 16,996 |
| Other uncultivated land (pastures/trees/shrubs etc.) | 32,311 | 25,832 |
| Permanent and current fallow | 24,546 | 26,182 |
| Forest | 67,460 | 71,794 |

Source: Land use Classification All India Summary Table (DACNET), eands.dacnet.nic.in/LUS-2010–2011/All-India-1.pdf (accessed on 8 May 2018)

has been a drastic reduction in land use classes like barren and unculturable land and also other uncultivated land (pastures/trees/shrubs etc.). The barren and unculturable land has been reduced by 13,213,000 ha, while the area under permanent pastures, grazing lands trees and shrubs have reduced by 6,479,000 ha. These changes have significant impacts on the livelihood of the rural poor, mainly the landless, herders, Dalits and marginal rainfed farmers. It also impacts a 'balanced' land use pattern that is required for environmental sustainability, as these lands are not only livelihood spaces for the rural poor but also ecological spaces, performing certain ecological functions within the overall landscape. Besides the rainfed cultivated land, the focus of the current watershed approach needs to be on grazing and pasture lands and culturable wastelands, so as to address the issues of environmental degradation and livelihood security of the poor. However, these types of lands are getting more and more alienated from individual and community ownership.[6]

While there are significant changes in land use at the national level, its distribution in the states is uneven. Almost 20 states show a reduction in cultivable area during the last ten years. Odisha leads with a reduction of 606,000 ha; reduction in other states include Maharashtra 167,000 ha, Punjab 188,000 ha, West Bengal 267,000 ha, UP 208,000 ha and so on during the 2001–2011 period. Gujarat and Jammu & Kashmir are two of the states which report an increase in the cultivable area.[7] Some of these states, like West Bengal, most parts of UP, Punjab etc., are not in the traditionally degraded land belts such as Rajasthan, Maharashtra or Gujarat, which may lead to the conclusion that even good lands are being converted from agricultural to non-agricultural use.

## Changes in other land uses

In the overall land use pattern, there is an increasing area coming under urban agglomeration, mining and Special-Economic Zones (SEZs), which is putting an increasing pressure on the other lands. As per the data in 2001, 2.52 per cent (77.37 lakh ha) of area was categorized as urban (Town and Country Planning Organisation 2001), which would have increased considerably, given the fact that the number of cities and towns has increased to 7,935 in 2011 from 5,161 in 2001.[8] This in itself is not a major issue – however, the new phenomenon of urban growth and sub-urbanization, and the spill over to adjoining rural agricultural belt due to the spiralling land prices, would be an issue of concern in the near future. Mining constitutes 0.17 per cent (could be noted as reported area under legal mining) of the total land area while industries occupy around 1 per cent (Department of Land Resources 2013). SEZ is a new phenomenon, which is taking up lands which otherwise were part of the livelihood sources of the rural poor. Total area under SEZ across India is expected to be over 200,000 hectares, an area the size of the National Capital Region. This land – predominantly agricultural and typically multi-cropped – is capable of producing close to one million tonnes of foodgrains. Estimates show that close to 114,000 farming households (each household on an average comprising five members), and an additional 82,000 farm worker families dependent upon these farms for their livelihoods, will be displaced. In other words, at least one million people, who primarily depend on agriculture for their survival, will face eviction. Experts estimate that the total loss of income to farming and the farm worker families is at least Rs 212 crore a year. This does not include other income lost (for instance, of artisans) due to the demise of local rural economies (GoI n.d.).[9]

## Occupational changes in rural India

The land use transformation is also accompanied by changes in agrarian relations and occupational patterns. The agrarian situation is witnessing a change where not only is the contribution of agriculture to the overall GDP shrinking, but slowly the population engaged in agriculture as a prime livelihood source or 'work', is also receding. While the share of workers engaged in farming and agriculture labour has come down by 13 per cent in 1991–2011, there is a perceptible increase in the number of non-agricultural labour, especially casual labour, in the rural population.

*Table 4.2* Percentage of Workers Engaged in the Agriculture Sector, 1991–2011

| *Year* | *Cultivators* | *Agriculture labour* | *Total workers engaged in agriculture* |
|---|---|---|---|
| 1991 | 39.7 | 27.4 | 67.1 |
| 2001 | 31.7 | 26.5 | 58.2 |
| 2011 | 24.6 | 29.9 | 54.5 |

Source: Office of the Registrar General & Census Commissioner, India (Census of India 1991, 2001 and 2011)

*Table 4.3* Change in Agricultural Occupation in Rural Areas, 1951–2011

| *Year* | *Cultivators (in million)* | *Agricultural labour (in million)* |
|---|---|---|
| 1951 | 69.6 | 27.3 |
| 1961 | 99.6 | 31.5 |
| 1971 | 78.2 | 47.5 |
| 1981 | 92.6 | 55.5 |
| 1991 | 110.7 | 74.6 |
| 2001 | 127.3 | 106.8 |
| 2011 | 118.7 | 144.3 |

Source: Various Census of India Reports

The National Sample Survey Office (NSSO) 66th round data for June 2010 concludes that, in rural India, the proportion of the employed (both principal and subsidiary status) male workers engaged in agricultural activities declined gradually from 81 per cent in 1977–1978 to 63 per cent in 2009–2010, whereas for the female workers, the decline was less – from 88 per cent to 79 per cent during the same period (NSSO 2013a). The 68th round for 2012 (NSSO 2013b) notes that nearly 59 per cent of the male workers and nearly 75 per cent of the female workers were engaged in the agricultural sector. Among the male workers, 22 per cent and 19 per cent were engaged in the secondary and tertiary sectors, respectively. The corresponding proportions for the female workers were 17 per cent and 8 per cent respectively. Even though these figures are slightly higher than the census figures (probably due to the methodological differences in enumeration), the increasing trend as per both the reports suggests the moving away of labour from agriculture. Another striking aspect, as per the census data, is the decline in 'farmers/cultivators', which has decreased even below the category of agricultural labour for the first time since independence.

The latest data on the occupational profile of rural households (Socio Economic and Caste Census 2015) shows a very interesting picture – less than one-third of the households earn a livelihood through cultivation while more than half of the households' main source of livelihood is manual casual labour, showing a relatively high level of proletarianization and marginalization of the occupation than what is otherwise often considered as an agriculture-rural link of the economy and livelihood among the rural working population (Table 4.4).

*Table 4.4* Occupational Profile of the Rural Household

| *S. no.* | *Categories* | *No. of households (% to total rural HH in parenthesis)* |
|---|---|---|
| 1. | Total Rural Households | 17.91 crore |
| 2. | Cultivation | 5.39 crore (30.10%) |
| 3. | Manual Casual Labour | 9.16 crore (51.14%) |
| 4. | Part-time or Full-time Domestic Service | 44.84 lakh (2.50%) |
| 5. | Rag picking, Scavenging etc. | 4.08 lakh (0.23%) |
| 6. | Non-Agricultural Own Account Enterprise | 28.87 lakh (1.61%) |
| 7. | Begging/Charity/Alms | 6.68 lakh (0.37%) |
| 8. | Others (including government service, private service, PSU employment etc.) | 2.50 crore (14.01%) |

Source: Various Census of India Reports

The situation assessment survey of farmers (NSSO 2003) reports that about 27 per cent of farmers did not like farming because it was not profitable. In all, 40 per cent felt that, given a choice, they would take up some other occupation. The occupational shift is important from the perspective of understanding the rural livelihood issues and developmental strategies that focus on creating sustainable livelihoods. Already there are suggestions that the latest Socio-Economic Caste Census (SECC) data would be key in reorienting the targets of various developmental programmes including the National Rural Employment Guarantee Scheme (NREGS), the largest employment generation and assets building intervention in rural India. These transformations have considerable significance for watershed development: balancing the environmental, agricultural production and livelihood enhancement objective, and, at the same time, making the intervention more inclusive and sustainable.

## Changes in land holding and agriculture production

The human-land ratio, in general, and the cultivator-agricultural land ratio, in particular, are shrinking rapidly (Bhalla 2014). This change is accompanied by the increasing share of marginal farmers and women farmers among the cultivators as agriculture is becoming a non-profit enterprise, as many studies show. While the percentage of landless households in terms of not owning an operational holding is around 31 per cent,[10] more than 85 per cent of the operational holdings are in the category of marginal/small group having less than 2ha.

In 1970, 70 per cent of the holders, who constituted marginal and small farmers, operated 21 per cent of the land, while 85 per cent of the farmers in the same category operate 44.3 per cent of the land now. However, the inequity is still very high: 5 per cent of the holders at the top own 32 per cent of the operational land. In 2002–2003 (kharif season), as high as 79 per cent of the rural households possessed land of size 1 ha or less. About 32 per cent possessed less than 0.002 ha of land as per the NSSO 59th round survey in 2003. The large holders, whose number is declining, would also be, in reality, having the best land, even though agriculture census does not look into access to irrigation etc. The Gini coefficient for 2003 based on NSSO data on land and livestock survey shows high inequality at 0.73 (Rawal 2008). Addressing the specific needs of marginal and small farmers as part of watershed development would require not only inclusive planning and resource allocation at the watershed level but also technological and institutional innovations.

There are other profound changes afoot in the agriculture sector in terms of cropping and cultivation (Table 4.6). Starting from 2005–2006, we notice a significant decrease in the area under millets (jowar, bajra and ragi), pulses and oilseeds, whereas there has been a perceptible increase in the area under wheat, cotton and sugarcane, which require irrigation water.

The trend of cultivation of marketable and high value agricultural products is going to be on the rise as the demand for them is increasing due to demographic and spatial shift of the population, together with the changing consumption pattern (Department of Agriculture and Cooperation 2013). Crops which have a higher labour input are becoming non-profitable for the farmers, and, if own labour and household inputs like manure are factored into the cost, then most of the cultivation, especially of cereals, would be non-remunerative. Livestock, the mainstay of Indian rural economy, is also showing a decline. The NSSO data on land and livestock show a decreasing trend in all categories of livestock except that of the buffalo. One of the reasons could be the shrinking of common and pasture lands due to land use changes. The number of sheep and goats in the rural areas declined from 85 per 100 rural households in 1991–1992 to 64 per 100 households in 2002–2003.

*Table 4.5* Percentage of Operational Holdings in Different Categories

| *Category* | *1970–71* | *1975–76* | *1980–81* | *1985–86* | *1990–91* | *1995–96* | *2000–01* | *2005–06* | *2010–11* |
|---|---|---|---|---|---|---|---|---|---|
| Marginal (<1 ha) | 50.98 | 54.58 | 56.39 | 57.79 | 59.44 | 61.58 | 62.88 | 64.77 | 67.04 |
| Small (1–2 ha) | 18.92 | 18.06 | 18.08 | 18.45 | 18.84 | 18.73 | 18.92 | 18.52 | 17.93 |
| Semi medium (2–4 ha) | 15.04 | 14.30 | 14.01 | 13.64 | 13.06 | 12.34 | 11.69 | 10.93 | 10.05 |
| Medium (4–10 ha) | 11.16 | 10.07 | 9.08 | 8.15 | 7.11 | 6.14 | 5.48 | 4.93 | 4.25 |
| Large (>10 ha) | 3.90 | 2.99 | 2.44 | 1.97 | 1.55 | 1.21 | 1.03 | 0.85 | 0.73 |
| Total | 100.00 | 100.00 | 100.00 | 100.00 | 100.00 | 100.00 | 100.00 | 100.00 | 100.00 |

Source: Agriculture Census Division 2015

*Table 4.6* Decadal Change in Cropping Pattern and Cultivation

| *Years* | *Crops (area in thousand ha)* | | | | | | | | |
|---|---|---|---|---|---|---|---|---|---|
| | *Millets (Jowar, Bajra, Ragi)* | *Wheat* | *Rice* | *Pulses* | *Oilseeds* | *Cotton* | *Fruits & vegetables* | *Sugarcane* | *Spices* |
| 2005–2006 | 20,075 | 26,687 | 43,920 | 23,672 | 30,504 | 8,713 | 9,917 | 4,644 | 2,896 |
| 2014–2015 | 15,290 | 32,078 | 44,238 | 21,707 | 28,424 | 12,660 | 9,980 | 5,565 | 3,458 |
| Change | –4,785 | 5,392 | 318 | –1,965 | –2,080 | 3947 | 62 | 921 | 562 |

Source: Directorate of Economics and Statistics n.d.

## Watershed development: potential and prospects

While the challenge for policies and programmes is to make the marginal small holder cultivation profitable and sustainable, there is also a need for addressing the changing aspirations of the rural population, especially the emerging generation, who are not tied to the land and whose aspirations are different from what was previously considered as part of the rural farming life. Rural development programmes and policies do not seem to pay much attention to the latter. Even the NGO sector involved in rural development work, including watershed development programmes, does not seem to be sensitive to this change taking place in the rural areas. While watershed development has the potential to address the specific farm needs in terms of drought proofing and, to some extent, help in climate resilient cropping for the marginal farmers, the aim of making agriculture a profitable enterprise depends on many other issues related to policy framework, institutional mechanisms, technology, investments and convergence. One of the critical questions that we need to ask is whether the watershed development strategy, as being practised today, can take account of these changing rural aspirations. Unless we acknowledge and engage with this issue, the task of attracting the new generation in rural areas to agriculture would remain a serious challenge.

Watershed-based rural and agricultural development has a long history in the country, starting with the catchment conservation programmes. The programme was reviewed periodically, and approaches and strategies were modified. The reviews mostly focused on the performance of the intervention, and new approaches and strategies were adopted to enhance the efficacy of the intervention introducing new operational guidelines. The transformation of the 'context' and its impact on the programme was seldom assessed; nor was a mechanism evolved to streamline the intervention in tune with the changing context.

The experience of watershed projects since the mid-1990s suggests that the projects have been successful in enhancing crop productivity to a large extent, but the impact on stability (or drought resistance) and diversification of farm activities has been rather limited. There are many studies[11] highlighting the impact of watershed development on biophysical and socio-economic components. For example, the Meta Analysis by ICRISAT, covering a large number of impact studies, shows the following results (Joshi *et al.* 2008):

*Table 4.7* Impact of Watershed Development

| *Indicators* | *Unit* | *Number of studies* | *Mean value from various studies* | *Minimum reported* | *Maximum reported* |
|---|---|---|---|---|---|
| Employment | Person days ha/yr | 99 | 154.50 | 5 | 900 |
| Increase in irrigated area | % | 93 | 51.50 | 1.23 | 204 |
| Increase in cropping intensity | % | 339 | 35.50 | 3 | 283 |
| Runoff reduced | % | 83 | 45.30 | 0.34 | 96 |
| Soil saved | t/ha/yr | 72 | 1.10 | 0.10 | 2 |
| BC ratio | Ratio | 311 | 2 | 0.80 | 7.3 |
| IRR | % | 162 | 27.40 | 2 | 102.70 |

Source: Joshi *et al.* 2008

The Eleventh Plan documents some of the achievements of watershed development, drawing extensively from studies, evaluations etc. (GoI 2007: 25). Some of the key findings are as follows:

- Soil loss and surface runoff reduced by 52 per cent and 58 per cent respectively in completed watersheds.
- Area under irrigation increased from 34 per cent to 100 per cent in different watersheds.
- The area under sowing increased. The cropping intensity increased.
- The productivity/yield of the crops increased, and the net returns also increased (up to 63 per cent).
- The cost benefit ratio of watersheds ranged from 1.10 to 15.72, depending on the earlier factors.
- The availability of drinking water and the groundwater situation improved in all the project villages.
- Other benefits such as fodder availability, employment opportunities (and also equal wages in a limited number of cases) and income generation opportunities improved significantly in all the villages where watershed projects were implemented.

There are other large-scale studies such as the one by Kerr *et al.* (1998); Rapid Assessment of Watersheds in Maharashtra, Karnataka and

Madhya Pradesh covering 1,020 watersheds by the Forum for Watershed Research and Policy Dialogue (Samuel *et al.* 2009); two large-scale studies (837 micro watersheds implemented during 1997–2002 and 947 watershed implemented between 2002 and 2005) undertaken by National Institute for Rural Development (NIRD 2011–12) in collaboration with national agencies, that show that watersheds bring direct tangible benefits with regard to ecosystem resources, productivity potential, livelihoods and the general rural economy, besides several indirectly attributable benefits such as education, credit uptake, food security etc. However, most of the studies also show declining benefits after a few years of implementation, mainly resulting from institutional and investment vacuum.

## Challenges in the existing programmes

Most of these studies also highlight many concerns in terms of poor management of assets, skewed distribution of subsidy in private lands ignoring Common Property Resources (CPRs), withering away of institutions, poor capacity to manage resources, discontinuity in benefits after the initial impacts, poor drought proofing potential in deficient rainfall years etc. If we take large cross sections of projects cutting across regions and modes of implementation, the results that would emerge could be considered 'average', while those cited as 'successful' would turn out to be 'deep' facilitated projects in terms of investments, institutional support and continuity of facilitation. These are the key lacunae that have been identified by research studies, evaluations and experiences emerging out of the field.

The Technical Committee of 1994, known as Hanumantha Rao Committee (Ministry of Rural Development 1994) noted the issue of continued land and environmental degradation resulting from increased pressure on resources, thus highlighting the need for sustainability. The Working Group of the Tenth Plan, while highlighting the impacts emerging out of rainwater conservation, points out that increases in agricultural production did not last more than two years while structures created were abandoned and there was no mechanism for looking after the common lands (GoI 2001). The report also noted that there were no systematic evaluations and that government departments implemented projects without having adequate technical staff. These observations about the projects of the 1990s are also echoed in reports pertaining to subsequent projects. The Technical Committee on Watershed Programmes in India (2006) gives a detailed analysis of the lessons learnt and the need for changing the various components of implementation with reference to technology, processes and institutional and project management mechanism. It highlights the issues related to poor application of scientific and technological parameters such as geo-hydrology, groundwater issues, local specificity such as agro-climatic factors, soil conditions and project planning and implementation enhancing tools such as GIS/GPS etc., lack of participatory mechanisms for building stakes, and ownership of the developmental intervention. These result from a top-down approach, a lack of creative dialogue between the agencies and the people, a mechanical implementation of some of the strategies to enhance participation, and a general lack of transparency and trust at the local level.

Most studies also highlight gaps in institutional mechanisms to address concerns of equity resulting from unequal resource access, and social factors such as caste and gender. These result from social and economic stratification or location-specific inequalities that would be difficult to resolve through a project, but, at the same time, impact the distribution of the project benefits. The problem of equity in watershed interventions is further compounded by the lack of strategies or institutional arrangements for project-specific equity concerns such as effective representation, timely and due wage receipts, effective mechanisms for ensuring assured and preferential access to usufructs from common land/pool resources in favour of the poor etc. In the absence of these considerations, watershed development tends to strengthen existing inequalities (Shah, Samuel and Joy 2011).

Studies also show that while the impacts on environmental resources such as soil, water and productivity are 'good' in the initial stages, they fail to sustain in the medium to long term. This results from the unsustainable use of regenerated resources, lack of maintenance, lack of additional investments and incentives for sustainable practices. It has been noticed that watershed development is followed by increased groundwater exploitation, even to the extent of its falling to a critical level.

Projects are implemented in departmental silos and fail to complement one another. This results in duplication of efforts, wastage of human resources, lack of or inadequate resource flows towards real needs etc. (GoI 2013). As watershed development is a land-based intervention, a large chunk of households gets automatically excluded from the major benefits and require other support interventions to ensure some amount of livelihood security. With changes in the occupational profile, as seen earlier, convergence and integrated approaches to livelihood promotion need to be the focus.[12]

## Reorienting watershed-based development

While policies and programmes around watershed development have tried to address these concerns from the operational deficiency perspective, it is important that challenges emerging from the larger socio-economic transformation are also accounted for, to make it more effective. This would call for introducing changes in the conceptual, technical and institutional mechanisms, besides formulating the programme as an adaptive mechanism, with a set of dynamic strategies and tools. Since most of these transformations are going to stay, and the levels of aspirations are also on the rise in the 'rurban' context, a dynamic approach, building on the existing learnings, could address some of the concerns thrown up by the emerging challenges and further sustainable land use and livelihood development, which is economically viable and inclusive.

Watershed development could move from the currently practised conservation package at micro-watershed scale to land use planning at various scales, which would help in prioritizing land and water for various uses and needs, viz. food security and agricultural development, non-agricultural development related to manufacturing and services, socio-cultural needs, recreation and aesthetics. At present, there is neither any systematic approach to land use planning nor are there legal and institutional frameworks for the same. Another important challenge for watershed development is to address the development and productivity enhancement of the pastures and culturable wastelands, which, at present, is the lowest priority in the watershed conservation strategy, as evident from field data. This is important from the perspective of equity and environmental sustainability besides integrating livestock into the farming system – moving towards a livestock-based farming system.

Non-canal-based irrigation accounts for 75.5 per cent of the irrigation in the country, as per the data available for 2011–2012. It mainly comes from private investments and anticipated returns. The increasing share of groundwater in irrigation is going to be on the rise, as the focus of groundwater development shifts to eastern India. At the same time, there would be increasing demand on groundwater from other competing needs and requirements slowly getting unleashed by the socio-economic transformation. Watershed development could contribute to its sustainable development as an integrated land and water resource planning and development approach. This could help in planning for livelihood requirement, economic use and other environmental and cultural needs of water. In fact, contending water uses – domestic, agricultural and industrial – have resulted in many water-related conflicts in the country (Joy *et al.* 2011).

Probably, there is also a need to adopt what is generally known as a biomass-based planning approach to watershed development. This approach can tie together both the sustainability and livelihood needs, opening avenues for non-farm incomes that can, at least partially, meet the growing aspirations of the rural people. As per this approach, if a typical farmer family of five members can either produce or get access to about 18 tonnes of biomass (dry weight) in a year, it can meet all its livelihood needs like food, fodder, fuel and re-circulable biomass for the agriculture system. Over and above, it also gives three tonnes of surplus biomass for cash income. The conventional way is to produce these three tonnes surplus biomass in the form of perishable commodities like vegetables and fruits and sell them in the market directly to meet cash requirements. Sometimes, efforts are also made to process them (into tomato ketchups, jams, pickles, various eatables etc.) and turn them into consumer products for sale. Though there is some value addition potential here, it often suffers from market saturation. The other non-conventional way is to produce non-perishable, bulk biomass (like small dimension timber, bamboo, fibre etc.) that becomes the main input for the decentralized processing units in the rural areas. In fact, over the last two to three decades, a considerable amount of work has been done in this area of using biomass in various infrastructure sectors like buildings, roads, water systems etc. Now, off-the-shelf technologies are available. This can pave the way for a dispersed industrial set up, with tremendous potential for value addition and incomes for the rural toilers. It can also help to reduce the use of fossil-based materials in infrastructure and could therefore be a part of a wider climate mitigation strategy. Thus, there is a potential synergetic relationship between alternative technologies and the increased biomass production as a result of watershed development (Joy and Paranjape 2004; Datye 1997; Paranjape and Joy 1995).

Small holders are going to be the reality and making farming profitable and sustainable would be the challenge that watershed development could strategize for. This could be through conservation agriculture, sustainable agriculture practices, access to certain amount of applied water, biomass-based processing and value addition facilities as part of a decentralized agro-industrial system, better extension services, institutional innovations for inputs and markets, convergence with other schemes and agencies and so on. Currently, there are very isolated experiments in this direction as part of watershed development by a few implementing agencies and farmer groups but mainstreaming and up-scaling them would be a new challenge. Technical and institutional innovations for working with the small holders, and making agriculture profitable and sustainable, would be an area for watershed development to focus on in the future.

We would be witnessing the issues related to changes in the composition of the 'workers' involved in agriculture, as more and more of the new generation opt out of agriculture. Data also suggest that rural unemployment and underemployment are on the rise among the educated (above secondary education), which also indicates their lack of interest in agriculture. Local evidence also suggests the lack of interest of the educated youngsters in agriculture (Shah 2013). One of the avenues for watershed development is to build the skills of the educated youth, and build around them service-providing institutions, agro and biomass processing industries, and marketing agencies and so on. Urbanization is also on the rise, and rural-urban linkage through marketing of products would be one of the avenues for this section of the population.

## Concluding discussion

With the changing rural and agrarian context, it is important for watershed development to adopt new approaches, strategies, technology innovations and institutional arrangements to be relevant and meaningful in the fast-changing agrarian context. While the present implementation has thrown up many insights into the problems of implementation and helped fine-tune the watershed-based approach to rural development, some of the key concerns still remain. Most often they have links to the larger changes occurring in the socio-economic and political context. To respond to this changing context, watershed development in the country has to build a dynamic and receptive set of strategies and tools by drawing on the innovative experiences and strategies for managing land-water-agriculture and rural livelihoods.

## Notes

1 Social scientists argue that the binary distinction between rural and urban (or for that matter, traditional vs modern) is slowly eroding as rural areas are changing rapidly. Many urban characteristics in terms of occupational profile, market penetration, communication and media coverage and general aspirations, cultural habits, like food, clothing, way of living etc., are changing in the rural areas and expressions such as 'Rurban' are gaining popularity (see Gupta 2015).

2 Estimates of the extent of degraded land vary from 55 Mha to 175 Mha, depending upon the definition of wasteland and also the source of information. The latest attempt to harmonize the aforementioned data by ICAR – National Remote Sensing Agency [NRSA] – NRAA Expert Group has brought out that the degraded land which has the potential for development under watershed development projects amounts to a total of 64 Mha, consisting of 50 Mha of water eroded, 5 Mha of wind eroded and 9 Mha in notified forest (as given in GoI 2007: 28). There is also an attempt to estimate and prioritize the rainfed area in the country using the Natural Resource Index and Livelihood Index by the NRAA (NRAA 2012).

3 The objectives of watershed development have evolved over time as the watershed development policies and programmes have now incorporated production enhancement and livelihood promotion as part of their objectives, shifting from purely environmental functions such as catchment stabilization as envisaged in the earlier phases.

4 IWMP introduced the idea of common guidelines (Department of Land Resources 2012) for all the government supported watershed projects moving away from the departmental silos. It introduced dedicated institutions at the centre, state, district, project and watershed level, increased the unit cost to Rs 12,000–15,000/ha from the previous cost of Rs 6,000/ha, introduced livelihood and production component, earmarking around one fourth of the unit cost and also allocating a cluster of micro-water sheds to the tune of around 5,000 ha of area as part of one watershed project. There are many other innovations in the guidelines. Even though the policies were more progressive, they failed to capture the emerging realities, and implementation continues as it used to be by various state government departments.

5 Each state has prepared a state perspective and strategic plan for watershed development which elaborates the extent of land available for watershed development, demarcated into micro-watersheds, watersheds, sub-basins, basins, etc. It has also put up the institutional, human resource and financial requirement for developing those areas till the end of the 14th FYP (by the end of 2027). It is a fairly detailed and technically elaborate document prepared by all the states.

6 During a field work analysing the institutional issues of IWMP projects in Janjgir Champa district, Chhattisgarh, where numerous thermal power plants are coming up, the village *pradhans* brought to our notice that even productive lands are being classified as culturable waste or fallow by the Revenue Departments so that land use transformation and acquisition can be easily facilitated. The community also expressed that even the owners/farmers are willing collaborators as it gives better 'returns' than putting it into agriculture which is a losing proposition as reported by many. However, Janjgir Champa is one district in Chhattisgarh where more than 70 per cent of the cropped area is irrigated.

7 Jaffrelot (2015) attributes the increase in agricultural land in Gujarat to the increased availability of irrigation, both from surface and groundwater, prompting farmers to cultivate the land otherwise left fallow.

8 A recent report by World Bank on urbanization in South Asia argues that the process of urbanization is hidden and messy. It says that the population living in urban like features are 55.3 per cent against the official

figure of 30.9 per cent if we use the agglomeration index for classifying the urbanization process. Urban agglomeration has expanded to the adjacent geographies of cities and towns, taking into its fold considerable land resources (as reported by Express News Service 2015).

9 For micro-level assessment of impacts of SEZ on land and livelihood in Gujarat, see Shah (2013).

10 Data on landlessness (households that do not cultivate any land) is very confusing in the Indian context. Using the 59th round of NSSO data, Rawal (2008) estimates that 41.63 per cent of the households do not own any land other than homestead, and, of this, 31.16 per cent do not have any land as part of homestead that could be cultivated, making them effectively the landless who do not own any cultivated land. The SECC estimates that 56.25 per cent of the rural households do not own any agricultural land, with Bihar, West Bengal, Andhra Pradesh and Tamil Nadu having landlessness (ownership of agricultural land) ranging from 65 to 73 per cent. This is in tune with the households that depend on casual manual labour for livelihoods in India which is pegged at 51 per cent of the rural households in the country.

11 There are a large number of studies on impacts of watershed development projects in the country. They vary according to the research objectives, indicators assessed, sample size of the study, timing of the study, the agency undertaking the evaluation/study etc. Here we have only focused on studies that covered a large sample size, cutting across states and agroclimatic regions, so that we get a representative picture.

12 There have been some policy initiatives towards convergence. See Department of Rural Development (NREGA Division) 2009.

## References

Agriculture Census Division. 2015. 'All India Report on Agriculture Census 2010–2011', Department of Agriculture, Cooperation & Farmers Welfare, Ministry of Agriculture & Farmers Welfare, Government of India (GoI), http://agcensus.nic.in/document/ac1011/reports/air2010-11complete.pdf (accessed on 23 May 2018).

Bhalla, S. 2014. 'Scarce Land: Issues, Evidence and Impacts', IHD Working Paper Series, Institute for Human Development.

Chaturvedi, B. K. 2011. 'Report of the Committee on Restructuring of Centrally Sponsored Schemes (CSS)', Member, Planning Commission, Government of India (GoI), New Delhi, September.

Datye, K. R. (assisted by Suhas Paranjape and K. J. Joy). 1997. *Banking on Biomass: A New Strategy for Sustainable Prosperity Based on Renewable Energy and Dispersed Industrialisation*. Ahmedabad: Centre for Environment Education.

Department of Agriculture and Cooperation. 2013. *State of Indian Agriculture. 2012–2013*. Department of Agriculture, Government of India (GoI).

Department of Land Resources. 2012. *Common Guidelines for Watershed Development Projects*. Ministry of Rural Development, Government of India (GoI).

Department of Land Resources. 2013. 'National Land Utilisation Policy: Framework for Land Use Planning & Management' (Draft). Ministry of Rural Development, Government of India (GoI), July, https://smartnet.niua.org/sites/default/files/resources/draft_national_land_utilisation_policy_july_2013.pdf (accessed on 23 April 2018).

Department of Rural Development (NREGA Division). 2009. 'Guidelines for Convergence between NREGA and Integrated Watershed Management Programme (IWMP) of Department of Land Resources (DOLR)', Ministry of Rural Development, Government of India (GoI), www.nrega.net/csd/circular/convergence-documents/Convergence_Guidelines.pdf/view?searchterm=None (accessed on 23 May 2018).

Directorate of Economics and Statistics. n.d. 'Land Use Statics at a Glance – State Wise', Department of Agriculture, Cooperation and Farmers' Welfare, Ministry of Agriculture and Farmers' Welfare, Government of India (GoI), http://eands.dacnet.nic.in/LUS_1999_2004.htm (accessed on 23 May 2018).

Directorate of Economics and Statistics. 2013. 'Land Use Classification – All India and States', Ministry of Agriculture, eands.dacnet.nic.in/LUS-2010–2011/All-India and states-1&2.pdf and excel (accessed on 30 July 2013).

Express News Service. 2015. 'India's Urbanisation Messy, Hidden: World Bank', *The Indian Express*, 25 September, https://indianexpress.com/article/business/business-others/indias-urbanisation-messy-hidden-world-bank/ (accessed on 13 June 2018).

Government of India (GoI). n.d. 'Report of the Committee on State of Agrarian Relations and the Unfinished Task of Land Reforms', Ministry of Rural Development, GoI, http://southasia.oneworld.net/Files/MRD%20Commitee%20Report.pdf (accessed on 25 April 2018).

Government of India (GoI). 2001. *Tenth Five Year Plan (2002–2007)*. Planning Commission, Government of India.

Government of India (GoI). 2007. *Eleventh Five Year Plan (2007–2012)*, Volume 3. Planning Commission, Government of India (GoI).

Government of India (GoI). 2013. *Twelfth Five Year Plan (2012–2017)*, Volume 1 & 2. Planning Commission, Government of India.

Gupta, D. 2015. 'The Importance of Being Rurban: Tracking Changes in Traditional Setting', *Economic and Political Weekly*, 50(24).

Jaffrelot, C. 2015. 'The Promised Land', *Indian Express*, 18 May, http://indianexpress.com/article/opinion/columns/the-promised-land/ (accessed on 8 May 2018).

Joshi, P. K., A. K. Jha, S. P. Wani, T. K. Sreedevi, and F. A. Shaheen. 2008. 'Impact of Watershed Programme and Conditions for Success: A Meta Analysis Approach', Global Theme on Agro Ecosystems, Report No. 46, p. 24. International Crops Research Institute for the Semi-Arid Tropics (ICRISAT), Patancheru 502 324, Andhra Pradesh.

Joy, K. J. and S. Paranjape (with inputs from A. K. Kiran Kumar, R. Lele and R. Adagale). 2004. *Watershed Development Review: Issues and Prospects*. Bangalore: Centre for Inter-disciplinary Studies in Environment and Development (CISED).

Joy, K. J., P. Sangameswaran, Latha Anantha, S. Dharmadhikary, M. K. Prasad, and K. P. Soma. 2011. *Life, Livelihoods, Ecosystems, Culture: Entitlements and Allocation of Water for Competing Uses*. Position Paper by the Thematic Subgroup on Water Entitlements and Allocations for Livelihood Needs and Ecosystem Needs. Pune: Forum for Policy Dialogue on Water Conflicts in India.

Kerr, J., G. Pangar, L. V. Pangare, and P. J. George. 1998. *The Role of Watershed Projects in Developing Rainfed Agriculture in India*. New Delhi: Study Report Submitted to ICAR and the World Bank, ICAR.

Ministry of Rural Development. 1994. *Report of the Technical Committee on Drought Prone Areas Programme and Desert Development Programme*. New Delhi: Department of Land Resources, Ministry of Rural Development, Government of India (GoI), http://dolr.gov.in/sites/default/files/Tech CommitteeReport1994.pdf (accessed on 23 May 2018).

NIRD. 2011–2012. *Comprehensive Study of Impacts of Investments in Watershed Development*. Centre for Water and Land Resources (CWLR), NIRD, Ministry of Rural Development, Government of India (GoI).

NRAA (National Rainfed Areas Authority). 2012. *Prioritization of Rainfed Areas in India: Study Report 4*. Planning Commission, Government of India (GoI).

NSSO (National Sample Survey Office). 2003. *Situation Analysis of Farmers*. NSS 59th Round Ministry of Statistics and Programme Implementation, Government of India (GoI).

NSSO. 2013a. *Employment and Unemployment Situation Among Major Religious Groups in India*. NSS 66th Round, 2009–2010, Ministry of Statistics and Programme Implementation, Government of India (GoI).

NSSO. 2013b. *Key Indicators for Employment and Unemployment in India*. NSS 68th Round, 2011–2012, Ministry of Statistics and Programme Implementation, Government of India (GoI).

Office of the Registrar General & Census Commissioner, India (Census of India 1991, 2001 and 2011). *Economic Activity*. Ministry of Home Affairs, Government of India (GoI).

Paranjape, S. and K. J. Joy. 1995. *Sustainable Technology: Making the Sardar Sarovar Project Viable – A Comprehensive Proposal to Modify the Project for Greater Equity and Ecological Sustainability*. Ahmedabad: Centre for Environment Education.

Rawal, V. 2008. 'Ownership Holding of Land in Rural India: Putting the Facts Straight', *Economic and Political Weekly*, 43(10), 8 March.

Samuel, A., K. J. Joy, S. Paranjape, E. Kale, R. Adagale, and R. Pomane. 2009. *Watershed Development in Maharashtra: A Large Scale Rapid Assessment*. Pune: ForWaRD, Society for Promoting Participative Ecosystem Management (SOPPECOM).

Shah, A. 2013. 'Mainstreaming or Marginalisation? Evidence from Special Economic Zones in Gujarat', *Economic and Political Weekly*, 48(41), 12 October.

Shah, A., A. Samuel and K. J. Joy. 2011. 'Equity in Watershed Development: Imperatives for Property Rights, Resource Allocation, and Institutions', in

S. P. Wani, J. Rockstrom and K. L. Sahrawat (eds.), *Integrated Watershed Management in Rainfed Agriculture*. London: CRC Press.

Socio Economic and Caste Census (SECC). 2015. 'Provisional Findings', http://secc.gov.in/reportlistContent (accessed on 25 April 2018).

Technical Committee on Watershed Programmes in India. 2006. *From Hariyali to Neeranchal: Report of the Technical Committee on Watershed Programmes in India*. Department of Land Resources, Ministry of Rural Development, Government of India (GoI), January.

Town and Country Planning Organisation. 2001. 'Ministry of Urban Development (MoUD)', Government of India (GoI). This was a PowerPoint Presentation and was Available on Their Website Till a Couple of Years Back.

# 5 Environmental flows in the Indian context

## Prospects and challenges

*Latha Anantha and Neha Bhadbhade*[1]

### The context and the need

The Global Biodiversity Outlook 3 of the Convention on Biological Diversity (CBD) had warned that 'rivers are becoming increasingly fragmented, often with severe disruption to their flows' (CBD 2010: para 9). The most fragmented rivers are in the industrialized regions like much of the United States and Europe, and in heavily populated countries such as China and India. 'More than 40 per cent of the global river discharge is now intercepted by large dams and one-third of sediment destined for the coastal zones no longer arrives' (CBD 2010: para 9). Nine of the 30 world river basins marked as global level priorities for the protection of aquatic biodiversity are from India due to their extensive and continuing development (Groombridge and Jenkins 1998). These basins include those of the Cauvery, the Ganges-Brahmaputra, the Godavari, the Indus, the Krishna, the Mahanadi, the Narmada, the Pennar and the Tapi. With an exception of the Ganges-Brahmaputra, all these basins have also been categorized as 'strongly affected' by flow fragmentation and regulation (Nilsson *et al.* 2005). This is indeed symptomatic of the level of degradation of the river systems in India and the urgent need to revive them.

'Flow' is the most critical indicator of the health and life of a river. Very few rivers remain in India whose flows have not been fragmented or reduced or altered by human interventions. We have the classic case of the Krishna river whose summer outfalls into the sea are dwindling due to over withdrawal and reduced summer recharge. Before 1960, the river discharge into the oceans equalled 57 billion cubic metres (BCM) a year. Since 1965, it steadily decreased, falling to 10.8 BCM in the year 2000, and falling further, close to nil, in 2004, thus impacting the coastal ecosystems (Joy *et al.* 2011). Although the impacts of reduced flows on ecosystems are not quantified properly, there is well-documented evidence of downstream environmental degradation in the lower Krishna basin, manifesting in soil and groundwater salinization, increasing pollution, disappearing mangroves and wetland desiccation (Venot 2008). Deforestation of the catchments for mining and agriculture, dams and diversions for hydropower and irrigation, sand mining and over-extraction of surface and groundwater are the major causes of such a distressing state of our rivers. Pollution from industries and sewage has affected the quality of both surface and groundwater. Among these, dams remain, without doubt, the most direct, often irreversible, modifiers of river flows, damaging its ecology and morphology.

India is the world's third largest dam builder with more than 5,100 large dams built to date (Anantha 2013). Multi-purpose and storage dams can significantly affect the flow regime on a daily and seasonal basis. Similarly, the operation of a hydropower dam, peaking or base load, controls the timing, frequency and duration of high and low flows and alters the natural hydrograph of the river. For instance, if the proposed 1750 MW Lower Demwe HEP planned across the Lohit sub-basin of the Brahmaputra river in Arunachal Pradesh materializes, the flow in the lean season in winter will fluctuate between a high flow (1,729 cumecs) and a low flow (35 to 70 cumecs) cyclically on a daily basis during peak hour generation which the river ecosystem has never experienced (Rahmani n.d.).

In cascading run-of-the-river type dams, the river is diverted through tunnels over considerable distances. For example, the Luhri project in the Sutlej basin will divert close to 60 km length of the already over-dammed Sutlej through tunnels (Agarwal, Asher and Bhandari 2011). In the Ravi, the Avay Shukla Committee (2010) had pointed out that when all the four hydro-electric projects in the 70 km stretch between Chambal and Kajoli get commissioned, just 3 km of the river would flow through the original river bed. The lack of flows between the dams in the cascades affects the river ecology and morphology as well as community dependence in between dam stretches, destroying its ecological integrity. A similar fate awaits most other rivers in the western and north-eastern Himalayan region where hundreds of dam cascades are planned and are at various stages of clearance and construction. In the Western Ghats too, several rivers have very low or negligible flows especially during summers (the Idukki HEP, the Sharavathi Tail Race HEP, the Mullaperiyar, the Parambikulam Aliyar group of dams, the Siruvani diversion etc.).

Dams have adversely impacted fish migration and their population. Recent estimates show that inland fisheries are collapsing mainly due to changes in the natural flow regime and deterioration of water quality affecting the livelihoods of millions of fisher folks across the country. According to the Central Inland Fisheries Research Institute (CIFRI), severe and drastic changes in the entire hydrological cycle of the river by dams and water abstractions have affected recruitment of most species, especially large carps, which like flowing water. Larger dams are the major cause of degradation of aquatic environment and disruption of livelihood for the communities dependent upon the fishery along the rivers (Pathak and Tyagi 2010).

Apart from destroying river and riparian habitats, allocation of water from dams and multi-purpose projects for irrigation and industries also leads to numerous intra-sectoral, inter-sectoral and inter-state water conflicts in the country. The Cauvery, the Mahanadi and the Mhadei are some of the examples of active inter-state water conflicts in the country.

It is only since 2007–2008 that the Ministry of Environment, Forest and Climate Change (MoEFCC) has made e-flow allocation a mandatory part of the environmental impact assessments (EIAs) for obtaining environment clearances for river valley projects (Thakkar 2012). At the beginning of 2011, many studies were carried out by several government and non-government agencies to assess e-flows in the Indian river basins, especially the Himalayan and the Eastern Himalayan river basins. A review of these studies showed that the flows arrived at have been much lower than those actually needed by the river. Social and livelihood aspects were not considered and most of the studies lacked proper objective setting (Anantha, Dharmadhikary and Bhadbhade 2017).

Therefore, the importance of e-flows cannot be over-emphasized and now that e-flows as an approach is gaining recognition in policy and regulatory regimes in India, it is important that this approach be studied and applied properly, using a sound scientific methodology involving the riparian communities in the entire process.

## What constitutes environmental flows?

There are several interpretations of environmental flows. The Brisbane Declaration (2007) endorsed by more than 750 scientists across 50 countries perhaps captures the essence of environmental flows most succinctly. It is described as the 'quantity, timing and quality of water flows required to sustain freshwater and estuarine ecosystems and the human livelihoods and well-being that depend on these ecosystems' (International Water Centre 2007). The International Union for Conservation of Nature (IUCN) defines environmental flows as the water regime provided within a river, wetland or coastal zone to maintain ecosystems and their benefits, where there are competing water uses and where flows are regulated (Dyson, Bergkamp and Scanlon 2003). The International Water Management Institute (IWMI) describes environmental flow regimes as discharges of a particular magnitude, frequency and timing, which are necessary to ensure that a river system remains environmentally, economically and socially healthy (IWMI 2005).

There has been considerable debate on what is the right perspective regarding water for environmental needs. Is 'apportioning', 'ensuring' or 'allowing' the water for ecosystems the correct perspective? '*Who are we to decide how much water should be allocated for environmental needs, or the evolutionary and ecological needs of rivers?* because "water itself is part of nature"' (Iyer 2007: 206).

Another perspective believes that environmental water requirement should include both terrestrial and aquatic ecosystems since these are connected. This perspective argues that water is needed for direct evapo-transpiration through forests, wetlands and other lands, all supporting distinct ecologies and other functions of terrestrial ecosystems, apart from aquatic ecosystems. The latter would then be understood as 'environmental flows', and both together would constitute 'water to be left for ecosystem needs' (Mohile and Gupta 2005).

In the Indian context, water to be left in the river for cultural and religious needs also assumes significance.

> Flows are needed for maintaining the river regime, making it possible for the river to purify itself, sustaining aquatic life and vegetation, recharging groundwater, supporting livelihoods, facilitating navigation, preserving estuarine conditions, preventing the incursion of salinity, and enabling the river to play its role in the cultural and spiritual lives of the people.
>
> (Iyer 2007: 207)

All the interpretations agree upon the most critical aspect: that a river needs its flow regime to remain environmentally, economically and socially healthy. From an ecosystem perspective, it is not only the amount of flows that are important, but also their timing, quantity, quality and duration. The appropriate flow regime through different seasons of the year for enabling the various ecosystem functions like migration, feeding and breeding of fish and other aquatic life is of prime importance. Equally critical aspects include sediment and nutrient transport, deposit of sand, flushing out of pollutants, enriching and safeguarding riparian, floodplain, mangrove, backwater and delta ecosystems, replenishing groundwater and protecting water quality. Based on the understanding that all land broadly falls within some watershed boundary, the flow regime to be left for the environment, right from the first order stream watersheds to the main river basin, denotes the water for environmental needs at a river basin level (Joy *et al.* 2011).

Meanwhile, it is very important to acknowledge that e-flows is ultimately a compromise. It surely cannot maintain the pristine condition or functions of a freely flowing fully protected river. It can only maintain the ecological function of the river to a certain desired state as close as possible to the natural flow regime which, in itself, is ultimately a societal judgement or decision. And achieving a balance between water allocation for environmental and human needs in already overused river basins is the most challenging task politically.

## Assessment of e-flows – a brief overview

The approaches to e-flows setting have been classified into two distinct categories, namely, objective-based flow setting and scenario-based flow setting.

### *Objective-based flow setting*

In this approach, the desired status of the river flows is arrived at based on the objectives, which maybe set jointly by all river communities or water management experts or even by the government. WWF-India's study on assessment of e-flows in the upper stretches of the Ganga considered objective-based flow setting wherein the geomorphologic, ecological, socio-economic and cultural objectives of the river were first established by the expert groups and then the river flow regime was established using hydraulic and hydrologic modelling to meet these objectives (O'Keeffe *et al.* 2012). Objective-based flow settings are basically prescriptive.

### *Scenario-based flow setting*

In this approach, several scenarios of flow regimes/flow allocations are examined, and the best option is arrived at. For instance, under the Lesotho Highland Water Project, various scenarios of e-flows release from dams were considered. For each scenario, the impacts on the downstream river ecosystems and dependent livelihoods were determined (King, Brown and Sabet 2003). These scenarios permitted the Lesotho government to assess the trade-offs presented by different e-flow options. Scenario-based flow settings are basically interactive approaches, more complex than objective-based ones.

There are four typologies of e-flows assessments based on the two approaches that include the following (discussed in the subsections).

### *Hydrological methods*

Hydrological index methods are mainly prescriptive desktop approaches relying primarily on historical flow records or modelled flow data to make flow recommendations for the future. These methods determine a fixed percentage/proportion of flow for the environmental requirements of the river. About 60 per cent of the e-flow methodologies that have been developed fall under this category. Some of the important methodologies include the Tennant Method (Montana Method), the Flow Duration Curve Analysis (FDCA) and the Texas Method. They are rapid desktop analysis methods relying on long historical flow data and are hence most appropriate at the reconnaissance level of water resources development. No ecological data is used or measured in these methods which make them ad hoc, especially in situations where trade-offs over water allocation are involved (Islam 2010).

### *Hydraulic rating*

The relationship between the changes in flows and changes in the hydraulic characteristics of the river, taking parameters like wetted perimeter, velocity, depth of water in the river etc. are used to arrive at the acceptable flow considered as the flow needed by the river environment. A cross section of the river which serves as surrogate for the entire biological habitat is taken for the assessment. E-flows are determined from a plot of the hydraulic variable(s) against discharge, commonly by identifying curve breakpoints where significant percentage reductions in habitat quality occur with decreases in discharge (Arthington *et al.* 2004). The methodologies rely on the highly simplistic assumption that a single hydraulic variable or group of variables can adequately represent the flow requirements of a target species for a particular activity. This method is only applicable to in-stream and not out-of-channel river flow-related components like riparian vegetation, floods plains etc.

### *Habitat simulation*

These methodologies, also sometimes referred to as habitat rating methods, are used to derive e-flow requirements based on how changes in micro-habitats occur with changes in river discharge. Discharges are modelled based on hydraulic variables like depth, velocity of flow and composition of substratum (King, Tharme and Villiers 2008). These methods are most suitable for conservation of target species and their habitats and require ecological expertise. The limitation of these methodologies is that they are extremely data intensive. Some of the most widely used habitat simulation methods include In-Stream Flow Incremental Methodology (IFIM) and River Hydraulics and Habitat Simulation Program (RHYHABSIM) (King, Tharme and Villiers 2008; King and Tharme 1994).

### *Holistic methodologies*

Holistic methodologies are considered as superior approaches in e-flow assessment and the science of river basin management as they try to consider the entire riparian and directly dependent terrestrial ecosystem rather than the needs of only a few keystone species. They are based on the concept of maintaining the natural flow patterns of the river. The common objective of holistic methodologies is to maintain and/or restore fluvial processes thus improving the health of the groundwater systems, floodplains and downstream estuaries and coastal wetlands. Currently, only 8 per cent of the total e-flow assessment methodologies are holistic in nature (Arthington *et al.* 2004). Holistic methodologies broadly fall under two categories, namely 'top-down approach' and 'bottom-up approach'. The fundamental principle of the top-down approach is based on 'what is the maximum permissible limit of flow alteration/modification from natural flow conditions of the river' (Arthington *et al.* 2004). In the bottom-up approach, e-flows are derived based on specific requirements, starting with zero flows. The commonly used holistic methodologies include Building Block Methodology (BBM), Downstream Response to Imposed Flow Transformation (DRIFT), Flow Restoration Methodology (FLOWRESM) etc.

## E-flows assessment and implementation in India – the challenges

Over 200 methodologies have been developed and tried out till date. However, the rate of actual implementation is less than 5 per cent.

India is still at the knowledge generation and refinement stage of e-flows. There are several issues and challenges related to the e-flows assessment and implementation process in India. Only a few critical ones are discussed here.

### *Understanding the ecological and hydrological linkages*

At a conceptual level, the lack of a proper understanding of the Ecological Limitations of Hydrological Alterations (ELOHA) (Poff *et al.* 2010) is a very seminal problem which decides how the flows would be viewed and managed by the decision makers and the diversity of users. This also includes surface-groundwater interactions, pollution-flow linkages, flow-floodplain and riparian linkages, source to sea functions of the river etc.

### *Absence or lack of data*

E-flows determination is also a scientific process and one of the pre-requisites for this aspect is data regarding several parameters like hydrology, morphology, ecology and so on. Unfortunately, in India, the lack of valid and reliable data is a major impediment. Local communities have significant knowledge regarding terrestrial and aquatic flora and fauna, the flows of the rivers, the response of aquatic species to changes in flows etc. but it is dispersed and needs to be integrated with other structured knowledge streams (Anantha, Dharmadhikary and Bhadbhade 2017).

### *Inputs from experts*

Apart from data, e-flow assessment also needs involvement of experts from fields like hydrology, morphology, ecology and so on. In Indian conditions, experts having basin-specific knowledge are very few. Moreover, their inputs can often imply significant financial costs (Anantha, Dharmadhikary and Bhadbhade 2017).

### *'Minimum flows' are not environmental flows*

Environmental flows are conceptualized as 'minimum flows' in India which itself is an incorrect premise to start with. Even the National Water Policy (NWP) (Section 14.3) has used the term 'minimum flows' (Ministry of Water Resources 2002: 6). Iyer (2007) correctly pointed out that while the idea of a 'minimum flow' or 'environmental flow' in streams and rivers is welcome in so far as some flow is better than no flows, this may not necessarily imply any major change in thinking; abstractions and diversions continue to be the norm and 'minimum flow' clearly implies maximum abstraction. If 'environmental flow' is understood as a synonym of 'minimum', then the only change is in semantics. This is precisely the problem with e-flow recommendations as most of the e-flow requirements are determined as some percentage of 90 per cent dependable flows. These are almost equivalent to minimum flows, and e-flow allocations end up a mere formality. Therefore, currently, e-flows are being used as a measure to justify more river valley projects under which minimum flow requirements for the river are derived.

### *Standardizing e-flow requirements of the river*

The Government of India has been trying to standardize e-flows methodology and allocation. Earlier, mostly desktop assessments were followed, which do not provide a holistic assessment of e-flows. A few Cumulative Impact Assessments (CIAs) have attempted BBM methodologies, though inadequately, as our analysis reveals (Anantha, Dharmadhikary and Bhadbhade 2017). The report on the Ganga river basin by the National Ganga River Basin Authority (NGRBA) says:

> The BBM methodology is found to be robust with high confidence level. However, specific flow recommendations are difficult to justify at this stage and will have to be worked out afresh. The major uncertainties are centred on the hydrological and hydraulic models due to the lack of availability of reliable data.
>
> (IIT 2011)

This reveals the data deficit context in which BBM methodology is applied in India.

However, the bigger concern is that the current ToR for applying for environmental clearance for River Valley projects states that the minimum e-flow shall be 20 per cent of the average four lean months of the 90 per cent dependable flow and 30 per cent of the monsoon flow during the monsoon season. During post-monsoon months, the flow shall be decided by the committee based on the hydrology and the available discharge. Fish diversity studies also need to be carried out for the estimation of e-flow (MoEFCC 2015). Very significantly, the ToR states: 'A site specific study on minimum environment flow should be carried out'. 'Site specific minimum e-flows' is an advancement from the earlier just 'minimum flows approach'. However, the inherent lacuna of the recommendation of the 2015 ToR is that 'site specific minimum environmental flows assessment' should be the norm.

### *Lack of clarity in setting objectives and relegation of Environmental Management Class (EMC) in e-flow assessment*

O'Keeffe and Le Quesne (2009) have rightly stated that

> there is no one correct environmental flow regime for rivers – the answer will depend on what people want from a river. Different sorts of rivers are likely to have different requirements and priorities, for example differing approaches for a river in a protected area in contrast to a river in a major irrigation or urban area. Choice and judgement, particularly when deciding on environmental objectives, are an essential part of the environmental flow process.

Hence, setting objectives is the most critical part of e-flows assessment. Human interventions in rivers will undoubtedly lead to deviation of the river from its original pristine flow regime and these interventions will put a constraint on the level of flows that can be maintained in the river. Conversely, the level of flows we want in a river would set limits on the kind and extent of its uses. E-flows determination is essentially a process of choosing a balance between the two. Thus, it is the objectives that will determine which uses, roles and functions of the river are to be prioritized (Anantha, Dharmadhikary and Bhadbhade 2017).

Who sets the objectives is another critical aspect and the very process suggests that setting the objectives should involve all the key stakeholders, in particular, the river basin communities. However, presently, the objectives for setting e-flows are a technical choice and a bureaucratic decision. Genuine local concerns about impact on fisheries, riparian farming, downstream impacts, cultural and spiritual values of the river do not find a reflection in e-flows allocation. And, there is no existing mechanism – legal, institutional, administrative or social – which will ensure the participation of all and attempt to set the objectives for a river.

Also, in an analysis of CIA studies and basin studies, it has been routinely found that the Environment Management Class (EMC) set for the riverine stretches is unacceptably low. In the CIA Study of Hydro-electric Dams in the Alakananda and Bhagirathi Basins, the agency Alternate Hydro Energy Centre (AHEC) of IIT, Roorkee has 'assumed' an EMC of C and D for these rivers at various cross sections, especially at the *Prayags* (sites of confluence of two rivers, of very high cultural significance) (Alternative Hydro-Energy Centre 2011). This has automatically resulted in low e-flows allocation for these stretches. As for the Lohit basin study in the northeast, which is an unpolluted, undammed free-flowing river with excellent water quality and biodiversity, the e-flows assessment using 'Tennants Method' says: *'Assume fair and degrading conditions prevail in the basin!'* (WAPCOS 2011: 285). Making the correct assumptions and setting the right objectives, which reflect not only the ecological class of the river, but also reflect the livelihood, social and cultural dependence and value of a river is a crucial prerequisite before assessing e-flows (Anantha and Dandekar 2012).

### *The challenge of bringing e-flows within the policy-legal framework*

Currently, e-flows assessment and implementation find very limited space in legal, policy, institutional and regulatory regimes in India (Anantha, Dharmadhikary and Bhadbhade 2017). Since the dominant view has been to maximize extraction, it is obviously very difficult for e-flows approach to be at the centre of planning and management of river basins. However, since the 1990s, concerned citizens and river basin communities have raised issues regarding the downstream impacts of the dams.

The NWP of April 2002 was the first document to recognize the need to maintain flows in the river. As quoted in para. 14.3: 'Minimum flow should be ensured in the perennial streams for maintaining ecology and social considerations' (MoWR 2002: 6). However, the policy talks about maintaining 'minimum flows', which is different from the concept of e-flows.

Himachal Pradesh was the first state to introduce e-flows in its hydropower policy and the state's High Court Directive mandates that all run-of-river dams release 15 per cent of the mean inflow as e-flows (TERI 2015).

The 2012 National Water Policy reflects a better understanding of what e-flows mean. It states, in the basic principles section, that 'water is essential for sustenance of ecosystem, and therefore, minimum ecological needs should be given due consideration' (MoWR 2012: 3).

And further that 'ecological needs of the river should be determined, through scientific study, recognizing that the natural river flows are characterized by low or no flows, small floods (freshets), large floods etc., and should accommodate developmental needs. A portion of the river flows should be kept aside to meet ecological needs, ensuring that the low and high flow releases are proportional to the natural flow regime, including base flow contribution in the low flow season through regulated groundwater use (MoWR 2012: 4).

The proposed National Water Framework Law, in its Draft Bill (GoI 2016), also has provisions for mandating e-flows. Its Clause 6 (6) states that

> environmental flows adequate to preserve and protect a river basin as a hydrological and ecological system shall be maintained and a portion of the flows should be kept aside to meet the ecological needs ensuring that low and high flow releases are proportional to the natural flow regime, including base flow contribution.
>
> (*ibid.*: 9)

However, currently, this bill does not seem to have any roadmap in terms of enacting the law for ensuring e-flows in our rivers. Also, the other issue is that water is a state subject, thus posing additional hurdles for the enactment of such central legislation. As far as the states are concerned, several states do recognize the need for e-flows.

### *E-flows in a changing climate*

With the changing climate, there is change in the rainfall and monsoon patterns. In recent years, it has been causing excessive flooding in some places and droughts in some other places at the same time in the country. A recent study by Ghosh *et al.* (2016) showed that there was a significant decrease in the monsoon over the major 'surplus' river basins. These research insights question the feasibility of the river inter-linking project, the main purpose of which is to transfer water from surplus basins to deficit basins to increase water and food security and also for flood mitigation and drought proofing.

In the last few years, India has faced some severe droughts which have affected millions of lives. In Maharashtra, the Jal Yukta Shivar campaign was launched under which mass scale dredging operations were carried out in the different rivers of the state, especially in the eastern region, where under the pretext of removal of silt, rivers were deepened, widened and straightened in order to increase their water carrying capacity. The idea of increasing the water availability by widening, deepening and straightening is also scientifically flawed. Widening of the channels destroys the natural banks which can eventually lead to more erosion. Natural meanders act as energy dissipators and therefore help in reducing the intensity of floods. Deepening of the river channels can destroy the natural in-stream habitats like riffles and pools which support certain aquatic species. Therefore, canalizing of river systems is not a scientific solution for drought proofing. Canalizing of the river is also contradictory to the idea of e-flows.

The combined effects of climate change and other human pressures on ecosystem structure and functions result in loss of resilience and, thus, in a downward shift of the services provided by ecosystems. Protection of rivers and associated ecosystems like wetlands, floodplains, mangroves, deltas and riparian ecosystems, and ensuring e-flows which revive the connectivity between the river and these ecosystems can help communities and governments to adapt better to climate change uncertainties.

### *Between environment and irrigation needs*

The experiences of countries like Australia reveal that where e-flows are being integrated into the river basin management framework and when diverse stakeholders are involved in the water sharing process, ultimately the conflict narrows down to the allocation of water between the environment which needs water the most and irrigation which has maximum water demand within the basin (Swainson, de Loë and Kreutzwiser 2011). Often this is also a conflict of value systems wherein the environmentally conscious people consider water as a common property, with the environment having a legitimate share over its water, versus the irrigators and concerned department which considers water as a service they pay for or which the government should provide for them. Irrigation being the highest water user within river basins in India, this is a political challenge which one needs to be prepared for in the e-flows allocation.

### *Addressing political priorities*

Allowing water for the environment is a political decision or choice in India rather than a purely eco-hydrological allocation. Even if the correct allocations have been made, the priorities of the ruling political party from local to interstate to transboundary may ultimately decide how much flows would be finally allocated or left in the river and for what use. The long-pending Teesta Agreement between India and Bangladesh over sharing of the Teesta waters and allowing flows into downstream Bangladesh still remains an unresolved issue due to the differing political priorities between India and Bangladesh and between West Bengal and the Indian Government. The other example is that of the Cauvery Tribunal Award. Despite allocating 10 thousand million cubic feet (TMC ft) of water for minimum flows, the releases are yet to materialize due to political reasons.

## E-flows approach in river basin planning

It is very important that all the diverse communities, departments, industries, agencies who use and share a river from source to sea, should respect, understand and recognize the dynamics of the river, its changing seasonal flows. The management and restoration of e-flows depends upon the feeling of stewardship and common responsibility shared among the different stakeholders. In fact, e-flows should be considered as the central guiding principle for setting limits on water use, after securing the water for drinking and for livestock. To achieve this, it is imperative that the following occurs:

1. E-flows should be seen as an integral part and parcel of a robust river basin planning strategy which includes aspects like environmental clearance of dams, industries, thermal and nuclear power plants, groundwater use, and water quality, apart from basic and livelihood needs of the people directly dependent on the river and requirements of urbanization.
2. Objective-setting should be clearly defined in the ToR of the project. They cannot be standardized. They should be realistic such that both human needs and river ecology can be sustained. Also, it is important to understand that objectives can be set only within the ecological and hydrological limits of the river. Hence, objective setting would also mean making the people aware of the limits to development of the river basin and beyond.
3. E-flows should be set apart as 'beneficial use' on par with other water uses as recommended in Joy *et al.* (2011). Basic and livelihood rights and ecosystem needs shall be given top priority.
4. E-flows assessment by any agency or government should respect the fundamental principles of equity, sustainability and gender equality.
5. Participation of stakeholders should be the basic principle followed in the e-flow assessment and implementation process. Special efforts need to be made in bringing in the local wisdom from the riparian communities in a more articulate and structured manner while deciding the appropriate e-flow assessment methodology/approach.
6. Regulation of water allocation or banning of new development projects requiring constant supply of water from river or groundwater should be made mandatory in over-allocated river basins.

The entire process of assessment, implementation and monitoring of e-flows shall be carried out with participation of the direct river-dependent local communities (tribals, fisher folk, boatmen and direct river-dependent farmers).

7 The flow regime and allocation for different sectors shall be made public and placed before the river basin stakeholders for discussion, consensus and negotiation before actual implementation. The principle of subsidiarity to the lowest scale of management shall be adhered to.
8 Review of the e-flows allocation once a year shall be mandatory. Since a river is a dynamic entity, e-flows are also a dynamic process and hence need adaptation.
9 Compliance of e-flows regime arrived at shall be legally mandatory. Violation of compliance shall be a punishable offence.
10 Reallocation strategies between existing massive water uses (users) and domestic/drinking water/ecosystem needs and uses should be given preference.

## Concluding discussion

The future of our riverscapes is totally dependent on what kind of development we seek and what impact it will have on our rivers. Therefore, e-flows will play a critical role in river basin planning and management. For this, e-flows need to be seen beyond the dam discourse. Also, e-flows are currently being used under best management practices and to justify as many dams on a river as possible. It is important to understand that e-flows just mimic the natural flows of the river and therefore cannot be arbitrarily used as a surrogate for natural flows in the river. The sector-based approach used for the planning of the river valley projects does not have adequate measures to attain participatory and multi-sector management. Therefore, river experts, river communities, civil society organizations (CSOs) and local government authorities need to come on one single platform when deciding the objectives for river basin planning, e-flows assessment and management. As water is a state subject, policies for mandating e-flows cannot be limited to the central level but need to happen at the state level too. Lastly, the first right over the water should be that of the river itself. It should be allowed to flow and carry enough sediments and nutrients to support and sustain aquatic habitats. It should be able to carry out the necessary processes towards self-purification. This can happen only when all the different flows occurring in nature are maintained in the river. Therefore, e-flows should not be treated as something that goes against economic development because in trying to gain more in the short term, we may lose our precious rivers which would otherwise have been able to provide for all our needs over centuries.

## Note

1 With inputs from Shripad Dharmadhikary, Partha Jyoti Das and Samir Mehta.

## References


Agarwal, N., M. Asher and P. Bhandari. 2011. *A Critique of the Luhri Hydro-electric Project on the Sutlej River.* Himachal Pradesh: HIM DHARA, Environment Research and Action Collective, www.himdhara.org/wp-content/uploads/2011/12/Critique-of-Luhri-HEP_english.pdf (accessed on 28 May 2018).

Alternative Hydro-Energy Centre. 2011. 'Assessment of Cumulative Impact of Hydropower Projects in Alakananda and Bhagirathi Basins', www.indiawaterportal.org/sites/indiawaterportal.org/files/assessment_of_cumulative_impacts_of_hydropower_projects_in_alaknanda__bhagirathi_basin_ahec_iit-roorkee_report_2012.pdf (accessed on 15 February 2018).

Anantha, L. 2013. 'Dam Decommissioning as an Environmental Priority', http://sandrp.in/dams/Dam_Decommissioning_as_Env_Piroirty_India_March2013.pdf (accessed on 15 February 2018).

Anantha, L. and P. Dandekar. 2012. 'Towards Restoring Flows into the Earth's Arteries: A Primer on Environmental Flows', www.internationalrivers.org/sites/default/files/attached-files/eflows_primer_062012.pdf (accessed on 24 May 2017).

Anantha, L., S. Dharmadhikary and N. Bhadbhade. 2017. 'E-flows in Indian Rivers: Methodologies, Issues, Indicators and Conditions: Learnings from Hasdeo Basin', Forum for Policy Dialogue on Water Conflicts in India, Pune.

Arthington, A. H., R. E. Tharme, S. O. Brizga, B. J. Pusey, and M. J. Kennard. 2004. 'Environmental Flow Assessment with Emphasis on Holistic Methodologies', Proceedings of the Second International Symposium on the Management of Large Rivers for Fisheries. FAO, www.fao.org/docrep/007/ad526e/ad526e07.htm (accessed on 24 May 2017).

Convention on Biological Diversity. 2010. 'Global Outlook 3', www.cbd.int/gbo3/?pub=6667&section=6708 (accessed on 15 February 2018).

Dyson, M., G. Bergkamp and J. Scanlon (eds.). 2003. *Flow: The Essentials of Environmental Flows.* IUCN, Gland, Switzerland and Cambridge, https://cmsdata.iucn.org/downloads/flow___the_essentials_of_environmental_flow___dyson_et_al.pdf (accessed on 17 June 2018).

Ghosh, S., H. Vittal, T. Sharma, S. Karmarkar, K. S. Kasiviswanathan, Y. Dhanesh, K. P. Sudheer, and S. S. Gunthe. 2016. 'Indian Summer Monsoon Rainfall: Implications of Contrasting Trends in the Spatial Variability of Mean and Extremes', *Plos One*, doi:10.1371/journal.pone.0158670, http://journals.plos.org/plosone/article/file?id=10.1371/journal.pone.0158670&type=printable (accessed on 11 September 2018).

Government of India (GoI). 2016. *Draft National Water Framework Bill, 2016*. New Delhi: Ministry of Water Resources, Government of India.

Groombridge, B. and M. Jenkins. 1998. 'Freshwater Biodiversity: A Preliminary Global Assessment: World Conservation Monitoring Centre (WCMC) Biodiversity Series No. 8', World Conservation Press, https://portals.iucn.org/library/sites/library/files/documents/WCMC-008.pdf (accessed on 28 May 2018).

IIT (Indian Institute of Technology). 2011. 'Environmental Flows: State-of-the-art with Special Reference to Rivers in the Ganga Basin', Ganga River Basin Environmental Management Plan. Report Code: 022_GBP_IIT_EFL_SOA_01_Ver 1_June 2011, http://52.7.188.233/sites/default/files/022_EFL.pdf (accessed on 28 May 2018).

International Water Centre. 2007. 'The Brisbane Declaration', www.watercentre.org/news/declaration (accessed on 24 May 2017).

International Water Management Institute (IWMI). 2005. *Environmental Flows: Planning for Environmental Water Allocation*. Colombo, Sri Lanka: International Water Management Institute (IWMI): 6. (IWMI Water Policy Briefing 015) doi:http://dx.doi.Org/10.3910/2009.332 (accessed on 15 February 2018).

Islam, M. S. 2010. 'Nature and Limitations of Environmental Flow Methodologies and its Global Trends', *Journal of Civil Engineering (IEB)*, 38(2): 141–152.

Iyer, Ramaswamy R. 2007. *Towards Water Wisdom: Limits, Justice, Harmony*. New Delhi: Sage.

Joy, K. J., Priya Sangameswaran, Latha Anantha, Shripad Dharmadhikary, M. K. Prasad, and K. P. Soma. 2011. 'Life, Livelihoods, Ecosystems, Culture: Entitlements and Allocation of Water for Competing Uses', Position Paper by the Thematic Subgroup on Water Entitlements and Allocations for Livelihoods and Ecosystem Needs). Pune: Forum for Policy Dialogue on Water Conflicts in India.

King, J., C. Brown and H. Sabet. 2003. 'A Scenario-based Holistic Approach to Environmental Flow Assessments for Rivers', *River Research and Applications*, 19(5–6): 619–639.

King, J. M. and R. E. Tharme. 1994. 'Assessment of the Instream Flow Incremental Methodology and Initial Development of Alternative Instream Flow Methodologies for South Africa', Water Research Commission Report No. 295/1/94. Water Research Commission, Pretoria: 590.

King, J. M., R. E. Tharme and M. S. de Villiers. (eds.). 2008. 'Environmental Flow Assessments for Rivers: Manual for the Building Block Methodology', Water Research Commission Technology Transfer Report No. TT131/00. Pretoria, SA, Water Research Commission: 340.

Ministry of Environment, Forest and Climate Change. 2015. 'Standard Terms of Reference (TOR) for EIA/EMP Report for Projects/Activities Requiring Environment Clearance Under EIA Notification, 2006', www.moef.gov.in/sites/default/files/final%20Booklet.pdf (accessed on 24 May 2017).

Ministry of Water Resources. 2002. 'The National Water Policy', www.karnataka.gov.in/minorirrigation/pdf/national_water_policy.pdf (accessed on 15 February 2018).

Ministry of Water Resources. 2012. 'The National Water Policy', http://mowr.gov.in/sites/default/files/NWP2012Eng6495132651_1.pdf (accessed on 15 February 2018).

Mohile, A. D. and L. N. Gupta. 2005. 'Environmental Water Requirement: Concept and Coverage', Abstracts of the NIE/ IWMI Workshop on Environmental Flows. New Delhi: 3–4, March.

Nilsson, C., C. A. Reidy, M. Dynesius, and C. Revenga. 2005. 'Fragmentation and Flow Regulation of the World's Large River Systems', *Science*, 308(5720): 405–408.

O'Keeffe, J., N. Kaushal, L. Bharati, and V. Smakhtin. 2012. 'Assessment of Environmental Flows for the Upper Ganga Basin', http://awsassets.wwfindia.org/downloads/wwf_e_flows_report.pdf (accessed on 24 May 2017).

O'Keeffe, J. and T. Le Quesne. 2009. 'Keeping Rivers Alive', A Primer on Environmental Flows and Their Assessment. WWF Water Security Series, 2, http://assets.wwfindia.org/downloads/keeping_rivers_alive.pdf (accessed on 11 September 2015).

Pathak. V. and R. K. Tyagi. 2010. 'Riverine Ecology and Fisheries, vis-à-vis Hydrodynamic Alterations: Impacts and Remedial Measures', CIFRI, ISSN 0970–0616X.

Poff, N. L., B. D. Richter, A. H. Arthington, S. E. Bunn, R. J. Naiman, E. Kendy, M. Acreman, C. Apse, B. P. Bledsoe, Mary C. Freeman, J. Henriksen, R. B. Jacobson, J. G. Kennen, D. M. Merritt, J. H. O'Keeffe, J. D. Olden, K. Rogers, R. E. Tharme, and A. Warner. 2010. 'The Ecological Limits of Hydrologic Alteration (ELOHA): A New Framework for Developing Regional Environmental Flow Standards', *Freshwater Biology*, 55(1): 147–170.

Rahmani. n.d. 'Report of Dr A. Rahmani, Member of the Team for Site Inspection of the Proposed DEMWE Lower Hydroelectric Project in Arunachal Pradesh', www.moef.nic.in/downloads/public-information/REPORT-Dr-A-REHMANI-DEMWE-HEP.pdf (accessed on 15 February 2018).

Shukla, A. 2010. 'Report of the One-Man Committee to Monitor Environmental Compliance of Hydel Projects in CWP No. 24/09'.

Swainson, B., R. C. de Loë and R. D. Kreutzwiser. 2011. 'Sharing Water with Nature: Insights on Environmental Water Allocation from a Case Study of the Murrumbidgee Catchment, Australia', *Water Alternatives*, 4(1): 15–34.

TERI. 2015. *Green Growth and Hydro Power in Himachal Pradesh*. New Delhi: The Energy and Resources Institute.

Thakkar, H. 2012. 'Rivers: Legal and Institutional Issues in India', http://re.indiaenvironmentportal.org.in/files/file/Rivers_Legal_and_Institutional_Issues_in_India.pdf (accessed on 24 May 2017).

Venot, J. P. 2008. 'Drawing Water for Thirsty Lands: Stories of the Closing Krishna River Basin in South India' Paper Presented at the 13th World Water Congress, Montpellier, 1–4 September.

WAPCOS. 2011. 'Basin-level Impact Assessment Study of the Lohit River', A Study by WAPCOS and Ministry of Environment and Forests.

# 6 Changing water use practices of the urban middle class in India

## Insights from Metropolitan Calcutta

*Kuntala Lahiri-Dutt**

### Introduction: the urban middle class as (water) consumers

An inescapable part of growing up in India in the 1970s was living with labels the western world used to describe its population; if much of the rest of the world was divided into the 'first' and the 'second', we in India were designated citizens of the 'third' world. Academic texts and popular media originating in the first world introduced us to our third world cities before we could form our own impressions of them. Calcutta, we were told, was a city of peasants – the definition offering a simple, homogenized view of the city's inhabitants. Although the quintessential 'primate city', it was nonetheless presented as a city of the third world, tying everyone living in Calcutta to rural origins and rural ways of life that contrasted with those of first world cities. In particular, third world cities such as Calcutta were seen as lacking in those material goods, amenities and services that made life comfortable elsewhere, and hence constituted an object of study by first world experts.

Until the 1980s, India followed its own version of a centrally planned, command-and-control economy. The desire to nurture domestic industry – and the culture of economic protectionism that followed in its wake – conspired against the importation of what were regarded as 'world class' goods and services into the country. Neoliberal economic measures led to abandonment, in 1991, of the socialist economic model in favour of an open economy. Part of the agenda for India's planners was to set about reconstructing its cities in terms of western, consumer-driven values, filling vacant spaces and replacing dilapidated building stock with high-rises and shopping malls. Changes in economic policy led to a surge of economic growth and put India somewhat suddenly in the throes of manifold changes, creating winners and losers, as with rapid growth elsewhere in the world. In response, social and economic inequalities increased: a large proportion of its population continues to live in abysmal poverty. The changes also had social and cultural repercussions: the pervasive mindset of the prior four decades – of protectionism, endemic corruption and bureaucratic control – was under challenge (Haynes *et al.* 2010).

There was also a new phenomenon: the rise of the middle class. Scholars began to notice that some Indians were transforming into voracious consumers. Clearly, changes in economic policy had paved the way for, among other things, 'a middle-class based culture of consumption' (Fernandes 2006: 19). The culture of consumption was slower to affect eastern India – where the metropolis of Calcutta is located – than metropolitan Delhi and western India, indicating the close attachment of consumerist culture to distinct political and regional proclivities. In eastern India, the rise of the middle-classes was presided over by the pro-China Communist Party, which ruled the state of West Bengal for three decades and, in its effort to re-inscribe history, changed the name of the city from Calcutta to Kolkata.

The sizeable and growing (IMF 2010; Varma 1998) middle class is a magnet for multinational corporations wanting to conduct business in India (Shrivastava and Kothari 2012: 323). The consumption culture this class represents is unprecedented in India's history, and is beginning to attract scholarly analysis.

In India, the change in perception of what makes water 'clean' and 'pure', and in domestic water use practices, has constituted one part of the rise in middle-class consumerism. Water has symbolic value in Indian cultures, and that symbolism is crucial for a deeper understanding of domestic water consumption. Regrettably, though, more has been written about the ongoing scarcity of water supply to urban homes than this symbolic value, which is reflected in how water is perceived to be 'clean' and 'pure'. Such perception leads to the use of tools and technology of purifying water that – ostensibly – provide convenience. A close analysis of these practices reveals that a deeper relationship of mutual exploitation exists between superficial commercial sentiment and consumer idealism – a relationship that finds common ground in middle-class aspirational ideals related to social status.

## Practices of material consumption

In addition to this large middle class, there are those waiting at its margins and interstices, in smaller urban centres as well as in the metropolises, to join this amorphous group. The contemporary view is that the sociological category of 'middle class' has enormous internal diversity or subsumes many contested identities; is fluid; and performs ideological work that challenges the ascription to it of a sociological category. The defining feature of the new middle class is material consumption – those in it are voracious users, and those outside aspire to become so. The old middle class of India was defined largely by its cultural outlook and political allegiances; it was the foundation stone of the Nehruvian developmentalist state, constituted in terms of the historical materialist conditions that prioritized specific concerns. As a political construction, the category has sometimes seen its dominance lead to the reproduction of inequalities in Indian society (Fernandes 2006). Different from this group is the 'new' middle class, the post-liberalization aspirational group, large in sheer numbers but small in terms of its proportion within the Indian population, holding 'the middle-class culture of public life' (Nandy 1998: 4). Ray (2010: 314) defines this class as a 'proper noun', in terms of its members' self-perception, cultural performances and enactments, which – Ray argues – reproduce an imagined 'middle class-ness'. It is marked by certain shared characteristics, which in the case of India includes aspirationalism, and also the necessity of negotiating the imagined and actual worlds of east and west, of tradition and modernity (Brosius 2010). New ways of consuming material goods underpin these characterizations and, therefore, the idea of being middle class. The concept thus becomes

> an identity constructed through consumption [that] is far more empowering and controllable than that which is dependent upon production . . . there is a clear preference for consumers to be able autonomously to employ their resources for the self-construction of their individual and social identity.
>
> (Miller 1995: 38)

If consumption underlies the ideas of being middle class, then consumption, by default, also becomes a means for those on its margins to join that class. For the individual, familial and group mobility strategies of the new, heterogeneous middle class, 'consumption assumes a long-term dimension, oriented towards present and future' (Osella and Osella 1999: 990). It is no wonder then that the middle class in India is endeavouring to find new ways of being – hungrily consuming resources such as water and energy that were hitherto out of the reach of ordinary Indians.

Understanding the material practices of this new middle class requires study of Indian households. Home has been sacred to the Indian way of life for a very long time, acting as the prime location of indigenous culture and cultural practices. The location of native tradition and culture within the private domain in India is considered the result of contact with European culture and is concomitant with colonization. This contact created a binary division between the public and private spheres (noted by Chatterjee 1993), fostering the image of the archetypal Indian as a product of colonialism: someone who is tradition-bound at home while juggling modernist ideals in public life. For the first time since it came into being through British cultural contact, this binary division is beginning to blur, as a rising middle class develops and adopts new ideas and new ways of being at home. Within a short span of 20 years, a number of cultural practices have changed fundamentally, symbolizing a deeper shift in the value system and cultural ethos of the middle class.

Increasingly, social and individual practices are being studied in order to develop an understanding of consumption. Practice theory, a loosely connected body of work, considers practice to be the location of all that is 'social', allowing us to move away from the conceptual binaries of structure and agency, and placing practices at the centre of human action. Practices are seen as routines, the indivisible unit of social enquiry and the site of analysis:

> [P]ractice (*Praktik*) is a routinised type of behaviour which consists of several elements, interconnected to one other: forms of bodily activities, forms of mental activities, 'things' and their use, a background knowledge in the form of understanding, know-how, states of emotion and motivational knowledge.
>
> (Reckwitz 2002: 249–250)

It does not follow that because practices are routinized behaviour, they do not change; crisis of routine leads to changes in practice. With increased pace of life, and rates of innovation and obsolescence, crises of routine have become more frequent, leading to more frequent changes in practice (Reckwitz 2002; Shove 2009). Consumption is considered to take place as a part of carrying out a practice. Put differently, most practices involve consumption of one kind or the other (Warde 2005). Therefore, if practice is the unit of social enquiry, examining household practices should yield insights into social processes. This is the logic that provided the foundation for a large study of 'water-using practices of households' in the south and southeast of

England (Pullinger *et al.* 2013). Based on this logic, one may hope to explore how changing values of water are reshaping water practices among the transforming Indian middle class. Calcutta's particularities offer a fascinating opportunity for investigation into material practices of water in middle-class homes. These include its location in economically stagnant eastern India; its unique history of the separation of private from public social spaces; the early development of a middle class in the city due to colonial British influence; and its Communist rule and deep attachment to Marxist materialist ideology.[1]

## The domestic spaces of middle-class household in Calcutta

Bengali intellectuals describe the Calcutta social milieu as a 'microcosm of Indian society' (Roy 1986: 9). Yet, the city is very different from other metropolises of India, on several counts – the foremost being the Bengali culture that was inscribed over 200 years of colonial rule (Mukherjee 1972). The general lack of economic buoyancy in its hinterlands, the decay of old industries like the jute mills and the refugee influx after the partition caused the city to burst at its seams. Munshi (1975: 11) notes that the civic services were 'not very far from a total breakdown'. In spite of the establishment of the Calcutta Metropolitan Development Authority (CMDA) – the apex planning body for the city – Calcutta's urban growth has in general been haphazard. Since the 1970s, its concrete sprawl has extended into the south – away from the traditional 'native' North Calcutta, or the old or 'black' town (Munshi 1975). Broadly, the original pattern of elongated growth along the levee of the Ganga gradually changed, as the wetlands in the eastern parts of the city were filled up to make way for new residential areas. As urban life flowed and shifted away from the core, 'the merciless property boom extended deeper and deeper southward' (noted by Chaudhuri 2013: 288) and, eventually, devoured the remaining swamplands.

During the summer months of 2012, 21 households in a predominantly middle-class neighbourhood of south Calcutta were surveyed and their water-related practices were observed for one full day each. These households were self-selected; the survey's aims and objectives were initially described informally in a meeting at which participants expressed their interest to join the study. An overview of the survey was offered to interested participants either over the phone or by email before meeting them in person. Within the household, the option to be interviewed was again open to each of the members; those members decided which one person from each household would participate in the study. The interviews were semi-structured, allowing the respondents to veer into topics close to their interests. Of those interviewed, 60 per cent were women, and the average age of the respondents was 43 years, safely allowing the inference that most were well-established in their jobs and life. An average household comprises roughly four members, two of whom are income earners, providing two income sources within each household. All households have at least one part-time domestic helper; yet, all complained of the difficulties of running the household. The average family income was 25,300 INR per month; that is, nearly 380 US dollars – although translated into US dollars this amount fails to convey its value within the community. Suffice to say the households in this study can afford a number of the trappings of modern life on their income. All of them have bank accounts, and life and medical insurance. A considerable 72 per cent own smartphones and go out once a week to malls to shop, watch a movie or dine.

These households live in apartments. They are middle class in their earnings and residences – and in their worldviews. Over the past few years, as Calcutta has transformed into a global city, their tastes and behaviours in consumption, ideas of cleanliness and comfort have changed fundamentally. Conforming to these changes, water use practices have also altered significantly; on an average day, 90 per cent of the households have at least three members who use water for a full-body shower.[2] Previously, women would sit on a low stool in the bathroom, but a standing shower has now become more common. As with western sensibilities, the purposes of showering are to maintain bodily hygiene, minimize bodily odour, remove perspiration and feel clean. Men usually shave outside of the shower area, and in over half the households, brushing and combing hair also took place outside the bathroom, usually in a basin meant for washing hands before and after meals.

One key aspect of intra-household water use is the application of electronic technology intended to reduce labour at home (as noted by Hand, Shove and Southerton 2005). All the households have, in the past decade or so, introduced a variety of appliances – flush toilets, washing machines, water heaters and, most importantly, water purifying machines, along with more, and varied kinds of, taps – in their homes for use in water-related chores. All households use electrical water filters; 84 per cent use geysers or electric water heaters; 72 per cent use washing machines; but, surprisingly, only 8 per cent of households own dishwashers. Following Woolgar (1991), one might deduce that this snapshot of appliance use is influenced by the ease with which a particular appliance accommodates the social and cultural context of the respondent household. Practice innovation, thus, links existing cultures with new technologies. Washing machines in India have been modified to wash garments that are unique to India, such as saris (some Samsung washing machines have a 'sari mode'), and kitchen appliances have been adapted to culturally rooted food preferences (such as the 'browning' facility in some microwave ovens meant mainly for the South Asian market). Interestingly, dishwashers are not yet designed to accommodate typically large and numerous Indian utensils, and the particular stove-top style of cooking in many Bengali households has yet to be addressed by electronic white goods manufacturing design. Practices are differentiated when they travel across the social spectrum (as noted by Warde 2005); the near-ubiquitous presence of the part- or full-time domestic help is also crucial in determining who uses what and when in Calcutta. The households with dishwashers have strong overseas links (employment in the merchant navy; residence in the United Kingdom), connections which perhaps have predisposed the residents to accommodate a dishwasher in the kitchen. Such exposure to different ways of consuming may well have influenced respondents' consumption patterns – based on the acquisition of conspicuous, tangible objects, rather than on the practicalities of their use.

To explain the practices of such consumption technologies, Shove (2003: 11–12) underlines that goods and objects should not be analysed in isolation without noticing 'the pre- and co-requisite systems and technologies on which they [consumer durables] depend, or the reconfiguration of ideas, actions and habits associated with their use and appropriation'. Indeed, the constant endeavour of the middle classes to find new ways of being within the microcosm of the home is exemplified by the entrance of these new technologies, which also creates new global citizens out of Calcuttans. The routines of everyday life are 'situated and inscribed in tools, devices and material objects' (Shove 2003: 13); yet, it is necessary to go beyond theories of consumption. One might note here that the perceived and almost universal need for domestic help in urban middle-class homes was not reduced by the presence of dishwashers or, for that matter, any of the other gadgets. Thus, more than the savings in domestic labour through its regular use, ownership of a dishwasher reflects the middle-class adoption of the notions of comfort conveyed by use of that appliance, and the accompanying status associated with it, even though the meanings of these technologies are site specific. This example demonstrates why in Calcutta the use of water- or energy-efficient technologies does not directly conform to western models of consumer use.

## Supplying water to Calcutta homes

Water has distinctive meanings for urban households in Calcutta, a gigantic metropolitan city that began its urban journey in three villages located on the natural levee of the river Ganga. Indeed, Calcutta barely rises above the sea level, and is 'balanced upon a huge natural raft of clay, literally floating on an enormous reservoir of water stored within the sand grains underneath' (Das Gupta 1995: 2). One would expect water to be abundant in such a context; yet, since colonial times, there were obsessive concerns over accurate planning of not merely the supply of water but also its purity.[3] Naipaul (1990: 281) describes Calcutta as:

> the British-built city of India. . . . In the building of Calcutta, known first as the city of palaces, and later as the second city of the British Empire, the British worked with immense confidence, not adapting the styles of Indian rulers, but setting down in India adaptations of the European classical style as emblems of a conquering civilization.

For this second most populous city in the Empire after London, and a key colonial depot for the British, built with the image of London in mind, obtaining clean water supplies was paramount from the early days of Calcutta's history. Understandably, the original source of water for Calcutta was the river Ganga – once known at the mouth of the Bay of Bengal as Hooghly, now rechristened Hugli. A number of water works followed, which lifted water from the Hooghly river for distribution to some areas of Calcutta. As the river carried large quantities of silt, and flowed through the industrial backyards of Calcutta, the quality of water soon became a problem. During the peak of summer (April–May) and during the monsoon months it was either too saline or silty. Therefore, numerous tanks and wells were built in the city to store freshwater from monsoon rains. The largest of these was 'The Great Tank' in Dalhousie Square – now known as the Binoy Badal Dinesh Bag – which developed as the central business district due to its proximity to river and ocean transport: the port, the warehouses, the *ghats* (the stopping points along the river) anchoring barges carrying goods from the interior and Fort William. This tank was deepened and extended in 1809 to afford the garrison at the old Fort access to sufficient freshwater. As the city grew, an increasing volume of water was required, and, between 1805 and 1836, more and larger tanks were excavated to enhance water supplies.[4] The turbid water was clarified using alum and fine cloth strainers, a practice that today has almost entirely fallen out of use. Some larger households stored the fresh February water in jars for use during the monsoon months. Similarly, some Europeans harvested rainwater to store in Pegu jars, while wealthier households had water carried into the home by water bearers.[5]

The Bengal Landholders' Attendance Act of 1848 (also known as the 1848 Act)[6] first overrode a private landowner to acknowledge the need for public (drinking) water supply in Calcutta. Following enactment of this legislation, an expert was deputed to carry out elaborate analyses of the water sourced from the River Hooghly between December 1861 and January 1863. Largely as a result of these tests, construction of the water works began at Pulta in 1868. Water was drawn through cast iron pipes from Pulta to the Tala Tank, where another pumping plant delivered the water to the residential neighbourhoods, part of it being directed to another subterranean reservoir at the Wellington Square, where a further pumping station was built.[7] Together, the reservoirs at Tala and Wellington Square had the capacity of three million gallons, or 660,000 litres (Ray 1901). By 1870, all the major residential areas of Calcutta had access to piped water, and the daily consumption was nearly 20 million litres. Subsequently, further pumping stations and overhead tanks were added to the system. Regardless, until the 1950s, the primary source of water had remained the river.

The Kolkata Municipal Corporation (KMC) is the institution responsible for the supply of water to resident households in Calcutta. The Calcutta Municipal Act of 1951 formally established the body in 1952 that is now responsible for water supplies in this metropolis. The total rated capacity of water supply to the area from several pumping stations and water treatment plants now stands at about 1400 million litres per day for its 10 million-plus residents in the Municipal Corporation area; and about 79 per cent of households have access to water – defined as potable water piped into the house – on an average of 8.3 hours of uninterrupted supply per day (ADB 2007).[8]

The rapid increase of urban sprawl in Calcutta has not been matched by an expansion of services – the geographical boundaries of the corporation area currently represent a correspondingly small proportion of Calcutta's urban extent, which depends largely on non-piped water supplies. Even within the corporation area, most urban residents depend on a mix of sources: treated surface water from the Hooghly, deep tubewells or borewells and hand pumps. Most middle-class households are dependent on either the KMC supply or groundwater. Excessive use of groundwater has caused a significant decrease in piezometric levels, leading to ground subsidence in certain areas.

Sahu *et al.* (2013) add to this that lowering of the groundwater table may be associated with the threat of arsenic contamination. Several studies show that the subsoil in a number of areas is contaminated by dangerous levels of arsenic, which leaches into the groundwater, causing chronic and life-threatening illness. Altogether, this has created a crisis in Calcutta's water supply; Basu and Main (2001: 41) argue that the crisis 'encompasses mutually reinforcing problems of efficiency, equity and the environment'. Consequently, debates over water in Calcutta have assumed two dimensions: that of quality and availability.

These water debates are closely connected to the overall urban decay resulting from the inability of Calcutta's urban service delivery system to cope with the post-partition influx of millions of refugees from East Bengal. The consequent pressure on water supply saw not only the decline of older uses of water such as the washing of streets, but also the emergence of new sources of water such as hand pumps in poorer areas and deep tubewells for high-rises. Since the 1980s high-rise boom, most middle-class Calcuttans rely on underground water lifted by deep tubewells. Today, very few households rely exclusively on KMC-supplied water; in lower-income areas, however, public taps also play an important role. Public knowledge of arsenic poisoning that ensues from excessive withdrawal of groundwater and the health risks from drinking untreated municipal water have driven behaviour change as ideas of water purity and portability have fundamentally changed. Consequently, almost every middle-class household has now introduced water filters to be used as the norm. In public spaces outside the home, preventive measures such as using bottled water, especially when eating in a restaurant, have become standard practice for most respondents, and very few households report having suffered waterborne diseases. When they do occur, the diseases – upset stomach or diarrhoea – are routinely identified by respondents as the result of consuming water from a public source outside the home.

Historically, domestic help in middle-class households was tasked with household chores including washing, cleaning and fetching of water. While piped water is available today and households are equipped with time-saving appliances – usually a washing machine – domestic help continues to be a regular household fixture. Consequently, most households employing domestic help continue to require the performance of water-related chores such as washing and cleaning. Household use of water in the form of washing cars and bikes are also the tasks of drivers and/or external help; these are washed with varying frequency ranging from daily to once or twice per week, with buckets of water usually sourced from a local public tap.

Although Delhi, Mumbai and Bangalore eclipse it today, until 1981, Calcutta was the largest Indian metropolis. Controversially referred to as either the 'dying city' or the 'city of hope', today it is choked with sewage and people; slums and shanties exist side by side with apartment blocks and air-conditioned shopping complexes. For a good part of the last quarter of the 20th century, but especially since the early 1990s, the middle class of Calcutta has been moving into small – 700–1200 square feet (65–112 square metres) – two-bedroom apartments in high-rises. This movement, in many ways, encapsulates a break from the past and the tradition and culture associated with that past.

## Water consumption narratives

How have water use practices changed? For an intimate view, it might be useful to look at how the respondents themselves viewed the transformations and narrated them. These narratives, collected as 'stories' during the qualitative interviews over the course of the research, allow us intimate access to the changing values of water. Let me narrate a water story as truthfully as I can from the taped interview of Respondent 10, a 61-year-old woman who has been a housewife all her life and has lived all her life in Calcutta. For the interview she spoke in Bangla, as she is more fluent in this language. Her husband is 69 and is now retired from his position with the central government. They have one son, a 36-year-old software engineer in a multinational organization and a divorcee, who lives with them. The respondent's 93-year-old father was sitting next to her during the interview, and often interjected to correct her memories of how water was used in their household or how practices used to be carried out in public spaces. The fascinating story of water they narrated together exemplifies my point: that the attention of the middle class has shifted gradually from access to quality – that is, from receiving adequate piped water in the home to being able to choose better-quality water for drinking. It also offers intimate views of water practices of urban middle-class homes in the past.

According to them, until about the 1920s, most households did not have piped water supply because only the richer, whiter parts of the city and the homes of a few aristocratic families were connected to the corporation pipeline. Indeed, as they recalled, Calcutta had a much smaller population in the 1920s than it does today, with sprawling houses inhabited by joint families. The woman respondent noted that many middle-class neighbourhoods had their own wells from which water was drawn by one of the household helpers – buckets were carried into the house by domestic servants. The old man recalled that the servants would pour the water into large *jala*s – earthenware pots – that would then be covered with muslin to filter out the particulate matter. The woman respondent observed that water stored in the *jala*s was used for drinking; the earthen pots also kept the water cool during muggy Calcutta summers. The old man recalled that many *bhadralok* – genteel folk – required their servants to carry smaller earthen jars – *kalsi*s – so that cool drinking water was at hand even when they travelled. Vendors at the railway stations sold these pots to passengers.

The old man recalled that by the mid-1930s, water pipes were laid across most of the northern and central parts of the city, and in parts of the south, extending piped water to middle-class Bengali families. During the same pre-WWII period, unfiltered river water became available through street-side hydrants. Although these were intended for washing the roads, most of the poorer families depended on these hydrants for bathing and for washing utensils. At the time of independence in 1947, water pipes had been laid in all the existing middle-class neighbourhoods, such as Ballygunge, Alipore and Tollygunge. Since then, the underground water system has been extended across the corporation area, serving most middle-class neighbourhoods that reside within the formal urban boundary. Those on the outer fringes or the frontiers of the sprawl are not served by piped water or sewage systems at all.

Despite the municipal water system, however, the preferred source of drinking water was still the tubewells, also constructed by the corporation. Underground water was thought to be purer – described by the respondents as *swachha*[9] – containing fewer disease-causing bacteria. The method of collecting drinking water was labour-intensive, but it was invariably the cheap labour of domestic workers, who used two large jars or buckets hanging from the ends of a wooden pole to carry the water into the kitchen for storage. Nonetheless, on occasion, particularly on hot summer days, some people filled a glass of drinking water straight from the tap without any filtration; knowledge of waterborne diseases at the time was not as widespread as it is today.

The old man recalled a severe epidemic of jaundice during the summer of 1960 as the crucial factor in creating the first panic among the Bengali middle classes concerning the quality of water being supplied by the corporation. As other waterborne diseases related to gastroenteric ailments were identified, doctors began to advise citizens to boil the water before consumption. The respondent noted that the first water filtration devices made their appearance in middle-class households at about this time. The early contraptions comprised two ceramic or stainless-steel containers, one sitting on top of the other. The upper container incorporated a porous ceramic cylinder that filtered out impurities – only particulate matter – into the lower container, which included a tap from which drinking water could be drawn. They were relatively expensive for the time, so some households fell back on the practice of dipping alum into water in the hope of purifying it. By the 1970s and 1980s, almost every middle-class household possessed one of the two-container water filters as a necessary part of everyday life.

During the 1980s, the existing technology was adapted for convenience – this took the form of a porous polypropylene moulded cylinder – referred to as a filter 'candle', with the now generic product name Aquaguard – attached to the kitchen tap (Muralidhararao and Rao 2005). Another, newer technology was Zeoline, a liquid product that could be carried around in one's pocket or handbag, one drop of which would purify a glass of drinking water within a minute. Comprised of sodium hypochlorite, Zeoline left a slight chlorinated smell and altered the taste of the water.[10] More sophisticated filtering options began to appear only during the late 1990s, and now most middle-class homes boast of at least one of these devices.

Let me now look at how other respondents' views about the quality of water have changed over the recent years. Respondent 11, a Bengali male aged 57, with two incomes, has been renting and living in a high-rise apartment for the past 18 years. His apartment receives water from the KMC. About 16 years ago, Respondent 11 began to feel that the water was not clean enough for drinking. He purchased a large aluminium pot to boil water to sterilize it. Then, he would cool the water and strain it through a piece of cloth. Within a year or so, the process proved costly and time-consuming, so he purchased a water filter, a steel jar about 1 metre high and fitted with ceramic filtering candles. However, the filtering process was also time and labour intensive, so he purchased an electricity-powered filter to provide the family with drinking water. He went through these changes because he felt that the 'quality of water is very important for all uses', and that 'life is easier' with water-filtering devices. In his view, pure water that is fit for drinking 'is free from iron and sediments'. Tap water supplied by the KMC did not meet this standard as it contained sediment. In his office, Respondent 11 drinks filtered water, but whenever he is in a restaurant, he purchases mineral water. He feels that bottled water is superior in quality to the filtered water he uses at home.

Around the same time as Respondent 11 began to use a water filter, he also installed in his house a flush toilet, as he views it as 'more hygienic and scientific', although he recognizes that it uses more water than the old-fashioned Indian toilet (which used to be a composting pit toilet). He also uses an electric water heater – a geyser – for 'more comfortable showers'. To make life more convenient, Respondent 11 does not rely only on electrical appliances; he also engages domestic workers to take care of domestic chores, including washing and cleaning.

Respondent 3 shares an apartment with her husband and two children. She is 41 years old. Her family bought the apartment in 2009, when they moved back from the United Kingdom after spending considerable time in that country. In addition to other commonly found water-related electrical appliances, Respondent 3 also owns a dishwasher. She did not use a water filter in the United Kingdom but finds it necessary to use it in Calcutta even though her apartment is supplied water from a deep tubewell. The family owns a car, which is washed daily. Safety and convenience form the basis of her decisions. Using a water filter was not an option as 'once we came back to India we had to use a water purifier as our systems were not equipped for normal water'. Although Respondent 3 recognizes that she is 'so used to a washing machine, dishwasher, *etcetera*, that I need them as everyday tools for a modern, comfortable life', she also feels that she requires the comfort provided by servants, which she employs to provide domestic help. Respondent 3 also uses flush toilets; she considers the traditional Indian toilet 'inconvenient and obsolete'.

Most respondents cite convenience as the reason for adopting new time-saving devices. Respondent 6 was pressed for time: 'since both my husband and I work, and the children go to school/college, we needed convenience . . . so the gadgets were purchased'. But if the service of domestic help is being used, convenience alone cannot be the entire reason for using time-saving appliances. Sufficient evidence exists to suggest that using electric and electronic appliances to perform domestic chores does not increase free time (see, for example, Schor 1991). 'The valuing of convenience is itself indicative of further transformation. Any number of devices and solutions are sold in the name of convenience and sold to those who believe themselves to be harried, hurried and harassed' (Shove 2003: 2). Therefore, one can reason that the everyday consumption of an essential resource such as water is driven by what is *thought of as being convenient* – along with what is seen as being clean.

The diversity of sources of water used by respondents' households exemplifies this assertion. Most households rely on deep borewells in conjunction with the KMC domestic water supply; very few rely on the municipal water supply alone. This reliance on a wider basket of sources implies the need to have choice and indicates a larger trend among the middle class in India: they consider state-provided amenities and services unreliable or unsatisfactory and replace or augment them with private service providers – be it security (gated communities), health (private hospitals and clinics), education (private schools), electricity (captive power via large generators) or water (private deep borewells). The middle class is wealthier, more aware, empowered and vocal than other social, economic and political groupings, and its increasing reliance on private provision of services could further affect service provision by the state.

None of the households report using untreated tap water for drinking. In most households, the practice of using some kind of treating mechanism was introduced at least a decade ago. Many households started with the simple practice of boiling and straining water, and using ceramic candle filters, but most households use electric filters now.

Two aspects concerning safe drinking water stood out: only a particular type of water is considered safe – irrespective of evidence – and any kind of technology is no longer understood to provide safe water as soon as a better technology becomes available. In other words, what is considered safe now may not be considered safe tomorrow. The water extracted from great depths through deep borewells is believed to pose minimal chances of contamination (Escamilla *et al.* 2011) for uses other than drinking. Similarly, most households relying on KMC water felt that the water supplied was 'more or less safe', agreeing that 'drinking water has become safer and more readily available', while nonetheless purchasing and regularly using water filtration devices. The same respondents also felt that a shift to filtered water was a logical choice because 'waterborne diseases are rampant here in Calcutta'.

Most households also reported using bottled water when consuming water outside the home, especially when in restaurants. The reason once again concerns the quality of tap water and its deleterious impact on health. Many respondents described 'pure, good quality water' as bottled water. One respondent's remarks regarding what they considered pure, good quality water suggests the extent to which their decisions are influenced by consumer marketing and the values attached to commercial campaigns: 'Like Pepsi's Aquafina – *clean water*' [author's emphasis]. Despite the claims of multinational drinks retailers, there is ample evidence from India to suggest that bottled water may not be safe (CSE 2003). An important concern arising from this circumstance is whether bottled water should be considered safe. Indian manufacturers claim that bottled water is pure, but this claim is not vouchsafed by a competent independent authority. Such advertising lacks sufficient regulation or legislative control, and is motivated by corporate interests, almost to the exclusion of public health concerns. Why do consumers overlook this lacuna? Why is there a focus on water when there are many other ailments such as respiratory diseases among the young and the elderly living in large, polluted cities? Is it a matter of what citizens can and cannot control through their consumption?

Water filters are not the only technology that has changed in middle-class households in India; the design of mechanisms for the disposal of faecal and urinary waste has also altered considerably. While the use of flush mechanisms connected to plumbing in toilets was only introduced a few decades ago, it is now commonplace among middle-class households. Respondent 4 recalled that his house 'used to get tubewell water from the roadside. Then the corporation started providing piped water and plumbing was done to take advantage of it'.

Householders tend to prefer modern toilets to the now outdated non-flushing Indian toilets, referring to these as 'inconvenient' and 'cumbersome' (Respondent 5). Respondent 8 called modern toilets 'fashionable and scientific', while Respondent 20 remembered that 'in the Behala house where I lived with my parents, I had to carry a bucket of water to flush. It was embarrassing when there were guests and inconvenient too'. Interestingly, convenience is linked here with social status, which is often an accurate gauge of class in India. Thus, one can see how water technologies also represent an imagined class ladder, which is a primary motivator in redefining convenience. Convenience sold successfully to consumers can morph into a status concept that can then inconspicuously merge with other factors such as the need for personal space and privacy.

Until about the time of independence, the Indian sense of cleanliness and the available technology was such that, in most households, toilets remained external to the home. The physical presence of toilets was considered polluting; in the urban context, where the entire property was indoors, houses were often designed with the toilet either in one corner of the ground floor or at the farthest permissible distance from the main sleeping and cooking areas. Piped water and plumbing were the first steps in making toilets an integral part of the household. As with the rest of Indian municipalities, in Calcutta, infrastructure and services constructed over decades have been vital in introducing new practices while dispensing with old ones. Yet, they have followed a model that has now created practices that municipal resources and infrastructure are hard-pressed to keep pace with. Every apartment built for the middle-class household is now equipped with at least one modern flush toilet that devours the limited supply of water.

## Fluid practices of the situated, fluid self

The emerging research on middle-class consumerism in India focuses on public spaces such as shopping malls, multiplexes and gated communities; the political construction of a social group that is a beneficiary and proponent of economic liberalization; and on the interaction of the middle-class with the human and non-human worlds around it, including nature tourism, adventure tourism and birdwatching (Urfi 2012). Scholarly studies have addressed the public spaces of consumption, in which people interact within a controlled environment and, in doing so, display a right to belong, a kind of citizenship mediated by the ability to consume. These community spaces, and their new economics and governance, exclude the marginalized elements of society and separate them from middle-class consumers (Voyce 2007). Within households, too, new practices divide the present from the past and class from class: 'I have always seen and am familiar with piped water and flush toilets. Public tubewells are used by the poor and slum dwellers' (Respondent 1). New practices also reflect the sense of entitlement of a middle-class consumer satisfied with nothing but the best: 'sure of pure water, always' (Respondent 1).

Since the 1990s, the ideas of purity, bathing and self-cleansing have become a vital component of the new culture of material consumption adopted by the middle classes. Srinivas (2002) suggests that the story of the bathroom conveys the story of the acceptance of western modernity and commodification in Indian households. Aided and abetted in no small measure by persuasive advertising in the mass media, and by the design of products and services that reinforced these emerging practices, the definition of hygiene, safety, personal well-being and the good life in general altered, and the practices around them changed dramatically. The reasoning of one respondent for using water filters was instructive in this regard: 'it is the safest thing to do for the family; the children need protection' (Respondent 19). These words form the backbone of every advertising campaign for water filters.

A key aspect in the changing practices of water in middle-class urban homes is the use of tools and technologies – no longer just to store and consume water but to alter its constitution through processes of purification, just as the consumer's body is purified through association with this technologically cleansed product. These new tools have imparted new values and meaning to water. Water is no longer regarded as a scarce resource. Most respondents estimate their daily household water consumption to be between 100 and 150 litres per day, but these estimates are not confirmed by an independent authority. While almost all respondents are aware of water shortages, none feel the need to question their own water consumption. Consumers do not consume water any longer, they consume ideals of the aspirational class: the convenience of a washing machine, the comfort of a geyser, the safety of a water filter. Once embedded, practices engendered by a desire for comfort, cleanliness and convenience are difficult to reverse.

Technologies and tools reflect changing human behaviour as the embodiment of human desires and ambitions. As new technologies change the meaning of 'pure' and 'clean' in the context of water, these recast the subjects in a mutual relationship in which the individual and technology is co-constructed. The practice of using new technologies represents new ways of being that recreate the middle-class subject as one who embraces change in the aspiration to join the conventional global consumer model of over-consumption. New consumptions, and new ways of consuming things like water, allow the middle classes to become global citizens, and this radical transformation is expressed not only in behaviour in public spaces but also in the intimate space of the home.

## Conclusion: implications of changing practices of domestic water use

It is crucial to understand how a basic good such as water is turned into a commodity, the actors that are involved in the process and the differential impacts it might have on different communities. In the current discourses, 'the community' is often broadly seen in urban India as a homogeneous group comprising victims of poor water governance; ageing infrastructure, due to the lack of investment capital; and a looming water crisis. This group is supposed to resist the commodification of water, a foundational pillar of life. However, in reality, urban India is marked with rifts along class, caste, ethnicity and religious lines. Therefore, when consumption of one group changes, it has to have a series of impacts or effects on the other groups. Changing consumptions and water practices of the middle class might adversely impact those of less powerful groups. Therefore, whereas access to water is undoubtedly a basic universal entitlement of citizenship, 'the community' is also an aspiring citizen, and commands more power than poor, rural communities. The political economy and political ecology of water are such that the poor often pay the price of the consumerism of those who are better off (Swyngedouw 2009). When two equal rights meet, Bakker (2003) argues, the group with greater voice and political power leads.

The global consumer that middle-class urban Indians are now are poorly linked to the debates and discourses over the commodification of water in India. As their incomes rise, changes occur in their perception of the basic need of pure, clean and potable water; to secure this basic need, this middle-class consumes selectively, leading to remarkable changes in the uses of water at home.

Epistemological implications of this chapter are no less crucial and pertain primarily to the scale of analysis. As Fam, Lahiri-Dutt and Sofoulis (2015) have shown, the household is not a mere building block of some larger social unit, nor a convenient site for accessing individuals and their psychologies but is an entity worth studying in its own right. The household exists at a unique scale, though its particular characteristics and dynamics are driven by logics of capital, class, gender, culture and resource distribution that also operate at other sites and on larger social scales. This is part of what makes the household a prime site for the transmission and reproduction – and potentially, for the abandonment, transformation or innovation – of social, technical and cultural norms and routine practices. This chapter has shown that commodification occurs at the microscopic scale of the household, where consumerist identity is located. Understanding changes at the household-level is at the heart of scaling down in thinking about water and can have far-reaching policy implications. Critiques of neoliberal policy reforms, or scholars of Indian water and experts on urban service provision, have so far focused their attention on the 'big pictures': broad-brush assessments of declining per capita availability of water volume and quality in Calcutta (Engel *et al.* 2011), and economic analyses of the willingness to pay for water (Roy 2012). Whilst these areas of inquiry are important, greater insight into consumer behaviour has the capacity to replace notions of the 'average consumer' with closely observed knowledge of the diversity of water use practices in domestic spaces. Such studies will help to demonstrate how water demand shifts, how different factors shape that demand and how new practices can reorient distributed demand. Introducing such a critical lens to contemporary water studies relies upon the realization that effective analysis of domestic water practices involves understanding both the social context of water consumption in its entirety and the cultural meanings intertwined with the habitual and inconspicuous routines of everyday life.

## Notes

* I acknowledge the assistance of Mohit Chaturvedi in reviewing the literature on practice theory and in analysing the qualitative data for this chapter, and of Soumit Dutt and Amrita Kamalini Bhattacharyya's assistance in collecting data. This chapter benefitted from the comments of reviewers of

*ACME: An International E-Journal for Critical Geography*, where a version of this chapter was published as 'Researching World Class Watering in Metropolitan Calcutta', *14*(3): 700–730. Another version of the study, with more quantitative data, was published as Juran, Luke and K. Lahiri-Dutt, 2017. 'Waterscapes in Transition: Changing Uses and Perceptions of Water in Middle Class Homes in Kolkata, India', *Water History*, 9(4): 433–451, doi:http://link.springer.com/article/10.1007/s12685-017-0202-5.

1 It is well known that Marxism in this part of India was widely adopted as a guiding philosophy by upper-caste, urbane, educated communities, giving it a *bhadralok* (gentleman's, or genteel) culture. How far this Marxist political history played a role in influencing the material culture of Bengalis is, however, beyond the scope of this chapter.
2 Although the term 'bathing' is used widely in India, it connotes showering, rather than bodily immersion, as is the case in a western context.
3 Datta (2012) offers a detailed perspective on early planning in Calcutta to emphasize the planners' preoccupation with cleanliness as a means of achieving desirable urban forms and with ensuring an adequate supply of water throughout the municipality.
4 Information in the two following paragraphs is sourced largely from Goode's (1916) authoritative work on Calcutta's municipal history.
5 Also see Kolkata Metropolitan Water and Sanitation Authority ('Retrospect: Water Supply in Old Days'), available from www.kmwsa.gov.in/html/retros.html (accessed 20 June 2014).
6 A landholder, Bon Behari Mondal, contested the Bengal government's right to acquire part of his land for public purposes, that is, for building a water reservoir and for higher compensation. His case was nullified by the High Court under the proviso of Act II of 1948.
7 Data from Kolkata Metropolitan Water and Sanitation Authority ('Retrospect: Water Supply in Old Days'), available from www.kmwsa.gov.in/html/retros.html (accessed 20 June 2014).
8 This figure is disputed by the KMC, which claims that 94 per cent of the city's households are connected to piped water and that water is supplied continuously for up to 20 hours per day.
9 (In Bangla) clean, pure and clear; also, *parishkar* or *parichhanna*.
10 This statement is verifiable. See www.sastasundar.com/index.php/product/details/MzU4Nw==/188 (accessed 21 June 2014).

## References


ADB (Asian Development Bank). 2007. *Benchmarking and Data Book of Water Utilities in India*. Manila: Asian Development Bank.

Bakker, K. 2003. *An Uncooperative Commodity: Privatizing Water in England and Wales*. Oxford: Oxford University Press.

Basu, S. K. and H. A. C. Main. 2001. 'Calcutta's Water Supply: Demand, Governance and Environmental Change', *Applied Geography*, 21: 23–44.

Brosius, C. 2010. *India's Middle Class: New Forms of Urban Leisure, Consumption and Prosperity*. New Delhi: Routledge.

Chatterjee, P. 1993. *The Nation and Its Fragments: Colonial and Postcolonial Histories*. Princeton: Princeton University Press.

Chaudhuri, A. 2013. *Calcutta, Two Years in the City*. London: Union Books.

CSE (Centre for Science and Environment). 2003. 'Analysis of Pesticide Residues in Bottled Water (Delhi Region)', https://cdn.cseindia.org/userfiles/Delhi_uploadfinal_sn.pdf (accessed on 28 May 2018).

Das Gupta, S. P. 1995. 'The Site of Calcutta: Geology and Physiography', in S. Choudhuri (ed.), *Calcutta: The Living City. Vol. 1: The Past*, pp. 2–4. Oxford: Oxford University Press.

Datta, P. 2012. *Planning the City – Urbanization and Reform in Calcutta, c. 1800–c. 1940*. New Delhi: Tulika.

Engel, K., D. Jokiel, A. Kraljevic, M. Geiger, and K. Smith. 2011. *Big Cities, Big Water, Big Challenges: Water in an Urbanizing World*. Berlin: World Wildlife Fund.

Escamilla, V., B. Wagner, M. Yunus, P. K. Streatfield, A. van Geen, and M. Emch. 2011. 'Effect of Deep Tube Well Use on Childhood Diarrhoea in Bangladesh', *Bulletin of the World Health Organization*, 89: 521–527.

Fam, D., K. Lahiri-Dutt and Z. Sofoulis. 2015. 'Scaling Down: Researching Household Water Practices', *ACME: An International E-Journal for Critical Geographies*, 14(3): 639–651.

Fernandes, L. 2006. *India's New Middle Class: Democratic Politics in an Era of Economic Growth*. Minneapolis: University of Minnesota Press.

Goode, S. W. 1916. *Municipal Calcutta: Institutions in Their Origin and Growth*. Calcutta: Bengal Secretariat Press.

Hand, M., E. Shove and D. Southerton. 2005. 'Explaining Showering: A Discussion of the Material, Conventional, and Temporal Dimensions of Practice', *Sociological Research Online*, 10(2), www.socresonline.org.uk/10/2/hand.html (accessed on 10 February 2018).

Haynes, D. E., A. McGowan, T. Roy, and H. Yanagisawa (eds.). 2010. *Towards a History of Consumption in South Asia*. Oxford: Oxford University Press.

IMF (International Monetary Fund). 2010. *World Economic Outlook Database*. IMF, April.

Miller, D. 1995. 'Consumption as the Vanguard of History: A Polemic by Way of an Introduction', in D. Miller (ed.), *Acknowledging Consumption*, pp. 1–57. New York: Routledge.

Mukherjee, S. N. 1972. *Calcutta: Myths and History*. Calcutta: Subarnarekha.

Munshi, S. K. 1975. *Calcutta Metropolitan Explosion: Its Nature and Roots*. New Delhi: People's Publishing House.

Muralidhararao, S. and T. N. V. V. Rao. 2005. 'Developments in Sediment Filtration in India', www.wcponline.com/2005/10/15/developments-sediment-filtration-india/ (accessed on 28 May 2018).

Naipaul, V. S. 1990. *India: A Million Mutinies Now*. New Delhi: Minerva.

Nandy, A. (ed.). 1998. *The Secret Politics of Our Desires: Innocence, Culpability and Indian Popular Cinema*. New Delhi: Oxford University Press.

Osella, F. and C. Osella. 1999. 'From Transience to Immanence: Consumption, Life-Cycle and Social Mobility in Kerala, South India', *Modern Asian Studies*, 33(4): 989–1020.

Pullinger, M., A. Browne, B. Anderson, and W. Medd. 2013. 'Patterns of Water: The Water-Related Practices of Households in Southern England, and Their Influence on Water Consumption and Demand Management', Final Report of the ARCC-Water/SPRC Patterns of Water Projects, London.
Ray, A. K. 1901. *Calcutta Town and Suburbs, Volume 7, Part 1, Short History of Calcutta*. Calcutta: Census of India.
Ray, R. 2010. 'The Middle Class: Sociological Category or Proper Noun?' *Political Power and Social Theory*, 21: 313–322.
Reckwitz, A. 2002. 'Toward a Theory of Social Practices: A Development in Culturalist Theorizing', *European Journal of Social Theory*, 5(2): 243–263.
Roy, J. 2012. *An Economic Analysis of Demand for Water Quality: A Case from Kolkata City*. Kolkata: Department of Economics, Jadavpur University.
Roy, N. R. 1986. *Prasanga: Kolkata*. Calcutta: Navana.
Sahu, P., H. A. Michael, C. Voss, and P. K. Sikdar. 2013. 'Impacts on Groundwater Recharge Areas of Megacity Pumping: Analysis of Potential Contamination of Kolkata, India, Water Supply', *Hydrological Sciences Journal*, 58(6): 1340–1360.
Schor, J. 1991. *The Overworked American: The Unexpected Decline of Leisure*. New York: Basic Books.
Shove, E. 2003. *Comfort, Cleanliness and Convenience: The Social Organization of Normality*. Oxford: Berg.
Shove, E. 2009. *Time Consumption and Everyday Life: Practice Materiality and Culture*. Oxford: Berg.
Shrivastava, A. and A. Kothari. 2012. *Churning of the Earth: The Making of Global India*. New York: Viking.
Srinivas, T. 2002. 'Flush with Success: Bathing, Defecation, Worship, and Social Change in South India', *Space and Culture*, 5(4): 366–386.
Swyngedouw, E. 2009. 'The Political Economy and Political Ecology of the Hydro-Social Cycle', *Journal of Contemporary Water Research & Education*, 142: 56–60, August.
Urfi, A. J. 2012. 'Birdwatchers, Middle Class and the "Bharat-India" Divide Perspectives from Recent Bird Writings', *Economic and Political Weekly*, XLVII(42): 321–329.
Varma, P. 1998. *The Great Indian Middle Class*. New Delhi: Viking, Penguin Books India.
Voyce, M. 2007. 'Shopping Malls in India: New Social "Dividing Practices"', *Economic and Political Weekly*, 2055–2062, 2 June.
Warde, A. 2005. 'Consumption and Theories of Practice', *Journal of Consumer Culture*, 5(2): 1311–1353.
Woolgar, S. 1991. 'Configuring the User: The Case of Usability Trials', in J. Law (ed.), *A Sociology of Monsters: Essays on Power, Technology and Domination*, pp. 571–572. London: Routledge.

# 7 The centralized approach to wastewater management and implications for sanitation governance

## An analysis of the intent and practice of the national urban sanitation policy in India

*Neelam Rana and N. C. Narayanan*

### Background

A major reason for pollution-free status of water bodies in the cities of the global north is the success of water-carriage and treatment technology (Abeysuriya, Mitchell and Juliet 2010; Sedlak 2014) by providing a resolution to the 'crises' of unmanaged sanitation prevailing in the 18th century (Abeysuriya, Mitchell and Juliet 2010). There has been an improved public health scenario in sewered cities (Wilsenach *et al.* 2003). This involves complex and capital-intensive infrastructure for collecting wastewater from a variety of sources (households, commercial areas, industrial plants and institutions) and conveying it through the sewerage network to a treatment unit, usually far from the point of its origin (Crites and Tchobanoglous 1998; Wilderer and Schreff 2000). This conventional approach of municipal wastewater management, also termed as Centralised Waste Water Management (CWWM) has dominated the physical delivery of services and the administrative control in urban sanitation since the late 19th century (Abeysuriya, Mitchell and Juliet 2010).[1] Replication of this sanitary revolution with access to piped water supply, flush latrines and treatment plants is the major policy approach in developing countries (Konteh 2009). However, the collection and centralized treatment of wastewater requires pumps, piping materials and energy, thus increasing the cost of the system (Wilderer and Schreff 2000; Giri, Takeuchi and Ozaki 2006; Go and Demir 2006), with collection costs accounting for more than 60 per cent of the total budget (Massoud, Tarhini and Nasr 2009).

Problems of the conventional approach related to financial and environmental sustainability and equity are widely acknowledged, especially in the context of developing countries. This crisis thus provides the 'necessary precondition' for search and emergence of new solutions (Kuhn 1970 in Abeysuriya, Mitchell and Juliet 2010) as alternative to the prevailing CWWM approach. The idea is to adopt from a wide range of technically feasible, economically and financially affordable and socio-culturally acceptable sanitation options (Kalbermatten *et al.* 1982; Mara 1996). In India, alternatives to CWWM such as shallow sewers, natural systems, decentralized stand-alone systems have been tried and tested in a variety of contexts to varied levels of success.[2] Even though some alternatives have found place in documents – such as the sewerage and sewage treatment manual (CPHEEO 2013), which is important for the practitioners – these still remain at the firm level, mainly due to the lack of efforts in institutionalizing such knowledge and experiences in mainstream policy making and sanitation planning at the city level. Launched in 2008 by the Ministry of Urban Development (MoUD), Government of India, the National Urban Sanitation Policy (NUSP), the first ever policy concerning urban sanitation, shows conceptual consistency with this alternative paradigm and provides a framework to approach the same at the city level.

First and foremost, the NUSP gives national goals along with a set of measurable process and output indicators in line with the nation's commitment towards MDGs. Second, it places responsibility of sanitation services on the Urban Local Bodies (ULB), in accordance with the 74th Constitutional Amendment Act (CAA), to provide the much-needed institutional clarity in sanitation services and governance. Third, while addressing the issue of exclusion, it questions the sustainability of past investments in sanitation for universal coverage and the failure to address contextual diversity. The NUSP thus suggests that cities formulate City Sanitation Plans (CSPs) in accordance with their need, demand and capacity (technical, financial, institutional) in a decentralized and participative manner through institutions like the City Sanitation Task Force (CSTF). Taking a holistic approach to sanitation planning, the framework enables CSPs to be embedded in the city budget and to be linked to other services like health, water and education (Walker *et al.* 2014). CSPs are not legally binding documents but certainly reflect the intent of the decision makers and their response to societal demands. As of 2011, about 137 cities have taken the initiative to develop CSPs. But do cities conform to the overall philosophy and recommendations of the NUSP? How did cities of different classes and infrastructural needs respond to it? To understand how the intent of the NUSP got translated into practice at the city level, we conducted a review of 26 CSPs and a few State Sanitation Strategies (SSSs) belonging to cities of different classes, sizes, financial health and water and sanitation services. The objective was to determine whether the aforementioned factors have any bearing on the choices made under CSPs.

The following sections highlight how the conventional approach to sanitation infrastructure and services governance has led to the exclusion of smaller cities and the urban poor in the Indian context. In the next section, key NUSP recommendations are described, followed by a brief explanation on the methodology adopted to study the CSPs. It then discusses how policy recommendations got adopted at the city level under three headings: strengthening urban sanitation governance; addressing problems of the urban poor and slums; and technological choices: appropriateness to the city context. The next section attempts to reason the study findings within the national policy context, followed by conclusions.

## Problems of the conventional approach: disparity and neglect of small towns/urban poor

The centralized approach to municipal wastewater management that dominated sanitation planning in India since the colonial rule has triggered disparities in sanitation where the poorer sections are neglected (Chaplin 2011). By design, a substantial segment of the poor remains outside the conventional formal water supply and sewerage systems (Kundu 1991) mainly due to the lack of land ownership (GoI 2008). As per Census 2011, about 12.2 per cent of the total urban households defecate in the open while 32.7 per cent (with individual toilet facility) are connected to public sewers (CPHEEO 2012). The service for urban slums is even worse, with only 24.5 per cent households connected to public sewers. Among different classes, the lower order towns have significantly higher infrastructural deficit in wastewater and related services (CPCB 2005; NIUA 2016). For smaller cities, the backlog of services and wastewater infrastructure is 80–100 per cent whereas it is 50–65 per cent for bigger cities (HPEC 2011: 225).

Historically, the capital-intensive nature of water and wastewater projects coupled with apparent shortage of funds and organizational resources led to higher preference being given to water and 'nationally important cities' in urban development schemes (GoI 1971a, 1971b). The mutual exclusivity between water and wastewater along with the focus on bigger cities led to a gap in sanitation services in general and for smaller towns in particular, which continued during the ambitious Jawaharlal Nehru National Urban Renewal Mission (JNNURM) period.[3]

The conventional CWWM approach has been questioned for being capital, water, energy and operations and maintenance (O&M) intensive. In order to cover all urban households by sewers, India needs a capital investment of INR 2,427 million over 2012–2031 (HPEC 2011: XXV) and INR 2,369 million to cover the O&M for new and old assets (ibid 226). The HPEC estimates account only for domestic users, with significantly higher total investment requirement if other user types are included. This would certainly be an uphill task since the majority of the water/wastewater public utilities can recover only 30 to 35 per cent of the total O&M expenses in India (ADB 2007, as cited in HPEC 2011; PMIDC 2013). With not a single Indian city of any class/size recovering the full O&M (WSP 2011), most of the sewage treatment plants (STPs) have been found to be running at sub-optimal capacity in the periodic assessments of the Central Pollution Control Board (CPCB).[4] The board attributed such anomalies in infrastructure development and maintenance to the lack of funds and organizational capacities of government agencies. Interestingly, contractors hired by the government agencies to operate and maintain the treatment unit(s) still get the full payment even if the unit is functioning at sub-optimal capacity.[5]

Studies have found that smaller order towns are more disadvantaged in adopting CWWM as (1) the cost per capita of laying sewers is comparatively higher (HPEC 2011: 226) and (2) they do not have the capacity to raise the required capital and O&M funds. Even though various urban development programmes like JNNURM have tried to bring in the required capital, the cities have either failed to arrange land or to provide sewer connections, leading to significant time and cost overruns (IIHS 2011; Avashia and Garg 2016), which is a typical feature of big infrastructural projects. The result is idle investments that effectively make such systems a non-productive investment which could have been utilized elsewhere (Lovins 2002). It is safe to say that such endeavours are a burden on the public exchequer and severely handicap the ability of cities to extend service provision.

Although it is clear that the CWWM approach might not be achievable by the smaller cities (constituting 30 per cent of urban population) or reach the slums (constituting 17.2 per cent of urban population), it continues to be the preferred choice. The failure in acknowledging differential capacities of cities and the needs of the urban poor compels one to question the relevance of the CWWM approach and the simplistic and homogeneous understanding of complex sanitation issues on the part of the decision makers.

## NUSP in practice: a study of CSPs

The NUSP 2008 provides a framework to adopt alternative approaches to sanitation services at the city level. As primary constraints, it identifies (1) poor awareness about sanitation-health-environment linkages, (2) fragmented institutional roles, (3) lack of integrated city-wide approach as opposed to piecemeal investments and (4) land tenure issues (GoI 2008: 6–9). Addressing the question of exclusion, it recommends (1) delinking sanitation services from land ownership, earmarking funds/land, using a differentiated approach in technology choice to extend good quality services to poor/slums (ibid: 25), (2) assigning institutional home and earmarking funds for sanitation and (3) city-wide participative-consultative, context specific, multi-stakeholder sanitation planning. It provides tools such as CSPs, SSSs and an institutional framework (CSTF) to realize the recommendations and sanitation goals.

To understand whether the intent matches the practice, a review of CSPs and SSSs was conducted. The section starts with a brief description on methodology, followed by a discussion on how cities conform to key recommendations concerning the strengthening of urban sanitation governance, the solving of sanitation issues for the urban poor and the appropriateness of technological choices to city context, forming the three sub-sections.

### *Methodology for CSP analysis*

The MoUD website (as on 2016) provides a list of 73 cities that have developed CSPs. We selected 26 cities belonging to different classes, financial health and stages of sanitation services from those retrievable online (refer Appendix 7.1). The class of the city is understood as its population, and financial health as cost recovery and efficiency in collection of user charges in water supply and sanitation (WSS). The indicators of financial health assessment are as per the Service Level Benchmarks (SLBs) of the MoUD. Sanitation services is taken as a percentage of sewerage coverage (refer Appendix 7.2 for details).[6] Since CSPs available online were more in number for medium and above towns, we selected our samples accordingly to account for this factor (Table 7.1). The study reviews available SSSs of Orissa, Uttar Pradesh, Tripura, Bihar and Kerala.

*Table 7.1* Class/Category of the Cities Studied

| *Population category* | *Class* | *Cities* |
|---|---|---|
| 20,000–50,000 | Class-III or Small Town | Attingal, Varkala |
| 50,000–100,000 | Class-II or Medium Town I | Kottayam |
| 0.1–0.5 million | Class-I or Medium Town II | Shimla, Rourkela, Dewas, Ahmednagar, Akola, Udaipur, Nellore |
| 0.5–1 million | Class I (large city) | Sangli Miraj Kupwad, Ulhasnagar, Nanded – Waghala, Kochi, Mira – Bhayander, Mysore, Solapur |
| 1–5 million | Class I (sub-metropolis) | Navi Mumbai, Aurangabad, |
| | Class I (metropolis) | Varanasi, Agra, Thane, Nagpur, Lucknow, Pune |
| 5–10 million | | Ahmedabad |

Source: NIUA (2016: 38–39) and HPEC (2011: 230)

We followed a two-fold approach to review the CSPs: (1) assigning a score to the CSP's content against the self-review checklist provided in the NUSP, comprising 22 indicators[7] and (2) thematic analysis based on study objectives. The indicators pertain to (1) situation analysis, (2) assigning institutional home for sanitation, (3) institutional overlaps/gaps assessment, (4) technology assessment and (5) implication of proposed solutions for users and service providers etc. We followed the guidelines given in the NUSP to assign a score to the CSPs. Since the checklist does not cover important aspects (like land tenure, earmarking funds) that the current research is interested in, we rely on thematic analysis of CSPs/SSSs as well. We identified and analysed how each of the three major themes from the NUSP (urban poor, sanitation governance and technology choice) figured in each CSP (Braun and Clarke 2006; Mayring 2000). We conducted key stakeholder open-ended semi-structured interviews from selected towns in the country – Maharashtra (Alibaug), Karnataka (Bangalore), Kerala (Alappuzha and Nedumanagadu), Orissa (Bhubaneswar) and Delhi.

We identify key limitations of the present work as follows: (1) it is primarily a desk study; a series of interviews with the stakeholders involved would have strengthened the key arguments. We have tried, however, to draw learnings from our previous experiences in other cities; (2) it provides limited analyses of the CSP development process and (3) CSPs were in draft stage at the time of analysis, hence, the unavailability of final or approved version could mean lack of complete information to review, which may alter study inferences.

### *Strengthening urban sanitation governance*

To strengthen sanitation governance, the NUSP recommends that states/cities (1) identify an institutional home for sanitation, (2) constitute participative multi-stakeholder institution (CSTF) for effective coordination and implementation, (3) identify gaps and overlaps in institutional arrangements and propose improvement action plan, (4) have dedicated funds for sanitation and (5) establish the link between health and sanitation. This section reviews how the cities adopted these recommendations in the CSPs.

- **Apathy in Assigning Institutional Home:** Water and sanitation are state subjects under the Indian Constitution. The 74th Constitutional Amendment (1992) suggested that state governments transfer functions including Water Supply and Sanitation (WSS) to the Urban Local Bodies (ULBs) in a bid to give them the status of being the third-tier of governance.[8] Although the Central government claims that such devolution has been achieved in most of the existing municipal laws (GoI n.d.), our study could not find mention of such provisions in any of the CSPs. Except for Nanded-Waghala, none of the cities explicitly mention or recognize the ULB as the 'institutional home' for sanitation. The study found that a large number of CSPs (~69 per cent) fail to acknowledge and thus ignore the existence of overlaps in institutional roles and responsibilities.
- Interestingly, sanitation services in relation to the ULBs have been understood in a narrow sense, i.e., provision or maintenance of public/community toilets and street sweeping. Despite passing Municipal Acts, as observed in Kerala, infrastructure establishment and maintenance of WSS is still under the purview of parastatal agencies like the Kerala Water Authority (KWA).[9] Even for

cities like Udaipur where the health and sanitation services come under the ULB's purview, the scope of work does not include sewerage and water supply services.[10] Such governance practices reinstate the argument of lack of capacity and resources of the ULBs to undertake big infrastructural projects.[11] For example, Bihar, Uttar Pradesh and Tripura on the one hand identify the ULBs as the nodal agency, and on the other hand admit that the ULBs lack capacity and thus continue to depend on para-statal agencies.

- **Non-existent or Non-Functional Participative Sanitation Institutions:** The policy suggests formation of a sanitation steering committee at the state level and a CSTF at the city level in order to 'take up sanitation in a mission mode and to mobilise joint actions from different public and non-government agencies' (GoI 2008: 11). The CSTF is supposed to be a nodal agency to appoint the implementing agency (preferably the ULB), to approve the CSPs and monitor the project progress. All 26 cities constituted the CSTF as per the CSPs. In fact, many cities proposed other kinds of supporting institutions as well, such as City Sanitation Cells (15 out of 26 cities) to deal with various sanitation aspects.[12] To coordinate various district/city/ward level sanitation institutions, Mysore proposed a state level urban sanitation cell. The effectiveness of such institutions, specifically CSTF, is difficult to evaluate due to the absence of any related information in the public domain. Hence it is doubtful whether CSTFs are currently functional in any of the cities.
- **Limitations in Identification of Institutional Overlaps and Gaps:** The NUSP identifies fragmented institutional roles and responsibilities as one of the key policy issues in sanitation (ibid: 7). It recommends that cities identify overlaps and gaps with respect to planning, financing, creation of physical infrastructure, O&M, training and capacity building, monitoring of outcomes, communications and regulation, with specific actions to resolve the same. Our study shows that only 8 out of the 26 cities attempted to identify the gaps but failed to develop improvement plans to deal with institutional fragmentation.[13] Cities seem to be clueless with respect to functions and funds specifically in O&M and monitoring/evaluation. The evident failure in identifying and assigning clear responsibilities could be due to the failure of state governments in devolving power, funds and functions to the ULBs under the 74th CAA.
- **Few Initiatives in Earmarking Funds:** One of the ways to deal with the sanitation disparity is to ensure dedicated funds in state and city

budgets for asset creation and O&M. We found that the majority of the cities (except Attingal, Varkala, Kottayam, Agra, Shimla, Akola, Dewas and Nagpur) and states (except Kerala and Tripura) failed to make this provision.[14] This reveals the lack of earnestness of the government agencies in resolving sanitation issues.

- **Absence of Genuine Efforts to Establish Health-Sanitation Linkages:** One of the key issues identified is the low priority accorded to sanitation due to the poor awareness about its inherent linkages with public health (GoI 2008: 7). The NUSP recommends (1) collection of baseline data on health-related indicators on WSS, (2) coordination between health and WSS departments and (3) awareness generation on the perceived linkages. As far as inclusion of sanitation-health indicators in CSPs is concerned, only four cities discuss this aspect, with none admitting the presence of data gaps or proposing action plans in this regard.[15] Though the NUSP specifically suggests that cities identify data gaps on various sanitation aspects and present action plans, only six cities (Varanasi, Attingal, Kottayam, Varkala, Mysore and Pune) have managed to incorporate this, with some suggesting the establishment of the Management Information System (MIS). States like Kerala have taken one step forward by launching a Health Policy (2013) for effective coordination between different departments.[16] Aurangabad city proposes to have a health committee at the city level to ensure coordinated efforts in sanitation. Even though cities proposed to constitute different types of institutions to initiate communication between various departments, the CSTF remains the preferred choice.
- The constitution of such institutions/committees does not automatically translate into better coordination as the majority of the CSPs fail to elaborate upon the improvement plan needed to realize effective coordination. In the absence of this, cities propose simpler tasks such as awareness generation and capacity building.

### *Addressing problems of urban poor and slums*

In obtaining affordable access to safe sanitation for the urban poor and slums, the NUSP identifies three main limiting factors: (1) lack of tenure, (2) space or economic constraints (GoI 2008: 7) and (3) lack of differential approach (ibid: 25). It asserts that basic sanitation provision should not be linked with land tenure and recommends that states 'resolve tenure, space and affordability constraints' (ibid: 14). In line with this, the NUSP (unlike JNNURM) makes specific recommendations to provide at least 20 per cent of the total funds dedicated to the sanitation needs of the urban poor (ibid: 14).[17] It emphasizes that 'a differentiated approach is necessary to extend good quality sanitation services to the poor' (ibid: 25). Further, cities have to adopt different techno-financial and management models to deal with the diverse needs of the different sections instead of a singular approach. Hence the NUSP recommends that cities first 'take stock of the legal and non-notified settlements' (ibid: 26) as part of CSP development. Let us examine how these recommendations figured in the CSPs.

- **Reluctance to Earmark Land and Funds:** The very first requirement placed by the NUSP, to ensure improved services to the poor, is to identify, clarify and classify different categories of settlements and associated land titles. Our study shows that only half of the cities have taken this step. Except for a few (Attingal, Kottayam, Varkala and Thane), many do not even acknowledge this particular data gap or its importance, indicating lower priority given to the sanitation issues and needs of the poor. Making budgetary provisions is recommended by the NUSP to ensure effective delivery of sanitation services to the urban poor. However, our study shows reluctance among cities to make budgetary provision for sanitation projects for the poor as only five cities (Attingal, Varkala, Kottayam, Kochi and Lucknow) recognize this aspect, with only two (Kochi and Lucknow) actually having made concrete provision.[18] Similarly, cities and states seem to be reluctant in assigning dedicated land for the poor as only one (Lucknow) has made such a provision.[19] Cities like Varanasi and Ahmedabad are already implementing programmes for the settlements with no clear land titles.[20] Even though a large number of CSPs fail to take concrete steps in ensuring land security to the urban poor, 50 per cent of the cities acknowledge the importance of delinking land ownership from basic service provisioning.[21] For example, Attingal, Varkala, Kottayam and Kochi suggest amendments in municipal acts to delink service provision from land ownership. Mysore acknowledges 'right to sanitation' and calls for universalized (100 per cent) provision of sanitation facilities without any barrier of cost and land tenure.

### *Technological choices: appropriateness to city context*

The NUSP recommends that cities 'account for the full cycle of safe confinement, treatment and safe disposal' (GoI 2008: 7) of human waste in their CSPs. The technology choices should aim to address the city-wide nature of the challenge and, thus, 'a mix of (technology) options must add up to addressing the issue completely' (ibid: 25). Addressing the issue of sustainability of investments (ibid: 7) and contextual diversity (existing sanitation services, climate, physiographic, economic, social and political), it suggests that cities/states 'formulate their own sanitation strategy and CSPs, in overall conformity to the national policy' (ibid: 9). Essentially, cities and states are required to plan sanitation infrastructure and services as per their need, demand and capacity (technical, financial, institutional). Addressing these concerns, the policy suggests that cities (1) conduct detailed evaluation, including cost-benefit analysis (CBA) to address financial sustainability concerns of different technologies, (2) propose interventions for the entire city and (3) assess O&M implications of proposed technologies on the users (like tariff increase, willingness to pay) and on the service providers (like financial capacity).

Interestingly, all CSPs, based on a self-review checklist, scored an average 65–72 per cent – meaning that these fulfilled the content quality requirement for 14–16 out of the total 22 indicators. The most neglected areas for which quality assessment is missing in the CSPs include techno-financial assessment and O&M implications of proposed technology interventions. The self-reviewing process by the ULBs can itself be questioned for inherent bias. For example, even though Nanded-Waghala city gave full score to its CSP, our detailed review reveals that all indicators have not been addressed.

- **Preference to One-Size-Fits-All Technological Choices:** The majority of the cities do consider the entire area for sanitation planning. However, only 50 per cent of the CSPs present proper information and some degree of assessment of different sanitation technology options. Further, only 4 out of the 26 CSPs discuss clearly the O&M implications of suggested options on the users and the implementing agency.[22] The CBA for available and proposed technology options is missing from all the CSPs. This could mean that the implementing agency does not want to consider different options and instead favours the conventional approach as indicated by the choice of CWWM in implementation/investment plans of 14 out of the 26 CSPs. Even though about 46 per cent of the CSPs consider mixed technological options, only two accommodate the same in their investment plans. Septage management is found to be another neglected area as the majority of the CSPs fail to provide analysis of the current situation or available technology options. This is especially worrisome when cities with low sewerage coverage (six out of 15 cities are below 45 per cent coverage) and high dependence on septic tanks propose to adopt CWWM, with a few exceptions including Kochi which proposed a separate department for on-site sanitation and septage management; Dewas which proposed a separate Septage Management Cell at the state level; Pune, Lucknow, Udaipur and Nellore which proposed decentralized management systems while Agra, Varanasi, Attingal, Varkala and Kottayam presented a situation analysis and proposed separate septage/faecal sludge management units.

The rationale behind the observed trend in technological choices under the CSPs has been analysed in relation to city class/size (population), financial health (specifically in sanitation/sewerage services), current level of WSS services and consultancy firm.

- *Technology choices and infrastructure needs:* Cities with higher infrastructural deficiencies should consider multiple technological options or differential approach over singular approach to achieve sanitation goals as stated in the NUSP. Our study could not find a clear relationship between the two variables, i.e., infrastructural gap in sewage and proposed technological options. Cities with relatively negligible/low and higher sewerage coverage seem to be more interested in the differential approach as compared to cities with medium coverage (25–75 per cent sewerage coverage).
- *Technology choices and city category:* One would expect lower order cities with negligible sewerage coverage or high dependence on septic tanks/soak-pits and weak financial health to choose the differential approach to ensure sanitation inclusion. Similarly, metropolitan cities having poor connectivity in the slums and in the outskirts are expected to opt for the differential approach over the conventional CWWM, on grounds of economies of scale. However, our study could not find a clear relationship between city size and proposed technological solutions under the CSPs. Both smaller cities and bigger cities discussed various technological options but medium-sized cities (population 5–10 lakh) failed to accommodate this aspect.
- *Technological choices and city financial health:* Analysis revealed that on an average the financial performance of the cities in sewage services is very poor (average collection efficiency and cost recovery is 43 per cent) as compared to water

supply (average is 73 per cent). More number of cities under the study fall under extreme categories of financial health, i.e., nil and above 75 per cent. Cities seem to have performed better in collection efficiency as compared to cost recovery – meaning they are not able to generate enough (operating) revenues to fund the operating expenses. We found that a significant number of cities with poor financial performance opted for the differential approach. The relationship between financial health and proposed alternatives to CWWM is relatively clear for cities with lowest and highest (75–100 per cent) financial performance. Once again, several cities belonging to the middle category preferred the CWWM approach.

- ***Technological choices and consultancy firm responsible for developing CSP***: The study observed a clear relationship between the consultant agency responsible for CSP development and technology selection. The two organizations, the All India Institute of Local Self Government (AIILSG) and Deutsche Gesellschaft für Internationale Zusammenarbeit (GIZ), were responsible for about 65 per cent of the CSPs studied.[23] A major proportion of the cities (9 out of 12) that developed CSPs under the guidance of the AIILSG did not opt for the alternative approaches and scored poor (6–18 and average score is 12) against the self-review checklist. The CSPs developed under the GIZ scored well, especially with respect to detailed technology evaluation, O&M implication and septage management. Four out of five cities, supervised by the GIZ for CSP development, have opted for alternative approaches to sewage management and discussed possibilities of low-cost sewage technologies. The consultants' influence is evident, particularly in technology selection. For example, CSPs steered by the GIZ selected a technology developed and promoted by a German organization that is a part of the GIZ network and receives grants from it.[24]

## Uncovering power relations in sanitation governance

Sanitation, especially wastewater management, is an important but neglected issue in Indian towns. From our earlier discussions, it is clear that even though CWWM has been a conventional approach in sanitation, it has severe limitations, especially for small towns and the urban poor. The realization that the approach excludes major sections of the urban population has led to a growing understanding among planners and decision makers to look for more inclusive alternatives.

The NUSP 2008 draws attention to this continuing neglect in sanitation and questions the efficacy and sustainability of past investments in the sector. It provides a set of recommendations and decentralized planning framework to ensure effective sanitation governance and improved sanitation services to the urban poor, with suggestions for contextual appropriateness of technical choices at the city level. Our study of CSPs and SSSs examined as to what degree cities and states conform to the NUSP. The objective was to determine whether size, class, WSS services and financial health of the cities have any bearing on the choices proposed under the CSPs and on the overall compliance with the NUSP. Even though CSPs scored an average 65 per cent against the self-review checklist, the widespread neglect of the NUSP recommendations make us question whether the CSP development process was actually a participative and consultative exercise – i.e., whether the CSPs were developed 'for the city by the city'.

The failure to make budgetary provision or resolve land tenure issues highlights the low priority given to the needs of the urban poor. The NUSP itself has conflicting understanding – on the one hand it sees access to sanitation service delinked from land titles and on the other it mentions that the 'provision of basic services would not entitle the slum dweller to any legal right to the land on which he/she is residing' (GoI 2008: 14). The land rights have always taken a backseat, be it the CSPs or City Development Plans (under JNNURM) or slum development programmes like Rajiv Awas Yojana (Mahadevia 2006; Hazards Centre 2007, 2008; Kamath 2012). The linkages between access to basic services and land tenure under these initiatives have imagined just provisioning of multi-storied housing projects (Kundu and Samanta 2011).[25] Since such projects typically find place only in the city outskirts, government agencies find it difficult to connect these with centralized sewerage network with no provision for economies of scale. Thus, the cycle of sub-optimal services continues for the urban poor.

The cities and states failed miserably to make provisions needed to ensure effective sanitation governance as well. First and foremost, except for few, none of the cities visualized the ULBs as the institutional home for sanitation. Second, sanitation in relation to the ULBs has been understood in a narrow sense as provision of toilets or general maintenance of public premises. This could either be due to the failure of the states to comply with the 74th CAA or the lack of the ULBs' capacity to carry out big infrastructural projects. This might also explain why the ULBs were not part of the consultant selection process for CSP development, why state governments or MoUD took upon themselves to decide consultants and why across cities we find concentration of only a few selected consultants. The appointment of the AIILSG for more than 19 cities in Maharashtra was done by the Water Supply & Sanitation Department (WSSD), Government of Maharashtra.[26] Similarly, the GIZ became a major part of the CSP development process as it collaborated with the MoUD under an eight-year-long programme called 'Support for NUSP' (Dube 2012).[27] The result is that CSPs appear to be 'copy-paste' type documents, with same technologies, or the technologies of partner organizations of the consultancy firm, finding place in the plans.

The study helped in uncovering power relations between the centre, state, ULBs and consultants in decisions related to sanitation technology choices as the majority of the cities ignored context appropriate options and selected CWWM. Whereas these choices are partly because of practical reasons (land availability, local resistance and lack of capacity with ULB/implementing agency), for the most part, they are outcomes of policy decisions taken at the state and central government levels. For example, Odisha makes it mandatory (under the Water Works Rule) for the ULBs to gradually phase out all the septic tanks (HoUDD 2011: 40). The policy implication is such that even though Rourkela recommended cost-effective options (small bore system) in its CSP, it could not be implemented. Similarly, since cities already have funds and projects under the JNNURM, they do not want to look beyond CWWM, even if it is not contextually appropriate. Kochi city, through another assessment study, realized that shallow sewers might be more appropriate in its case. However, the city could not include it in the CSP financial plan as funds under the JNNURM were already approved to establish CWWM.

The Centre's decision of linking the performance of the ULBs, against Service Level Benchmarks (SLBs), to the grant release (under the 13th Finance Commission, 2010–2015) (WSP 2009a) is further limiting the ULBs to choose appropriate sanitation interventions.[28] Interestingly, these standards did not envisage monetary incentives when launched initially as part of the NUSP (GoI 2008: 35). When the SLBs propose 100 per cent sewerage coverage at the city level, they have to consider both CWWM and alternative systems to reach the target (MoUD n.d.: 42). However, our study showed that the cities seem to have either misjudged or ignored the nuances of this parameter, as, irrespective of their size, class, need or capacity, they proposed to target CWWM. One of the key issues with the SLB framework is that, unlike previous differential approaches – such as Zakaria Committee1963; CPHEEO 1980; NIUA 1987; Ninth Five Year Plan (Government of India (GoI) 1999 as cited in NIUA 2007) – it does not take into consideration size (cities, human habitation), class and financial health of the cities in WSS (refer to NIUA 2007). The major implication of the Finance Commission's decision is that even cities with better financial health like Nagpur (in its CSP) showed concern regarding higher expectations placed under the SLBs. When the issue related to mismatched financial capacity and ambitious targets given to the ULBs was raised by the smaller towns in a national-level workshop, it was suggested that they follow an incremental approach with the SLBs (WSP 2009b).

Endorsement of the SLBs by the Finance Commission legitimizes and incentivizes the single idea of best practice in sanitation services, which makes service provisioning more difficult for the public sector due to limited options and flexibility than the private sector (Lundvall and Tomlinson 2002; Tillema 2007). Another argument in favour of benchmarking is that this is supposed to introduce competition and peer-to-peer learning within the sector. However, such approaches might work for the private sector where companies have very similar goals and other organizational characteristics (Lundvall and Tomlinson 2002) but not for the public sector, as different components of services are managed by different agencies with limited clarity on roles and responsibilities.

The SLB framework, adopted as a universal set of indicators with a purpose 'to create consensus of the desired service standards' (MoUD n.d.),[29] is made on the basis of investment assessments in the urban sector (like High Power Expert Committee (2011) of the Government of India). Such focus on assets creation of a certain variety diverts attention from issues of equity, governance and need for better sanitation planning. Even though these estimates are debatable (IIHS 2011), they still hold a prominent place in urban development literature without really being questioned for their relevance as the desired level of service standards in the Indian context. Why were such concerns not addressed appropriately by higher level decision makers during the SLB pilot testing phase or during CSTF meetings or during the CSP development phase? The SLB dominance in sanitation raises questions on the efficacy of participatory processes and institutions in the making of the CSPs. And, to answer these questions, we might have to dig deeper into the structure of bureaucracy, dominant ideas and triggering influences in the policy processes, which is beyond the scope of this study.

## Conclusions

Even though centralized wastewater management is seen at the top of the sanitation ladder and is projected as the ultimate solution, its effectiveness is questionable in the context of the developing countries. Although the MDGs and SDGs present inclusive understanding of what entails sanitation services in varied contexts, the conventional centralized management continues to dominate the urban development programmes in India. This is often triggered from a desire to make cities global and transgressed from the imagination of cities as engines of growth. While the imagination has drawn major capital that went to bigger cities, it has made sanitation issues a simple act of asset creation. With no scope for participation in the centralized approach, the concerns such as land tenure, sanitation-health linkages and city capacities (technical, financial, institutional) have been side-lined, leading to exclusion and further deepening of the sanitation divide for the urban poor and smaller cities. The lack of clarity in institutional structure – funds, functions and functionaries – even after two decades of passing the 74th CAA, makes the sanitation services delivery further difficult.

The National Urban Sanitation Policy (2008), Government of India, tries to address the inclusivity concerns through the adoption of a variety of contextually appropriate technology options in participative city sanitation plans – situating the ULBs at the centre of sanitation governance. However, half-hearted efforts by the cities in translating policy recommendations has led to the adoption of a centralized approach and the development of generic plans. One of the major factors that hindered the efficacy of these processes includes previous commitments of cities to other urban development programmes like JNNURM, leading to the lock-in of technology. Second, the centre's decision to link universal standards of service provisions with the grant release incentivizes and limits cities into adopting certain kinds of technology – piped sewer systems in this case. Third, selection of consultancy firms by the centre and state governments greatly influenced the content of sanitation plans and technology selection. Last, failure to view ULBs as a nodal sanitation institution due to assumptions of capacity deficit has resulted in plans imposed from elsewhere that are not in tune with the capacity and demand of the cities.

This centralization of policy and lack of support for local capacity is one of the major institutional barriers to implement alternative approaches and inclusiveness (Medema, McIntosh and Jeffrey 2008).

Hence, the centralized approach beyond merely a technology option is a governance mechanism to deliver sanitation services and decide responsibility for delivery. The study of sanitation needs to go beyond techno-financial understanding to include contexts, institutions, actors and policy processes. Although our study showed that the CSPs are not addressing many of the prominent urban sanitation issues, the NUSP as a policy has clearly opened countless windows and triggered a process of mainstreaming sanitation alternatives in the right direction.

## Notes

1 Municipal wastewater may consist of domestic wastewaters and/or industrial discharges (CPCB 2009).

2 Refer to the Centre for Science and Environment (www.cseindia.org/node/3798) for case studies on technology alternatives in sanitation and wastewater. Refer to the Consortium for DEWATS Dissemination (CDD) Society (www.cddindia.org/) for applications specific to shallow sewers and natural technology (DEWATS).

3 Data compiled from JNNURM website: http://jnnurm.nic.in/wp–content/uploads/2014/08/state-wise-details.pdf and http://jnnurm.nic.in/wp-content/uploads/2014/05/approved-projects-statewise.pdf (accessed on 10 June 2016).

4 Status of sewage treatment in India (CPCB 2005); evaluation of operation and maintenance of sewage treatment plants in India (CPCB 2007); status of water supply, wastewater generation and treatment in Class-I cities and Class-II towns of India (CPCB 2009). The CPCB produced similar reports in 1978, 1989 and 2000. Performance evaluation of sewage treatment plants under the National River Conservation Directorate (NRCD) (CPCB 2013); inventorization of sewage treatment plants (CPCB 2015a); River Stretches for Restoration of Water Quality (CPCB 2015b) status of sewage treatment plants in the Ganga basin (CPCB 2003).

5 Personal communication with the Executive Engineer, Bangalore Water and Sewerage Services Board, November 2015.

6 Cost recovery = Total annual operating expenses and total annual operating revenues. Collection Efficiency = Current revenues collected in the given year and total operating revenue billed during the given year.

7 For details on self-review checklist, refer to: http://moud.gov.in/upload/uploadfiles/files/CSP_Checklist_for_cities.pdf (accessed on 12 January 2018).

8 For details refer http://indiacode.nic.in/coiweb/amend/amend74.htm (accessed on 11 January 2018).

9 While Kerala Municipality Act (1994) and amendments therein require the municipal corporations to maintain and arrange water and sewerage services, the KWA continues to provide water services in all municipal corporations except Thrissur (Attingal Municipality n.d.: 99).

10 Udaipur and Dewas Municipal Corporation have two departments: Health and Sanitation and Public Works Department (PWD). The former is responsible for basic sanitations services (looking after solid waste

management and sanitation issues, such as collecting and disposing of solid waste, sweeping streets and cleaning public toilets. It also operates and maintains the necessary sanitation equipment) while the PWD is responsible for providing infrastructure and services for collection of wastewater and treatment.

11 Personal communication with the Executive Engineer, Bangalore Water and Sewerage Services Board, November 2015.

12 City Sanitation Cell by Dewas, Ahmednagar, Ulhasnagar, Sangli Miraj Kupwad, Mira Bhayander, Agra, Nagpur, Lucknow, Attingal, Kottayam, Varkala, Solapur, Varanasi. Shimla proposes cell for Sewerage System Cell, Water Supply Cell, Solid Waste Management Cell, Storm Water Drainage Cell, Public Sanitation Cell. Attingal, Varkala and Kottayam propose solid waste management cell.

13 Akola, Aurangabad, Ahmednagar, Sangli Miraj Kupwad, Thane, Mira Bhayander, Udaipur, Nellore.

14 Attingal, Varkala, Kottayam, Agra and Shimla talked about earmarking certain amount in the municipal budget for sanitation whereas Akola and Nagpur request the state governments to allocate dedicated funds. Dewas expects resources to be earmarked for water and sanitation development within municipal and state budgets. Kerala proposed to create a separate centralised State Urban Sanitation Fund (SUSF) to be pooled from a variety of resources such as bilateral and multi-lateral organizations, the State Finance Commission and the Central Finance Commission and both tied/untied funds to make sustained effort in environmental sanitation (GoT n.d.: 13).

15 Thane provides a detailed discussion, with some mention by Ahmedabad, Akola and Ulhasnagar. For Ahmedabad, the online source (CSP) does not contain complete information on the health indicators.

16 Attingal Municipality n.d.: 13

17 Under JNNURM, provision of internal earmarking of funds within local bodies' budget for basic services including sanitation is a mandatory reform.

18 Kochi: 2 per cent of the Municipal Corporation's own revenue is earmarked for poverty alleviation schemes and ULB to earmark dedicated funds for the sanitation sector and O&M of public sanitation facilities. The Lucknow Nagar Nigam has earmarked INR 14 crore from the total development budget of INR 57 crore, i.e., 25 per cent in 2010–2011 (as part of JNNURM's mandatory reform).

19 The city has reserved 20–25 per cent of developed land in all housing projects for the urban poor through amendments in housing policies.

20 Varanasi is implementing the Integrated Low-Cost Sanitation Scheme, which mandates provision of sanitation services irrespective of the tenure in urban poor pockets. Ahmedabad under the old no objection certificate schemes provides basic services where land titles are not clear.

21 Small towns: Attingal, Varkala; Medium Towns: Kottayam, Shimla, Rourkela, Udaipur; Large city: Kochi, Mira – Bhayander, Mysore; Metropolitan cities like Pune and Ahmedabad.

22 Dewas and Lucknow evaluated willingness to pay whereas Shimla evaluated detailed implications of septage management.

23 AIILSG was responsible for Ahmednagar, Akola, Sangli Miraj Kupwad, Ulhasnagar, Nanded, Mira Bhayander, Solapur, Navi Mumbai, Aurangabad,

Thane, Nagpur and Pune. GIZ was responsible for Shimla, Kochi, Mysore, Varanasi and Dewas and SSSs for Himachal Pradesh, Andhra Pradesh, Kerala and Chhattisgarh.

24 The Decentralised Waste Water Treatment System (DEWATS) has been developed by the Bremen Overseas Research and Development Association (BORDA) and propagated in India by the Consortium for DEWATS Dissemination (CDD) Society. The association of GIZ with the MoUD led to the adoption of DEWATS-based projects in cities like Shimla (with the help of the CDD Society).

25 For detailed discussion on linkages between land rights and basic services and how the issue has been dealt with in various urban and slum development programme, refer to Mahadevia (2009); Mahdevia and Datey (2012); Zimmer (2012); Simpreet and Bhise (2014); Chamaraj (2014).

26 WSSD submitted proposal for CSP development for 19 Municipal Corporations to the MoUD and received sanction. The Sangli Miraj Kupwad Municipal Corporation was communicated, by the WSSD, to prepare the CSP (letter no CSP 2010/CR49/WS – 21 dated: 13 April 2010) and about the appointment of AIILSG (Mumbai) for capacity building of the Municipal Corporations for CSP preparation (SMKMC 2011:10).

27 The first phase (2011–2014) included support to the NUSP, SSS and CSP implementation and technical assistance. The MoUD in 2010 requested GIZ to support CSP development in 10 Indian cities namely Shimla, Varanasi, Raipur, Dewas, Nasik, Tirupati, Vasai Virar, Vikarabad, Mysore, and Kochi. www.sswm.info/sites/default/files/reference_attachments/dube%202012%20experiences%20and%20perspectives%20of%20state%20and%20ulbs%20in%20india.pdf (accessed on 6 August 2016) and GIZ (2011).

28 Recommendations have been accepted under the 14th Finance Commission (2015–2020) as well.

29 Refer MoUD website. http://moud.gov.in/policies/servicelevel (accessed on 15 June 2016).

## References

Abeysuriya, Kumudini, Cynthia Mitchell and Willets Juliet. 2010. 'Urban Sanitation Through the Lens of Thomas Kuhn', in John R. McNeill, José Augusto Pádua and Mahesh Rangarajan (eds.), *Environmental History: As if Nature Existed*, pp. 65–84. New York: Oxford University Press.

ADB (Asian Development Bank). 2007. In High Powered Expert Committee (HPEC). 2011. 'Report on Indian Urban Infrastructure and Services: For Estimating the Investment Requirements for Urban Infrastructure Services', Ministry of Urban Development. Section 2.3.5: 47.

Avashia, Vidhee Kiran and Amit Garg. 2016. 'Have the Reforms Delivered: Urban Infrastructure and Governance Mission under JNNURM?' *Economic & Political Weekly*, 51(2): 41–57.

Braun, Virginia and Victoria Clarke. 2006. 'Using Thematic Analysis in Psychology', *Qualitative Research in Psychology*, 3: 2, 77–101, www.tandfonline.com/doi/pdf/10.1191/1478088706qp063oa?needAccess=true (accessed on 12 February 2018).

Chamaraj, Kathyayini. 2014. 'Undermining RAY', www.infochangeindia.org, October, http://infochangeindia.org/agenda-issues/urban-poverty/9448-undermining-ray (accessed on 17 June 2018).

Chaplin, Susan E. 2011. *The Politics of Sanitation in India: Cities, Services and the State*. New Delhi: Orient BlackSwan.

CPCB (Central Pollution Control Board). 2003. 'Status of Sewage Treatment Plants in the Ganga Basin', Ministry of Environment & Forests, Government of India (GoI).

CPCB (Central Pollution Control Board). 2005. 'Status of Sewage Treatment in India', http://cpcb.nic.in/newitems/12.pdf (accessed on 9 June 2016).

CPCB (Central Pollution Control Board). 2007. 'Evaluation of Operation and Maintenance of Sewage Treatment Plants in India', Control of Urban Pollution Series: CUPS/68/2007, http://cpcb.nic.in/openpdffile.php?id=UmVwb3J0RmlsZXMvTmV3SXRlbV85OV9OZXdJdGVtXzk5XzUucGRm (accessed on 24 February 2018).

CPCB (Central Pollution Control Board). 2009. 'Status of Water Supply, Wastewater Generation and Treatment in Class – I Cities & Class – II Towns of India', Control of Urban Pollution Series: CUPS/70 / 2009–2010, www.cpcb.nic.in/upload/NewItems/NewItem_153_Foreword.pdf (accessed on 9 June 2016).

CPCB (Central Pollution Control Board). 2013. 'Performance Evaluation of Sewage Treatment Plants Under NRCD', http://cpcb.nic.in/upload/NewItems/NewItem_195_STP_REPORT.pdf (accessed on 9 June 2016).

CPCB (Central Pollution Control Board). 2015a. 'Inventorization of Sewage Treatment Plants', Control of Urban Pollution Series: CUPS/ / 2015, www.cpcb.nic.in/upload/NewItems/NewItem_210_Inventorization_of_Sewage–Treatment_Plant.pdf (accessed on 9 June 2016).

CPCB (Central Pollution Control Board). 2015b. 'River Stretches for Restoration of Water Quality: Monitoring of Indian National Aquatic Resources Series', MINARS/37 /2014–2015. Ministry of Environment, Forests & Climate Change, February, http://cpcb.nic.in/RESTORATION–OF–POLLUTED–RIVER–STRETCHES.pdf (accessed on 8 August 017).

CPHEEO (Central Public Health and Environmental Engineering Organisation). 1980. *The Manual on Sewerage and Sewage Treatment*. New Delhi: Ministry of Urban Development, Government of India (GoI).

CPHEEO (Central Public Health and Environmental Engineering Organisation). 2012. *An Analysis of 2011 Census Data on Household Amenities with Respect to Drinking Water Sources and Latrine Facilities in Urban Areas of the Country*. New Delhi: Ministry of Urban Development, Government of India (GoI), http://urbanindia.nic.in/programme/uwss/AnalysisHouseholdAmenities.pdf (accessed on December 2012).

CPHEEO (Central Public Health and Environmental Engineering Organisation). 2013. 'Manual on Sewerage and Sewage Treatment', http://cpheeo.nic.in/Sewerage.aspx (accessed on 11 August 2016).

Crites, R. and G. Tchobanoglous. 1998. 'Small and Decentralised Wastewater Management Systems', in Sharon Hophmayer-Tokich (2006) (ed.),

*Wastewater Management Strategy: Centralised v. Decentralised Technologies for Small Communities*. Boston: McGraw-Hill.

Dube, R. 2012. 'City Sanitation Plans: Experiences and Perspectives of State and ULBs in India: National Workshop on Improving Services in Urban Water Supply and Sanitation', New Delhi, 9–10 July, www.sswm.info/sites/default/files/reference_attachments/DUBE%202012%20Experiences%20and%20Perspectives%20of%20State%20and%20ULBs%20in%20India.pdf (accessed on 6 August 2016).

Giri, R., J. Takeuchi and H. Ozaki. 2006. 'Biodegradation of Domestic Wastewater Under the Stimulated Conditions of Thailand', *Water and Environment Journal*, 20(3): 109–202.

GIZ. 2011. 'Fact Sheet on City Sanitation Plans. Environmental Policy/Conservation and Sustainable Use of Natural Resources', www.urbansanitation.org/live/hrdpmp/hrdpmaster/hrdp-asem/content/e30293/e31169/e49811/e49812/CSPfactSheet-Final.pdf (accessed on 24 February 2018).

Go, E. and I. Demir. 2006. 'Cost Analysis of Alternative Methods for Wastewater Handling in Small Communities', *Journal of Environmental Management*, 79(4): 357–363.

Government of India (GoI). n.d. JNNURM Primers. 'Implementation of the 74th Constitutional Amendment and Integration of City Planning and Delivery Functions. State Level Reform', www.mumbaidp24seven.in/reference/1_2_Implementation_CAA_Planning.pdf (accessed on 3 January 2018).

Government of India (GoI). 1971a. 'The Fourth Plan: Mid Term Appraisal, Planning Commission', in Susan E. Chaplin (ed.) (2011), *The Politics of Sanitation in India: Cities, Services and the State*. Orient BlackSwan, December: 230.

Government of India (GoI). 1971b. 'Chapter 19: Regional Development, Housing and Water Supply. Fourth Five Year Plan', *Planning Commission*, http://Planningcommission.Nic.In/Plans/Planrel/Fiveyr/4th/4planch19.Html (accessed on 6 October 2016).

Government of India (GoI). 1999. *Ninth Five Year Plan, 1997–2002*, Volume II & I. Planning Commission, Government of India.

Government of India (GoI). 2008. 'National Urban Sanitation Policy, 2008', http://moud.gov.in/upload/uploadfiles/files/NUSP_0.pdf (accessed on 26 August 2017).

Government of Tripura (GoT). n.d. 'Tripura Urban Sanitation Strategy (Draft)', Urban Development Department, www.Sswm.Info/Sites/Default/Files/Reference_Attachments/Got%202011%20tripura%20urban%20sanitation%20strategy.Pdf (accessed on 24 February 2018).

Hazards Centre. 2007. *Urban Renewal or Cities of Exclusion: A Report*. New Delhi.

Hazards Centre. 2008. *Challenges to a Mission*. New Delhi.

HoUDD (Housing and Urban Development Department). 2011. 'City Sanitation Plan Draft Report', Rourkela Municipality, Government of Orissa.

HPEC (High Powered Expert Committee). 2011. 'Report on Indian Urban Infrastructure and Services: For Estimating the Investment Requirements for Urban Infrastructure Services', Ministry of Urban Development.

Government of India (GoI), http://icrier.org/pdf/FinalReport–hpec.pdf (accessed on 26 August 2017).
IIHS (Indian Institute for Human Settlements). 2011. 'Urban India 2011: Evidence', 22 November. India Urban Conference (IUC): Evidence and Experience (IUC 2011).
Kalbermatten, John M., DeAnne. S. Julius, Charles G. Gunnerson, and D. Duncan Mara. 1982. *Appropriate Sanitation Alternatives: A Planning and Design Manual*. Baltimore: International Bank for Reconstruction and Development/The World Bank, Johns Hopkins University Press, http://documents.worldbank.org/curated/en/701511468740361506/pdf/multi-page.pdf (accessed on 24 February 2018).
Kamath, Lalitha. 2012. 'New Policy Paradigms and Actual Practices in Slum Housing: The Case of Housing Projects in Bengaluru', *Economic and Political Weekly*, XLVII(47–48): 76–86.
Konteh, Frederick Hassan. 2009. 'Urban Sanitation and Health in the Developing World: Reminiscing the Nineteenth Century Industrial Nations', *Health & Place*, 15(1): 69–78. Elselvier (accessed on 24 February 2018).
Kuhn, Thomas S. 1970. *The Structure of Scientific Revolutions*, 2nd ed. Chicago: University of Chicago Press, https://projektintegracija.pravo.hr/_download/repository/Kuhn_Structure_of_Scientific_Revolutions.pdf (accessed on 9 February 2018).
Kundu, Amitabh. 1991. 'Micro Environment in Urban Planning Access of Poor to Water Supply and Sanitation', *Economic and Political Weekly*, 26(37), www.epw.in/system/files/pdf/1991_26/37/micro_environment_in_urban_planning_access_of_poor_to_water_supply_and_sanitation.pdf (accessed on 8 June 2016).
Kundu, Debolina and Dibyendu Samanta. 2011. 'Redefining the Inclusive Urban Agenda in India', *Economic and Political Weekly*, 46(5): 55–63. 29 January. http://indiagovernance.gov.in/files/inclusive-urban-agenda.PDF (accessed on 3 January 2018).
Lovins, Amory B. 2002. *Small Is Profitable: The Hidden Economic Benefits of Making Electrical Resources the Right Size*. Colorado: Rockey Mountain Institute Snowmass.
Lundvall, Bengt-Åke and Mark Tomlinson. 2002. 'International Benchmarking as a Policy Learning Tool', in Maria João Rodrigues (ed.), *The New Knowledge Economy in Europe: A Strategy for International Competitiveness and Social Cohesion*. Cheltenham, UK, Northampton, MA: Edward Elgar.
Mahadevia, Darshini. 2006. 'NURM and Poor in Globalising Mega Cities', *Economic and Political Weekly*, 41(31): 3399–3403.
Mahadevia, Darshini. 2009. 'Urban Land Market and Access of the Poor in India', India: Urban Poverty Report 2009, pp. 199–221. Ministry of Housing and Urban Poverty Alleviation. New Delhi: Oxford University Press, www.undp.org/content/dam/india/docs/india_urban_poverty_report_2009_related.pdf (accessed on 3 January 2018).
Mahdevia, Darshini and Abhijit Datey. 2012. 'The Status of Pro-Poor Reforms in Indian States', October. Working Paper – 17. Centre for Urban Equity. CEPT University. An NRC for Ministry of Housing and Urban Poverty

Alleviation, Government of India (GoI), http://cept.ac.in/UserFiles/File/CUE/Working%20Papers/17CUEWP17_The%20Status%20of%20Pro-Poor%20Reforms%20in%20Indian%20States_Resize.pdf (accessed on 3 January 2018).

Mara, D. Duncan. 1996. *Low Cost Urban Sanitation*. New York: John Wiley.

Massoud, May A., Akram Tarhini and Joumana A. Nasr. 2009.'Decentralized Approaches to Wastewater Treatment and Management: Applicability in Developing Countries', *Journal of Environmental Management*, 90(2009): 652–659. Elsevier (accessed on 25 February 2018).

Mayring, Philipp. 2000. 'Qualitative Content Analysis', *Forum Qualitative Sozialforschung/Forum: Qualitative Social Research*, 1(2), Art. 20, http://nbn-resolving.de/urn:nbn:de:0114-fqs0002204 (accessed on 24 February 2018).

Medema, W., B. S. McIntosh and P. J. Jeffrey. 2008. 'From Premise to Practice: A Critical Assessment of Integrated Water Resources Management and Adaptive Management Approaches in the Water Sector', *Ecology and Society*, 13(2): 29.

NF Infratech Service (Delhi). n.d. 'City Sanitation Plan (Draft): Udaipur City'.

NIUA. 1987. *Maintaining Gujarat Municipal Services – A Long Range Perspective*. New Delhi: National Institute of Urban Affairs (NIUA).

NIUA. 2007. 'Norms and Standards of Municipal Basic Services in India', NIUA WP 07–01, www.indiawaterportal.org/sites/indiawaterportal.org/files/Norms_standards_municipalbasic_services_in_India_NIUA.pdf (accessed on 3 February 2018).

NIUA. 2016. 'Towns of India: Status of Demography, Economy, Social Structures, Housing and Basic Infrastructure', HSMI – HUDCO Chair – NIUA Collaborative Research, http://smartnet.niua.org/sites/default/files/resources/Hudco%20Phase%20III.pdf (accessed on 10 January 2016).

PMIDC (Punjab Municipal Infrastructure Development Company). 2013. 'Challenges of Service Delivery in Water and Sanitation', http://icrier.org/Urbanisation/events/20–Feb–2013–Chandigarh–CII/Session%202/Mr%20Rakesh%20Verma,%20Municipal%20Commissioner%20Ludhiana.pdf (accessed on June 2013).

Sedlak, David. 2014. *Water 4.0: The Past, Present, and Future of the World's Most Vital Resource*. New Haven, London: Yale University Press.

Simpreet, Das Chandana and Raju Bhise. 2014. *Slum Free India: Myths and Realities: A Status Report on Rajiv Awas Yojana, 2014*. New Delhi: National Desk, Youth for Unity and Voluntary Action (YUVA), www.yuvaindia.org/Data/reports/RAY%20Status%20Report_V1.2.pdf (accessed on 9 January 2017).

SMKMC (Sangli Miraj Kupwad Municipal Corporation). 2011. 'City Sanitation Plan' (Zero Draft). Sangli Miraj Kupwad Municipal Corporation, May, www.prudaonline.com/aiilsg/jdownloads/City%20Sanitation%20Plans/CSPMS/csp_sangli_miraz_kupwad.pdf (accessed on 24 February 2018).

Tillema, Sandra. 2007. 'Public Sector Organizations' Use of Benchmarking Information for Performance Improvement: Theoretical Analysis and

Explorative Case Studies in Dutch Water Boards', *Public Performance & Management Review*, 30(4): 496–520, Taylor & Francis Ltd.

Walker, R. Kennedy, B. Evans, J. Amezaga, and C. Paterson. 2014. 'Challenges for the Future of Urban Sanitation Planning: Critical Analysis of John Kalbermatten's Influence', Review Paper, *Journal of Water, Sanitation and Hygiene for Development*, 4(1):1–14. IWA Publishing, http://washdev.iwaponline.com/content/4/1/1 (accessed on 24 February 2018).

Wilderer, P. A. and D. Schreff. 2000. 'Decentralised and Centralised Wastewater Management: A Challenge for Technology Developers', *Water Science and Technology*, 41(1): 1–8 in Sharon Hophmayer – Tokich (n.d.), *Wastewater Management Strategy: Centralised v. Decentralised Technologies for Small Communities*.

Wilsenach, J. A., M. Maurer, T. A. Larsen, M. C. M van Loosdrescht, and M. E. Van Loosdrecht. 2003. 'From Waste Treatment to Integrated Resource Management', *Water Science and Technology*, 48(1): 1–9.

WSP (Water and Sanitation Programme). 2009a. 'Phase II – Benchmarking Urban Water Utilities in India', http://wwwwds.worldbank.org/external/default/WDSContentServer/WDSP/IB/2009/01/08/000333037_20090108222255/Rendered/PDF/470570WSP0Box31Benchmarking11Report.pdf (accessed on February 2015).

WSP (Water and Sanitation Programme). 2009b. 'Improving Water and Sanitation Service Delivery in India Lessons from a National Workshop on Service Level Benchmarking', Nagari: 18th Meeting of the Urban Think Tank. New Delhi, 14–15, December, www.wsp.org/sites/wsp.org/files/publications/WSP–nagari–improvingwatersanitation–india.pdf (accessed on 11 August 2016).

WSP (Water and Sanitation Programme). 2011. 'Cost Recovery in Urban Water Services: Select Experiences in Indian Cities'.

Zakaria Committee. 1963. 'Augmentation of Financial Resources of Urban Local Bodies. Report of the Committee of Ministers', Constituted by the Central Council of Local Self Government.

Zimmer, Anna. 2012. 'Enumerating the Semi-Visible: The Politics of Regularising Delhi's Unauthorized Colonies', *Economic & Political Weekly*, 47(30): 89–97.

# Appendix

## 7.1: City Sanitation Plans examined for the study


Administrative Staff College of India (ASCI) and Directorate of Municipal Administration Government of Karnataka. n.d. *City Sanitation Plan Report for Nellore.*

Administrative Staff College of India (ASCI) and Directorate of Municipal Administration Government of Karnataka. 2010. *City Sanitation Plan: Agra.*

Administrative Staff College of India (ASCI) and Directorate of Municipal Administration Government of Karnataka. 2011. 'City Sanitation Plan Mysore', Karnataka (Draft Report).

Ahmednagar Municipal Corporation and All India Institute of Local Self Government (Mumbai). n.d. *City Sanitation Plan* (Zero Draft).

Ahmedabad Municipal Corporation and Urban Management Centre. 2012. *City Sanitation Plan Ahmedabad.*

Akola Municipal Corporation. 2011. *City Sanitation Plan* (CSP).

Attingal Municipality. n.d. *City Sanitation Plan (Final Draft): Towards Town Wide Sanitation.*

Aurangabad Municipal Corporation. 2011. 'Zero Draft City Sanitation Plan for Aurangabad', www.prudaonline.com/aiilsg/jdownloads/City%20 Sanitation%20Plans/CSPMS/csp_aurangabad.pdf (accessed on 24 February 2018).

Corporation of Cochin and GIZ. 2011. 'City Sanitation Plan, Volume I: Main Report', www.urbansanitation.org/live/hrdpmp/hrdpmaster/hrdp-asem/content/e30293/e31169/e49836/e49818/e49819/1.KochiDraftCSP-VolumeI-Main.pdf (accessed on 24 February 2018).

CRISIL Risk and Infrastructure Solutions Limited and Japan International Cooperation Agency. 2011. *Final City Sanitation Plan for Lucknow.*

Mira-Bhayander Municipal Corporation. 2011. *City Sanitation Plan.*

MoUD (Ministry of Urban Development) n.d. 'Handbook of Service Level Benchmarking', Government of India (GoI), www.wsp.org/sites/wsp.org/files/publications/service_benchmarking_india.pdf (accessed on 24 February 2018).

Municipal Corporation Shimla and GIZ-ASEM. 2011. 'City Sanitation Plan for Shimla', www.shimlamc.org/file.axd?file=2011%2F10%2F2+R-CityStrategy-Final-111012.pdf (accessed on 24 February 2018).

Nagpur Municipal Corporation and All India Institute of Local Self Government (Mumbai). 2011. 'City Sanitation Plan'.

Nanded Waghala City Municipal Corporation and All India Institute of Local Self Government. 2011. 'City Sanitation Plan' (Zero Draft). Vol. 1. Report.

Navi Mumbai Municipal Corporation. 2011. 'City Sanitation Plan'.

Pune Municipal Corporation and All India Institute of Local Self Government. 2011. 'Pune City Sanitation Plan'.

Rourkela Municipality. 2011. 'City Sanitation Plan' (Draft), Housing and Urban Development Department, Government of Orissa.

Solapur Municipal Corporation. 2011. 'Solapur City Sanitation Plan' (Final Draft).

Thane Municipal Corporation. n.d. 'City Sanitation Plan'.

Varanasi Municipal Corporation, Consortium for DEWATS Dissemination, CEPT Research & Development Consultancy, Alchemy Urban Systems (P) Ltd. and GIZ-ASEM. 2011. 'City Sanitation Plan for Varanasi (Draft): Main Document'.

Varkala Municipality. n.d. 'City Sanitation Plan (Final Draft): Towards Town Wide Sanitation'.

Ulhasnagar Municipal Corporation. 2011. 'Draft City Sanitation Plan (Part I of II)'.

United States Agency for International Development (India), Alchemy Urban Systems (P) Ltd. and Consortium for DEWATS Dissemination Society. 2011. 'City Sanitation Plan for Dewas'.

# Appendix

## 7.2: Details of the Selected Cities

| *Name* | *Population** | *Class* | *Population category* | *Category* | *Sewage network coverage (%)** | *Financial health in WSS** | |
|---|---|---|---|---|---|---|---|
| | | | | | | *SLBs for water services Cost recovery =100% Efficiency in collection of user charges = 90%* | *SLBs for sewerage services Cost recovery = 80% Efficiency in collection of charges = 90%)* |
| Attingal (Kerala) | 37,346 | Class – III | 20,000–50,000 | Small town – II | nil | Collection efficiency 75% | NA |
| Varkala (Kerala) | 40,048 | | | | nil | 77% and 78% | NA |
| Kottayam (Kerala) | 55,374 | | 50,000–1,00,000 | Medium Town – I | nil | NA | NA |
| Shimla (Himachal Pradesh) | 1,69,578 | Class – I | 0.1–0.5 Million | Medium Town II | 60–70% | NA | NA |
| Rourkela (Orissa) | 272,721 | | | | 95% of area without sewerage | 21% and 65.5% | NA |
| Dewas (Madhya Pradesh) | 289,550 | | | | 8% | 55% and 66% | 10% and 30% |

| | | | | | | | |
|---|---|---|---|---|---|---|---|
| Ahmednagar (Maharashtra) | 350,859 | | | | 40% of city covered with sewerage | 60% and 60% | 17% and 17.5% |
| Akola (Maharashtra) | 425,817 | | | | nil | 52% collection efficiency | NA |
| Udaipur (Rajasthan) | 451,100 | | | | 4% of houses connected | NA | NA |
| Nellore (Andhra Pradesh) | 499,575 | | | | 11% | 90.6% and 86.1% | Nil |
| Sangli Miraj Kupwad (Maharashtra) | 502,793 | Class I (large city) | 0.5–1 Million | Large City | 32.5% | 95% and 70% | 62.13% and 64.49% |
| Ulhasnagar (Maharashtra) | 506,098 | | | | 60% | 45•50% ανδ 60% | 50% and poor collection efficiency |
| Nanded – Waghala (Maharashtra) | 550,439 | | | | 67.40% | 80.8% and 75.50% | 75.90% ανδ 85.50% |
| Kochi (Kerala) | 602,046 | | | | 5% | NA and 22% | NA |
| Mira Bhayander (Maharashtra) | 809,378 | | | | 11.60% | 100% and 92% | 90% and 61% |
| Mysore (Karnataka) | 893,062 | | | | 78% | 62% and 70% | NA and 26% |
| Solapur (Maharashtra) | 951,558 | | | | 53% of toilet seats connected to sewerage | 85% and 56% | 0% and 24.37% |

(Continued)

| *Name* | *Population** | *Class* | *Population category* | *Category* | *Sewage network coverage (%)** | *Financial health in WSS** | |
|---|---|---|---|---|---|---|---|
| | | | | | | *SLBs for water services Cost recovery =100% Efficiency in collection of user charges = 90%* | *SLBs for sewerage services Cost recovery = 80% Efficiency in collection of charges = 90%)* |
| Navi Mumbai (Maharashtra) | 112,0547 | Class I (Sub – Metropolis) | 1–5 Million | Metropolitan City I | 99% | 97.25% and 90.32% | 117.18% and 85% |
| Aurangabad (Maharashtra) | 117,5116 | | | | 60% | 100% and 40% | Nil |
| Varanasi (Uttar Pradesh) | 1,198,491 | | | | 78% (does not include slums) | NA | 44.31% and 56.51% |
| Agra (Uttar Pradesh) | 1,585,704 | | | | 17% | NA | Negligible recovery |
| Thane (Maharashtra) | 1,841,488 | | | | 17%<br>38% of population | NA | 100% and 80% |
| Nagpur (Maharashtra) | 2,405,665 | | | | 60% of city is covered | 93% and 73% | 100% and 60% |
| Lucknow (Uttar Pradesh) | 2,817,105 | | | | 40–43% houses connected | 64% and 84% | 53% and 82% |
| Pune (Maharashtra) | 3,124,458 | | | | 97.57% | 70.67% and 90.93% | 76.05% and 68% |
| Ahmedabad (Gujarat) | 5,577,940 | Class I (Metropolis) | 5–10 Million | | 95%<br>65% slum area connected | 78% and 81% | 83% and 83% |

Note: * as per the respective CSPs. NA (Not Available)

Source: Respective CSPs for Column 2, 6 and 7; NIUA 2016; HPEC 2011

# 8 Canal irrigation performance and impacts

## Applying contingency theory to irrigation management in India

*Tushaar Shah*[1]

### Introduction: canal irrigation at crossroads

Indian irrigation is at crossroads; and its irrigation policy, in a state of flux. Agrarian stagnation during the 1990s and thereafter has been blamed on the slowdown in public investment in agriculture, mostly irrigation. However, scores of evaluations of large canal irrigation projects have found them under-performing when compared to their planning goals and targets. Over a century ago, in the preface to the second edition of his book *Irrigation Works of India*, Burton Buckley (1905: Preface) wrote eloquently about the 'benefits which [the great irrigation works of India] confer on the people of India [which] cannot but tend to display the true beneficence of British rule in the great continent'. Buckley was able to boast that during the seven-year period between the first and second editions of his book, the 'area watered by irrigation works controlled by the Government of India increased by fifty per cent' (ibid.). Some hundred years later, the scenario is markedly different. Between 1990 and 2004, governments of India and its various states invested INR[2] 130 billion (US $ 28.9 billion at US $ = INR 45) in building new public irrigation systems and rehabilitating the old ones under the Accelerated Irrigation Benefits Programme. However, benefits from government irrigation systems have declined, as the area served by public irrigation projects was reduced by over 3 million ha (Shah 2009). 'No acceleration, little irrigation, minuscule benefit', quipped a Delhi-based think-tank (SANDRP 2006).

Poor performance of canal irrigation and its reasons have generated a vast literature within India and elsewhere in the developing world. But, essentially, the 'problem-shed' of canal irrigation is located in the interplay between three components of canal irrigation systems: (1)

management agency, (2) farmers and (3) physical system, as outlined in Figure 8.1.

*Reform Irrigation Bureaucracy:* During the 1970s, unaccountable irrigation bureaucracy, which was interested in construction more than in operation and maintenance, crippled the canal irrigation system (see, e.g., Blair 1985; Wade 1992). With a view to improving performance (Wade and Chambers 1980), a massive programme of training and capacity building for irrigation bureaucracy was initiated, besides investments in 16 Water and Land Management Institutes across the country.

*Rehabilitate Old Infrastructure:* The next proposition was to improve the physical infrastructure which has led to large investments in rehabilitation of old infrastructure. Soon, however, governments and international financial institutions found that irrigation systems were often ready for a second round of rehabilitation even before the first was over. Farmers, the key beneficiary, did little towards the upkeep of the infrastructure.

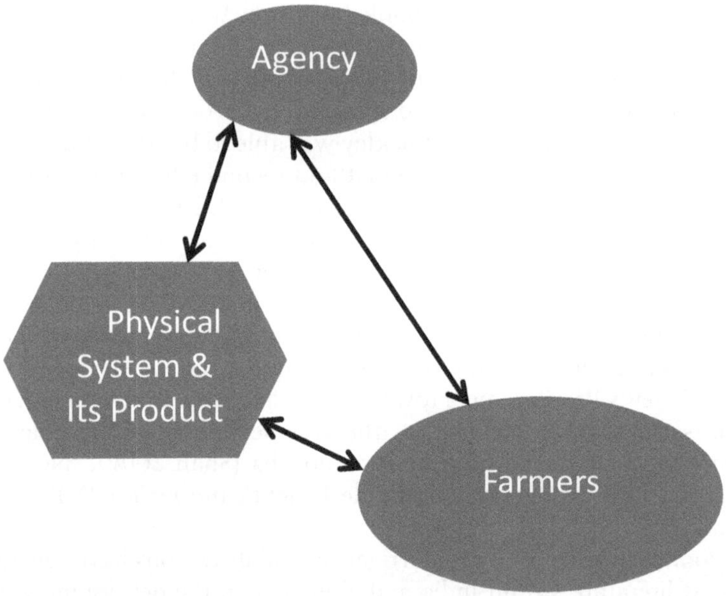


*Figure 8.1* The Canal Irrigation Problem-Shed

Source: Shah *et al.* 2012

***Modernization Drive:*** The next wave went beyond physical deterioration and argued that most Indian irrigation systems were designed at a time when farmers were happy with a much lower level of irrigation service than they demand today (Plusquellec 1998).[3] If farmers have to take active interest in maintaining them, irrigation systems need not only rehabilitation but also modernization, with greater room for providing farmers the differentiated level of water control and irrigation services that they demand today. The way to end the build-neglect-rebuild syndrome is to modernize not only infrastructure but also irrigation institutions.

***Participatory Irrigation Management* (PIM):** Since the highly centralized and top-down approach has resulted in poor service delivery, it was thought that the PIM could create a more effective water management system. Indeed, there are some outstanding Indian examples of PIM projects supported by NGOs – such as the Waghad project[4] in Maharashtra and Visnagar, Gujarat. Yet PIM/IMT (Irrigation Management Transfer) has proved far from being a panacea for ailing irrigation systems in India or elsewhere. Once considered a roaring success, Philippines's PIM programme has lost much of its sheen (Oorthuizen 2003). Many observers consider PIM successful even if all that it does is 'save money for the government, as it divests itself of the responsibility to finance routine costs of O&M of irrigation systems' (Vermillion 1996: 153), no matter whether PIM improves service delivery, water productivity, conflict resolution, and such like. PIM has produced sustainable revitalization in irrigation systems in a few countries, notably Turkey, Mexico and Columbia, with medium-to-large-sized land holdings but has failed to make a mark in small-holder farming contexts of Asia and Sub-Saharan Africa (Shah *et al.* 2002). Here, sustained intervention by support units from NGOs has animated farmer organizations, as exemplified by the work of the Development Support Centre in Gujarat; but withdrawal of such support often heralds the collapse of PIM (Shah *et al.* 2002; Shah 2009).

## The experience so far

Much available evidence suggests that canal systems in India and other developing countries performed better for a long time in the past than they do now. Of irrigation in mediaeval era, we only have sketchy accounts. However, we have better documentation of government irrigation systems during the colonial era. Table 8.1 outlines the colonial

*Table 8.1* Colonial Schools of Irrigation Design and Management[5]

| | *French in Indo-China* | *Dutch in Netherlands East Indies* | *British in South Asia* | *Soviets in Central Asia* |
|---|---|---|---|---|
| Originally designed for | French farmers | Dutch and local farmers | Local farmers | Soviet farmer collectives |
| Original design objectives | High economic returns | High economic returns | Maximizing land and water tax | Maximize cotton production |
| Level of local water control | High, with active management by agency staff | Moderate to high, with active management by local staff | Low; water regulation through '*warabandi*' and outlet size | High, with active management by Russian engineers and collectives |
| Original management objectives | High level irrigation service through local water control | High level irrigation service through local water control | Spread available water over largest area | Irrigation as part of a collective farming strategy |
| Choice of crops allowed | Controlled | Controlled | Not controlled | Controlled |
| Presence of expat staff at local level | High | Moderate | Low | Low |

Source: Shah *et al.* 2012

irrigation context in several parts of Asia by comparing the French, Dutch, British and Soviet 'schools'. And this suggests that many external conditions on which irrigation managers had little or no control helped better service delivery; many of these are, however, absent today.

Years after independence, the colonial design and management tradition continued to hold sway in all these countries. However, many external contingencies that shaped the working of irrigation systems changed. Crop control in command areas was abandoned everywhere. Land reforms in many countries changed the landscape of irrigation commands. Expatriate farmers with large commercial holdings were replaced by indigenous subsistence farmers with small holdings.

Colonial hard state gave way to a soft, welfare state. Commercial viability lost primacy; small holder development and food security became key objectives. Yet, irrigation design, planning and management changed little to achieve a better fit with these new contingencies.

In India, too, there is indirect evidence that irrigation systems were more vigorously managed as a commercial enterprise during the colonial era than today. A 1902–1903 account by Burton Buckley (1905) shows that colonial irrigation investments were not only attractive in financial and economic terms, but these were also prudently and tightly managed for techno-economic sustainability. Farmers paid high ISF (Irrigation Service Fees) and taxes; but they also received higher level of service. 'After all, even in a colony, levying taxes without some guaranteed delivery of water was not done!' (Ertsen 2007: 5). For every Rs 100 invested in fixed capital, Rs 87 was the annual irrigated crop output, Rs 10 were collected as ISF, Rs 2.6 was spent on regular maintenance, and around Rs 5 was spent annually on O&M. About 100 years later, comparable figures were much worse: for every Rs 100 invested in fixed capital stock, value of irrigated crops was Rs 18, ISF collected was Rs 0.2; the annual O&M spend was down to Rs 2.53 and infrastructure maintenance was Rs 0.86 (Table 8.2). A virtuous 'build-serve-earn-maintain-grow' syndrome had given way to a vicious 'build-neglect-rebuild' one.

## A contingency approach

There is, therefore, a need to explore the factors that vitalized the interaction between the irrigation agency, farmers and the physical system (Figure 8.1) in ways that made irrigation systems more productive and sustainable in the past than they are at present. Learning from history suggests that the agency-farmer-system interaction in the historical past was influenced by four exogenous contingency clusters: nature of the state, nature of the society, state of agrarian institutions and state of irrigation technology. All of these have undergone a profound transformation between 'then' and 'now' as outlined in Table 8.3.

The Indian 'state' is softer today than it was during colonial and precolonial times[12] and the local authority structures are weaker today than they were in the past. Many state governments now levy land revenue as token rates, and many have abolished ISF, which, in colonial Punjab of the 1930s, generated more state income than even income tax did (Islam 1997). Forced labour for canal construction and maintenance was a rule then but is almost totally absent now in India. Due to high demographic

*Table 8.2* Symptoms of Managerial Decline in Indian Canal Irrigation

| | *Major and medium systems in British India, 1902–03* | *Major, medium and multi-purpose irrigation projects in India* | | *Major and medium irrigation systems in India, 2001* |
|---|---|---|---|---|
| | | 1977–1978 | 1986–1987 | |
| 1 Source | Burton Buckley 1905 | Vaidyanathan Committee Report (GoI 1992) | | CWC 2006 |
| 2 Capital investment in major and medium projects (nominal) | £ 30 million | Rs 3004 crores | Rs 26014 crores[6] | Rs 295,000 crores |
| 3 Area irrigated by all government schemes (m ha) | 7.4 | 18.75 | 25.33[7] | 18 |
| 4 Water fees collected as a percentage of capital investment | 10 | 1.43 | 0.3[8] | 0.2 |
| 5 Value of crops irrigated as a percentage of capital investment | 87 | NA | NA | 18.3[9] |
| 6 Water fees collected as a percentage of value of crops irrigated | 11 | NA | 2[10] | 1.2 |
| 7 Water fee collected as a percentage of working expenses | 280 | 45 | 20[11] | 7.9 |
| 8 Maintenance expenditure as a percentage of working expenditure | 53 | 42 | 38 | 34 |
| 9 Maintenance expenditure as percentage of capital investment | 2.6 | NA | NA | 0.95 |

Source: Shah *et al.* 2012

pressure on land today, intensive cultivation has been the key livelihood strategy for small farming households, in particular, the rice growing areas of Asia. Today, however, farmers everywhere want to diversify their land use to high value farming system as a pathway to agricultural growth. Naturally, irrigation systems designed for rice cultivation are

*Table 8.3* Canal Irrigation Contingencies: Then and Now

| | *Then* | *Now* |
|---|---|---|
| Nature of state | Hard state and strong authority structures with deep presence in rural society | Soft state and weak authority structures with thin administrative presence |
| | Land revenue the key source of state income; and public irrigation a commercial enterprise | Land revenue insignificant for the state; public irrigation |
| Nature of society | Forced labour was common | Forced labour is uncommon |
| | Low demographic pressure on farm land made extensive farming viable | High demographic pressure encourages intensive land use |
| | Most Asian irrigation systems irrigated rice | Irrigation systems support diversified cropping patterns |
| Institutions | No private land ownership with farmers | Farmers have secure ownership rights on land |
| Technology | Well irrigation was laborious and costly | Well irrigation is easy and, thanks to power and other subsidies, relatively cheap |

Source: Shah *et al.* 2012

today unable to offer farmers the level of services they need for their diversified cropping pattern. Agrarian institutions also supported communally managed canal irrigation under the authority of strong states and local overlords in the past because peasants seldom owned the land that they were cultivating. Local leaders and the state enjoyed greater power to enforce discipline and order and control the anarchy inherent in surface water distribution. With farmers having secure private ownership right on their lands, imposing discipline and controlling anarchy are harder today than ever in the past.

By far the most important difference is in the irrigation technology (Shah 2009). Development of tubewell technology and availability of affordable mechanized pumps and pipes has made private irrigation a powerful and widely preferred alternative to flow/canal irrigation systems. There used to be practices in many Indian irrigation systems where farmers routinely used to bribe irrigation managers to provide them service of required level (Wade and Chambers 1980). Today, with proliferation of tubewells in canal command, irrigation managers have almost lost their power of rent-seeking.

This comparative perspective of the socio-political environment in which irrigation systems functioned in the past and do today suggests that their performance has a great deal to do with their external task environment. In contrast, most initiatives to improve canal irrigation performance have focused on changing the agency-farmer-system interaction with little regard for the external task environment. We need, therefore, to work with a broader hypothesis to explain the factors that determine the performance of irrigation systems.

In organization theory, a widely accepted proposition, known as contingency theory, suggests there is no 'silver bullet' to improve the working of any organization. Applied to our problem, it suggests that there is no best way to organize and manage a canal irrigation system or to improve its performance. Instead, the optimal course of action is contingent upon its internal and external situation.

A reading of the current state of Asian irrigation suggests clusters of contingencies that define the external task environment of canal irrigation systems in different parts of Asia. Irrigation systems in China, North Korea and Myanmar face totally different contingencies compared to irrigation systems in central Asia or in peninsular India; and those in high-income Malaysia face an altogether different set of contingencies that is encouraging it to revert to the estate mode of irrigation agriculture, somewhat similar to what was practised in colonial Africa. There is thus no point in comparing the performance of an irrigation system in one cluster with that in another, though comparative performance analysis within clusters may make sense if key contingencies were identified and factored in properly. The strategies for improving the performance of irrigation systems under these different 'contingency clusters' – as well as the notion of management performance itself – have to be defined in a context-specific framework simply because what would work under one 'contingency cluster' is unlikely to work in another. Similarly, there is no 'silver bullet' that can revitalize canal irrigation throughout Asia at one fell swoop. The need is for a granular understanding of what are the internal and external context variables of irrigation systems in different socio-political settings so as to evolve a change management roadmap for each contingency cluster.

## 1. *Atomistic private tubewell irrigation as a dominant contingency*

Explosive growth in small-scale private tubewell irrigation has emerged as the dominant contingency facing canal irrigation on which its managers have little control. The relationship between groundwater development and canal irrigation in India has evolved in three distinct phases.

### *Phase 1, 1850–1970: surface irrigation drives out groundwater irrigation*

Around 1900, R. C. Dutt laid out the over-arching logic of Indian irrigation:

> Every province in India has its distinct irrigation requirements. In the alluvial basins of the Ganges and the Indus, the most suitable irrigation works are canals from these rivers; while away from the rivers, wells are the most suitable. In Bengal, with its copious rainfall, shallow ponds are the most suitable works, and these were numerous in the olden times, sometimes of very large dimensions. In Madras and Southern India, where the soil is undulating and the underlying rock retains the water, the most suitable irrigation works are reservoirs made by putting up large embankments and thus impounding the water descending from hill slopes. Such were the old reservoirs of Madras.
>
> (Dutt 1904: Vol. II, 119)

Right up to the mid-1960s, Indian irrigation lived up to this imagery. For centuries, the use of well irrigation was limited by the laborious human and animal driven technologies. The introduction of the Persian Wheel (*sakiya*, or *rahat*) by West Asians to northern India's peasantry hastened the spread of well irrigation (Hardiman 1998). Lifting water through the Persian Wheel became popular in many northern and western parts of Colonial India (Islam 1997; Habib 1999).

In colonial India, gravity flow from surface storages or rivers and streams always drove out well irrigation which, besides being laborious and time consuming, could cover only a small area. In undivided Punjab, with frenzied canal construction during the 19th and early 20th century, the area irrigated by wells declined from 1.86 million ha in 1868–1869 to 1.54 million ha in 1918–1919 to about 1.42 million ha in 1926–1927 (Randhawa 1983). Elizabeth Whitcombe estimated that in 1860, some 3 million to 4 million acres – one-seventh of the cultivated land in Oudh (present western Uttar Pradesh) – was irrigated by shallow earthen wells. But with the onset of the Ganga canal, W.A. Forbes in 1866 lamented that the inroad of canals had left most wells in disuse and that well sinking was 'now almost entirely abandoned' (Whitcombe 1971: 70). This trend continued even as independent India and Pakistan began building new dams and canal systems after 1947. The propensity of canals to crowd out wells created environmental crises in many parts, thanks to water-logging and secondary salinization. Amritsar's groundwater levels rose so high after canal irrigation that the town got depopulated in the early years of 20th century (Randhawa 1983). Much thinking began to figure ways to use tubewells as vertical drains in canal commands. Indeed, much research on design of tubewell strainers took place precisely to overcome the problem of water-logging in canal commands of Punjab (CBIP 1992). Yet, canal managers remained suspicious of wells within their commands since well-irrigators claimed exemption from payment of irrigation fees and betterment levies.

### *Phase 2, 1965–1990: groundwater development fosters conjunctive use in canal commands*

In a uniquely South Asian phenomenon, the adoption of surface irrigation at the expense of wells has been reversed since around 1965, with rapid spread of pump irrigation in many Indian canal and tank commands. In a World Bank sponsored study of 16 surface irrigation systems around the world, the only three that had substantial groundwater irrigation in their commands were all Indian systems (Burt and Styles 1999). Suspicious of booming well irrigation, canal managers actively discouraged wells in canal commands during the 1960s and 1970s, but as Vaidyanathan (1996: 187) showed for the Lower Bhavani project in Tamil Nadu, 'the enforcement was practically abandoned'. It was only when benefits of conjunctive use of ground and surface water began to get noticed that official thinking began to change. Researchers like Dhawan (Dhawan and Satya Sai 1988) considered the recharge of wells by canal irrigation to be a major benefit of canal projects, and Palanisami and Ranganathan (2004) showed the same benefits in the tank commands of Tamil Nadu. Water logging and secondary salinization had emerged as serious problems in many canal commands in India and Pakistan. Normally, such problems are avoided by constructing expensive drainage systems which South Asian governments often avoid for lack of resources. With World Bank support, Pakistan established the famous SCARP tubewell programme to use public tubewells as vertical drains as also to augment tail end water supplies in canals during the 1950s. This was a resounding failure primarily because management of government tubewells in bureaucratic format just did not work, as was found with public tubewell programmes in many Indian states (Steenbergen and Oliemans 1997). However, the boom in private tubewells that got subsequently catalysed achieved conjunctive use better than the failed SCARP programme (World Bank 2005). In the Indian Punjab, too, growth in tubewell irrigation during the 1960s and 1970s helped a great deal in arresting and reversing the water-logging tendencies that the Bhakra and Pong dams had created (Dhawan and Satya Sai 1988). Soon, however, concerns about water-logging were eased and in some places were replaced by groundwater depletion issues (Dhawan 1995). During the 1970s and 1980s, then, the rise of groundwater irrigation in canal commands appeared to be an unalloyed boon, as it proved a perfect substitute for lateral drainage systems that elsewhere use up much land and capital.

### *Phase 3, post 1990: groundwater boom and shrinking canal commands*

However, throughout South Asia, by around 1990, groundwater pumping began to replace gravity flow irrigation. The drivers were in three clusters. First, deteriorating public irrigation system soon after Independence; second, inequity in supply of water between head (which used substantially more water by raising water intensive crops like paddy, banana and sugarcane) and tail end areas (which starved for water); third, the rise of the groundwater boom insulated farmers in peripheral command from deteriorating system management and growing head-tail inequality.

The general outcome was the hastening of the deceleration in the performance of surface irrigation structures of all kinds. Flow irrigation from tanks, used for centuries to grow rice, especially in southern India, too began rapidly shrinking with growing profusion of wells in tank commands. Janakarajan and Moench (2006) found a strong positive correlation between the rapid growth of well irrigation and the decay of tanks. In Tamil Nadu, the heartland of tank irrigation, between 1960 and 2000, flow-irrigated area from tanks fell by a third, from 940,000 to 601,000 ha (Palanisami and Ranganathan 2004). According to Selvarajan (2002), Andhra Pradesh, Tamil Nadu, Karnataka and Orissa, which together accounted for 60 per cent of India's tank-irrigated area, lost about 37 per cent of their tank-irrigated area from 1965 to 2000.

Soon, large canal systems began going the way of the tanks. In the Bhakra command on the Indian side, canal irrigation at first drove out wells; however, especially since 1990, the trend has been reversed

(Dharmadhikari 2005), and now, 75 per cent of all irrigated areas in the Indian Punjab depend upon well and tubewell irrigation (Singh 2006: citing a Government of Punjab 2005 document).[13] Even the Punjab government's 2005 State of the Environment Report lamented a reduction of 36 per cent in the canal irrigation area since 1990 (PSCST 2005). According to Selvarajan (2002), Uttar Pradesh, Andhra Pradesh, Bihar, Orissa and Tamil Nadu – which account for 45 per cent of India's net irrigated area – all witnessed an absolute decline in canal-irrigated areas but large increases in pump irrigation from wells between 1985 and 2000. During the five-year period from 1997–1998 to 2002–2003, canal-irrigated area in Gujarat fell 46 per cent, from 0.78 million ha to 0.42 million ha.[14]

The year 1990 seems to be a watershed one; between 1990 and 2004, India invested well over INR 130,000 crore (US $ 28.8 billion at US $ = INR 45) on constructing new canal irrigation systems and modernizing old ones but got 3 million ha *less* canal irrigated area in return. In Pakistan, the story has been no different: areas irrigated with gravity flow from canals fell by more than 1 million ha – 13.3 per cent – between 1980–1981 and 2002–2003. Many argue that what tubewells pump is canal seepage. That may be; the point is that the *mode* of delivering water to crops – and the whole regime tied to it – is changing from flow to lift, collective to individual, public to private, formal to informal.

## 2. *Reconfigured river basins: planners propose, pumpers dispose*

Large surface irrigation projects in India take a long time between conception and completion, commonly 15 to 30 years and often more. Until the mid-1960s, planners could be reasonably confident that the hydraulic mosaic of the river basin or sub-basin would remain largely unchanged.while the plans were being implemented.

But, the change in this state of affairs explains a significant part of the underperformance of many surface irrigation projects in India. We can view this change by considering the development trajectory of a river basin in four phases over which Indian irrigation has evolved over 200 years. In phase 1 of a river basin in predevelopment state, one found some irrigated agriculture along the banks of the river and tributaries upstream. While the colonial government viewed canal irrigation investment as an opportunity to combine 'the interests of charity and the interests of commerce' (Whitcombe 2005: 677), the government of independent India viewed canal irrigation as an investment in agricultural growth, food security and poverty alleviation. Many new irrigation systems got planned to transform a hitherto dry area into a prosperous command area (Daines and Pawar 1987). This was phase 2 of the evolution of the river basin.

In India of the late 20th century, however, a third phase has begun in which a groundwater boom entered. Pockets of groundwater irrigation emerged upstream of the reservoir as well as in the proposed command area. Lifting directly from the river and tributaries also added to growth in intensive irrigation along the banks. In numerous small and medium surface irrigation systems throughout India, pump irrigation development upstream can make dams useless in most seasons; the reservoirs fill only in years of exceptionally good rainfall in the catchment areas.[15]

Even the planning of mega projects now is not safe from uncontrolled pump irrigation expansion. The Sardar Sarovar Dam on the Narmada – and the entire hydraulic infrastructure below it – is designed based on the annual allocation of 11 $km^3$ of water to Gujarat by the Narmada tribunal in 1978. Recent studies have shown that pump irrigation development upstream of the dam has increased annual consumptive use of groundwater by about 5 $km^3$ during this period (Ranade 2005; Kumar *et al.* 2005). Singh, Kumar and Ghosh (2005: 11) report that 'there are hundreds of thousands of individual farmers who are lifting water directly from the river'.

Much the same result follows when farmers upstream pump from groundwater instead of from rivers and canals. Growth in well irrigation in the upper Krishna basin, mostly Maharashtra, reduced the runoff coefficient by a third – from 0.22 to 0.15 between 1971–1974 and 1996–2000 – and contributed around half of the 46 per cent decline in the inflows into the downstream Sri Sailam reservoir in Andhra Pradesh, from 56 to 30.4 $km^3$, during that period (Biggs *et al.* 2007). Unlike the Narmada tribunal, the Bachawat tribunal on the sharing of the Krishna waters among Maharashtra, Karnataka and Andhra Pradesh stipulated that 'the use of underground water shall not be reckoned as the use of the water of river Krishna' (Government of India and KWDT 1973, 1976). In 1969, when the tribunal gave its award, the provision seemed inconsequential enough; 30 years later, however, runaway expansion in groundwater irrigation had defeated the spirit of the award.[16]

In phase 4 of the reconfiguration of many Indian river basins, reservoir inflows got further reduced as pump irrigators in catchment areas take to rainwater harvesting and groundwater recharge in a big way to sustain their irrigation agriculture against declining groundwater availability. Modifying dugwells for localized rainwater recharge is becoming increasingly common in many hard-rock aquifer areas. In Saurashtra and Kutch regions of Gujarat and many areas in Madhya Pradesh and Rajasthan, village communities built a cascade of small check structures on streams and rivulets to improve recharge. Large-scale, government-financed watershed treatment programmes also do much for *in situ* water harvesting and recharge, besides generating local employment. Water harvesting and groundwater recharge on a large-scale make pump irrigation sustainable in catchment areas and farming more drought resilient. But it reduces surface water flows all along the basin. Siltation has so far been considered the prime enemy of reservoirs; now, upstream water harvesting and groundwater recharge efforts threaten inflow into large reservoirs. Just 1 million tubewells[17] irrigating 2 million to 2.5 million ha and supported by decentralized recharge structures upstream of the Sardar Sarovar Dam can use up all 11 $km^3$ of Gujarat's share of Narmada water. And considering that India has added some 800,000 new groundwater wells every year over the 1990–2000 period, there is little doubt that pump irrigation is cannibalizing canal irrigation. That atomistic irrigation development in upstream catchments is significant, as evident in the hype that the Bharatiya Janata Party created in 2017 Gujarat assembly elections by accusing Ashok Gehlot, a former Congress chief minister, of promoting large-scale water harvesting and well irrigation in the catchment of the Mahi river so that Gujarat's *Sujalam Sufalam* project was undermined.[18]

### *3. Future of canal irrigation in India: reform or morph*

Today, within and outside canal commands, groundwater wells are the chief source of delivering water to crops. Ever since the 1970s when the value of wells as 'vertical drains' was recognized in canal commands, the discourse centred around integrating them in canal system management (Shah 1993: Chapter 8). That stage seems passé; the need now is to integrate canal systems into the groundwater irrigation economy. The major impediment to this is the failure of irrigation systems to spread surface water over larger areas for extensive, protective irrigation – which was the original design goal of many colonial and post-colonial systems that never got achieved.

In a typical Indian surface irrigation system's command, one commonly finds intensive canal irrigation of water-loving crops like rice, banana and sugarcane. These doubly benefit from abundance of ground as well as surface water. But this is a fraction of the area the system was originally designed to cover. There is an outer command where some canal water reaches at some time, but groundwater wells are the mainstay of irrigated agriculture where there is huge mismatch between recharge and extraction. Outside the outer command lie pure groundwater irrigated areas where farmers' constant demand is for energy subsidies.

A possible alternative scenario is of conjunctive management of surface and groundwater in the design command. In the process, canal deliveries on their own will prove insufficient for maturing crops but will recharge groundwater over a larger area. Is a move in this direction possible or likely? That depends on what path India's canal irrigation will take in the future, over say a 25-year time horizon. Many scenarios are possible; but I will explore here four, including the one in which nothing happens to change course.

*Business-as-usual scenario*

This is the most likely scenario and assumes that construction and management of canal irrigation projects will continue over the coming 25 years pretty much as they have done in the past 25. This will imply, among other things, that:

- Central and state governments will continue to construct and rehabilitate large public irrigation projects despite their poor track record of performance.
- Similarly, multi-lateral lenders will continue to fund new irrigation projects as well as rehabilitation/modernization projects that are attractive for making large loans that governments are happy to receive.
- Poor performance of irrigation systems will continue to be blamed on the anarchy below the outlet; despite being unsuccessful, PIM/IMT will continue to be peddled as blanket solutions.
- Since the best sites are already used up, new projects will be increasingly costly and unviable.
- To justify unviable projects, planners will continue to over-estimate the command area[19] and assume unrealistic irrigation duty.
- Political leaders will continue to score electoral brownie points in initiating and constructing grandiose projects, without paying much attention to the stringent institutional and management requirements.
- Irrigation departments will continue to remain supply-driven, construction-oriented with little interest in management of systems to achieve full potential.

- Even if bureaucracies were motivated and capacitated, canal irrigation performance is difficult to measure and monitor when land revenue and water fee collection have been trivialized.
- In some states, irrigation departments will continue to stagnate or even shrink in size; states like Gujarat have not hired an irrigation engineer in 20 years.
- Where irrigation departments are growing, with rising government salaries and stagnant irrigation fee collection, establishment costs will increase, with very little left for operation and maintenance.
- In overall terms, the public irrigation in India may continue with low level equilibrium; overall, more and more money invested will keep giving India less and less canal irrigation as has happened since 1991.
- The key socio-economic benefits of such projects – often more than gravity-fed irrigated areas – will be in terms of recharging the aquifers in the areas where they can reach water by gravity flow and feeding urban water supply schemes.

### EXPANDING THE AREA UNDER CONJUNCTIVE MANAGEMENT OF SURFACE AND GROUNDWATER

India's canal systems are designed to mobilize and move around 300 Billion Cubic Metre (BCM) of water in a normal year. While the Central Water Commission (CWC) estimates that public systems irrigate some 30 million ha at a gross duty of 10,000 $m^3$/ha at source, the land-use survey as well as the Minor Irrigation Census data shows that 14–15 million ha are irrigated by public canals, at 20,000 $m^3$/ha. In comparison, 230 BCM of groundwater storage gives India a gross irrigated area of 35.2 Mha according to LUS (land-use statistics) and 53 Mha according to the MIC (Minor Irrigation Census). Thus, the groundwater storage India needs to support an irrigated hectare is between 4300 and 6600 $m^3$/ha which is a quarter or a third of surface storage/hectare. And dwindling groundwater storage – evident in falling groundwater levels around the country – is India's central water and energy challenge.

This challenge can be substantially met by spreading canal waters on much larger areas to support groundwater recharge/irrigation. Around the world, a key problem in achieving such conjunctive use is the reluctance of canal irrigators to invest in groundwater wells. In the India (and Pakistan) of today, this is no longer a problem due to the vast prevalence of wells and tubewells in the canal commands.

Modernization of many canal irrigation projects aimed at reversing the degeneration trend by 'restoring derelict systems to their original potential', ended up spending huge sums on construction and little on management improvement and capacity building. Improving the management of main systems holds the key to unlocking value in India's public irrigation (Wade and Chambers 1980). But doing this requires reform and revitalization of irrigation bureaucracies more than PIM/IMT and spending billions on reconstruction.

### BUILDING ON FARMER MODIFICATIONS TO IMPROVE SYSTEM IMPACTS

Farmers' dissatisfaction with irrigation systems arises from three sources: (1) in its original planning, the level of irrigation service the system was designed to offer was less than what farmers expected at that time; (2) over time, the level of service actually offered has declined due to poor O&M, farmer vandalism, break-down of rules, etc.; (3) because of myriad external changes, farmers today demand a higher level of irrigation service than what they expected when the system was originally commissioned. Since irrigation managers make no effort to redress these issues, those farmers who can, modify or adapt the system to better meet their needs. Irrigation managers often view these adaptations as 'unauthorized'; but these can also be viewed as signals that farmers provide about an irrigation management scheme in which they will happily participate.

A sample of the many ways in which Indian farmers have done this is listed in Table 8.4. Regardless of whether system managers support these or not, these are emerging and playing a major role in water distribution in many systems. This is the closest that canal irrigation can come to mimicking the flexible, on-demand groundwater irrigation. The lesson for the system managers is to look for opportunities in such farmer adaptation and incorporate these into the system itself. The Indira Gandhi Nahar system in Rajasthan formally encourages and subsidizes farmers to construct farm ponds *(diggis)* to which canal water is delivered fortnightly for irrigation on demand. Another is the practice of using canal water to fill up tanks in Gujarat and system tanks in Tamil Nadu.

### REDESIGNING IRRIGATION PROJECTS AS HYBRID SYSTEMS WITH PUBLIC PRIVATE PARTNERSHIPS

Building on farmer adaptations is beneficial in incremental terms, but it is still patchwork. In new systems or systems under modernization,

*Table 8.4* Farmer Modifications and Adaptations of Canal Systems to Serve Their Needs

| # | *System modification and adaptation* | *Examples* | *How widespread is this in India?* | *Extent of farmer enterprise and investment* | *Precondition for farmer enterprise and investment* | *Presence of irrigation service institutions* |
|---|---|---|---|---|---|---|
| 1 | Classical Canal Irrigation: The system operates as designed; wells driven out by canals | Mahi in the early 1970s;[20] Bhakra command in the 1950s | Not at all | Negative | | Nil |
| 2 | Main system delivers water in farm ponds (diggis) fortnightly | Indira Gandhi canal, Rajasthan[21] | Not very | Low; individual | Canal supply to farm ponds | Nil |
| 3 | Canals water is used by farmers to fill up large open wells | Lower Bhavani system | Tamil Nadu | High | Sharing scarce canal water | WUAs |
| 3 | Main system delivers water in village ponds; farmers irrigate from ponds by gravity or lift | Sardar Sarovar; System; system tanks in South India | Some | Low; individual | Tanks replenished regularly | Irrigation Service Markets (ISM) |
| 4 | Main system delivers water into canals; farmers/groups lift and irrigate | Mahi system;[22] Upper Krishna;[23] Sardar Sarovar command[24] | Widespread throughout India | Substantial; private and co-operative | Perennial canals run at full-supply level (FSL) | High to very high presence of ISMs |
| 5 | Main system delivers volumetric water supply to a contractor allocates to farmers and collect water fees | Several systems in China[25] | This model is spreading in China | Substantial, private | Strong village authority backing the arrangement | High presence of ISMs |
| 5 | Main system recharges the aquifers; much irrigation takes place through tubewells | Bhakra;[26] Mahi;[27] Upper Krishna basin[28] Tamil Nadu[29] | Very, very widespread | Substantial, mostly private | Alluvial aquifers, unlined canals | High to very high presence of ISMs |
| 6 | Irrigation tanks support well irrigation in their command | Tamil Nadu;[30] AP[31] Karnataka, Eastern Rajasthan[32] | Very, very widespread | Substantial, mostly private | None | Some presence of ISMs |
| 7 | Irrigation tanks converted into percolation tanks | Much of Tamil Nadu;[33] Rayalaseema[34] in Andhra Pradesh | Rapidly spreading in South India | Substantial, mostly private | Consensus among tank irrigators | Some to high presence of ISMs |

Source: Author

a superior alternative may be to anticipate farmer enterprise and design hybrid systems that use entrepreneurial energies of private farmers or their organizations to take over the messiest task of water distribution while the agency confines its role to bulk water deliveries. The scenario then involves enlisting the water scavenging 'pump irrigation anarchy' as a comrade-in-arms and leverage it to enhance their reach and performance. A case for doing this in the Sardar Sarovar Project (SSP) in Gujarat has already been made. This was first rejected by a government-appointed Expert Committee (Shah *et al.* 2010) but is now under implementation in a modified form which is unlikely to work as well as the original suggestion. Another good example is also provided by developments in the upper Krishna basin in Maharashtra. In 1976, the Bachawat Award allocated 560 TMC ft of water to Maharashtra, which the state had to develop by 2000. Maharashtra was not able to build reservoirs and canal networks needed to use this water; by 1996, it had constructed only 385 TMC ft of storage and little by way of canal network in the Krishna basin. Therefore, the government first began allowing farmers to lift water from the Krishna and its tributaries. But this only encouraged small-scale private lift schemes, most of which could not convey water longer than 1–1.5 km distance. In 1972, only 200 private and co-operative lift schemes were operating in Maharashtra. As pressure to utilize the water mounted, the government adopted a far more pro-active posture towards lift irrigation schemes. It introduced a capital cost subsidy for irrigation co-operatives and also facilitated bank finance from nationalized and co-operative banks. Most importantly, the Irrigation Department (ID) constructed a series of Kolhapur Type (KT) weirs across many tributaries of the Krishna, to use them as storages for lift irrigation schemes. Each scheme has to be approved by the ID, whereupon it qualifies for an electricity connection and bank finance. Each scheme also has to pay irrigation fees to the ID for the actual area irrigated; it also has to pay the electricity charges to the State Electricity Board at prevailing rates for agricultural use. Between December and June each year, the ID implements a fortnightly schedule of water releases to fill up the dykes, starting with the last dyke first. This ensures that lift schemes will have access to reliable water supply during the irrigation season. A good example of the partnership between irrigation department and irrigation co-operatives is the Radhanagari project (constructed by Shahuji Maharaj in 1916) that serves 91 villages in Kolhapur district studied by Choudhury and Kher (2006), Padhiyari (2006) and Chandra and Sudhir (2010). If these studies are any guide, Radhanagari has performed better than government-managed gravity canal systems in all respects, in terms of farmer contribution to investment and operating costs, equitable water distribution, water availability on demand, payment of water and electricity charges, area irrigated as compared to planned, and the level of farmer satisfaction with irrigation service provided.

Radhanagari may appear an exception; this is not so. According to Government of India's Minor Irrigation Census III, in 2000–2001, Maharashtra had some 100,000 such schemes in operation for lifting and piped distribution of surface water, mostly in the Upper Krishna basin. Over 20,000 of these were owned and operated by farmer groups and co-operatives. These lifted water from rivers and streams and transported it mostly by buried pipelines to up to 30 km from source. Remarkably, none of these were operated by a government agency. Over 90 per cent of Maharashtra's lift schemes were constructed by farmers from their own funds and bank finance, with the present value of aggregate investment being around Rs 5,000 crore. Over 90 per cent schemes used electric pumps to lift water and 70 per cent had buried pipeline network for water distribution. Total horsepower of pumps installed in these schemes was around 590,000, equivalent to 440 MW, even though all the schemes involved a sizeable lift ranging from 20 metres to 185 metres. These irrigated a gross area of some 350,000 ha (including sugarcane area of over 100,000 ha). Maharashtra's lift irrigation schemes likely employed over 100,000 workers as *pankhyas* (water managers), if we count the fact that the 80,000 families operating private lift schemes had at least one family member each devoted full-time to work on the scheme operation.

Wherever canals offer reliable water supplies, private investors have invested in turning water into 'irrigation service' that mimics on-demand groundwater irrigation. At present, such private pump and pipe systems on canals are considered 'unauthorized', and their owners, 'water thieves'. But these can also be viewed as partners in redesigning canal systems as hybrid systems in which the agency promises to deliver bulk water at, say, a minor level, along a predetermined schedule and licenced ISPs (irrigation service providers), paying a volumetric water charge, assuming the responsibility of distributing water to their farmer-customers through a buried pipe network. Such hybrid systems involving piped distribution can have several advantages over the conventional gravity flow systems:

- Private partners take up a large part of the capital investment of a canal.
- Buried pipe distribution system faces much less 'right-of-the-way' problem that canals face.

- Piped distribution saves land used up for sub-minors and field-channels.
- Piped distribution minimizes water-logging.
- Piped distribution is considered too costly in comparison to earthen canals but is actually cost-effective if land required for canals is valued at market price.
- Piped distribution can prevent evaporation loss.
- Piped water delivery from canals mimics tubewell irrigation and raises productivity of irrigation water because users pay a higher price for the irrigation service.
- Done right, piped distribution can help spread canal water over a much larger area.
- Piped distribution can put into a place a regime of conjunctive use of ground and surface water.
- While pipelining is more energy-intensive compared to gravity canals, if managed well, it can significantly improve the overall farm energy balance by spreading surface water over a larger area, reducing the need for groundwater pumping, by integrating micro-irrigation technologies.
- Lastly, while farmer participation in canal irrigation management is found hard to come by, under such a hybrid PPP model, farmer participation in irrigation management begins at the construction stage itself (Shah *et al.* 2010).

If the Maharashtra experience is any guide, inviting farmers to participate in creating such hybrid systems is not difficult. To promote farmer investments in piped distribution in a planned and systematic manner, all that agencies need to do is the following: (1) not only recognize and legalize but also register and incentivize the lifting of water from canal systems; (2) make firm commitments during the irrigation season each year; (3) encourage existing tubewell owners to convert their electricity connections to canal lift; (4) offer electricity connections to approved piped distribution schemes planned by farmers, co-operatives and producer companies; (5) involve institutional financial agencies in providing finance to support farmer co-operatives for their investments in pumps and pipeline systems; (6) subsidize capital costs of approved projects in a manner that minimizes perverse incentives; (7) register each pipeline system and ensure that it pays irrigation fee for all the land irrigated with canal water; and (8) modify the traditional idea of 'irrigation command' to include any farming community that is willing to invest in piped distribution and pay a volumetric water charge.

## Concluding note

Indian thinking on designing and managing canal irrigation today has emerged out of the colonial irrigation experience and is unable to break out of the colonial mode to respond to the rapidly changing reality. The then authoritarian state used force to create order and enforce rules in irrigation commands where farmers had no alternative to gravity flow irrigation.

The reality of India's public irrigation systems is vastly different today; the state's budgetary stake in land revenue is minimal, as is the irrigation fee farmers are expected to pay. The vast colonial revenue and irrigation bureaucracy at local levels is replaced by an institutional vacuum. Strong colonial authority structures have given way to competitive populist party politics. Population pressure on farmlands is higher than ever before; India's small holder is under pressure to intensify the use of his shrinking land holding, which he can do with year-round groundwater irrigation more easily than with seasonal canal or tank water. Over time, the primary role canals and tanks play is of sustaining a booming groundwater economy through groundwater recharge. The key criterion for assessing the performance of canal and tank irrigation ought not to be the actual area commanded, but the area on which it sustains conjunctive use of ground and surface water. But India's public irrigation systems neither monitor the 'conjunctive management area' nor count it as a performance benchmark. In enlarging the 'conjunctive management areas' – by spreading canal waters over as large an area as possible – lies a vast scope for unlocking value in India's canal irrigation. This requires a transformation in the way agencies manage canal systems. How likely is such transformation to occur?

Applying Kurt Levin's force-field analysis[35] would suggest that big change for the better in the management of India's public irrigation will occur when drivers of change will outweigh the forces that restrain change. For the moment, the latter far outweigh the former and will make 'business-as-usual' (outlined previously) the most likely scenario. Indeed, one can find hardly any notable 'driver' that would create pressure for a major change programme in the public irrigation sector. Governments and donors have kept throwing good money after bad, and they will keep doing so regardless of what past investments delivered or failed to deliver. If a battery of 'change drivers' were to be created, the work would need to begin by creating a credible information and a monitoring system about how public irrigation systems are performing against their original designs, both in terms of 'conjunctive management area' they support, and vis-à-vis each other. In business, measuring performance is generally considered essential to managing it. This seems nowhere truer than in the public irrigation business in India today.

## Notes

1 The author is grateful to the Planning Commission, Government of India for commissioning a report on which this chapter is based. The chapter also benefited from learnings from a World Bank assignment to the International Water Management Institute and support from IWMI-Tata Water Policy Program.
2 INR = Indian Rupees
3 Herve 1998
4 Govardhan and Kulkarni 2014
5 I am grateful to Kai Wegerich for helping me develop this comparative picture.
6 GoI 1992: Annexure 1.5
7 GoI 1992: Annexure 1.7-A
8 Computed using irrigation charges collected as in Table 2.6 in GoI 1992 as a percentage of capital investment in row 3.
9 Assuming 18 million ha of canal irrigated area growing crops worth Rs 30000/ha at 2000–2001 prices.
10 'The Irrigation Commission had suggested that water rates should be fixed at around 5 per cent of gross income for food crops and 12 per cent for cash crops. At present, the actual gross receipts per ha of area irrigated by major and medium projects is barely 2 per cent of the estimated gross output per ha of irrigated area, and less than 4 per cent of the difference between output per ha of irrigated and unirrigated areas' (GoI 1992: 2.25).
11 Computed from Table 2.6 in GoI 1992.
12 'all the various types of social indiscipline which manifest themselves by deficiencies in legislation and, in particular, law observance and enforcement, a widespread disobedience by public officials and, often, their collusion with powerful persons and groups . . . whose conduct they should regulate. Within the concept of the soft states belongs also corruption' (Myrdal 1970: 208).
13 Between 1990 and 2002, gross sown area in Punjab increased by 440,000 ha, but the area served by flow irrigation from canals fell by 589,000 while that served by tubewells soared by 837,000 (Down to Earth 2005).
14 See *Divya Bhaskar* 2007: 3.
15 Gidwani (2002) shows how well irrigation in upstream areas has been an old and foolproof device to sabotage surface water sharing agreements by analysing the disputes around Khari River in Gujarat.
16 An excellent account by Neelakantan (2003) of the socio-economic transformation in Chettipalayam, a Tamil Nadu hamlet, and its surrounding areas over the past 50 years offers a vivid case study of how the arrival of pump irrigation made short work of the original engineering and institutional design of a public irrigation project, including a long-defended

system of riparian rights. The same dynamic is described by Steenbergen (1995) to explore the decline of *karezes (qanats)* in Baluchistan.

17 Each is assumed to pump an average of 15,000 $m^3$ per year, and two-thirds of the pumped water is consumptively used.

18 Lad 2017

19 For example, the Sardar Sarovar Project is planned to irrigate 1.8 million ha on the assumption that the project will ration canal water at a delta of 53 cm/year. If we take the total water circulating in Indian canal systems as 300 BCM and divide it by the 17 m ha this irrigates, the storage per net ha irrigated comes to 17640 $m^3$. As a project representative of Indian canal irrigation sector, the SSP cannot command more than 0.55 million ha.

20 Shah 1993

21 Amarasinghe *et al.* 2008

22 Choudhury and Shah 2005

23 Lohar *et al.* 2006; Birari *et al.* 2003; Choudhury and Kher 2006; Padhiyari 2006

24 Talati and Shah 2004; Talati and Pandya 2007; Singhal and Patwari 2009

25 Shah, Giordano and Wang 2004; Wang *et al.* 2003

26 Dharmadhikari 2005; Down to Earth 2005

27 Shah 1993; Shah 2009; Kolavalli 1986

28 Venot 2008; Biggs *et al.* 2007

29 Sivasubramaniyan 2008

30 Palanisami and Easter 1991; Palanisami and Balasubramanian 1998

31 Rao 2003

32 Shah and Raju 2001

33 Palanisami 1995; Palanisami 2005

34 Rao 2003

35 Burnes and Cooke 2013

## References


Amarasinghe, U., S. Bhaduri, O. P. Singh and B. K. Anand. 2008. *Managing Unreliability of Canal Water: Case Study of Diggis in Rajasthan*. Colombo, Sri Lanka: International Water Management Institute.

Biggs, T. W., A. Gaur, C. A. Scott, P. Thenkabail, P. G. Rao, M. Krishna Gumma, S. K. Acharya, and H. Turral. 2007. 'Closing of the Krishna Basin: Irrigation, Streamflow Depletion and Macroscale Hydrology', Research Report 111. International Water Management Institute, Colombo, Sri Lanka.

Birari, K. S., D. S. Navadkar, D. V. Kasar, and M. S. Yadav. 2003. 'Cooperative Lift Irrigation Schemes for Sustainable Use of Water', *Indian Journal of Agricultural Economics*, July–September.

Blair, H. W. 1985. 'Reorienting Development Administration', *Journal of Development Studies*, 21(3): 449–457.

Buckley, R. B. 1905. *The Irrigation Works of India*. London: E. & F.N. Spon Ltd.

Burnes, Bernard and Cooke, Bill. 2013. 'Kurt Lewin's Field Theory: A Review and Re-evaluation', *International Journal of Management Reviews*, 15(4): 408–425, October.

Burt, C. and S. Styles. 1999. 'Modern Water Control and Management Practices in Irrigation: Impact on Performance', Water Reports No.119. Food and Agriculture Organization of the United Nations, Rome.

Central Board of Irrigation and Power (India). 1992. *History of Irrigation in Indus Basin* Publication 230. New Delhi: Government of India (GoI).

Central Water Commission. 2006. 'Financial Aspects of Medium and Major Projects', http://cwc.gov.in/main/webpages/publications.html (accessed on 28 May 2018).

Chandra, A. and C. Sudhir. 2010. A Study of Kolhapur Lift Irrigation Cooperatives', MTS Report, Institute of Rural Management, Anand.

Choudhury, N. and V. Kher. 2006. 'Public Private Partnership in Surface Water Irrigation: A Case of Kolhapur', IWMI-Tata Water Policy Program, Anand.

Choudhury, N. and Z. Shah. 2005. *Long Term Socio-Economic Impacts of Displacement: Case Study of Mahi Bajaj Sagar Dam*. Anand: IWMI-Tata Water Policy Program, Unpublished Report.

Daines, S. R. and J. R. Pawar. 1987. 'Economic Returns to Irrigation in India, SDR Research Groups Inc. & Development Group Inc', Report Prepared for U.S. Agency for International Development Mission to India, New Delhi.

Dharmadhikari, S. 2005. *Unravelling Bhakra: Assessing the Temple of Resurgent India*. Bhopal: Manthan Adhyayan Kendra.

Dhawan, B. D. 1995. *Groundwater Depletion, Land Degradation and Irrigated Agriculture in India*. New Delhi: Commonwealth Publishers.

Dhawan, B. D. and K. J. Satya Sai. 1988. 'Economic Linkages among Irrigation Sources: A Study of the Beneficial Role of Canal Seepage', *Indian Journal of Agricultural Economics*, 43(4): 569–579.

Divya Bhaskar. 2007. 'Ahmedabad Edition', 4 September, p. 3.

Down to Earth. 2005. 'The Lie of the Land', 31 May, pp. 36–38.

Dutt, R. 1904, reprint 1989. *The Economic History of India*, Volumes I and II. New Delhi: Government of India (GoI), Ministry of Information and Broadcasting.

Ertsen, M. W. 2007. The Development of Irrigation Design Schools or How History Structures Human Action', *Irrigation and Drainage*, 56: 1–19.

Gidwani, V. 2002. 'The Unbearable Modernity of "Development"? Canal Irrigation and Development Planning in Western India', *Progress in Planning*, 58(1): 1–80.

Govardhan, R. and G. R. Kulkarni. 2014. 'Waghad Project Level Water User Association – A Case Study', National Convention of Presidents of Water User Associations, organised by MoWR RD & GR. – India NPIM at Delhi, 7–8 November.

Government of India (GoI). 1992. *Report of the Committee on Pricing of Irrigation Water*. New Delhi: Planning Commission of India.

Government of India (GoI) and Krishna Water Disputes Tribunal (KWDT). 1973, 1976. *The Report and the Further Report of the Krishna Water Disputes Tribunal with the Decision*. New Delhi: Central Water Commission.

Habib, I. 1999. *The Agrarian System of Mughal India 1556–1707*. New Delhi: Oxford University Press.

Hardiman, D. 1998. 'Well Irrigation in Gujarat: Systems of Use, Hierarchies of Control', *Economic and Political Weekly*, 33(25): 1533–1544.

Islam, M. M. 1997. *Irrigation Agriculture and the Raj, Punjab, 1887–1947*. New Delhi: Manohar Books.

Janakarajan, S. and M. Moench. 2006. 'Are Wells a Potential Threat to Farmers' Well-Being? Case of Deteriorating Groundwater Irrigation in Tamil Nadu', *Economic and Political Weekly*, 41(37): 3977–3987.

Kolavalli, S. 1986. 'Economic Analysis of Conjunctive Use of Water: The Case of Mahi-Kadana Irrigation Project in Gujarat India', Ph.D. Thesis, Urbana IL: University of Illinois, Chapter 6, pp. 100–124.

Kumar, M. D., S. Ghosh, O. P. Singh, R. Ranade, and R. Ravindranath. 2005. 'Changes in Groundwater Ecology and Its Implications for Surface Flows: Studies from Narmada River Basin, Madhya Pradesh, India', Water Policy Research Highlight 25. IWMI-Tata Water Policy Program, Anand.

Lad, Mahesh. 2017. 'When Gujarat Govt. Wanted to Supply Water to North Gujarat, Ashok Gehlot had Vehemently Opposed it: Modi', *Desh Gujarat*, http://deshgujarat.com/2017/10/16/when-gujarat-govt-wanted-to-supply-water-to-north-gujarat-ashok-gehlot-had-opposed-it-modi/ (accessed on 28 May 2018).

Lohar, N. S., R. R. Mane, S. N. Patil, and M. B. Nichit. 2006. 'Comparative Economics of Lift Irrigation Schemes Operated in Kolhapur District of Western Maharashtra', *Indian Journal of Agricultural Economics*, July–September.

Myrdal, G. 1970. 'The "Soft State" in Underdeveloped Countries', in P. Streeten (ed.), *Unfashionable Economics: Essays in Honour of Lord Balogh*. London: Weidenfeld and Nicolson.

Neelakantan, S. 2003. 'A Gossipmonger's Revisit to Chettipalayam: Water Conflict and Social Change in Amaravathi Basin', Working Paper 182. Madras Institute of Development Studies, Chennai.

Oorthuizen, J. 2003. *Water, Works and Wages: The Everyday Politics of Irrigation Management Reform in the Philippines*. New Delhi: Orient Longman.

Padhiyari, H. K. 2006. 'Water Service Markets in Surface Irrigation Systems: Institutions and Socio-Economic Impact', Paper Presented at the *IWMI-Tata Annual Partners' Meet*, IWMI-Tata Water Policy Program, Anand, February 2005.

Palanisami, K. 1995. 'Hydro-Economic Integration and Conversion of Tanks into Percolation Ponds, CGWB Project Report', Tamil Nadu Agricultural University, Coimbatore.

Palanisami, K. 2005. 'Sustainable Management of Tank Irrigation Systems in South India', Working Paper Series No. 2. Afrasian Centre for Peace and Development Studies, Kyoto, Japan.

Palanisami, K. and R. Balasubramanian. 1998. 'Common Property and Private Prosperity: Tanks vs Private Wells in Tamil Nadu', *Indian Journal of Agricultural Economics*, 53(4), October–December.

Palanisami, K. and K. W. Easter. 1991. 'Hydro-economic Interaction in Tank Irrigation Systems', *Indian Journal of Agricultural Economics*, 46(2), April–June.

Palanisami, K. and C. R. Ranganathan. 2004. 'Value of Water in Tank (Surface) Irrigation Systems', Water Technology Centre, Tamil Nadu Agricultural University, Coimbatore.

Plusquellec, Herve. 1998. 'Modernization of Irrigation Systems and the Role of the World Bank', Paper Presented at ITIS V Workshop, Aurangabad, http://siteresources.worldbank.org/INTARD/841438111130534002/20434273/Herve.pdf (accessed on 25 October 2010).

Punjab State Council for Science and Technology (PSCST). 2005. 'State of the Environment, Punjab: 2005', Punjab State Council for Science and Technology, Chandigarh.

Ranade, R. 2005. "Out of Sight, Out of Mind": Absence of Groundwater in Water Allocation of Narmada Basin', *Economic and Political Weekly*, 40(21): 2172–2175.

Randhawa, M. S. 1983. *A History of Agriculture in India*, Volume III. New Delhi: Indian Council of Agricultural Research.

Rao, G. B. 2003. 'Oases of Rayalaseema: SPWD's Tank Restoration Program in Southern Andhra Pradesh', *Wastelands News*, 19(1): 64–72.

SANDRP. 2006. 'Accelerated Irrigation Benefit Program: Why It Is a Complete Misnomer: No Acceleration, Little Irrigation, Minuscule Benefits', *Dams, Rivers and People*, 4(7–8): 8–9.

Selvarajan, S. 2002. *Sustaining India's Irrigation Infrastructure*. Policy Brief 15. New Delhi: National Centre for Agricultural Economics and Policy Research.

Shah, T. 1993. *Groundwater Markets and Irrigation Development: Political Economy and Practical Policy*. Bombay: Oxford University Press.

Shah, T. 2009. *Taming the Anarchy: Groundwater Governance in South Asia*. Washington, DC: RFF Press.

Shah, T., M. Giordano and J. Wang. 2004. 'Irrigation Institutions in a Dynamic Economy: What is China Doing Differently from India?' *Economic and Political Weekly*, 39(31): 3452–3461.

Shah, T., B. V. Koppen, D. Merrey, M. D. Lange, and M. Samad. 2002. 'Institutional Alternatives in African Smallholder Irrigation: Lessons from International Experience with Irrigation Management Transfer', Research Report 60, Colombo, Sri Lanka: International Water Management Institute.

Shah, T., S. Krishnan, P. Hemant Kumar, S. Verma, A. Chandra, and C. Sudhir. 2010. 'A Case for Pipelining Water Distribution in the Narmada Irrigation System in Gujarat, India', Colombo: IWMI Working Paper 141.

Shah, T. and K. V. Raju. 2001. 'Rethinking Rehabilitation: Socio-Ecology of Tanks in Rajasthan, India', *Water Policy*, 3(6): 521–536.

Shah, Tushaar & Anwar, Arif & Amarasinghe, Upali & Thai Hoahn, Chu & Junna, Mohan & Molle, Francois & Mukherji, Aditi & Prathapar, Sanmugam & Suhardiman, Diana & Qureshi, Asad & Wegerich, Kai. (2012). *Applying Contingency Theory to Irrigation System Management in India 2.* Conference Paper, IWMI-TATA Water Policy Program, 2012.

Singh, O. P., M. D. Kumar and S. Ghosh. 2005. 'Changing Water Use Hydrology of Narmada River Basin: Implications for Basin Water Allocation', Water Policy Research Highlight 19. IWMI-Tata Water Policy Program, Anand.

Singh, S. 2006. 'Credit, Indebtedness and Farmer Suicides in Punjab: Some Missing Links', *Economic and Political Weekly*, 41(3): 3330–3331.

Singhal, N. and V. Patwari. 2009. 'Evolving Arrangements for Local Water Diversion-Delivery in SSP', MTS Report, Institute of Rural Management, Anand.

Sivasubramaniyan, K. 2008. 'Irrigation Management and Its Effect on Productivity Under Parambikulam Aliyar project in Tamil Nadu', Proceedings of the 7th Annual Meet of IWMI-Tata Water Policy Program, I1: 820–841. Hyderabad: International Water Management Institute.

Steenbergen, F. van. 1995. 'The Frontier Problem in Incipient Groundwater Management Regimes in Balochistan (Pakistan)', *Human Ecology*, 23(1): 53–74.

Steenbergen, F. van and W. Oliemans. 1997. 'Groundwater Resource Management in Pakistan', in A. Schrevel (ed.), *Groundwater Management: Sharing Responsibility for Open Access Resource: Proceedings of the First Wageningen Water Workshop, October 1997*, pp. 93–109. Special Report. The Netherlands: International Land Reclamation Institute.

Talati, J. and D. Pandya. 2007. 'Issues in Canal Infrastructure: Development and Canal Irrigation Management', *Economic and Political Weekly*, 42(33): 3422–3429.

Talati, J. and T. Shah. 2004. 'Institutional Vacuum in Sardar Sarovar Project: Framing "Rules-of-the-Game"', *Economic and Political Weekly*, 39(31): 3504–3509.

Vaidyanathan, A. 1996. 'Depletion of Groundwater: Some Issues', *Indian Journal of Agricultural Economics*, 51(1–2): 184–192.

Venot, J. P. 2008. 'Why and Where Are the Krishna Waters Disappearing?' *Economic and Political Weekly*, 43(6): 15–17.

Vermillion, D. 1996. *The Privatization and Self-Management of Irrigation: Final Report.* Colombo: International Irrigation Management Institute.

Wade, R. 1992. 'How to Make "Street Level" Bureaucracies Work Better: India and Korea', *IDS Bulletin*, 23: 51–54.

Wade, R. and R. Chambers. 1980. 'Managing the Main System: Canal Irrigation's Blind Spot', *Economic and Political Weekly*, 15(39): A107–112.

Wang, J., Z. Xu, J. Huang and S. Rozelle. 2003. 'Incentives in Water Management Reform: Assessing the Effect on Water Use, Production and Poverty in the Yellow River Basin', Chinese Council for Agricultural Policy (draft paper), Beijing.

Whitcombe, E. 1971. *Agrarian Conditions in Northern India*. Berkeley: University of California Press.

Whitcombe, E. 2005. 'Irrigation', in D. Kumar and M. Desai (eds.), *The Cambridge Economic History of India, c.1757–c.1970, Volume* 2, pp. 677–737. Hyderabad: Orient Longman.

World Bank. 2005. 'Pakistan – Country Water Resources Assistance Strategy: Water Economy Running Dry', Report 34081-IN. Agriculture and Rural Development Sector, South Asia Region. Washington, DC.

# 9 Out of balance

## Agricultural growth and groundwater depletion in two backward states of India

*P. S. Vijayshankar and Himanshu Kulkarni*

### 1. Introduction

It is by now well known that India is heavily dependent on groundwater for irrigation and drinking water (Shah 2009; World Bank 2010; MoA 2013). In the Indian sub-continent (which includes Bangladesh, India and Pakistan), annual groundwater use soared from about 10–20 km$^3$ before 1950 to 240–260 km$^3$ in 2009 (Shah 2009). Groundwater contributes about 65 per cent to India's net irrigated area (Kulkarni and Vijayshankar 2009; Vijayshankar, Kulkarni and Krishnan 2011) and more than 80 per cent of rural drinking water is sourced from groundwater. Much is written about India's unique groundwater story in terms of the increased vulnerability from over-extraction (Moench 1992; Macdonald *et al.* 1995; Shah 2009) and co-emergent issues of contamination (Susheela 2001; Kumar and Shah 2003; Krishnan 2009). With over 30 million wells and a crudely estimated 3 million springs, groundwater has often been the case of 'out of sight, out of mind': it has gone unnoticed in the shaping of many of India's policies. What seems more alarming is that groundwater crisis is now moving beyond the traditional Green Revolution belt of Northwest and South India and moving into the hitherto agriculturally low productivity states such as Rajasthan and Madhya Pradesh. These states seem to have adopted a growth path out of poverty, which appears to be pushing them in the direction of an environmental disaster similar to what the core Green Revolution areas experienced earlier.[1] Does this mean that there is an inevitable trade-off between agricultural growth and environmental quality? The question is all the more important because it is likely that elected governments in other high poverty states such as Uttar Pradesh, Bihar, Jharkhand and Odisha might soon start emulating Rajasthan and Madhya Pradesh in taking up aggressive farm support policies targeting groundwater extraction. Hence, we need to examine how an ecologically balanced growth path can be charted out for the high poverty regions of the country.

The rest of the chapter is organized as follows. Section 2 gives a snapshot picture of agricultural growth in Madhya Pradesh and Rajasthan. Section 3 highlights the role of groundwater irrigation in improving the rate of growth of these states. Section 4 discusses the status of groundwater resources and the emerging scenario of groundwater overuse there. Section 5 outlines the alternative approach that explores ways of combining growth with environmental stability. Section 6 summarizes the major conclusions of the chapter.

## 2. Agricultural growth in Rajasthan and Madhya Pradesh

It is now accepted that there has been an unmistakable turnaround growth in Indian agriculture between 2004 and 2014. The 1990s were not a good decade for Indian agriculture. The trend of slow growth and stagnation of the 1990s seems to have been somewhat reversed as the value of output from agriculture showed a growth rate close to 3.5 per cent in the 11th Plan period (2007–2012) (Planning Commission 2013; Chand and Parappurathu 2012). The reasons for this turnaround are listed in many ways: revival of capital investment in agriculture (mainly in the private sector), improved supply of key inputs such as seeds, fertilizers and electricity, shift in terms of trade in favour of agriculture, new technology, greater access to institutional credit etc. (Chand and Parappurathu 2012). What is remarkable about this reversal of trend is that growth has mainly taken place in states and crops which have hitherto been laggards in terms of agricultural performance. Thus, low productivity states with a sizeable rainfed agriculture segment and growing coarse cereals, pulses and oilseeds showed considerable growth dynamism between 2004–2005 and 2011–2012 (Planning Commission 2013).

It was during this period (2000–2010) that states such as Rajasthan and Madhya Pradesh moved into a high growth path (over 4 per cent per annum), which led to descriptions like ‘agricultural powerhouse’.

The livestock sector, which contributes to over one-third of the total value of production of agriculture in Rajasthan and MP respectively, also reported rates of growth of over 4 per cent. Since these are predominantly agrarian states, the slow growth of agriculture and allied activities has been one of the main reasons for endemic poverty and malnutrition. The recent spurt in growth may, therefore, have led to

*Table 9.1* Annual Rate of Growth of Gross State Domestic Product (GSDP) from Agriculture and Allied Activities, 1982–2012 (at constant 2004–2005 prices)

| | *1981–1982 to 1993–1994* | *1994–1995 to 1999–2000* | *2000–2001 to 2004–2005* | *2005–2006 to 2011–2012* |
|---|---|---|---|---|
| High productivity states | 4.1 | 2.9 | 2.5 | 2.1 |
| Medium productivity states | 3.0 | 2.4 | 2.1 | 3.7 |
| Low productivity states – of which, | 3.6 | 2.6 | 2.5 | 5.1 |
| Madhya Pradesh | 4.9 | 1.6 | 2.2 | 4.4 |
| Rajasthan | 5.9 | 5.5 | 10.9 | 5.5 |
| **All-India** | **3.4** | **3.3** | **1.7** | **3.7** |

Source: Planning Commission 2013

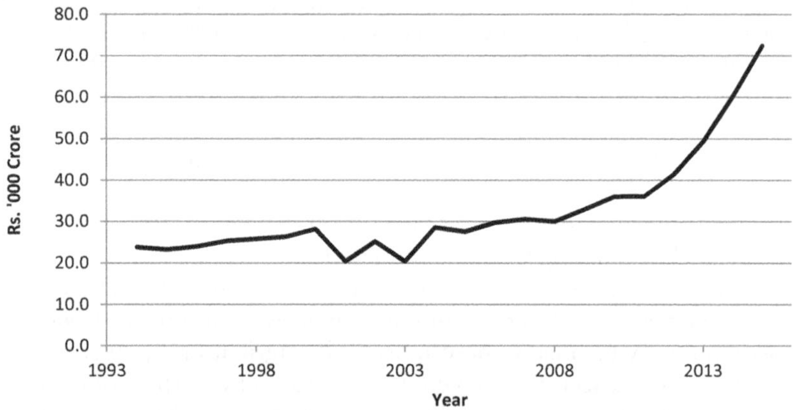


*Figure 9.1* State Domestic Product from Agriculture, Madhya Pradesh, 1994–2015, at constant 2004–2005 prices

Source: Calculated from MoSPI and CSO 2016

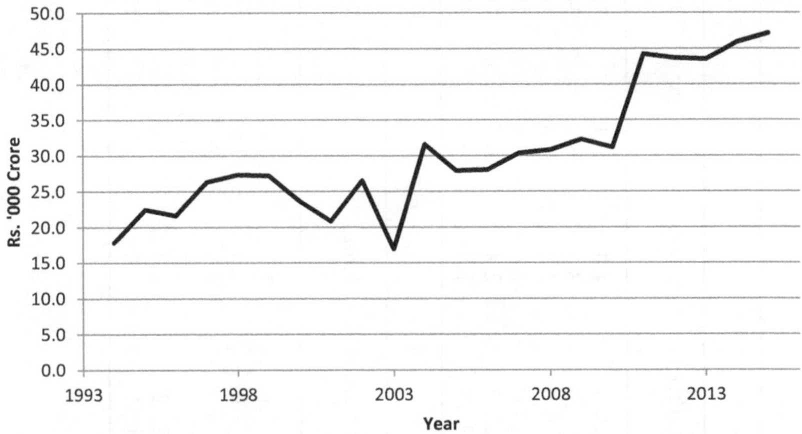


*Figure 9.2* State Domestic Product from Agriculture, Rajasthan, 1994–2015, at constant 2004–2005 prices

Source: Calculated from MoSPI and CSO 2016

greater poverty reduction and caused significant improvement in their nutrition levels.

Table 9.2 summarizes the changes in cropping pattern in Madhya Pradesh (including Chhattisgarh) and Rajasthan over a 50-year period from 1962–1965 to 2012–2016. Foodgrain crops occupied 84 per cent of the gross cropped area (GCA) in Madhya Pradesh in the 1960s, which came down to 66.6 per cent in 2012–2016. The area under oilseeds (soybean being the main oilseed crop) moved up from 10 per cent in the 1960s to 25.8 per cent by 2012–2016. Similarly, in Rajasthan, the area under foodgrain crops declined from 76 per cent in 1962–1965 to 52 per cent in 2012–2016 and the area under oilseeds (rapeseed and mustard being the mail oilseed crop) went up to nearly 20 per cent of the gross cropped area. Hence, we notice a somewhat similar trend of a shift away from foodgrains to oilseeds in both the states. Even within the foodgrains group, it is noticeable that there has been an expansion in the area under wheat whereas the area under 'coarse cereals' has declined in both the states. There has been no procurement or price support for coarse cereals, while oilseeds soybean (in both the states) and rapeseed and mustard (in

*Table 9.2* Changes in Cropping Pattern, 1962–2016 (Per Cent of GCA)

*Madhya Pradesh*

| | *Rice* | *Wheat* | *Coarse cereals* | *Pulses* | *Foodgrain* | *Oilseeds* | *Fibres* | *Others* | *Total* |
|---|---|---|---|---|---|---|---|---|---|
| 1962/65 | 22.8 | 17.3 | 23.0 | 20.4 | 83.5 | 10.0 | 4.4 | 2.1 | 100.0 |
| 1970/73 | 21.7 | 16.6 | 22.8 | 20.8 | 82.0 | 9.3 | 3.5 | 5.2 | 100.0 |
| 1980/83 | 22.3 | 15.7 | 22.1 | 22.2 | 82.2 | 9.5 | 2.9 | 5.4 | 100.0 |
| 1990/93 | 21.7 | 15.6 | 16.0 | 20.2 | 73.5 | 18.6 | 2.4 | 5.6 | 100.0 |
| 2005/08 | 21.0 | 15.9 | 10.0 | 21.0 | 67.8 | 22.9 | 2.4 | 6.7 | 100.0 |
| 2012/16 | 19.4 | 19.2 | 6.7 | 21.3 | 66.6 | 25.8 | 1.9 | 4.5 | 100.0 |

*Rajasthan*

| | *Rice* | *Wheat* | *Coarse cereals* | *Pulses* | *Foodgrain* | *Oilseeds* | *Fibres* | *Others* | *Total* |
|---|---|---|---|---|---|---|---|---|---|
| 1962/65 | 0.7 | 7.9 | 45.5 | 21.7 | 75.9 | 7.6 | 1.7 | 14.8 | 100.0 |
| 1970/73 | 0.8 | 8.9 | 45.3 | 21.1 | 76.0 | 7.0 | 1.9 | 15.1 | 100.0 |
| 1980/83 | 0.8 | 10.1 | 40.0 | 19.2 | 70.1 | 6.9 | 2.1 | 20.9 | 100.0 |
| 1990/93 | 0.7 | 10.1 | 35.7 | 17.3 | 63.8 | 17.3 | 2.5 | 16.3 | 100.0 |
| 2005/08 | 0.5 | 9.7 | 32.9 | 17.0 | 60.0 | 21.2 | 2.0 | 16.7 | 100.0 |
| 2012/16 | 0.6 | 12.4 | 24.3 | 14.8 | 52.1 | 19.6 | 1.8 | 26.4 | 100.0 |

Source: Bhalla and Singh 2012; GoI 2016

Rajasthan) enjoyed substantial public investment support and stable market price, which explains their remarkable growth. In Rajasthan, area under 'other crops' (notably guar and fodder crops) maintained a steady share of the cropped area, largely due to high industrial demand (for guar gum) and demand from the booming livestock economy in the state.

The structure of the value of production from Agriculture and Allied (A&A) sectors corresponds to and reflects the changing cropping pattern in the states. While the crop sector contributed to about 72 per cent of the total value of output of the A&A sector in MP, the corresponding figure for Rajasthan was only 58 per cent. Oilseeds and fruits and vegetables together contributed roughly one-third of the value of output of the A&A activities in MP, whereas in Rajasthan 'other crops' held a similar share. The remarkable fact is the high share of the livestock products, particularly milk, in the total value of output of the A&A sectors in both the states – 19 per cent in Madhya Pradesh and 32 per cent in Rajasthan. Indeed, it is the faster growth of the livestock economy which could have contributed significantly to the faster overall agriculture growth in both the states.

*Table 9.3* Share (%) of Crop Groups and Allied Sectors in Total Value of Output of Agriculture and Allied Sectors (at constant 2004–2005 prices)

| | | *Madhya Pradesh* | | *Rajasthan* | |
|---|---|---|---|---|---|
| | *Crop group* | *2011–2012* | *2013–2014* | *2011–2012* | *2013–2014* |
| 1 | Cereals | 18 | 18 | 12 | 10 |
| 2 | Pulses | 8 | 9 | 4 | 4 |
| 3 | Oilseeds | 15 | 11 | 11 | 11 |
| 4 | Cotton | 3 | 2 | 2 | 2 |
| 5 | Condiments and spices | 1 | 3 | 3 | 2 |
| 6 | Fruits & vegetables | 15 | 18 | 1 | 1 |
| 7 | Others | 8 | 8 | 24 | 28 |
| | **Total agriculture** | 71 | 72 | 58 | 58 |
| 8 | Livestock | 18 | 19 | 32 | 32 |
| 10 | Forestry | 10 | 8 | 10 | 9 |
| 11 | Fisheries | 1 | 1 | 0 | 0 |
| | **Total agriculture and allied sectors** | 100 | 100 | 100 | 100 |

Source: MoSPI and CSO 2016

## 3. Role of irrigation development

The earlier analysis of changes in the cropping pattern and structure of the value of output from A&A sectors brings out clearly that it is the irrigated segment of the economy, including irrigated crops and livestock products that have enjoyed considerable state support and hence have grown faster than others. At the national level, the value of India's irrigated economy covering irrigated crops and livestock products is estimated to be Rs 14,575 billion or roughly 60 per cent of the total value of A&A sector (GoI 2016). Fast-paced irrigation development has been one of the hallmarks of the process of agricultural growth in these two states. The pace of irrigation expansion increased between 2004–2005 and 2013–2014, in which period Madhya Pradesh and Rajasthan added 3.73 and 2.77 million hectares to their irrigated area respectively.

Interestingly, unlike the all-India pattern, both surface and groundwater sources contributed to this increase, though the contribution of groundwater sources has been more significant. In these predominantly rainfed states, surface water sources account for less than one-third of the total irrigated area, the rest of the irrigation being sourced from groundwater. The share of wells and tubewells providing groundwater irrigation in gross irrigated area was roughly between 65 per cent and 67 per cent in 2013–2014 in both the states.

This share has remained constant despite the growth of gross irrigated area, which implies that irrigation development in these states has been made possible by an aggressive exploitation of groundwater sources.[2]

*Table 9.4* Growth of Gross Irrigated Area in Rajasthan and Madhya Pradesh, 2004–2014

| | *Madhya Pradesh* | | | *Rajasthan* | | |
|---|---|---|---|---|---|---|
| | *GCA* | *GIA* | *GIA/ GCA %* | *GCA* | *GIA* | *GIA/ GCA %* |
| 2004–2005 | 20203 | 6193 | 30.7% | 21062 | 7093 | 33.7% |
| 2007–2008 | 20416 | 6567 | 32.2% | 22208 | 8088 | 36.4% |
| 2010–2011 | 22046 | 7421 | 33.7% | 26002 | 8322 | 32.0% |
| 2013–2014 | 24047 | 9919 | 41.2% | 26120 | 9865 | 37.8% |

Source: GoI 2016

*Table 9.5* Net Irrigated Area by Source (%) in Madhya Pradesh and Rajasthan, 1994–2014

| | *Madhya Pradesh* | | | | *Rajasthan* | | | |
|---|---|---|---|---|---|---|---|---|
| | *Canals* | *Tanks* | *Wells & Tubewells* | *Others* | *Canals* | *Tanks* | *Wells & Tubewells* | *Others* |
| 1993–1994 | 22.4 | 2.6 | **61.1** | 13.9 | 29.9 | 3.7 | **65.5** | 1.0 |
| 2000–2001 | 19.5 | 2.1 | **64.1** | 14.3 | 27.6 | 0.8 | **70.8** | 0.9 |
| 2004–2005 | 16.8 | 2.1 | **66.3** | 14.6 | 27.5 | 1.2 | **70.1** | 1.5 |
| 2009–2010 | 16.3 | 2.1 | **68.0** | 13.5 | 28.9 | 0.2 | **69.9** | 1.0 |
| 2013–2014 | 18.0 | 2.7 | **65.4** | 13.8 | 30.2 | 0.7 | **67.4** | 1.7 |

Source: GoI 2016

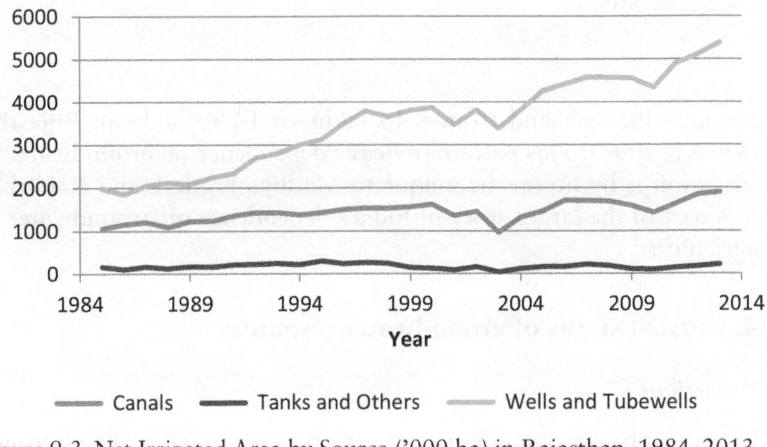


*Figure 9.3* Net Irrigated Area by Source ('000 ha) in Rajasthan, 1984–2013
Source: GoI 2016

The increasing prominence of groundwater in irrigation is also brought out by the data from Minor Irrigation (MI) Census on the approximate number of irrigation structures.[3] Between the first (1986–1987) and fourth MI Census (2006–2007), the number of wells and tubewells went up from about 7.47 lakhs to over 16.66 lakhs in

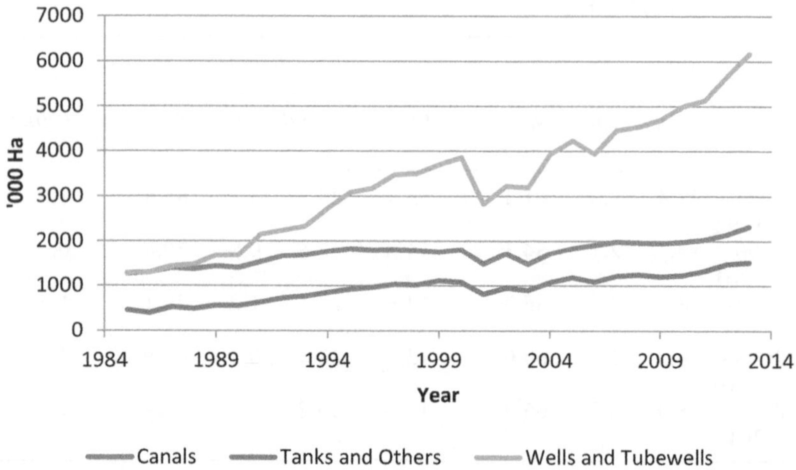


*Figure 9.4* Net Irrigated Area by Source ('000 ha) in Madhya Pradesh, 1984–2013

Source: GoI 2016

Madhya Pradesh and from 8.46 lakhs to 14.99 lakhs in Rajasthan (MoWR 2007). This pattern of heavy dependence on groundwater for irrigation is by no means unique to Madhya Pradesh and Rajasthan. It is part of the larger story of India's dependence on groundwater for agriculture.

## 4. Current status of groundwater resources

### *Rajasthan*

Given this background, let us now see how the assessments of groundwater resources in these two states have moved. India's groundwater resources are periodically assessed by using the ratio of groundwater extraction to the 'replenishable' quantity of groundwater available annually in a block/taluka (CGWB 2006, 2011, 2014). This methodology was developed initially by the Groundwater Resources Estimation Committee (MoWR 1997) and revised later in 2009 (MoWR 2009). An index called 'Stage of Groundwater Development' is the ratio of groundwater draft to the net annual groundwater availability in this assessment. Net annual groundwater availability is defined as the annual groundwater potential (total annual recharge from the monsoon and non-monsoon seasons) minus the natural discharge during the non-monsoon season (estimated at 5–10 per cent of the total annual groundwater potential). When the value of the 'Stage of Groundwater Development' of an area (district or sub-district – taluka/block/mandal) is less than 70 per cent, it is considered *safe*; when between 70 per cent and 90 per cent, it is deemed *semi-critical*; when between 90 per cent and 100 per cent, it is identified as *critical*; and more than 100 per cent is termed *overexploited*. It is the stage of development of an area along with the long-term decline in either pre- or post-monsoon water levels that makes it semi-critical, critical or overexploited.

The trajectory of increased irrigation from groundwater in Madhya Pradesh is of relatively recent origin. It started in the late 1990s, with the real take-off after 2000. In comparison, Rajasthan has had a longer history of groundwater irrigation, beginning in the late 1980s and accelerating after 2000. Analysis of the Central Groundwater Board (CGWB) data over the years has shown that the groundwater balance has alarmingly worsened in both the states (CGWB 2006, 2014, 2016). In Rajasthan, the Stage of Groundwater Development (ratio of annual groundwater draft to annual utilizable recharge) rose alarmingly from 125 per cent in 2004 to 140 per cent in 2013, indicating that the groundwater resources of the state were in a precarious position. Of the 248 assessment units in the state, 204 (821 per cent) were in the critical and overexploited category in 2013.

*Table 9.6* Estimated Volume of Groundwater Resource (BCM) in Rajasthan

| | | *2004* | *2011* | *2013* |
|---|---|---|---|---|
| **Rajasthan** | | | | |
| 1 | Net groundwater availability | 10.38 | 10.83 | 11.26 |
| 2 | Total annual draft, of which | 12.99 | 14.84 | 15.71 |
| | – Irrigation | 11.60 | 13.13 | 13.79 |
| | – Domestic and industrial uses | 1.39 | 1.71 | 1.92 |
| 3 | Annual groundwater deficit (1–2) | (–) 2.61 | (–) 4.01 | (–) 4.45 |
| 4 | Stage of groundwater development (%) | 125 | 137 | 140 |
| 5 | Number of critical and overexploited blocks/total blocks | 190 / 237 (80%) | 196 / 243 (81%) | 204 / 248 (82%) |

Source: CGWB 2006, 2014 and 2016

Rajasthan forms a part of the northwestern region of India, which includes Punjab, Haryana, parts of Western UP and Delhi. While much of Punjab, Haryana and Western UP is underlain by thick, extensive, largely unconsolidated sediments belonging to the Indo-Gangetic River System, Rajasthan shows a mixed geology. More than half of Rajasthan is underlain by loose unconsolidated sediments of both alluvial and Aeolian origin. Southeastern portions are characterized by crystalline rock formations that also constitute the Aravalli mountain range. Volcanic rock formations are exposed in the southern part of the state adjoining Madhya Pradesh (Banswara, Dungarpur and Jhalawar districts) and in parts of the Jaisalmer district. Canal irrigation in the state is limited to parts of northern and southern Rajasthan. Five districts (Ganganagar, Hanumanthgarh, Kota, Bundi and Bikaner) account for over 75 per cent of canal irrigation in the state. The rest of the state is heavily dependent on groundwater for irrigation. Groundwater resource in these hard rock systems[4] is characterized by limited productivity of individual wells, unpredictable variations in productivity of wells over relatively short distances and poor water quality in some areas. Sedimentary formations underlie parts of the Bundi, Kota and Baran districts located in the southern part of the state. Hence, aquifer systems in Rajasthan are far more diverse than those in Punjab, Haryana and Western UP, implying that the impact of overexploitation in these various aquifer settings will have different hydrogeological and socio-economic bearings. What is unique about the pattern of groundwater overexploitation in Rajasthan is that it has emerged across all the four hydrogeological settings present in the state. The hastening of agricultural growth in Rajasthan has resulted in most districts of north, northeast and south Rajasthan moving into a danger zone in terms of groundwater extraction.

### *Madhya Pradesh*

In Madhya Pradesh too, while the stage of groundwater development has moved from 48 to 58 per cent between 2004 and 2013, an estimated 85 blocks out of the total 313 (28 per cent) are categorized as semi-critical, critical or overexploited in terms of groundwater extraction in 2013.

Unlike Rajasthan, Madhya Pradesh does not have a large tract of 'alluvial' geology. Consolidated rock formations of igneous, metamorphic and sedimentary origin are present in different parts of MP, giving it a diverse hydrogeological constitution. However, aquifer

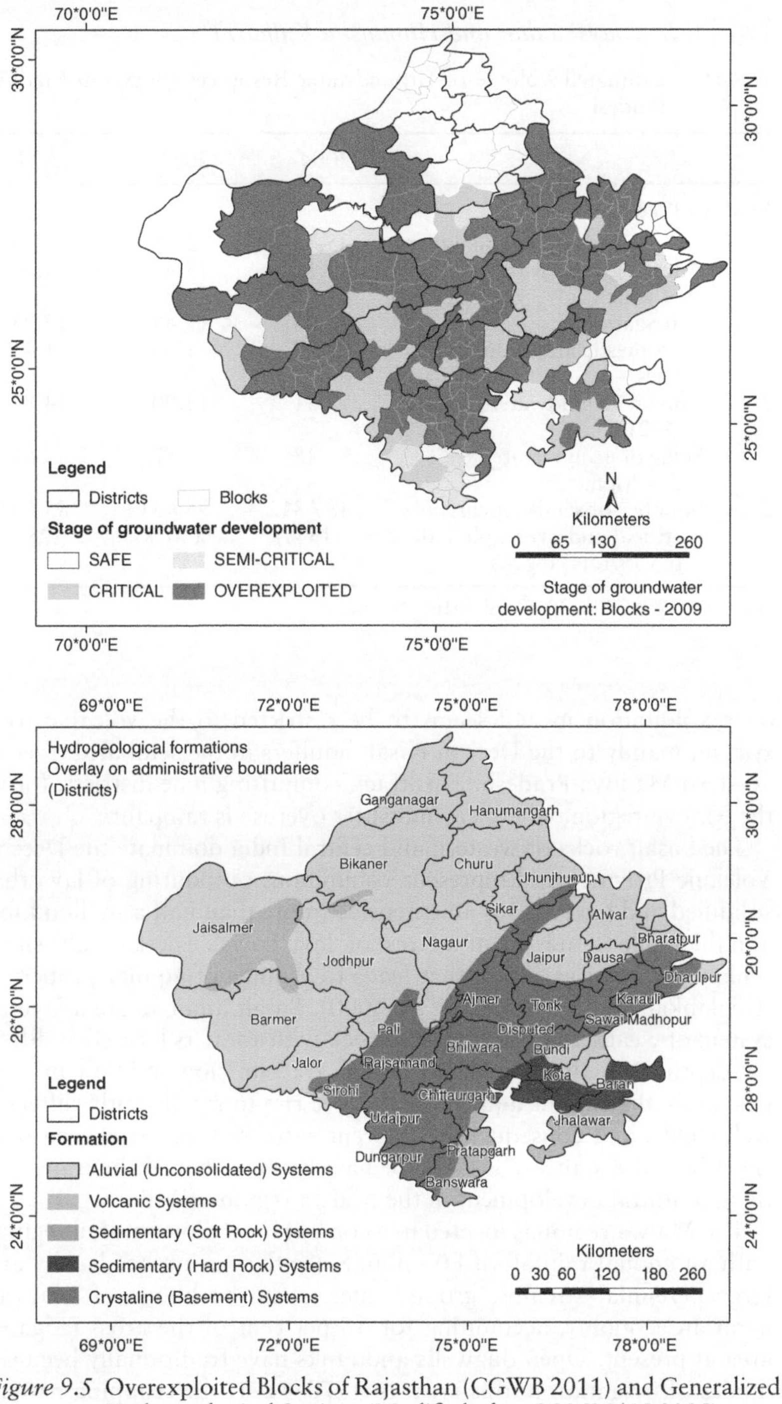


*Figure 9.5* Overexploited Blocks of Rajasthan (CGWB 2011) and Generalized Hydrogeological Settings (Modified after COMMAN 2005)

Source: GoI 2016

*Table 9.7* Estimated Volume of Groundwater Resources (BCM) in Madhya Pradesh

| | | *2004* | *2011* | *2013* |
|---|---|---|---|---|
| **Madhya Pradesh** | | | | |
| 1 | Net groundwater availability | 35.33 | 32.29 | 34.16 |
| 2 | Annual groundwater draft, of which | 17.12 | 18.83 | 19.36 |
| | – Irrigation | 16.08 | 17.48 | 17.95 |
| | – Domestic and Industrial Uses | 1.04 | 1.35 | 1.41 |
| 3 | Annual groundwater surplus (1–2) | 17.51 | 13.90 | 14.80 |
| 4 | Stage of groundwater development | 48 | 57 | 58 |
| 5 | Number of semi-critical, critical and overexploited blocks/total blocks | 48 / 312 (15%) | 95 / 313 (30%) | 85 / 313 (28%) |

Source: CGWB 2006, 2014 and 2016

overexploitation in MP seems to be restricted to the volcanic rock system, mainly to the Deccan Basalt aquifers in the semi-arid tract of Western Madhya Pradesh. This tract, comprising nine districts, forms the Malwa region, where groundwater overuse is rampant.

The basalt rocks of western and central India dominate the Deccan Volcanic Province and represent voluminous outpouring of lava that solidified and gave rise to an extensive (more than half a million km$^2$) and thick pile (hundreds of metres) of 'lava flows'. These basalts show a high degree of variation that leads to a range of aquifer properties (Deolankar 1980; Kulkarni *et al.* 2000). Basalt aquifers are a layered system of weathered and fractured rock with aquifers located at different depths. Variable conditions in their transmission and flow properties imply that basalt aquifers often give rise to significantly different well yields, and consequently different extraction patterns even over short lateral distances. This factor has crucially shaped the trajectory of agricultural development in the Malwa region of MP.

The Malwa region is located in a comparatively low rainfall regime, with an annual rainfall of 800 mm. Since this region has hardly any large perennial streams, groundwater is the backbone of Malwa's agrarian economy, accounting for 85 per cent of the gross irrigated area at present. Open dugwells and tanks have traditionally been the modes of irrigation in this area. In 1970–1971, the cropping pattern of this area was dominated by rainfed crops, with only 6 per cent of

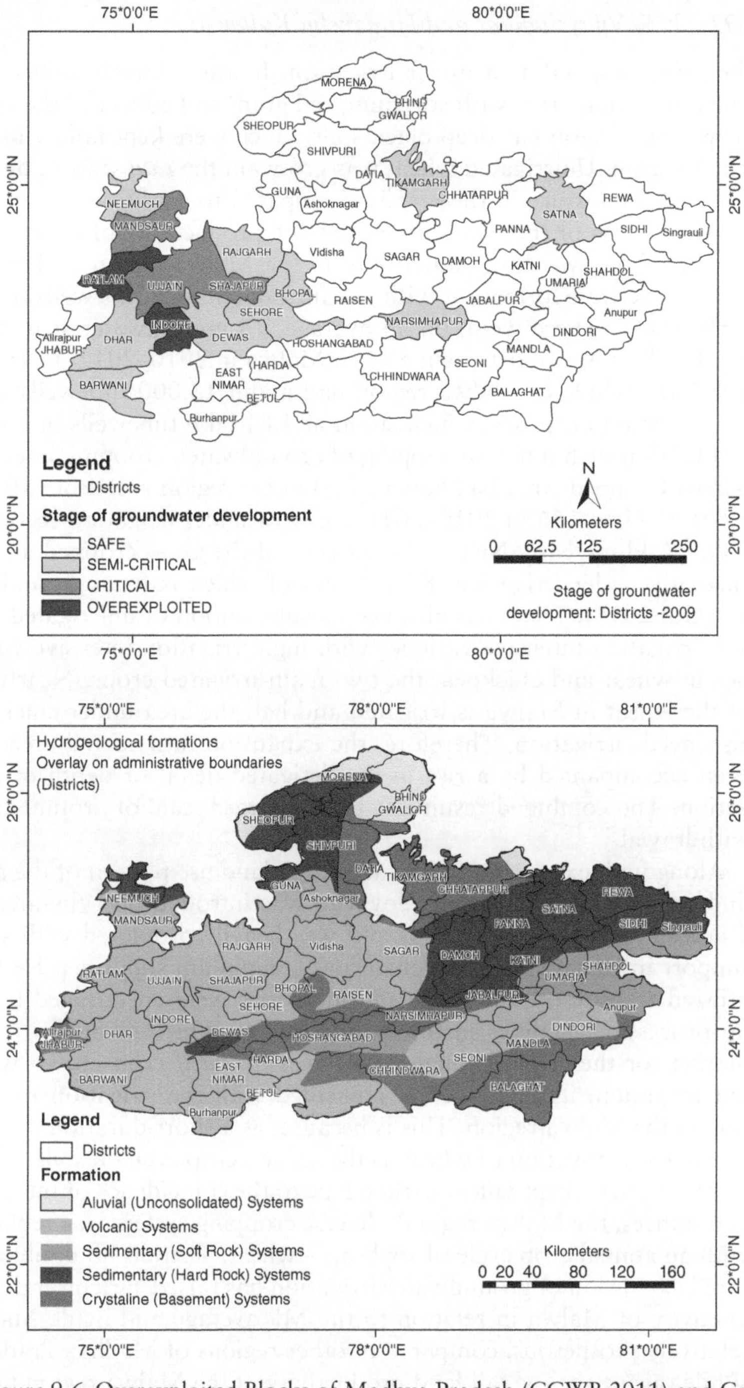


*Figure 9.6* Overexploited Blocks of Madhya Pradesh (CGWB 2011) and Generalized Hydrogeological Settings (Modified after COMMAN 2005)

Source: CGWB 2006, 2014 and 2016

the gross cropped area under irrigation. It was a largely millet and pulses-growing area, with sorghum, red gram and cotton as the main crops. The region has deep black soils which were kept fallow in the rainy season. Unirrigated wheat was grown in the *rabi* season, on the conserved moisture in these soils. Compared to traditionally wheat-growing areas of the Narmada valley, the productivity of agriculture on the whole was low. Agriculture in the Malwa region underwent a dramatic transformation with the introduction of tubewells in the early 1980s. There were, on an average, 18 groundwater structures per 100 hectares of net sown area in Malwa in 2010–2011. In 1986–1987, the whole of Malwa region had about 13,000 tubewells used for irrigation purposes, which stood at 1.61 lakh tubewells in 2010–2011. With such intensive tapping of groundwater, cropping intensity (Gross Cropped Area/Net Sown Area) in the region rose from 109 in 1970–1971 to 166 in 2010–2011 and area under irrigation recorded a nine-fold increase. Nearly 33 per cent of the gross cropped area is currently under irrigation, 85 per cent of which is from groundwater (GoI 2016). There has also been a substitution of unirrigated and low irrigation-intensive varieties with high irrigation-intensive varieties in wheat and chickpea, the two main irrigated crops. Nearly all of the wheat in Malwa is irrigated and half the area under chickpea also needs irrigation. Therefore, the expansion in irrigated area has been accompanied by a rise in the 'irrigated delta' or depth of irrigation. The combined result has been a larger scale of groundwater withdrawal.[5]

Along with expansion of irrigation, the land use pattern of the area underwent a radical change. Soybean was introduced in the area as a new crop in the early 1980s and was heavily promoted with state support in the area. The mechanism of minimum support price was utilized to promote the crop, and industries were encouraged to set up processing facilities in towns like Indore, which created a ready market for the crop. Though soybean is a *kharif* crop grown without irrigation, its introduction coincided with the irrigation revolution in the Malwa region. This is because, as a short-duration crop, it facilitated cultivation of wheat as the second crop even on soils which were otherwise kept fallow earlier. Due to the coincidence of these circumstances, the Malwa region's diverse cropping system was replaced with an annual crop cycle of soybean – wheat. There is no doubt that rapid expansion of groundwater irrigation has raised agricultural productivity of Malwa in relation to the MP average and made Malwa relatively prosperous, compared to other regions of Madhya Pradesh. While raising the overall land productivity of the Malwa region (and, of course, moving many small and marginal farmers out of poverty), this cycle not only eliminated all other crops but put an enormous strain on the limited water resources of the region.

The experience of both the states also shows that supportive public policies would also have contributed to agricultural growth and, indirectly, to groundwater depletion. For example, Madhya Pradesh has embarked on an ambitious public procurement drive (mainly wheat) since 2008 and has now emerged as the second largest contributor to public procurement of wheat in India, after Punjab (Krishnamurthy 2012). In 2012–2013, Madhya Pradesh procured 8.5 million tonnes of wheat, which came down to 7.31 million tonnes in 2015–2016 (41 per cent of the state's total production). Even though Madhya Pradesh is the largest producer of pulses in India, accounting for 31 per cent of production and 22 per cent of the area under cultivation, there is no public procurement of pulses in operation till date. Similarly, Rajasthan is a major state in the production of millets, but public procurement of millets is zero in the state.

Another indicator of the state support to agriculture is the ratio of public expenditure on agriculture and allied activities to total public expenditure. The most recent data is summarized in Table 9.8.

The table shows that both Rajasthan and Madhya Pradesh have been making considerable fiscal commitments (ranging, on an average, between 15–20 per cent of total development expenditure and 10–15 per cent of revenue expenditure) in their annual budgets to agriculture and allied sectors during the period 1990–2010. Even though this support is potentially available for all agrarian regions within each state, only a few regions seem to have gained by it. These states have also spent considerable amount of money on rural electrification, which has been one of the main reasons for the rapid growth of groundwater irrigation in these states.

*Table 9.8* State-wise Share (%) of Public Expenditure on Agriculture, Rural Development and Irrigation in Total Public Expenditure, 1990–2010

| *State* | *Share in development expenditure* | | | | *Share in total revenue expenditure* | | | |
|---|---|---|---|---|---|---|---|---|
| | *1990–1995* | *1995–2000* | *2000–2005* | *2005–2010* | *1990–1995* | *1995–2000* | *2000–2005* | *2005–2010* |
| Madhya Pradesh | 31 | 27 | 23 | 28 | 21 | 17 | 13 | 16 |
| Rajasthan | 28 | 21 | 19 | 21 | 18 | 12 | 11 | 13 |
| **All states** | **30** | **26** | **21** | **21** | **19** | **15** | **12** | **12** |

Source: Reserve Bank of India Various Years

## 5. Is there a trade-off between agriculture growth and environmental balance?

Does the recent growth experiences of Rajasthan and Madhya Pradesh support the conclusion that there is an implicit trade-off between agricultural growth and environmental balance in these high poverty states?[6] Are these states setting a model for other high poverty states such as Uttar Pradesh, Bihar, Jharkhand and Odisha to copy? The conceptual formulation of an inevitable trade-off between economic growth and environmental quality is found in the 'Environment Kuznets Curve' (EKC) hypothesis.[7] Named after the economist, Simon Kuznets, who proposed an inverted-U-shaped relationship between income growth and economic inequality, the EKC hypothesis postulates that rapid economic growth will lead to a disruption of environment balance in the early stages of growth. But as per capita income increases, environmental degradation will eventually be reversed, and balance would be restored (Barbier 2002). Hence, environmental degradation is reversible and self-correcting, and economies will 'grow out of' environmental problems in the long run (Beckerman 1992). The EKC hypothesis is schematically shown in Figure 9.7.

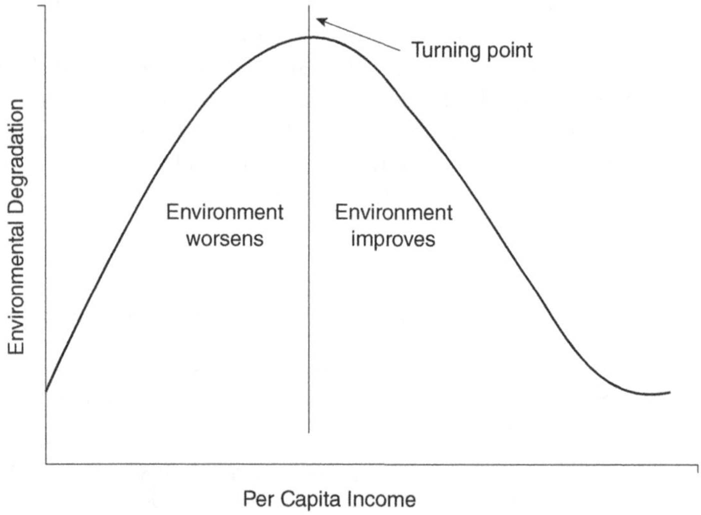


*Figure* 9.7 Schematic View of EKC Hypothesis Showing Trade-off between Per Capita Income and Environment Quality

Source: Adapted by authors

The EKC hypothesis was initially proposed to show the relationship between economic growth and air quality. But soon it was also extended to include stocks of environmental and natural resources ('natural capital') where it was posited, first, that the economic processes are reversible in terms of their impact on the environment and, second, that it is possible to substitute natural capital with man-made physical capital. Both presumptions are clearly wrong when applied to the stock of natural resources. Natural resources such as land, water, rivers, forests and the atmosphere – or *ecosystems*, in general – have the capacity for self-regeneration, but can nevertheless undergo degradation and depletion through human usage (Dasgupta 2013). Resource gets depleted when their rate of current consumption exceeds the rate of regeneration and such depletion can be irreversible. There could be several reasons for this high current consumption of natural capital, leading to a reduction in the productive base of the society and a reduced flow of future benefits (Arrow *et al.* 2004). Under-pricing of natural resources in relation to its social cost is one of the prime reasons for this high present consumption and overuse. In the case of groundwater, under-pricing arises on account of the poorly defined property rights regimes and the failure of the market mechanism to incorporate negative externalities (Arrow *et al.* 2004). Estimation of the value of the direct and indirect benefits from groundwater as an ecosystem is also fraught with several problems commonly encountered in valuation of ecological services, including the choice of a socially acceptable discount rate (Daily *et al.* 2000).

On account of these, it is clear that the trade-off proposed in the EKC hypothesis cannot apply if environmental stocks are depleted. As shown earlier, the prime mover of the process of getting out of poverty in Rajasthan and Madhya Pradesh has been an intensification of the use of groundwater reserves. Depletion of the stock of groundwater can have several long-term impacts on the ecosystem, which are not captured in the EKC framework. There is also the question as to 'who pays for the trade-off', assuming they do exist. Clearly, the ones gaining from overuse of resources and those who are likely to face the negative impact are not the same group of people. Environmental degradation hence will have implications for equity and justice in society. The recent experience of Rajasthan and Madhya Pradesh seems to indicate that more careful and integrated approaches to groundwater regulation and management are needed.

### *Participatory groundwater management*

Groundwater is a Common Pool Resource (CPR), access to which is difficult to restrict. But it is reducible in the sense that each unit extracted by one user is no longer available to other users. What makes management of groundwater especially tricky is that it is a highly mobile resource. This makes it difficult to establish and enforce private and exclusive rights over groundwater. Beyond a point, especially in times of increased scarcity, groundwater use transcends farm boundaries and generates negative externalities such as falling water tables, well interference, increased dissolved solids and even sea-water ingress in coastal areas. Many of these externalities are driven by an implicit competition between various users (Kulkarni and Vijayshankar 2014).

India's groundwater challenge is also about the disparity between *the scales of information and action*. The aggregated picture provided by assessments like those done by the Central Groundwater Board (CGWB) cannot form the basis for action. Actions on groundwater management require information at different scales, including data at the aquifer scale. Understanding aquifers is important in the management of groundwater. Moreover, aquifers seldom exist in isolation. The complex layering of rock strata with varying aquifer properties gives rise to specific *groundwater typologies*. Groundwater typologies are not just entities in physical space. They follow a historically governed pattern of access to groundwater and the social processes that regulate its use. While the physical structure broadly sets out the range of options available, the trajectory of the development of groundwater resources in a specific historical context is governed by the social processes and forces controlling them. Groundwater typologies then need to be seen as a socio-physical category. The first step in sustainable management of groundwater is to carefully construct a disaggregated picture by *mapping aquifers* and delineating *aquifer typologies*, incorporating variations in hydrogeological and socio-economic contexts (Vijayshankar, Kulkarni and Krishnan 2011). Ideally, aquifer mapping should take place at the scale of watersheds of the order of 1,000 to 2,000 hectares. These maps can be then aggregated at a more regional scale rather than moving down from an aggregated picture.

An approach of adopting an aquifer typology not only provides insights to the hydrogeological diversity within a groundwater system but is also able to incorporate socio-economic situations that may drive patterns of groundwater usage (Kulkarni *et al.* 2009). Along with this, a comprehensive database on the groundwater flow systems and groundwater availability in each aquifer typology needs to be constructed. Disaggregated aquifer maps and database management systems will make it possible for the community of users to arrive at a sustainable yield management goal for an aquifer and watershed in a given hydrogeological setting. This involves working out *location-specific protocols* and agreements within the user community for sustainable use of water, including a growing acknowledgement of the fact that aquifers also render ecosystem services, the simplest indicator of which is the base flow in streams and rivers. Regulatory options at community level such as depth to and distance between wells and borewells, protection of drinking water sources, crop water budgeting for arriving at a cropping pattern that matches with water availability in the aquifer, will form part of these rules and norms of use, based on equitable use of groundwater in each management unit.

This groundwater management framework spelt out here brings the *community* to the centre stage of management. It also centrally focuses on environmental sustainability of the use of groundwater. In a recent study, scientists from the International Water Management Institute (IWMI) have strongly argued for the expansion of groundwater irrigation in the 112 most 'irrigation deprived' districts of India (Shah *et al.* 2016). The approach involves installation of 1–1.5 million groundwater structures in these districts to expand the area under irrigation. Such approaches are essentially lacking in any notion of sustainability, particularly in the absence of aquifer information, and the need to protect groundwater from overuse, which the *participatory, community-based groundwater management* necessarily embodies. Of course, it is obvious that community efforts need to be supported by an enabling/empowering legal framework, in place of the command-and-control rules that most legislative instruments are prone to become. Hence, a combination of community, science and law is at the base of the new framework for groundwater management being proposed here.

### *Surface storages to correct the 'Hydrological Disequilibrium'*

Studies have also indicated that there is a severe 'hydrologic disequilibrium' in both the economies. In Rajasthan, command areas of the Ganga canal and the upper Indira Gandhi Nahar Project (IGNP) areas are dependent mostly on surface water along with little groundwater, while the rest of the state is dependent mostly on groundwater. In Madhya Pradesh too, except the Chambal basin in the north and the Central Narmada Valley, the rest of the state is heavily dependent on groundwater for irrigation. As we saw previously, the groundwater dependent districts are also experiencing higher levels of agrarian dynamism, suggesting that farmers' demand for groundwater irrigation is unlikely to slow any time soon. This creates a basic lack of balance between surface and groundwater sources. This hydrologic disequilibrium could be corrected through a conjunctive use of surface and groundwater. The principle could be that as far as possible, the entire protective irrigation during the *kharif* season and the first irrigation in *rabi* could be met through surface water harvesting and storages, and the balance should be met out of groundwater. This would protect groundwater as a backup resource for ensuring drinking water security in summer.

We saw earlier that both Rajasthan and Madhya Pradesh have been able to increase area under canal irrigation in recent years. Madhya Pradesh, in particular, adopted several reforms on account of which its canal command area increased from less than 1.0 million hectares (Mha) in 2003–2004 to 1.44 Mha in 2012–2013 and then to 2.33 Mha in 2013–2014 (Shah *et al.* 2016). This was made possible by last-mile investments in lining big earthen canals, rehabilitation of several minor irrigation schemes and revitalizing the farmer organizations and Water User Associations. Such timely and appropriate investments can enhance the effectiveness of surface irrigation systems and reduce the pressure on groundwater.

### *Enhanced groundwater recharge*

Studies by the International Water Management Institute (IWMI) indicate that there is a huge untapped potential for managed aquifer recharge in Rajasthan. The need to awaken the people to take up groundwater recharge and rainwater harvesting, and also manage demand and make irrigation more efficient, have been stressed in a recently concluded multi-partner action research programme called MARVI (Maheshwari *et al.* 2014).

The state also has a long tradition of water harvesting through small storage structures like tanks. Tank irrigation has, over time, fallen into disuse and disrepair. Tanks are seldom de-silted. Using public investment funds from the Mahatma Gandhi National Rural Employment Guarantee Act (MGNREGA) and other programmes, the capacity of the existing storage tanks could be enhanced. Recent research has shown that the best strategy in tank rehabilitation is to view tanks as complex socio-ecological systems with multiple stakeholder groups. Instead of restoring tank irrigation to its original status at great cost, it is better to focus on a wider, river basin management approach and take into consideration the interests of this wide range of stakeholders (IWMI 2003). The example of NGOs such as PRADAN and Tarun Bharat Sangh, working at scale on the revival of 'paals' and 'johads', is relevant here. Madhya Pradesh has shown how MGNREGA could be used as an effective means of water harvesting and groundwater recharge by combining it with the watershed programme. This model, which attempts environmental regeneration through employment generation, could probably be scaled up and implemented in the groundwater-scarce areas of the state.[8]

## *Managing agricultural demand*

Since agriculture accounts for over 80 per cent of the water use, management of agricultural demand is the key to the effective protection of groundwater resources in both the states. A wide range of measures need to be adopted such as promotion of *crop varieties which require less irrigation*. In irrigated crops such as wheat, varieties are now available which can give a reasonably good yield with two or three irrigations (including the pre-sowing wetting of fields). Such drought-resistant varieties could be combined with *diversification of land use*, where available agricultural land is apportioned between irrigated and unirrigated crops. Crops like chickpea which require less water should be promoted. Improving water use efficiency through *water-saving technologies* like drip systems is another option. However, experience shows that unless these are combined with cropping system changes, the farmers might use the water saved for expanding area under cultivation (Fishman, Devineni and Raman 2015). Long-term changes in cropping systems and crop varieties grown require the support of *a strong system of incentives* from the government in the form of price support and public procurement. In Madhya Pradesh, recent procurement policies have given a clear signal to the irrigated wheat-growing farmers to expand the area under wheat. A similar system of incentives could be used to promote cropping patterns that require less amount of water. Crops such as pulses, sorghum and minor millets are still grown by farmers in many districts of Rajasthan and Madhya Pradesh. In view of the role of millets in the traditional food basket of the area and also considering their potential to withstand water stress, there is a strong argument for *extending the support price mechanism to millets and pulses*. Another area requiring urgent action is *agricultural extension*, which can play a vital role in the promotion of water-saving cropping systems. Public-funded extension has undergone a steep decline in most parts of India. The most important challenge for the future extension managers is to find innovative methods of knowledge management and dissemination. The agricultural universities through their colleges, regional research stations and Krishi Vigyan Kendras (KVK) could play a crucial role as centres of knowledge development, management and transmission to farming communities.

### *Reform of the power sector*

The close link between the water and power sectors, requiring co-management, is well-known. The dilemma is that heavy power subsidies have encouraged groundwater overuse and pauperized state electricity boards on the one hand, while, on the other, they have also improved livelihoods and incomes of small and marginal farmer households. In Rajasthan and Madhya Pradesh, there is a strong case for some rationalization in electricity pricing so that locally appropriate cropping systems are promoted, and resource degradation is controlled. The experience of the Jyotigram Yojana in Gujarat, which separated grids supplying power to farms from domestic supply, is now being repeated in states like Madhya Pradesh. It can be hoped that power rationing and assured availability of quality power would lead to some reduction in the amount of groundwater extracted. Use of solar power can help reduce the burden of subsidies but their effect on groundwater use is uncertain. In sum, without appropriate policy changes in the power sector, participatory groundwater management might remain a distant dream.

### *Legal and institutional arrangements*

Lastly, protection of groundwater resources has some major legal and institutional requirements. Though Madhya Pradesh and Rajasthan have enacted their own groundwater laws, the basic *legal principles* governing groundwater continues to be those laid down in British common law as early as the middle of the 19th century. These legal principles and rules give the landowner the right to take substantially as much groundwater as desired from wells dug on their own land. The right to water goes hand in hand with the right to land. Hence, landowners enjoy unlimited access as part and parcel of their ownership rights to the land. The present legal framework considers only the interests of landowners, completely overlooking the hugely important fact that groundwater serves the basic needs of life of many landless people as well (Kulkarni, Shah and Vijayshankar 2015). A change in this legal framework is essential. While a command and control type of legislation comes into conflict with the decentralized patterns of groundwater use, legal reforms for protection of participatory social processes in groundwater management can be visualized.

The recently formulated Model Bill for the Conservation, Protection, Regulation and Management of Groundwater, 2016 (MoWR 2016), emphasizes the principle of right to water for life as one of the guiding principles in groundwater law and management. It also provides for preparation of Groundwater Security Plans at the Gram Panchayat, Watershed and Block levels, for 'attainment of sufficient quantity of safe water for life and sustainable livelihoods by every person' and for 'ensuring water security even in times of emergencies such as droughts, floods etc.' (MoWR 2016). These provide a strong basis for a legal structure for protection of groundwater where it is threatened by overuse. Along with law, the *regulatory structures* in the water sector also need to be redesigned. These regulatory structures need to be conceptualized as a related but separate set of institutions that handle distinct governance functions and take important decisions (political/technical, normative/non-normative decisions).

## 6. Concluding observations

Both Rajasthan and Madhya Pradesh are states with a significant rainfed agriculture segment. These states till recently have been among the poorest and most backward of the Indian states. However, rapid agricultural growth, aided by groundwater irrigation, has pulled these states out of their poverty trap. However, in the bargain, the limited groundwater resources of these states have been badly stretched and are now under the threat of overexploitation. The way forward is to firmly establish a framework of equitable and sustainable management of groundwater and work out its implications for agricultural growth. This framework places communities at the centre of groundwater management and emphasizes the need to understand aquifer characteristics and the physical configuration of the groundwater systems before any plan for intensification of groundwater use is made. Taking the right to water for life as one of the guiding principles in groundwater law and management, we need to implement several important steps for protection of groundwater in these states, on which the life and livelihoods of millions of people depend.

## Acknowledgement

We are grateful to K. J. Joy of the Forum for Policy Dialogue on Water Conflicts in India for encouraging us to develop the idea of groundwater trajectories in Rajasthan and Madhya Pradesh into a paper for the Prof Ramaswamy Iyer Memorial Volume. We thank Dr Mihir Shah and Dr Mekhala Krishnamurthy for providing critical observations on various drafts of the chapter.

## Notes

1 Elsewhere, we have developed the hypothesis that it is the pressure on democratically elected governments to rapidly achieve poverty eradication ('competing coalitions') which may be driving the agricultural growth revival in these hitherto laggard states (Vijayshankar 2017).
2 For example, the net irrigated area in Rajasthan went up from 3.2 million hectares in 1984–1985 to 7.5 million hectares in 2012–2013. Much of this increase (over 80 per cent) has taken place through expansion in area under irrigation from groundwater (wells and tubewells). As a result, the area irrigated from groundwater in the state went up from about 1.99 million hectares in 1984–1985 to 5.38 million hectares in 2012–2013.
3 The figures for the number of wells and tubewells are not consistent across different rounds of the MI Census. The aggregation of opening stock and yearly additions to the stock of wells and tubewells gives a much higher figure than what the census reports. This difference is, presumably, on account of the number of wells and tubewells that become dysfunctional – which probably indicates a lowering of the water table because of excessive withdrawals from the aquifer (Mukherji, Rawat and Shah 2013).
4 'Hard rock' is a generic term applied to consolidated formation with aquifers of low primary inter-granular porosity (mainly for igneous and metamorphic rocks like granites, basalts, gneisses and schists).
5 It is a mistake often made to put the entire burden of expansion of tubewell irrigation on private investment. While farmers may have invested their own money in irrigation equipment, what indeed facilitated the expansion of such irrigation has been the public investment in rural electrification in the region. Electrification of villages in Malwa goes back to the 1980s and seems to have facilitated introduction of tubewells in the region.
6 Environmental externalities 'are the unaccounted for consequences for others (including future people) of decisions made by each one of us on reproduction, consumption, production and use of the natural environment' (Dasgupta 2013).
7 'Intellectual support for the viewpoint was offered in the World Bank's World Development Report 1992, where the authors used data on air quality in urban sites to conclude that there is a U-shaped relationship between GDP and environmental quality. The relationship was christened, inevitably perhaps, as the 'environmental Kuznets curve' (Dasgupta 2013).
8 This model, which had a successful run between 2008 and 2012, ran into problems subsequently due to implementation difficulties of

MGNREGA. However, we feel that this model is worth reconsidering and reviving in view of the growing problem of groundwater shortage in the state.

## References

Arrow, K., P. Dasgupta, L. Goulder, G. Daily, P. Ehrlich, G. Heal, S. Levin, K. G. Mäler, S. Schneider, D. Starret, and B. Walker, 2004. 'Are We Consuming Too Much?' *The Journal of Economic Perspectives*, 18(3): 147–172, Summer.

Barbier, E. B. 2002. 'The Role of Natural Resources in Economic Development', Discussion Paper No. 0227, Centre for International Economic Studies, Adelaide University, Adelaide.

Beckerman, W. A. 1992. 'Economic Growth and the Environment: Whose Growth? Whose Environment?' *World Development*, 20: 481–496.

Bhalla, G. S. and G. Singh. 2012. *Economic Liberalisation and Indian Agriculture: A District-level Study*. New Delhi: Sage.

CGWB. 2006. *Dynamic Groundwater Resources of India (as on March, 2004)*. Central Groundwater Board, Ministry of Water Resources. New Delhi: Government of India (GoI).

CGWB. 2011. *Dynamic Groundwater Resources of India (as on March, 2009)*. Central Groundwater Board, Ministry of Water Resources. New Delhi: Government of India (GoI).

CGWB. 2014. *Dynamic Groundwater Resources of India (as on March, 2011)*. Central Groundwater Board, Ministry of Water Resources. New Delhi: Government of India (GoI).

CGWB. 2016. *Dynamic Groundwater Resources of India (as on March, 2013)*. Central Groundwater Board, Ministry of Water Resources. New Delhi: Government of India (GoI).

Chand, R. and S. Parappurathu. 2012. 'Temporal and Spatial Variations in Agricultural Growth and Its Determinants', *Economic and Political Weekly*, XLVII(26–27), 30 June.

COMMAN. 2005. 'Managing Groundwater Resources in Rural India: The Community and Beyond', British Geological Survey Commissioned Report CR/05/36N.

Daily, G. C., T. Söderqvist, S. Aniyar, K. Arrow, P. Dasgupta, P. Ehrlich, C. Folke, A. Jansson, B. O. Jansson, N. Kautsky, S. Levin, J. Lubcheno, K. G. Mäler, D. Simpson, D. Starret, D. Tilman, and B. Walker. 2000. 'The Value of Nature and the Nature of Value', *Science*, 289(5478): 395–396, doi:10.1126/science.289.5478.395.

Dasgupta, P. 2013. 'The Nature of Economic Development and the Economic Development of Nature', *Economic and Political Weekly*, XLVII(51), 21 December.

Deolankar, S. B. 1980. 'The Deccan Basalts of Maharashtra, India – Their Potential as Aquifers', *Ground Water*, 18: 434–437, doi:10.1111/j.1745-6584.1980.tb03416.x

Government of India (GoI). 2016. *Indian Agricultural Statistics*. New Delhi: Department of Economics and Statistics (DES), Ministry of Agriculture, Government of India, http://eands.dacnet.nic.in/ (accessed on 28 May 2018).

Fishman, R., N. Devineni and S. Raman. 2015. 'Can Improved Agricultural Water Use Efficiency Save India's Groundwater?' *Environmental Research Letters*, 10(8): 1–9, doi:10.1088/1748-9326/10/8/084022

IWMI. 2003. 'Rethinking Tank Rehabilitation', Water Policy Briefing No. 7. IWMI-Tata Water Policy Programme, Colombo, Sri Lanka: International Water Management Institute.

Krishnamurthy, Mekhala. 2012. 'States of Wheat: The Changing Dynamics of Public Procurement in Madhya Pradesh', *Economic and Political Weekly*, 48(52), 29 December.

Krishnan, S. 2009. 'The Silently Accepted Menace of Disease Burden from Drinking Water Quality Problems', Paper prepared for the Mid-Term Appraisal of the 11th Five Year Plan of Government of India. CAREWATER, INREM Foundation, Anand.

Kulkarni, H., U. Badarayani, H. Dhawan, D. Upasani, and R. Gupta. 2009. 'Groundwater Management in India: From Typology to Protocols and Community-Driven Pilots', in H. Kulkarni, U. Badarayani and D. (eds.), *Groundwater Management: Typology of Challenges, Opportunities and Approaches*. ACWA-H-09-2, Pune: Advanced Centre for Water Resources Development and Management (ACWADAM).

Kulkarni, H., S. B. Deolankar, A. Lalwani, B. Joseph, and S. Pawar. 2000. 'Hydrogeological Framework of Deccan Basalt Ground Water Systems, West-Central India', India. *Hydrogeology Journal (Springer – Verlag)*, 8(4): 368–378.

Kulkarni, H., M. Shah and P. S. Vijayshankar, 2015. 'Shaping the Contours of Groundwater Governance in India', *Journal of Hydrology: Regional Studies*, 4(Part A): 172–192, http://dx.doi.org/10.1016/j.ejrh.2014.11.004.

Kulkarni, H. and P. S. Vijayshankar. 2009. 'Groundwater: Towards an Aquifer Management Framework', *Economic and Political Weekly*, XLIV(5): 13–17, 7 February.

Kulkarni, H. and P. S. Vijayshankar. 2014. 'Groundwater Resources in India: An Arena for Diverse Competition', *Local Environment: The International Journal of Justice and Sustainability*, 19(9): 990–1011, http://dx.doi.org/10.1080/13549839.2014.964192 (accessed on 28 May 2018).

Kumar, D. and T. Shah. 2003. 'Groundwater Pollution and Contamination in India: The Emerging Challenge', *The Hindu Survey of Environment*: 7–12.

Macdonald, D. M. J., H. Kulkarni, A. R. Lawrence, S. B. Deolankar, J. A. Barker, and A. B. Lalwani. 1995. 'Sustainable Groundwater Development of Hard-rock Aquifers: The Possible Conflict Between Irrigation and Drinking Water Supplies from the Deccan Basalts of India', British Geological Survey NERC Technical Report WC/95/52: p. 54. Wallingford, UK.

Maheshwari, B., M. Varua, J. Ward, R. Packham, P. Chinnasamy, Y. Dashora, S. Dave, P. Soni, P. Dillon, R. Purohit, Hakimuddin, T. Shah, S. Oza, P. Singh, S. Prathapar, A. Patel, Y. Jadeja, B. Thaker, R. Kookana, H. Grewal, K. Yadav, H. Mittal, M. Chew, and P. Rao. 2014. 'The Role of Transdisciplinary Approach and Community Participation in Village Scale Groundwater Management: Insights from Gujarat and Rajasthan, India', *Water*, 6: 3386–3408, doi:10.3390/w6113386.

MoA. 2013. *State of Indian Agriculture: 2012–2013*. New Delhi: Department of Agriculture and Co-operation, Ministry of Agriculture, Government of India (GoI).

Moench, M. 1992. 'Drawing Down the Buffer', *Economic & Political Weekly*, XXVII: A7–A14.

MoSPI and CSO. 2016. Various Years. *National Accounts Statistics*. New Delhi: Central Statistical Organisation and Ministry of Statistics and Programme Implementation, Government of India (GoI).

MoWR. 1997. *Groundwater Resource Estimation Methodology: Report of the Groundwater Estimation Committee*. New Delhi: Ministry of Water Resources, Government of India (GoI).

MoWR. 2007. *Report of the 4th Minor Irrigation Census*. New Delhi: Ministry of Water Resources, Government of India (GoI).

MoWR. 2009. *Groundwater Resource Estimation Methodology: Report of the Groundwater Estimation Committee*. New Delhi: Ministry of Water Resources, Government of India (GoI).

MoWR. 2016. *Model Bill for the Conservation, Protection, Regulation and Management of Groundwater*. New Delhi: Ministry of Water Resources, Government of India (GoI).

Mukherji, Aditi, S. Rawat and T. Shah, 2013. 'Major Insights from India's Minor Irrigation Censuses: 1986–1987 to 2006–2007', *Economic and Political Weekly*, 48(26–27), 29 June.

Planning Commission. 2013. *Twelfth Five Year Plan (2012–2017): Faster, More Inclusive and Sustainable Growth*. Planning Commission, Government of India (GoI), Volume I. New Delhi: Sage.

Reserve Bank of India. Various Years. *State Finances: Study of Budgets*. Various Issues.

Shah, Tushaar. 2009. *Taming the Anarchy: Groundwater Governance in South Asia*. Washington, DC: Resources for the Future and International Water Management Institute.

Shah, Tushaar, Shilp Verma, Neha Durga, Abhishek Rajan, Alankrita Goswamy, and Alka Parlecha. 2016. 'Har Khet Ko Paani: Rethinking Pradhan Mantri Krishi Sinchayi Yojana (PMKSY)', IWMI Policy Paper. IWMI-Tata Policy Program, Colombo: International Water Management Institute.

Susheela, A. K. 2001. *A Treatise on Fluorosis*. New Delhi: Fluorosis Research and Rural Development Foundation.

Vijayshankar, P. S. 2017. 'India's Agricultural Development: A Regional Perspective', in R. Nagaraj and S Motiram (eds.), *Political Economy of Contemporary India*. Cambridge: Cambridge University Press.

Vijayshankar, P. S., H. Kulkarni and S. Krishnan. 2011. 'India's Groundwater Challenge and the Way Forward', *Economic and Political Weekly*, XLVI(2): 37–45.

World Bank. 2010. *Deep Wells and Prudence: Towards Pragmatic Action for Addressing Groundwater Overexploitation in India*. Washington, DC: The World Bank, p. 97.

# 10 Reducing water for agriculture for improving productivity

## Adapting and up-scaling innovative approaches

*Biksham Gujja and Hajara Shaik*[1]

### Introduction

The total renewable water resource (TRWR) is a broad indicator of water availability at the country level on an annual basis. It has two components, (1) surface water, which is from the rivers, streams, lakes and water harvesting structures such as tanks etc., and (2) groundwater, which is water pumped from digging an open well, borewell or deep borewell. India has about 1869 BCM of annual renewable water resources. Of that available water, approximately about 1121 BCM is 'utilisable' water resources. Of this TRWR, the surface water is approximately about 690 BCM (61 per cent) and the remaining 431 BCM is groundwater.

Both[2] surface and groundwater are interrelated and interconnected. It is not possible to use the entire TRWR for human needs due to various reasons, such as distribution, geography, topography and accessibility. The assessment by the Central Water Commission (CWC) and the Central Ground Water Board (CGWB) in 1997 has indicated that the surface water use was 399 BCM and the groundwater use was 230 BCM.

Out of the 1121 BCM of 'utilisable' water resources, by 1997, 629 BCM (56 per cent) had already been used. The FAO estimated that the total water use in 2014 was 761 BCM, out of which 688 BCM was for agriculture. If water use continues in such 'business-as-usual' mode, demand may reach 1180 BCM by 2050. This is more than the total 'utilisable' water resources available.[3] The water demand in 2050 has been estimated to be 197 per cent more for the domestic sector, 287 per cent more than the year 2000 levels, while the agricultural sector may need 5 per cent more at the 2014 level.[4] All these estimates indicate that, at this rate, India will not be able to meet the water demand of various sectors in the economy. Therefore, planners need to focus on demand-side management, which means that India needs to reduce its water demand without compromising its national socio-economic needs, goals and aspirations. The reduction needs to take place mainly in the agriculture sector, since it uses significantly large quantities of water.

Government figures from the Ministry of Water Resources (MoWR) indicate that the total utilizable water resources are estimated to be ≈1123 BCM, with the estimated demand of 710 BCM (2014). The water demand will rise to ≈1093 BCM by 2025. So, by 2025, which is in the next few years, the water demand will be the same as the entire 'utilisable' water available in the country. At the local level, the water situation has already reached water stress levels. Another way of understanding the nation's water wealth is 'per capita' water availability. At the national level, the per capita availability of water had declined from 3,089 $m^3$ per person in 1962 to 1,103 $m^3$ per person in 2014.

The gradual decline of the per capita availability of water is argued to be mainly due to an increase in population. By 2050, India's population is expected to reach 1.7 billion,[5] from the current level of 1.3 billion, due to increased life expectancy (from the current level of 68.8 years to 74.6 years plus added growth). Consequently, the per capita water availability is estimated to decline to 850 $m^3$ or less. By 2020, India's per capita water availability is projected to reach critical levels, which is below 1,000 $m^3$. Any country with per capita levels below 1,000 $m^3$ is categorized as a 'water stressed' country.

These figures are national averages and do not reflect the specific water availability and the 'water stress' at the local levels. 'Water stress' is therefore much more acute in specific regions and river basins compared to the national average. The aforementioned figures reflect water availability and its current usage, with approximate future projections but donot help in policy formulation and methodological interventions. Such specific interventions are possible only by methodological improvements, with specific uses at the regional, local and catchment levels of river basins.

This chapter focuses on the growing national water demand, specifically in the agriculture sector. The main aim of this chapter is to discuss water demands in the irrigation sector, which is the primary user of water. It also attempts to throw light on the financial investments and future policy directions by focussing on government expenditure in the irrigation sector since Independence. The contribution of the primary sector is about 18 per cent of the GDP, which is gradually declining. The primary sector includes total value of all crops, livestock products, forest products and fisheries. In 2014–2015, the contribution by value of the primary sector is about Rs 2,048,700 crores ($320 billion). Within that, the value of all-crops was Rs 1,227,700 crores ($190 billion). This is about 10.8 per cent of GDP. However, the value of all crops includes rainfed and irrigated ones. Since we are discussing the role of irrigation in improving agriculture productivity, the value added by irrigated crops will be even much less. For example, three major irrigated crops—paddy, wheat, sugarcane add Rs 170,400 cr, Rs 107,800 cr and Rs 76,000 cr respectively. The value of these three crops is Rs 354,200 cr ($55 billion). This indicates that only one-third of the value of all the crops comes from irrigated crops. Together, the value added to GDP by crops which use the bulk of irrigated water is less than 3.3 per cent of the national GDP (data from the Ministry of Statistics and Programme Implementation 2017).[6] But the water allocations and water management plans have not been updated to meet the emerging social and economic challenges. The primary aim of this chapter is to suggest a pragmatic 'water efficient' approach to improve agriculture productivity while reducing the water use at per unit level of cultivation and production. The last section of the chapter suggests specific solutions and proven methods to reduce the water demand significantly while increasing crop production and improving land productivity.

## Water demand

The water demand projections forIndia are based on two factors:

1 The projected increase in the area of irrigation due to population growth which is essential to produce agricultural commodities.
2 The urban and industrial requirements to meet the growing industrial production needs of the rural and the urban sectors.

According to the National Commission for Integrated Water Resources Development (NCIWRD), the annual water demand for 2025 has been estimated to be in the range of 784 to 843 BCM, while, for 2050, the figures range from 973 to 1180 BCM.

Freshwater withdrawals increased at the rate of almost 13 per cent per year since 1977, from 380 BCM in 1977 to 761 BCM in 2014. During the same period (1977 to 2014), the per capita internal renewal of water declined by almost 50 per cent. It is projected as being due to population growth and migration. However, the increase in water use, which is primarily for agriculture, has also been reflected in an increase in production of cereals or staple food from 138 million tonnes in 1977 to 295 million tonnes in 2014, which is more than a 100 per cent increase. Thus, while water has played a significant role in meeting the country's food needs and achieving food security so far, continuing the current approach may not be sustainable since water resources have reached their limit.

Though there is a variation in the figures of current water use and the future water demand projections, one thing is consistent and that is that even in 2050, the agriculture sector shall be demanding 65–70 per cent of the total water withdrawals. Note that the agriculture sector in India contributes less than 15 per cent to the GDP, and this shall be far less, i.e., 10 per cent by 2050.

However, the water demand projections by the Standing Committee on Water Resources for the Eleventh Plan (2007–2011) shows much higher average demand, and for each sector. Therefore, it can be inferred that:

- it is highly unlikely that India will have more 'utilisable water' than 1121 BCM;
- the projected demand for the agriculture sector is itself higher than the total 'utilisable water';
- the total demand far exceeds the total water availability.

## Reducing water withdrawals for agriculture: a significant challenge

Until now, political policy and resource allocation for planning in India has relied on the simple assumption that increased monetary resource allocation for irrigation planning will help agriculture and therefore farmers in rural India. It was initially a planning approach, with a genuine concern for the income gap between rural and urban India. To resolve this, providing more water for agriculture was presumed as good for the nation and its farmers. Consequently, financial allocation by each state in India for developing irrigation infrastructure was planned to the tune of several thousands of crores. The financial allocation will be discussed separately later.

Given such a political and policy context, reducing water allocations to the agriculture sector will be difficult, politically, socially and economically. The current policy understanding is that increased available water for agriculture will help the agriculture sector. As discussed earlier, there is an urgent need to change this perspective and acknowledge that there is no additional water available for the agriculture sector. Even if it is presumed as available, it is prohibitively expensive to add each ha of additional land into the realm of irrigation. Given the data (Table 10.1) for the past decades, it can be seen that even if the

*Table 10.1* Net Area under Irrigation, By Sources

(000 Hectares)

| *Source of irrigation* | | | | | | | | |
|---|---|---|---|---|---|---|---|---|
| *Year* | *Government* | *Private* | *Canal (Govt. + Pvt.)* | *Tanks* | *Tubewells* | *Other wells* | *Other sources* | *Net irrigated area* |
| 2001–2002 | 14,993 | 209 | 15,202 | 2,196 | 23,245 | 11,952 | 4,342 | 56,936 |
| 2002–2003 | 13,867 | 206 | 14,073 | 1,811 | 25,627 | 8,727 | 3,658 | 53,897 |
| 2003–2004 | 14,251 | 206 | 14,458 | 1,916 | 26,691 | 9,693 | 4,299 | 57,057 |
| 2004–2005 | 14,553 | 214 | 14,766 | 1,734 | 25,235 | 9,956 | 7,538 | 59,229 |
| 2005–2006 | 16,490 | 227 | 16,718 | 2,083 | 26,026 | 10,044 | 5,966 | 60,837 |
| 2006–2007 | 16,802 | 224 | 17,027 | 2,078 | 26,942 | 10,698 | 5,999 | 62,744 |
| 2007–2008 | 16,531 | 217 | 16,748 | 1,973 | 28,497 | 9,864 | 6,107 | 63,189 |
| 2008–2009 | 16,686 | 195 | 16,881 | 1,981 | 28,367 | 10,389 | 6,020 | 63,638 |
| 2009–2010 | 14,789 | 188 | 14,978 | 1,587 | 28,371 | 9,992 | 7,008 | 61,936 |
| 2010–2011 | 15,472 | 171 | 15,643 | 1,980 | 28,543 | 10,629 | 6,864 | 63,659 |
| 2011–2012 | 15,833 | 172 | 16,005 | 1,919 | 29,943 | 10,595 | 7,236 | 65,697 |
| 2012–2013 | 15,506 | 165 | 15,671 | 1,753 | 30,543 | 10,763 | 7,536 | 66,266 |
| 2013–2014 | 16,115 | 163 | 16,278 | 1,842 | 31,126 | 11,312 | 7,542 | 68,100 |

Source: GOI 2018a

state managed to add to the irrigation area, it would not be able to address the water demand issues or create any new employment or add to farmers' income.

Soon the most prominent challenge for India would be to reduce its water demand, as agriculture is the livelihood of the people, providing them employment, food security and social security. India's growth projections, economic development and social stability aredependent on water security. It can reduce its water use for agriculture without compromising on its targets of foodgrain production. To meet the challenge of keeping the growth of agriculture intact while cutting down on the usage of water, one would require a paradigm shift in the conventional cultivation practices. Based on the current data and future projections, it had been observed that:

- India is using far more water to produce far less agricultural commodities per unit of irrigated area. More water to agriculture is not translating into an increase in productivity or profitability for the farmer.
- India is pumping far more groundwater than any other country in the world. It is also pumping a lot faster than its natural systems can recharge. It might have serious consequences not only for farmers but also for the other sectors.
- India is polluting proportionally far more water per unit of industrial production.
- India is still making plans and investments to create more irrigated area than focusing on improving the productivity of existing irrigated area.
- India is spending its financial, human and institutional resources to increase water supply rather than focusing on supply-side management.

## Irrigation in India

Often policy papers on agriculture begin in the following way: 'agriculture in India even today continues to be vulnerable to the vagaries of the weather because close to 52 per cent of it is still un-irrigated and rain-fed' (GOI 2018b: 84)[7] (see Table 10.4). It implies that if the entire area is sown and changed to irrigated area, the problems of agriculture shall resolve themselves. There are two presumptions behind this kind of policy projection:

1 that all the uncultivated area in India can and should be transformed to irrigated area, and

2 that such conversion is going to resolve the rural issues of income gap, employment and so on.

Such assumptions are fundamentally flawed. Moreover, it is impossible to irrigate all the cultivated area in India no matter how much the government might be willing to spend, as there is a natural limt to TRWR in a country. The other flaw is to assume that the rural economic crisis, employment and the rural-urban income gap can be addressed by merely spending more money on agriculture. Despite significant investments in irrigation, there is a natural limit to crop production and soil productivity. Addressing rural crisis, especially when the agriculture sector growth is far below the overall economy, requires far more sophisticated thinking and responsible investments. Spending more money in the name of irrigating all the cultivable land will not add much to the net area. Besides, such efforts may result in unexpected ecological problems and increase the uncertainty of irrigated area due to the diversification of available utilizable water to a broader area. Thus, data seems to suggest that government spending on irrigation may have become part of the problem rather than the solution.

The Economic Survey 2018 presented in the parliament states that 'shortages of water and land, deterioration in soil quality, and of course climate change-induced temperature increase and rainfall variability are all going to impact agriculture' (GOI 2018b: 83–84). The following sub-sections discuss irrigation in India and its costs, benefits and impact on agriculture.

### *Irrigation: increased significantly in earlier decades*

Irrigation was undoubtedly part of the solution in the early decades after Independence. During the 1950s, 1960s and 1970s, the area of irrigation increased rapidly, resulting in an increase in cereal production. According to the Director of Economics and Statistics, Ministry of Agriculture, the net area of irrigation in the country during 2013–2014 was 68.1 Mha (Million hectares) for all the sources of irrigation. Area irrigated by source was as follows: Canals – 16.3 Mha; Tanks – 1.84 Mha; Tubewells – 31.1 Mha; Other Wells – 11.3 Mha; and Other Sources – 7.5 Mha (Table 10.1). The gross area irrigated was 95.77 Mha, which means about 27.67 Mha has been irrigated more than once for the second crop in the same year.

During the year 1950–1951, the net irrigated area in India was around 20.58 Mha, with the gross irrigated area at about 22.56 Mha. This indicates that by 1950, the area irrigated more than once was about 1.7 Mha (Table 10.2). The source-wise distribution of net irrigation in

*Table 10.2* Trend in Cropped and Irrigated Area

*(Million Ha)*

| *Year* | *Net area sown* | *Total cropped area* | *Net irrigated area* | *Gross irrigated area* |
|---|---|---|---|---|
| 1950–1951 | 118.75 | 131.89 | 20.85 | 22.56 |
| 1960–1961 | 133.20 | 152.77 | 24.66 | 27.98 |
| 1969–1970 | 138.70 | 162.27 | 30.20 | 36.97 |
| 1970–1971 | 140.86 | 165.79 | 31.10 | 38.20 |
| 1980–1981 | 140.29 | 172.63 | 38.72 | 49.78 |
| 1990–1991 | 143.00 | 185.74 | 48.02 | 63.20 |
| 2000–2001 | 141.34 | 185.34 | 55.20 | 76.19 |
| 2010–2011 | 141.56 | 197.56 | 63.66 | 88.93 |
| 2011–2012 | 140.98 | 195.69 | 65.70 | 91.78 |
| 2012–2013 | 139.94 | 194.14 | 66.27 | 92.25 |
| 2013–2014 | 141.43 | 200.86 | 68.10 | 95.77 |

Source: GOI 2017

1950 was as follows: Canal irrigation – 8.30 Mha, Tanks – 3.62 Mha, Groundwater – 5.98 Mha, and Other Sources – 2.97 Mha.

The following observations are essential in understanding the area and source of irrigation between 1950–1951 and 2013–2014. (For the annual figures refer to Table 10.1 and Table 10.2):

- Canal irrigation doubled: Canal irrigation increased by 8 Mha (from 8.3 Mha to 16.3 Mha), which is almost double the area.
- Tank irrigation declined by 1.84 Mha from 3.62 Mha, which is a drop of 50 per cent.
- Groundwater irrigation increased six times from 5.98 Mha to 42.4 Mha.
- Other sources of irrigation increased about two times from 2.97 Mha to 7.5 Mha (that is by 4.53 Mha).
- The area irrigated more than once increased from 1.7 Mha to 28 Mha.
- The gross area of irrigation by all sources increased from 23 Mha to 96 Mha, an increase of about 73 Mha.

While there is an increase in the area of irrigation, the role and contribution of major irrigation projects (which is canal irrigation) for this increase was minimal, despite enormous financial investments. We shall discuss later how this has happened.

### *Irrigated area: confusion over net and gross*

There is confusion over the extent of the area irrigated in the country. Often the figures projected by the Department of Irrigation are higher than the figures compiled by the Department of Agriculture. The irrigation potential created (IPC) in India is normally around 110 million ha (Muthyam 2017).[8]

The total area of irrigation (including area irrigated more than once) never exceeded 96 Mha according to the data published by the Ministry of Agriculture (Table 10.2). In addition to that, the Minor Irrigation (MI) and Major and Medium Irrigation (MMI) projects do overlap. For example, 'over 13 per cent MI schemes are located in the command area of major and medium irrigation projects, and 12.2 per cent irrigation provided through MI schemes was in the command area'.[9] Therefore, it is double counting of the area irrigated through different schemes.

The net increase in canal irrigation from 8.30 Mha (1950–51) to 16.27 Mha (2013–2014) is a 100 per cent increase. Therefore, the total increase of the area under MMI is just about 8 Mha from 1950–1951 to 2013–2014. The bulk of the money spent on major irrigation infrastructure resulted in a marginal increase in net area of canal (MMI) irrigation.

### *Groundwater resources and private funding*

The most impressive gains are in groundwater irrigation. The total irrigated area covered under groundwater irrigation increased from 5.98 Mha in 1950 (≈6 Mha) to 42.4 Mha in 2014. All the investments in groundwater irrigation came from small and marginal farmers, most of them with land ownership of less than one hectare. Since the First Plan, governmental investments in supporting minor irrigation had been almost minimal. Therefore, the private investments from marginal farmers in creating irrigation facilities are far more significant and result-oriented than public sector investments, which we shall analyse in later sub-sections.

Another notable factor was a remarkable decline of tank irrigation (ancient systems of flood and rainwater irrigation) from 3.62 Mha in 1950 to 1.8 Mha in 2014, which is a decline of almost 50 per cent. There are multiple reasons for this, but the most important ones are ignorance as well as deliberate neglect of maintenance by the Central Government and the large and medium farmers.

### *Government spending on MMI*

India had always prioritized and allocated massive investments for major irrigation projects. The actual figures may be different from published data, which may be exponentially high to exaggerate them as a political achievement of elected governments. This, in turn, may have influenced allocations for major irrigation projects to create an additional irrigated area.

The 12th Plan document states the following: 'There has been a massive increase in plan expenditure on irrigation and flood control over the last 60 years'. As can be seen from Annexure 5.1, MMI (Major and Medium Irrigation projects) outlays rose from Rs 376 crore in the first Five-year Plan to a projected outlay of more than Rs 341,000 crore in the 12th Plan (Planning Commission of India 2013)[10] (Table 10.3 and Figure 10.1). During this period from 1950 to 2012, the increase in irrigated area due to government investments is around 13 Mha.

The capital expenditure to create each hectare of irrigation has been increasing every year. For example, as per government data, the capital expenditure on MMI during the 15-year period (1990–1991 to 2006–2007) was about Rs 156,000 crores. During the same period, the working expenses on MMI irrigation was about Rs 105,000 crores, with a total expenditure of Rs 256,000 crores.

*Table 10.3* Plan-wise Financial Expenditure on Irrigation in India

| *S. no.* | *Period* | *Major & medium (Rs Crores)* | *Irrigation potential created ('000 ha)* | *Cost per Ha (Rs)* |
|---|---|---|---|---|
| 1 | 1st plan (1951–1956) | 376.2 | 2486 | 1,513 |
| 2 | 2nd plan (1956–1961) | 380.0 | 2143 | 1,773 |
| 3 | 3rd plan (1961–1966) | 576.0 | 2231 | 2,582 |
| 4 | Annual plans (1966–1969) | 429.8 | 1530 | 2,809 |
| 5 | 4th plan (1969–1974) | 1242.3 | 2608 | 4,763 |
| 6 | 5th plan (1974–1978) | 2516.2 | 4014 | 6,269 |
| 7 | Annual plans (1978–1980) | 2078.6 | 1895 | 10,969 |
| 8 | 6th plan (1980–1985) | 7368.8 | 1083 | 68,041 |
| 9 | 7th plan (1985–1990) | 11107.3 | 2225 | 49,920 |
| 10 | Annual plans (1990–1992) | 5458.8 | 821 | 66,490 |
| 11 | 8th plan (1992–1997) | 21669.2 | 2216 | 97,785 |
| 12 | 9th plan (1997–2002) | 49289.6 | 4097 | 120,307 |
| 13 | 10th plan (2002–2007) | 82195.2 | 5296 | 155,202 |

Source: Planning Commission Various Years

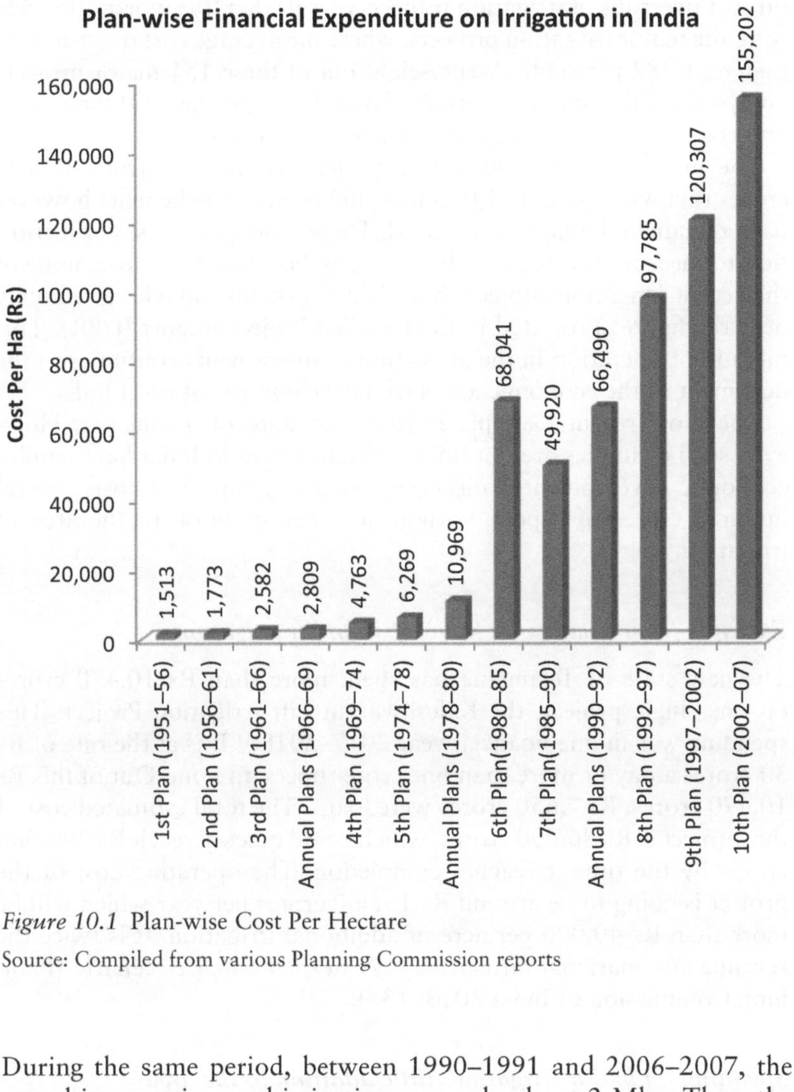


*Figure 10.1* Plan-wise Cost Per Hectare

Source: Compiled from various Planning Commission reports

During the same period, between 1990–1991 and 2006–2007, the actual increase in canal irrigation was only about 2 Mha. Thus, the spending amounted to Rs 10 lakhs (1 million) per ha of net irrigation. Often such high costs for irrigation projects were due to prolongation of work or non-completion of the project as scheduled. Lately, due to fluctuations of rupee parity vis-à-vis other currencies, the costs have increased manifold while the projected benefits have remained the same or fallen drastically.

A study carried out by the Twelfth Plan Working Group on MMI on cost overruns of irrigation projects reveals that 'the worst offenders were the major irrigation projects, where the average cost overrun is as high as 1,382 per cent. Twenty-eight out of these 151 major projects analysed witnessed cost overruns of over 1,000 per cent. Of these, nine had cost overruns of over 5,000 per cent' (Bhaduri 2013).

The project cost to complete a project has jumped from Rs 100 crores to a whopping Rs 1,000 to 5,000 crores. The benefits however have remained the same or reduced. There is no mechanism or institution to measure the accountability of any benefits. Therefore, none of the recent irrigation projects has yielded benefits anywhere remotely near the figures projected in the Detailed Project Report (DPR). This method of operation in the allocation of investments continues to the detriment of the economic and social development of rural India.

The most recent example is from the state of Telangana. However, such examples are not unique. Many states in India have similar economic development projects, where a single project costs several hundred crores of rupees, without any real addition to the area of irrigation.

### *Example from Telangana: Kaleshwaram lift irrigation*

The new state of Telangana has spent more than Rs 10,470 crores on one single project, the Kaleshwaram Lift Irrigation Project. This spending was in one financial year 2017–2018.[11] It is at the rate of Rs 30 crores a day or more than one crore rupees an hour. Out of this Rs 10,470 crores, Rs 7,650 crores were loans. The total estimated cost of this project is Rs 86,000 crores, which could quickly reach Rs 200,000 crores by the time it reaches completion. The operating cost of the project is going to be around Rs 13,000 crores per year which will be more than Rs 40,000 per acre of additional irrigation. It is twice the revenue any marginal farmer may get in the best-case scenario (Planning Commission of India 2013: 138).

### ***Spending on major irrigation: little addition to the area***

Currently, there are two ways of operation for different irrigation systems in India. One is planned and managed by the government, viz. the operated and subsidized irrigation system. These are primarily MMI projects constructed and operated by respective irrigation departments of the state governments. The Government of India too contributes and has shared in the capital expenditure of specific state projects. In this system, farmers do not have to contribute towards providing water. The water is delivered almost free at the farm level. The performance of this system is abysmal.

The Indian Institute of Management (IIM) Lucknow was asked by the Planning Commission of India to conduct the socio-economic impact of the Accelerated Irrigation Benefits Programme (AIBP). The IIM evaluated 10 sample projects in 10 different states and submitted a report in 2011. The findings indicate that there is a significant gap between irrigation potential created by the states and the utilization of that potential. The reasons identified are 'low water discharge, insufficient water distribution mechanisms, unequal water distribution to farmers located at different points, loss of water during distribution, incorrect recording of irrigated area and diversion of cultivable land to other purposes within the command area' (Planning Commission of India 2010).

The aforementioned reasons are related to inefficiency of water usage, which is a direct result of poor maintenance of the irrigation infrastructure. However, it is being interpreted to direct policy in a different direction, which could be burdensome to farmers. 'State governments are finding it difficult to finance the recurring costs of irrigation and to collect economic water charges from the farmers' (Planning Commission of India 2010). However, the report claims that the 'farmers in major irrigation projects are willing to pay an extra charge for assured water supply, indicating that access to water is more important than its cost' (Planning Commission of India 2010). In reality, farmers are unwilling to pay the appropriate water maintenance charges unless assured of water at a critical time for the crops. The government claims that unless farmers pay, they do not have the funds to maintain the system. Water efficiency is not merely water supply in time. Unless farmers are incentivized to use less water, they'll continue to use as much water as possible, fearing that it may not be available when it is needed. The larger question one has to ask is this: can the government maintain the irrigation infrastructure in a cost-effective way? Alternatively, is there a differentway of structuring these maintenance systems where farmers are willing to get involved and also pay for the system?

### *Private spending on irrigation has done well*

Minor irrigation has done well in the country. According to the 5th Minor Irrigation Census report, there are about 21.7 million MI schemes, which is an increase of 700,000 from the 4th Census report.[12]

All the capital expenditure for minor irrigation has come from farmers' private investments. Government spending on capital costs of minor irrigation is almost negligible. However, the operational costs of minor irrigation were subsidized by state and central governments, with free power and electricity to operate the pumps.

According to the 5th Census of the minor irrigation survey report,

> irrigation potential created (IPC) has increased from 84.03 million hectares in the 4th Census to 89.52 million hectares in the 5th Census. Similarly, irrigation potential utilized (IPU) has increased from 63.5 million hectares in the 4th Census to 71.3 million hectares in the 5th Census which shows an increase of around 12.3 per cent during this period.

While there is an increase of 6.5 per cent in IPC, the greater increase is in IPU. However, of this 89.52 million ha IPC, only 71.3 million ha is being used. Thus, 18 million ha is still not being used, mainly due to non-availability of groundwater. More than 88 per cent of the minor irrigation schemes are groundwater dependent and 99 per cent of them are owned by the private farmers.[13]

What is more interesting is that the 'majority of schemes (80.3 per cent) are being financed by own savings of individual farmers followed by bank loans (6.5 per cent), others (6.3 per cent), government funds (5.1 per cent) and money lenders (1.9 per cent)'.[14] The banks and the government together support less than 13 per cent of these irrigation assets. Poor farmers are investing in irrigation infrastructure with their own savings and loans including those from money lenders.

The average cost of each scheme is estimated to be approximately Rs 69,266, ranging from Rs 50,000 for a shallow tubewell to Rs 204,872 for a surface water flow scheme. The total cost of creating these schemes is estimated to be around Rs 117,000 crores (Rs 1170 billion). Since more than 90 per cent are under the private ownership of farmers, a significant chunk of contributions for minor irrigation came from the small farmers. The farmers have financed this entirely through personal borrowings, pledges and savings.

As mentioned earlier, the computed cost of the investments in MI is about Rs 117,000 crores. The cost of per ha irrigation potential created by the MI is Rs 13,928 (say Rs 14,000). Assuming there shall be optimum utilization of 63.5 Mha, the cost for each ha comes to nearly Rs 18,425 (see Table 10.3 and Figure 10.1).

Of this, 70 per cent of the money is from the savings of farmers, 3 per cent from money lenders, 13 per cent from bank loans and 9 per cent from government support. Thus these small irrigation infrastructures were predominantly created by small and marginal farmers with their savings. However, the cost estimation mentioned in the 4th MI Census Survey Report does not take into account the cost of farm labour, farmer's financial contributions and personal efforts to access groundwater resources.

Compare these individual efforts of farmers with the government investments on MMI projects which costs at least Rs 10,00,000 per ha (Table 10.3). Evidently, the MI is not only efficient and far more reliable, but it is also the one scheme where public-private partnerships can be initiated. The government is spending at least 50 times more for creating each ha of irrigation compared to that of the farmers who are contributing their own money for groundwater irrigation. Farmers are thus creating increased irrigation potential and utilizing water at a fraction of the cost compared to government-funded irrigation projects. This should be acknowledged and made into a future policy direction for public-private partnerships for any new technologies or schemes which increase water efficiency and reduce wastage of water.

When farmers are putting their own saving in creating the irrigation facilities, the government is not able to support the water use efficiency. In spite of all the talk, only 'about 1.9 per cent schemes used drip irrigation and about 3.3 per cent used sprinkler systems for water distribution'[15] and more than 53 per cent of schemes still used kaccha open channels. About 40 per cent of these schemes use pipes, which is again due to investments from the poor farmers. There is a lot of scope for water use efficiency in these schemes, but they need support. The reasons for farmers not being able to use these systems more efficiently are stated in the 5th Census report as: '"less discharge of water" in 60.9 per cent cases followed by 11.4 per cent due to "mechanical breakdown" and 7.8 per cent due to "non-availability of adequate fuel/power". Reasons like "non-availability of funds" and "lack of maintenance" contribute only 2.3 per cent and 3.3 per cent respectively'.[16]

### *Unutilized irrigation potential*

It is worth mentioning here that the Irrigation Potential Created (IPC) projected by the government is in its books and reports, whereas the result-oriented Irrigation Potential Utilized (IPU) by the farmers is the real figure on the ground. By 2007, the total surface water irrigation of IPU was 45.7 Mha, an increase from 29.64 Mha. Similarly, the ground IPU is 40.81 Mha, of which 34.3 Mha was added after 1950.

Therefore, since the 1950s, the actual increase in irrigation by surface water was far less than groundwater.

Irrigation through groundwater is primarily through investments by farmers from their savings or borrowings, as noted previously. There are 16.2 million electrical pumps in the country and 8.5 million diesel pumps. These 24.7 million pumps contributed to the growth of the irrigation potential. Overall, these pumps lift 220 BCM of water every year to irrigate the fields. On an average, each of the pumps lifts 9–10 thousand $m^3$ of water and irrigates 1.6 ha of land. On an average, each ha irrigated by groundwater consumes 30–40 per cent less water but produces almost the same quantity of grain.

Compared to the cost of major irrigation in 1950, which is less than Rs 3000 per ha, the current cost of over Rs 1 million is an increase of almost 300 times in the last 60 years. Even considering the devaluation of the rupee, this is still a massive increase of cost to provide irrigation. In addition to these yearly capital costs, significant amounts of money are being spent on maintaining the irrigation system. Hence, there is a need to look at the cost-benefit of the irrigation systems in India in order to re-direct the money for more demand-side management.

## Strategic direction and interventions

India needs to prioritize policy decisions which focus on reducing water consumption in agriculture. It is possibleby diverting a part of the investments allocated for MMI projects to technologies which directly benefit farmers. It can set an example for social cooperation and economic success through public-private partnerships. As the farmers have demonstrated their commitment towards and success in increasing the area of irrigation through groundwater resource utilization, a sympathetic and inclusive approach to use water sustainably is the need of the hour.

The components of such a strategy could include the following:

- Reduction of water for agriculture by 25 per cent by 2030: The national planning process must prioritize sustainable water usage. It can be done by reducing the significant quantity of water withdrawal, say 25 per cent, which is 170 billion $m^3$ of water to agriculture by 2030, by meeting all the production needs.
- Industry participation for zero pollution: Industry must be made part of the agenda to reduce pollution. 'Polluters will pay' must be the co-operative initiative of the government and the industry to achieve zero industrial pollution.

- Investing in water in an intelligent way: Redirecting government investments, NABARD loans and international investments towards focussing on water productivity targets rather than the construction of major irrigation projects.
- Water pricing: Creating a system of incentives and disincentives to save water through water pricing. Farmers can exchange credits they get for saving water; similarly, others can be asked to pay for exceeding their quota of water. This will protect the poor and also encourage water saving.

The suggestions may appear ambitious but many countries have addressed sustainable water withdrawal and usage issues only by positive interventions. Many small interventions have demonstrated the possibility at the microscopic scale when interventions at the larger scale have somehow failed to work.

### *Reducing water withdrawals in agriculture*

According to the FAO, in 2010, the Indian agriculture sector was withdrawing about 688 BCM of water. Of that, approximately 460 BCM was surface waterand 225 BCM was groundwater. Indian agriculture planners need to have a very bold vision to reduce the total water usage without compromising on productivity. Water use in agriculture can be limited to 520 BCM while increasing total production of agricultural commodities by 25 per cent. It would mean that India needs to reduce about 110 BCM of surface water to obtain 350 BCM and groundwater withdrawals of 60 BCM, thereby reducing a total of 165 BCM of water use. It should be set as a national target to be reached by 2030, with specific targets for each agricultural farm, each project and each state. In turn, it requires a specific target to improve the productivity of each crop using less water.

This target of reduced water use can be achieved by several policy incentives and disincentives. No additional investments are required. It requires diversion and reallocation of financial resources towards water efficiency, water productivity, water saving, water conservation and water storage. There are systematic approaches and water use technologies available for the farmers. Farmers will be willing to implement such approaches provided the incentives to increase productivity by using less water can be linked to the subsidies, received either directly or indirectly. Monetary incentives can be given for using less water without compromising the productive capacity of the land or decreasing crop productivity.

The total water withdrawal for agriculture must be targeted around 520 BCM. The initial and immediate reaction could be, 'it is not possible'. It would be useful to recall in this context that China withdraws less than 400 BCM of water annually but produces a lot more agricultural goods and services than India.

Two significant proven technological experiences which are popular in India are these: (1) System of Rice Intensification (SRI) and (2) Sustainable Sugarcane Initiative (SSI).

### *System of rice intensification (SRI)*

Rice cultivation is a very water-intensive activity. To produce one kilo of rice, 3,000–5,000 litres of water are required. About two or three times more water is needed for rice cultivation compared to other irrigated crops. It is estimated that irrigated rice receives 34–43 per cent of the world's irrigation water. It is projected that by 2025, 15–20 Mha of irrigated rice will suffer some degree of water scarcity.

Rice is a staple food for India and plays a significant role in India's diet, economy, employment, culture and history. Ninety per cent of the rice produced is consumed within the country. With 44 Mha, India has the most extensive area under the production of rice. Of that, 26.3 Mha (2013–2014) is irrigated. India produced 157 million tonnes of paddy (close to 100 million tonnes of rice in 2014). The productivity is 3.5 tonnes per ha. India produces 21 per cent of the global paddy production, i.e., 741 million tonnes, whereas China, with much less area (30 Mha), produces 207 million tonnes of paddy, with an average production of 6.8 tonnes/ha. The productivity of China is almost twice that of India. Therefore, India's focus should be more on productivity than the increase in area or increase in irrigation. For example, if India can produce six tonnes per ha on its irrigated area, it will be enough to meet its demand by 2050.

The total area under irrigated food crops was 44.14 Mha in 2013–2014. Of this, 55 per cent, which is 26.3 million ha of the area, was under irrigated paddy cultivation. This 26.3 Mha consumes more than 60 per cent of all the water drawn by agriculture. However, all the investments in major irrigation projects, which is supposed to be for irrigated food crops, added only 15 Mha of irrigated paddy.

The challenge currently, therefore, is to continue to grow rice under irrigated conditions but using much less water. SRI is about this, and it has been proven with positive results in many parts of India. State governments of Tamil Nadu and Bihar in collaboration with many non-governmental organizations have been promoting this method extensively.

SRI is based on four main principles:[17]

- Reducing seed, by planting young seedlings with broader spacing.
- Reducing water, avoiding standing water but keeping the soil saturated.
- Reducing the usage of inorganic fertilizers and pesticides.
- Employing mechanical weeding to create aeration.

The practices related to these principles have been well developed, and several manuals have been developed to practice SRI in a systematic way.[18] Detailed methodology and the practical steps to scale-up these proven methods have been extensively discussed and documented.[19] By adopting the SRI method, India can easily meet its future demand for rice production while reducing more than 30 per cent of the current water usage in paddy cultivation.

Table 10.4 summarizes these factors, assuming that SRI is practised on 20 Mha of rice (out of India's current 43 Mha under rice).

*Sustainable sugarcane initiative*

The next water intensive crop in India is sugarcane. Nearly 5 Mha of sugarcane is under cultivation, and 95 per cent of this area is irrigated.

*Table 10.4* Impact of SRI in India if Adopted on 20 Mha

| | *Level* | | *Total estimate* | | *Advantage due to SRI* |
|---|---|---|---|---|---|
| | *Current* | *SRI* | *Current* | *SRI* | |
| Seed use | 30 kg/ha | 7.5 kg/ha | 600 m tonnes | 150 m tonnes | 450 m tonnes saved |
| Irrigation water | 149 $m^3$ | 92 $m^3$ | 2,980 $Mm^3$ | 1,840 $Mm^3$ | 1,140 $Mm^3$ saved |
| Paddy production | 3.17 t/ha | 4.17 t/ha | 139 m tonnes | 183 m tonnes | 44 m tonnes extra production |

Source: Gujja and Thiyagarajan 2009

Moreover, sugarcane is an annual crop, and in some cases, the maturity requires more than one year. It is the only crop in India which is still on the ground in mid-summer. Once the crop has taken root after plantation, it needs irrigation throughout the year. Many conflicts arise during the summer on account of allocating water between sugarcane and human needs.

The seven main principles that govern SSI are as follows:[20]

- Raising seedlings in a nursery using single-budded chips extracted from healthy canes.
- Transplanting young seedlings when they are 25–30 days old, that is, while they are still at the two-leaf stage, with just two leaves fully emerged.
- Maintaining wide spacing between plants, both between rows and within rows.
- Seedlings are transplanted into the primary field, usually with a spacing of 4ft x 2ft or 5ft x 2ft, possibly with more spacing between the rows when the soil is very fertile.
- Providing sufficient moisture to the plants and soil but avoiding any flooding of the fields so that the soil is maintained in the most aerobic condition.
- Encouraging the use of organic matter for providing soil nutrients and plant protection.
- Practising intercropping between rows with pulses and other crops for efficient utilization of the land, by maintaining ground cover that inhibits the growth of weeds while enhancing nitrogen in the soil.

SSI saves at least 22 per cent of water at the planting stage. Since it involves wide spacing, the method facilitates drip irrigation, which further saves 20–25 per cent of water. Therefore, sugarcane cultivation can be made more water efficient while increasing its productivity. SSI produces at least 20 per cent more; in fact, many farmers reported an increase of more than 60 per cent of production.

The water savings and the increased production through the SRI and SSI technologies used by the farmers have been documented and independently verified by the Gold Standard.[21]

Similar approaches can be applied on many other crops and they can be grown with more efficient methods. These methods of 'More Production for Less Water' are being practised in India and many other parts of the world (SRI-Rice 2014).

### *Industry and business participation in improving the productivity of agriculture*

Industry uses about 17 BCM of water which is less than 3 per cent of water used for agriculture. In reality, the total water use by industry and business is a lot more. Many industries depend on raw materials produced by the agriculture sector. Therefore, industry needs to participate in water efficiency of agriculture for its own good. It can participate in several ways to influence the water efficiency in agriculture.

The industry and the business impact on water resources could be categorized into five types.

- Direct use: Water used within industries and businesses. This water is withdrawn directly by the industry, primarily for their production centre or operating area and is about 17 BCM.
- Water embedded in the raw materials: Industries use raw materials. Production of raw materials requires water, and this is drawn from the natural systems.
- Water required by the products going out of the industry: This is somewhat difficult to estimate, and some might argue about it, but many industries which produce goods and services require water after they are finished with production.
- Water itself is business: Water itself is business for bottled water companies. They are expanding but are not focusing on water use efficiency at the basin level or catchment level. Those companies need to be encouraged to protect sources of water in their own interest and the interest of affected communities. Unless water is treated as a raw material for the industry and relative profits are taxed accordingly, water efficiency cannot be plugged and integrated into the business.
- Water pollution: This is a known issue, but often ignored. In India, many industries use water to dilute its waste before releasing a part of it into the natural systems to comply with pollution standards. Therefore, it is essential to consider this parameter while estimating the water used by industry.

There are many 'case studies' documenting the role of industry in aggravating and addressing the water crisis. To understand their 'catchment', first they need to list the areas from where raw materials such as grain, fodder, water and ingredients are being procured. Each industry first needs to calculate its quantity of water needs and the corresponding area of water catchment which it is indirectly or directly affecting. Many big industries and big businesses are aware of such supply chain issues but have not internalized the approaches to deal with it. As part of moving from case studies to catchments, some specific steps have been suggested here.

1 Identifying the impact on catchment: Industries and businesses first need to map out the entire water use in their product and supply chain including water needs after it goes out of their factory. Next, one can estimate the water footprint of a particular industry on its water catchment. This step is to establish an area of influence, which is far higher than its production centre, the factory.
2 Estimating the total water footprint of each type of industry: It is also possible to fix the impact based on per unit of its produce or unit of its turnover/profit. It is like estimating the water component for each of the units, to quantify actual water withdrawal required to produce the product.
3 Targets to reduce water withdrawal over a period: It is possible to first fix either an industry-wide or a full-product target. For example, it is better to consider all factors to avoid some inherent or historical advantages of a particular situation or area. It is to set the full standard or measure to improve water productivity and to have a broader impact on water efficiency.
4 Zero pollution: Industry and businesses must adopt a policy of zero pollution both in their own interest and in national interest.

### *Redirecting the national and international investments*

Government policy in India has not yet evolved on the impact of financial investments on water usage, be it in the manufacturing of products or the location of the industry which chooses to discharge conveniently into the natural water bodies or unclaimed lands. Therefore, the impact of financial investments on water resources locally and regionally should be the criteria while deciding on the location or type of investments.

### *Water pricing*

Water pricing, like privatization, is debated in a very 'ideological' context rather than in a realistic or practical context. There are two types of general arguments on water pricing:

1 The argument against any water pricing because it will lead to further denial of water to the poor.

2 There is a claim for water pricing as the solution to all water problems. The argument is that since water is freely available, people do not value it and thus cause wastage.

It is possible to price water while protecting the needs of the poor and the socially disadvantaged sections. With the detailed study showing the full cost of water delivery, delivered to each of the major cities, one can develop a specific framework for pricing. By not recovering the full cost of water, it is not the poor who are benefitting but the rich and the middle classes who do not pay for the services they receive. It is possible to have proper water pricing and charging of the full cost to users to improve the service and reduce the cost per unit, provided the government has proper and independent regulatory mechanism in place. If water pricing were to be introduced in the future, the consumers would have to pay the cost of water through price integration in the product, instead of burdening farmers to absorb the cost of water.

## Conclusions and way forward

Currently, around 80 per cent of our water is allocated to agriculture. The government is still allocating vast financial resources to increase the irrigated area in the country. Such a policy needs to be changed. Investments need to be re-directed from water supply projects (such as major and medium irrigation infrastructure projects) to the adoption of water-efficient methods. The government needs to invest in innovations which reduce water use for agriculture while improving the yield. Its role needs to shift from being a water provider and builder of extensive infrastructure projects to being a facilitator of innovation, a supporter of practical solutions initiated by the public and private sector. The government's approach needs to shift from 'creating and increasing the irrigation potential' to 'improving the productivity and profitability of irrigated areas'.

The current focus on high spending on MMI is deepening the water crisis. The government is, in effect, spending to create crises and conflicts. There are innovations which can prove to be effective in reducing the water demand of major irrigated crops such as rice and sugarcane while significantly improving and increasing per unit of production. These are proven methods and are already popular with the farmers. However, they are relatively few and have an impact on only a microscopic scale. These methods need to be promoted on a large scale, with substantial investments, to create a significant impact at various levels. The focus should be on water efficiency, water productivity and cost-effectiveness of irrigated areas.

The entire system of irrigation in India follows an outdated approach by quantifying physical targets. It is usually in the form of quantity of water stored, quantity of water diverted, number of acres irrigated, amount of money spent and so on. There is an urgent need to change such an approach and move towards having national targets to raise the productivity per unit of water and the net income for the quantity of water. To implement such new targets, farmers need to get proper advice, training and support in methods, 'to reduce water usage but produce more'. Such interventions are already there but need significant hike in spending to get the water savings at the basin level. India needs to take the bold decision of entirely stopping any additional infrastructure investments on major irrigation for a decade and instead create incentives and disincentives to promote water use efficiency at the project, basin and farm level. It is possible but requires a significant shift in thinking and resource allocation.

The urban water sector is still focusing on quantity rather than quality. Bringing efficiency in the water supply to the urban sector will reduce costs. Currently, in the industrial sector, there is a lack of implementation of pollution control measures and lack of encouragement to treat the effluents, leading to water quality issues. Although industries are small users of water, they do affect water quality enormously, thereby causing an impact on public health. Therefore, incentives should be provided to improve water quality and promote technologies which enhance water treatment.

The water crisis is linked to the energy crisis. There are 25 million agriculture pumps in India, and most of them can be supplied with solar power. There should be interventions which support subsidies to farmers opting for solar energy. In this way, vast land resources required for solar panels can be decentralized.

Another tricky issue in India is water pricing. Water is priced in the urban water supply but there is a reluctance to recognize water pricing issues. For example, in many parts of rural India, drinking water is being purchased from small service providers. However, there is little recognition of this ground reality and thus regulation on the quality or pricing. Contrarily, farmers are paying the price for the irregular supply of water. So, it is better to recognize that there is a price for water and the policy needs to evolve with creative incentives to use water efficiently and productively. Water management as a concept and a practice needs to undergo a radical transformation in India. For that, the farmers, the private sector and the civil society need to have a composite dialogue.

Industry too is not focusing on water. Its current thinking is to somehow evade the issue of pollution by either diverting it somewhere or treating it partially or ignoring it. Some industries and business are doing better, but they too need to be more strategic rather than publicity-oriented.

The change in the water policy decisions must come from the demand-side management of irrigation. The allocation of resources, efficiency in water use, zero pollution in both urban and industry will largely determine the future course of India's social and economic development. Unfortunately, so far, the process of change is too slow and too insignificant to meet the challenge.

## Notes

1 The authors are thankful for the assistance provided by Sraban Kumar Dalai in data processing and preparation of figures.
2 Central Water Commission (CWC): 'Due to various constraints of topography, uneven distribution of resource over space and time, it has been estimated that only about 1123 BCM of total potential of 1869 BCM can be put to beneficial use, 690 BCM being due to surface water resources. Again about 40% of utilisable surface water resources are presently in Ganga-Brahmaputra-Meghna system' (CWC 2010: 5).
3 'The major difference in demand estimates is accounted for by irrigation: the 2030 Water Resources Group estimates at 1,200 BCM are almost double that of the Ministry of Water Resources' estimate of 650 BCM for 2030. It will be a major challenge to determine how to manage this demand-supply gap in a sustainable and cost-efficient manner' (Varma 2011: 4).
4 'Between 2025 and 2050, there is a projected demand gap of nearly 200 BCM. Considering from XII Plan onwards, the demand gap could be of the order of 250 BCM. Even if a fair percentage of this additional demand is borne by groundwater, the extra burden on surface irrigation will be of the order of 150 BCM to achieve self-sufficiency by 2050' (MoWR 2011: 11).
5 www.populationpyramid.net/india/2050/ (accessed on 9 March 2018)
6 Ministry of Statistics and Programme Implementation 2017: 14–30 (refer to Section 3.1 and Tables 1–10 for the exact values).
7 Economic Survey 2017–2018 reports that climate change is likely to lower farmers' income by 25 per cent, www.financialexpress.com/budget/economic-survey-2017-18-agriculture-climate-change-likely-to-lower-farmers-income-by-25/1035560/ (accessed on 19 March 2018).
8 'The massive development of a vast irrigation network has resulted in significant increase in I.P created from 22.6 Mha in 1951 to 110.07 Mha by the end of March 2009. However, the reliable data on actual I.P utilisation under different irrigation projects is not readily available for aggregation at river basin or national level. Wherever available, it lacks either in

consistency and/or reliability because of various data collection agencies involved in the process' (Shankar 2017).

9 MoWR 2017: IX

10 'An outlay of Rs 341,900 Crores is recommended for the MMI sector of which Rs 208,600 Crores would be in the state sector and Rs 133,300 Crores would be in the central sector' (See Ministry of Water Resources 2011: ii).

11 Newspapers in Telangana State reported on 7 March 2018 that this is the highest spending ever on a single project by any state government in India. This has been reported as a significant achievement since there are another 20 days in the financial year, this figure could reach Rs 11,000 crores. See *Andhra Jyoti*, Telangana Edition, a Telugu daily newspaper published from Hyderabad, 7 March 2018, www.andhrajyoti.com.

12 MoWR 2017

13 'Almost 97 per cent of the MI structures are being owned by private entities and only about 3% is in the domain of public ownership. This pattern is more dominant in groundwater schemes where almost all type of schemes has around 99% private ownership' (MoWR 2017: 33).

14 MoWR 2017: 34

15 MoWR 2017: IX

16 MoWR 2017: X

17 See for details: http://sri.ciifad.cornell.edu/aboutsri/methods/index.html#SRIprinciples (accessed on 12 April 2018).

18 SRI manuals are available at: www.agsri.com

19 Gujja and Thiyagarajan 2009

20 See Rott 2017.

21 https://www.goldstandard.org/our-work/water-registry (accessed on 19 April 2018).

## References

Bhaduri, Amita. 2013. 'Accelerated Irrigation Benefits Programme Gave Near-Exclusive Priority in 12th Five-Year Plan, But Will It Solve India's Water Problems?' India Water Portal, www.indiawaterportal.org/articles/accelerated-irrigation-benefits-programme-given-near-exclusive-priority-12th-five-year-plan (accessed on 12 April 2018).

Central Water Commission. 2010. 'Water and Related Statistics', Water Planning & Project Wing, Central Water Commission, p. 264.

Government of India (GoI). 2017. 'Agriculture Statistics at a Glance 2016', Ministry of Agriculture & Farmers Welfare. Department of Agriculture, Cooperation and Farmers Welfare, Directorate of Economics & Statistics, pp. 327–328, http://eands.dacnet.nic.in/PDF/Glance-2016.pdf (accessed on 14 April 2018).

Government of India (GoI). 2018a. 'Statistical Yearbook 2017', Ministry of Statistics & Programme Implementation, http://mospi.nic.in/statistical-year-book-india/2017/181 (accessed on 14 April 2018).

Government of India (GoI). 2018b. 'Economic Survey 2017–2018' (Vol. 1, Chapter 6 – Agriculture, Climate, and Climate Change). Ministry of Finance, Department of Economic Affairs, Economic Division, www.indiaenviron

mentportal.org.in/files/file/economic%20survey%202017-18%20-%20 vol.1.pdf (accessed on 10 April 2018).

Gujja, Biksham and T. M. Thiyagarajan. 2009. 'New Hope for Indian Food Security? The System of Rice Intensification', IIED (International Institute for Environment and Development), gatekeeper 143, November, http://indiaenvironmentportal.org.in/files/New%20Hope%20for%20Indian%20Food%20Security.pdf (accessed on 30 April 2018).

Ministry of Statistics and Programme Implementation. 2017. 'State-Wise and Item-Wise Estimates of Value of Output from Agriculture and Allied Sectors', Report by the Central Statistics Office, Government of India (GoI), www.mospi.gov.in (accessed on 11 April 2018).

Ministry of Water Resources (MoWR). 2011. 'Report of the Working Group on Major and Medium Irrigation and Command Area Development for the XII Five-Year Plan 2012–2017', p. 165.

Ministry of Water Resources (MoWR). 2017. 'Report of 5th Census of Minor Irrigation Schemes', www.indiaenvironmentportal.org.in/files/file/Report%20of%205th%20Census%20of%20Minor%20Irrigation%20Schemes.pdf (accessed on 13 April 2018).

Ministry of Water Resources, River Development and Ganga Rejuvenation. 2014. '4th Census of Minor Irrigation Schemes Report', Minor Irrigation (Statistics) Wing, November.

Planning Commission. 'Various Years: Annual Plan Document of Planning Commission – Central Water Commission (P&P Directorate)', MoWR. (Minor Irrigation Division) and Working Group Report of XI Plan (for Target), http://planningcommission.nic.in/plans/annualplan/ (accessed on 14 April 2018).

Planning Commission of India. 2010. 'Evaluation Study on Accelerated Irrigation Benefits Programme (AIBP)', PEO Report No. 214, New Delhi: Programme Evaluation Organisation, Planning Commission, Government of India (GoI), http://planningcommission.gov.in/reports/peoreport/peoevalu/peo_aibp.pdf (accessed on 12 April 2018).

Planning Commission of India. 2013. *Twelfth Five Year Plan (2012–2017): Faster, More Inclusive and Sustainable Growth*. New Delhi: Planning Commission, Government of India (GoI), http://planningcommission.gov.in/plans/planrel/12thplan/pdf/12fyp_vol1.pdf (accessed on 11 April 2018).

Rott, P. (ed.). 2017. 'Achieving Sustainable Cultivation of Sugarcane', in *Volume 1: Cultivation Techniques, Quality and Sustainability*. Cambridge: Burleigh Dodds Science Publishing.

Shankar, Muthyam. 2017. 'Assessment of Irrigation Potential Utilization in Major Irrigation Project Using Geospatial Data', *International Journal of New Technology and Research* (IJNTR) ISSN:2454-4116, 3(4): 95–99, April.

SRI-Rice. 2014. 'The System of Crop Intensification: Agroecological Innovations for Improving Agricultural Production, Food Security, and Resilience to Climate Change', Ithaca, NY: SRI International Network and Resources Centre (SRI-Rice), Cornell University and the Wageningen, The Netherlands: Technical Centre for Agricultural and Rural Cooperation (CTA), http://sri.

ciifad.cornell.edu/aboutsri/othercrops/SCImonograph_SRIRice2014.pdf (accessed on 12 April 2018).

Varma, Harish Kumar. 2011. 'ADB's Water Sector Operations in India: Review and Way Forward', South Asia working paper series, Asian Development Bank, www.adb.org/sites/default/files/publication/29246/adb-water-sector-operations-india-review-forward.pdf (accessed on 16 May 2018).

# 11 Gender and water

## Why we need alternatives to alternative discourses

*Sumi Krishna and Seema Kulkarni*

### Introduction

For over four decades women have figured in the discourses around water at the local, national and global levels. They have moved from the periphery of the discourse to seemingly more central locations (see, for instance, Green and Baden 1995; Zwarteveen 1997; Jackson 1998; Joy and Paranjape 2005; Harris 2009; Seager 2010). Over these years, the development sector as a whole has demonstrated the following: (1) the basic needs approach has given way to rights-based approaches;[1] (2) concerns about access to natural resources have evolved to encompass issues of resource control; and (3) the focus on women's roles has been firmly displaced by a deeper understanding of the importance of gender relations in determining women's lives and work. Each of these shifts in perspective reflects a more nuanced political understanding of development. But these alternative discourses have had limited impact in the shaping of policy and institutional initiatives. In this chapter, therefore, we seek to understand why the progressive terms of discourse and recent policy reforms have not led to a more gender equitable and sustainable system of water governance particularly in relation to women in India. We suggest that the gender and social aspects of natural resource management have to be integrated into the planning process. This could be achieved if, on the one hand, the gender and water discourse is embedded in an interdisciplinary and multi-sector approach to natural resources and, on the other hand, the broader political struggles for resources integrate feminist perspectives and engage with women's collective actions around water.

### Development planning approaches

The movement for India's Independence encompassed the protection of soil, water, vegetation and forests to ensure people's livelihoods (see the National Planning Committee 1948). But women's gendered responsibilities and productive roles in family provisioning were rather narrowly conceptualized. The early Five Year Plans located women, children and the disabled within a common social welfare framework (Sujaya 1995; Krishna 2004a). The gender gap in education was recognized but the gendered structures within which women live and work were not. Even '*Towards Equality*', the landmark Report of the Committee on the Status of Women (Government of India 1974), which provided an impetus to the modern women's movement in India, did not deal with women's gendered responsibilities for water, fuel and fodder. In the late 1970s, the buzz created by the international women's movement, and the strong position on women's rights taken by the autonomous women's movement in India (see Sangari and Vaid 1989) led to the recognition that women's concerns could not simply be subsumed under broad national plans. Thus, India's Sixth Five Year Plan (1980–1985) included a separate chapter on women, marking a shift in the national planning process. In the mid-1980s, the concept of 'gender mainstreaming' emerged at the Third World Conference on Women in Nairobi (1985) and was formalized at the Fourth World Conference in Beijing (1995). Mainstreaming became part of the discourse across many development sectors in India. Envisaged both as a goal and a strategy to integrate women along with men into all planning processes, this was an advance from the earlier policy of separate programmes for women.

At the level of discourse, gender mainstreaming led to the recognition that women contribute a major part of the labour in managing the land, water, plants and other livelihood resources, and further that they have a rich experiential store of knowledge about diverse landscapes (such as watersheds, forests and pastures) and varied resources (such as poultry, livestock and inland fishery). This understanding was reflected, for instance, in a new emphasis on gender in the Tenth Five Year Plan (2002–2007). Under the New Agriculture Policy, 2000, a Gender Resource Centre (GRC) was set up within the Indian Council for Agricultural Research as the nodal agency for all matters pertaining to gender and agriculture. But the GRC does not deal with critical issues related to the larger framework of agricultural change, the decline of common property resources that have increased women's labour, or changes in cropping patterns triggered by government policies related to land, water and forests. So, the GRC's transformative potential is limited (see Krishna 2009). This is characteristic of the way in which the Indian planning process incorporates rhetorical shifts in perspective, which are then blurred in the institutional mechanisms that are created supposedly in response to the alternative discourse.

The Eleventh Five Year Plan (2007–2012) too incorporated feminist views and language, as did the earlier National Water Policy, 2002, which recognized the need for structural changes to ensure the appropriate participation of women. It states (Para 12):

> Management of the water resources for diverse uses should incorporate a participatory approach; by involving not only the various governmental agencies but also the users and other stakeholders, in an effective and decisive manner, in various aspects of planning, design, development and management of the water resources schemes. Necessary legal and institutional changes should be made at various levels for the purpose, duly ensuring appropriate role for women.
>
> (GOI 2002)

The more recent National Water Policy of 2012, however, shows less explicit commitment to equity and social justice in general and more specifically to women. In para 9.6 it says:

> Local governing bodies like Panchayats, Municipalities, Corporations, etc., and Water Users Associations, wherever applicable, should be involved in planning of the projects. The unique needs and aspirations of the Scheduled Castes and Scheduled Tribes, women and other weaker sections of the society should be given due consideration.

In the 1990s, as the Indian economy was being liberalized, the community development model of the 1950s was also being shaped anew.[2] Decentralized community-based resource management programmes emphasized women's central roles. The emphasis on users, stakeholders and local bodies in the water sector resonated with the earlier focus from the 1950s and 1960s on community participation. Institution-building was foregrounded and the hope was that a new structure of governance would emerge. But, too often, interventions were premised on the homogeneity of communities, and of women, overlooking the differences in their ethnic, caste and class locations.

Since the mid-1980s, watershed development has been a primary focus of planning with the objective of improving the productivity of land, increasing the availability of food and easing poverty. Watershed projects were also intended to involve women; women's 'self-help' savings-and-credit groups and small enterprises were supported. Micro-watershed village-level studies in several states have shown, however, that the environmental benefits of watershed development have gone mainly to landowners and that women were certainly not among them.[3]

Viewed from a feminist perspective, there remains a gap between adopting the language of equity and establishing programmatic initiatives to achieve this. In varied cultural contexts across the country, poor women lack customary entitlements to land and resources. In many parts of the country, new rights to resources (such as the water sources created through public funds as in watersheds) have been circumscribed by the pre-existing system of rights. For instance, thousands of Water Users' Associations were formed in the late 1990s in Andhra Pradesh (then including the new state of Telengana), under the thrust for decentralization and local control of resources, but membership was based on land ownership and women did not own land (Jairath 2000; Krishna 2001, 2004a). Simply providing recognition at the policy level has not led to a strategy for incorporation into programmes. When the membership of Water Users' Associations is based on land ownership, this effectively excludes women and the landless. Indeed, without gaining rights to productive resources or recognition of their work in agriculture, women continued to be viewed in relation to the traditional 'womanly' areas of care (family provisioning, child health and nutrition) rather than as productive workers and farmers with needs, rights and responsibilities over a range of natural resources including water (Ahmed 2005; Krishna 2009; Kulkarni *et al.* 2009).

In the Indian context, the longer-term impact on praxis was probably the outcome of the 73rd and 74th Amendments to the Constitution, which mandated one-third reservation of seats for women in the elected local bodies. In time, this brought many more women into local decision-making, with the potential to affect local water management among other matters; yet it is only in a few instances that women elected members have been able to assert their control against the onslaught of private vested interests (See Krishna 2004a; 2004b).

## Women and drinking water

Over half a century ago, in 1961, social activist Mrinal Gore contested the local civic election to the then Bombay Municipal Council and won. In 1964, as a member of the civic body, she took up the struggle to bring a regular and safe drinking water supply to the slums of Goregaon, a suburb of north Mumbai, where 11 people had been killed in water riots. Known as '*Paniwali Bai*' (the woman who brings water), she went on first to become a member of the state legislature; then, in 1977, she won the Lok Sabha election to become a Member of the Indian Parliament. It is said that her slogan '*Paaniwalibai Dilli mein, Dilliwalibai paani mein*', 'Water woman in Delhi, Delhi woman (Prime Minister Indira Gandhi) in the water', was responsible for her landslide victory. Together with other progressive women leaders, Ahilya Rangnekar and Pramila Dandavate, she led the women's fight for food, water, shelter, housing and employment as part of a wider social and political struggle (Gavankar 2003).

The national and international perspective on drinking water, however, was not imbued with such an integrated vision. The preferred approach was to concentrate media attention, programmes and funding on a single issue at a time. Hence, international days, years and decades were held with much fanfare to mark a particular developmental problem. In 1977, the United Nations Water Conference affirmed: 'All peoples have the right to have access to clean drinking water in quantities and of a quality equal to their basic need'. This led to the launch of the first International Drinking Water and Sanitation Decade (1981–1990). The necessary technologies were viewed as relatively simple and cost-effective and the results were expected to be quickly and clearly visible – saving the time and labour of women and improving health for all. Community participation was projected as a key strategy, as emphasized at that time by the WHO, among others. Improvements in water supply, sanitation and health were seen to be interlinked and most effective when integrated with broader community development goals. The United Nations Development Programme (UNDP) Administrator claimed that the achievement of Decade goals would 'revolutionise the lives of rural women in every developing country' (Chauhan and Gopalakrishnan 1983: 7).

The Government of India adopted the global discourse of the international agencies, the Decade goals and strategy. The global image of the 'Third World' woman burdened by her load of water (or/and fuel wood) fitted neatly into the government's welfare approach to development. By the early 1980s, however, it became clear that what had seemed eminently achievable was not going to be possible. Improved water supply and sanitation for all was not just a matter of identifying and implementing engineering solutions. The social and gender aspects, the 'software' was as important as the hardware of pumps and pipes (Chauhan 1983; Krishna 1985).

Today, almost anyone who is connected to the government water supply network in urban India is being subsidized; yet, the poor often pay higher rates for water than their richer neighbours because the tariff is structured in large slabs, presumably for administrative convenience. With the state aiming to become a facilitator rather than a service provider of drinking water, the goal of the first Water Decade has been turned on its head. This has a gendered impact because water provision is women's work in most (though not all) parts of India.

## New principles and gendering the water sector: the post-1990s scenario

In the latter part of the 1980s, the discourse on water had begun to absorb some of the language of the global environmental and women's movements that had emerged in the previous decade. Sustainable development and women's centrality to resource management became critical premises. There was also the beginning of a shift in thinking to meld the technical with the social and economic factors. This is reflected, for example, in the 1992 International Conference on Water and Environment that adopted the 'Dublin statement on water and sustainable development'. The statement affirmed four 'principles' (United Nations 1992):

1 Freshwater is a finite and vulnerable resource, essential to sustain life, development and the environment.
2 Water development and management should be based on a participatory approach, involving users, planners and policy makers at all levels.
3 Women play a central part in the provision, management and safeguarding of water.
4 Water has an economic value in all its competing uses and should be recognized as an economic good.

The broad sweep that covered all women in the conventional development discourse also marked some of the more radical approaches to women like ecofeminism, which, for the first time, highlighted the critical connections between nature and women. The ecofeminist approach brought to light the interconnections between unbridled growth, ecological destruction and domination over women. Ecofeminists advanced the concept of an all-encompassing patriarchal domination that exploited women, resources and 'Third World' nations (see Mies 1986; Shiva 1988; Mies and Shiva 1993). Although this presented a new perspective, it was evident that women's knowledge of water was not a matter of their female biology but rather a consequence of the social shaping of their lives. Furthermore, not all women, nor women at all times and everywhere, have had such essential linkages with nature and natural resources (Agarwal 1992;

Krishna 1996; Rocheleau, Slayter and Wangari 1996; Leach 2003). When the discourse is framed with women as being intimately connected with nature, thus as privileged knowers, the onus of managing and conserving water is also placed on women. This was widely critiqued by sections of feminists (Ahmed 2005; Joshi and Fawcett 2005; Kulkarni *et al.* 2009) who argued that this was in effect an instrumental approach to women and natural resource management, and their participation in water. Furthermore, when women and communities are perceived as being homogenous, the underlying structures (of ethnicity, caste, class and other markers of identity) that determine access to water are overlooked. These critiques put forward a more nuanced approach to understanding gender and water, locating it in the larger framework of political ecology.

Among key lessons that emerged from the feminist political ecology critiques of the gender and water sector were that programmes and policies around water must ensure that the burden of women's unpaid work is not increased in the absence of rights and voice in decision-making. And, further, that stereotypical assumptions of women's work and women's relationship with water should not be the basis for policy making. Women's current roles as collectors of water for domestic use result in policies, which may engage women in deciding on the locations of taps, for example, but do not include women in making technological choices or decisions over rights to water usage. Feminist critiques also noted the disjunction between domestic water supply being treated as the women's realm and irrigation water as the men's, thus undermining women's productive roles and eliding over men's domestic responsibilities.

In the 21st century, the thrust for reform in the water and sanitation sector was accompanied by attempts to alter institutional structures at all levels. The approach to women, however, did not reflect the same reformatory impetus; the new programmes and institutional structures continued to restrict women at most to participation in community-based and domestic water programmes.

## World water forums and the gender and water alliance (GWA)

It is ironic that the 1992 International Conference on Water and Environment, which, for the first time, emphasized the importance of women's participation in water management, provided the basis for water being treated as a commodity. In the post-Dublin years, participation through decentralized planning and management and cost recovery through pricing were considered important measures in water management. The conference also marked a shift in water management from a techno-centric approach to institutional restructuring and economic reform. A series of World Water Forums since Marrakech in Morocco, in 1997, developed a 'Vision for Water, Life and the Environment in the 21st century'. At the second World Water Forum (held in Hague in 2000), gender issues were foregrounded with the formation of the Gender and Water Alliance.[4] International agencies acknowledged the need to involve men and women in planning for water (UN-Water 2003). As part of the Global Water Partnership formed in 1996, national water partnerships were set up in different countries and many South Asian nations established networks for 'women and water'.

These World Water Forums and the establishment of the Gender and Water Alliance seemed to reflect the growth and spread of an alternative discourse on water. The terminology of 'gender' decidedly replaced 'women' and both activism and research on gender and water grew rapidly. The emphasis was on certain areas and themes – domestic drinking water and sanitation issues (which re-emerged within the context of rural and urban human settlements); displacement and rehabilitation issues related especially to the construction of large river water projects and water for irrigation, livestock and other such purposes. Nuanced analyses, however, revealed the contradictions between policy and practice as also within each of these spheres – e.g., participatory management of a universal heritage of water versus the marketing of water as an economic commodity: burdening women almost exclusively with the labour and responsibility of safeguarding water versus addressing gendered rights to water. Despite these debates, however, policy makers and even practitioners continue to see women only as instruments to address the water crisis, especially at the micro level.

## The fallout of global policy changes

At the global level there is growing tension between recognizing that water is a human rights issue and treating it as an economic commodity; on both sides of this divide, gender remains unaddressed, if not unrecognized. Gender issues in the water sector have not been located in particular historical contexts nor approached in terms of the complex power relations between people, involving ethnicity and caste/class. Ignoring this context serves the vested interests of the state, capital and patriarchy. So, although the centrality of gender justice seems to receive wide acceptance in statements and documents, the practice lags behind.

Following international pronouncements, a spate of programmes was announced at the national and state levels, shaped largely by the requirements of international or multinational agencies. These programmes were designed to include women in water management, mainly through micro-level institutions concerned with domestic water. Thus, the gender component became a routine addition in policies and programmes. By the early 2000s, strong programmes had been devised and budgetary allocations too were made.

The Indian National Water Policy of 1987, revisited and updated in 2002 (highlighting human settlements and the environment), was again reviewed a decade later. The National Water Policy 2012 (GOI 2012) gives primacy to drinking water and sanitation, and to water as being critical for the ecology. Yet, it treats all water beyond these domains uniformly as an economic good. Water for livelihoods is thus not central to the policy document. The policy directions being taken by the post 2013 Government of India (under the Bharatiya Janata Party-led National Democratic Alliance) point to the erosion of regulations on land acquisition for the so-called public good because the social audits to safeguard the people's interests are not being undertaken. Therefore, the apprehension is that water sources too may be taken over without people's participation and consent.

## Water reforms and privatization

Post 1991, with decentralization and economic liberalization, the water sector has seen significant shifts in terms of economic and institutional restructuring. Typically, water reforms rearticulate the global shift from perceiving water as a social good to be provided free by the government to acknowledging that it as a scarce economic resource. This has led to the state withdrawing from its role as a provider to that of facilitating demand through so-called community participation. Consequently, key elements of the reform process are decentralization, charging users for the service, transferring operation and maintenance to the community, introducing regulatory bodies and the increasing involvement of the private sector. Added to this package is now the idea of Public Private Partnerships (PPPs).

As reforms in the water sector are largely being driven by economic and institutional restructuring, the only attention to gender is women's representation in micro-level water institutions. Policy documents either do not mention gender-differentiated water needs or do so minimally. There is also scarcely any recognition of women's role in water management. Women are simply subsumed under the general category of 'stakeholder participation'. It is not surprising, therefore, that policies and practice do not reflect an understanding of the varied facets of gender roles and relations, cutting across different social groups (Kulkarni *et al.* 2009).

## Moving beyond 'alternative perspectives'

Over the last four decades as various perspectives on women/gender and water have emerged, even entered mainstream discourse, there have been seeming shifts in policy. Theoretical insights, social activism and the political economy of development (including development aid/funding) have intersected in complex ways leading to an understanding that water issues are socially embedded along the axes of class, caste, ethnicity and gender. Water and sanitation issues have gained currency in international policy discourse along with the recognition of the politics of water in the nexus of water and society. Though this is now the new 'received wisdom' in the rhetoric of policy making, progressive terms of discourse are also being appropriated if not subverted for vested interests. Even at a rhetorical level, however, the alternative perspectives in the water sector do open the way for exploited sections of people to organize struggles around resource rights. Similarly, fore-grounding women's central role in water management has not transformed women's lives but does provide an opening for gendered struggles around the life-sustaining resource.

While the introduction of quotas in water-related institutions such as the water and sanitation committees or the Water Users' Associations in the irrigation context has undoubtedly created a space for women, recent studies on the working of decentralized institutions show how difficult it is for women to participate effectively in an inequitous terrain (Kulkarni *et al.* 2009). Despite this overwhelming constraint, women in the domestic water sector do seem to be more visible and to themselves be making a perceptible change as significant stakeholders in village politics. Thus, the idea of representation and participation in the public sphere has served women who did not otherwise possess a public voice and identity to at least demand that their points of view be heard. The right vested through public participation allows them a space to demand for change (see Krishna 2007). The Panchayat Raj Institutions have enabled women to formally enter public spaces and use that to their advantage. Therefore, women are a significant constituency for politicians and policy makers. The process is slow, and the benefits are highly differentiated across class, caste or tribal lines, so the commitment to decentralize has to be extended beyond the duration of any particular scheme (Ahmed 2005; Mukhopadhyay 2005; Kulkarni 2011; Kulkarni and Joy 2012).

We now need to ask how women's struggles around water can be *transformative* rather than just ameliorative. The scholarship on gender and water has grown apace in what seems to some observers a rarefied space extending our understanding of the issues manifold but with insufficient influence on praxis, even as the middle-class and urban feminist discourse in India is increasingly focused on issues of autonomy and violence that cut across class and caste and draw wide media coverage (Krishna 2015). The concerns of the poorest and most oppressed (whether urban, rural or tribal) are very specific to particular local situations of livelihood deprivation (see, for instance, Tewari-Jassal 2004; Lahiri-Dutt 2006; Krishnan 2009; Krishna 2012). Women's struggles for livelihoods, water equity and gender justice involve contestations, negotiations and conciliations that the alternative discourses have scarcely envisioned and rarely documented. The challenge is to find ways to engage critically with customarily embedded social practices, generate community feelings in secular settings, and rethink gender and water issues with intellectual rigour and practical effectiveness.

Both participation and representation for 'women' as a political category are major policy shifts but have diverted attention from re-hauling the water sector and rethinking the gendered division of labour. The challenge, therefore, is for research and action to move beyond the areas of participation and representation and to focus on enhancing our understanding of the ways in which macro policies are treating women's labour merely as a means of profit accumulation and are reducing the family itself into a consumption unit. Because gender and caste pervade everyday life, any initiatives in the gender-water sector have to address the grassroots social injustices that determine access and decision-making and this requires engagement with struggles that go beyond water.

Women's incentive for water management – underlying their agency – is not just related to their resource dependence, but also to social and institutional structures, which do not allow them the same access as men to resource rights, economic opportunities or decision-making. Engendering governance is not merely a technical exercise; increasing the number of women in organizations or political spaces, such as water committees, but about redefining the nature of public space and acknowledging that the private domain – where much gendered socialization takes place – cannot be seen as distinct or separate. Furthermore, there is little recognition of the implications of the public-private divide or the terrain of households and to a lesser extent, communities and the intra- and inter-dynamics of power that characterize institutional sites and that set the boundaries for participation by women and men (Ashworth 1996). 'Although governance is about getting institutions right for development' governance policies rarely concentrate on 'getting institutions right for women *in* development' (emphasis added, Goetz 1997; see also Kabeer 2005). Not only are institutions assumed to be neutral, the public-private divide that determines women's exclusion from the public domain is used to reinforce gendered power relations at all levels – in public, private and civil society organizations.[5]

Water management organizations, whether traditional or modern, are mainly masculine spaces with women having few decision-making roles or none at all. Customary socio-cultural practices too constrain women's agency in critical phases of natural resource management – such as harvesting tussar silk cocoons, storing paddy seeds, or managing water. But the culture of the modern water sector (premised on the masculine engineering ideal of the early 20th century) is itself a significant constraint. So too perhaps are the educational choices that young women make. Recent trends of engineering education show that the space for women is opening up slowly. A critical mass of women water professionals is important but it is not sufficient. Greater numbers of women in the water sector will not change practices and policies if the perspectives and the organizational culture remain unchanged. It is in this context that the work of the small number of women, who have been systematically engaging with water as activists, practitioners or professionals, becomes significant. There are many insights to be gleaned from their struggles and achievements in water and sanitation management, which have scarcely been documented (Kulkarni 2013; Krishna and De 2013). It is pertinent that struggles that may begin around water issues evolve to encompass a much wider swathe of women's lives and livelihoods.

Men who see women's roles as confined to the home find it difficult to accept their participation in the public sphere (assuming that 'women lack mental and educational skills to make decisions'), while organizational cultures tend to assign typically 'female tasks' to women staff or confine them to desktop rather than field-oriented positions. While these roles are being challenged, the shaping of women's lives cannot be understood without understanding the expectations and opportunities that also shape men's lives (see Nussbaum *et al.* 2003). Recent research on gender and governance in the water sector is also beginning to address questions of masculinity and the construction and implications of gendered identities in water bureaucracies and NGOs (see Cleaver 1998; Cleaver and Elson 1995). The greater focus on women, however, continues as women are still an under-researched and unrecognized constituency in water policy and management. Women's relationship with men, the structures of patriarchy that determine participation in water governance at various levels and how men perceive women's changing roles are important questions for research and for the community water institutions (see also Ramamurthy 1991; Seager 2010; Zwarteveen 1998, 2008).

Over four decades, new approaches have emerged and the discourse on gender and water has become more nuanced and complex. At the national and international levels, a range of policies and programmes has been put in place to enhance water resources through decentralized community management, local participation and increased representation for women. Yet, as with other natural resource sectors, these alternative perspectives and interventions have not succeeded in resolving the conflicts between social and private benefits and may even have aggravated them. These contradictions have for long been part of the Indian polity but in the present milieu in which private resource rights seem to be advancing at the cost of resource management for the poorest social groups, the sectoral approach to water governance needs to be questioned. At the same time, the discourse on gender and water needs to be strengthened by a deeper engagement with the spectrum of political struggles for resource rights.

## *Looking beyond water*

Our review of four decades of policy and practice around gender and water shows that the alternative perspectives that have emerged from mutual engagement between policy makers, academics and practitioners have had limited impact. While gender has been recognized as an analytic category, increasing women's representation in policy and programmes, there is a growing sense of discomfort among gender water researchers and practitioners because there is little evident change on the ground. The expectation of greater numbers of women in the waterscape, from the micro to the macro, has not happened. There have also not been notable policy responses to women's grassroots struggles against patriarchy and around water, although these have often significantly empowered the women.

Therefore, we argue that policies and programmes, action and research, need to look beyond water to women's grassroots political struggles that encompass their dignity as women, their lives and livelihoods. Such an alternative perspective would help to forge a truly transformatory practice.

## Notes

1 Rights-based approaches, generally, treat economic development as a human right: the goal of development is to transform relations of power by empowering those who have been denied their rights (like women in patriarchal societies) and by strengthening institutions to make positive interventions for transformative change. For a detailed discussion see, for instance, Nussbaum (1998) (see also Green and Baden 1998; Green, Joekes and Leach 1998).

2 In 1952, recently Independent India launched a massive country-wide community development programme, which became a model for other post-colonial nations. The community development blocks under a Block Development Officer and staff were responsible for the entire gamut of village development including drinking water supply. The concept of block development was closely interlinked with the elected village panchayats, which had replaced the traditional village panchayats (see Chauhan 1983; also Krishna 1996, 2009).

3 An extensive study on the social and private benefits in watershed development (Datar and Prakash 1999: 158–159) reveals that investments in soil and water conservation on private or public land, and subsidized energy costs, mainly benefited the landed. As bigger farmers used more groundwater for cultivating non-food crops, the benefits 'provided at public cost' became 'a privilege for a few'. Moreover, the emergence of 'water lords', who sold water 'to the poor and needy at exorbitant rates'. rendered poor women even more vulnerable.

4 See genderwateralliance.org

5 Institutions like the family, household or market serve varied socio-cultural, economic or political functions. Social institutions may be seen 'as the formal and informal rules, the norms that shape interactions among people and between them and the environment' (Krishna 2009: 408). Norms based on prescribed and enforced rules of conduct 'often reflect the interests of the more powerful sections and their perceptions of what is normal and appropriate' (ibid.: 413). In common usage, the term 'institution' is often confused with the term 'organization', which is 'a formal unit set up to achieve a particular purpose' (ibid.: 414). So, organizations may be viewed as players in a game in which institutions set the rules (see also Goetz 1995; Kabeer and Subramanian 1999).

## References

Agarwal, B. 1992. 'The Gender and Environment Debate: Lessons from India', *Feminist Studies*, 18(1): 119–158.

Ahmed, S. 2005. 'Why Is Gender Equity a Concern for Water Management?' in S. Ahmed (ed.), *Flowing Upstream: Empowering Women Through Water Management Initiatives in India*. New Delhi: Foundation India Books and Ahmedabad: Centre for Environment Education.

Ashworth, G. 1996. *Gendered Governance: An Agenda for Change*. Gender in Development Programme (GIDP). New York: United Nations Development Programme (UNDP).

Chauhan, S. K. 1983. 'Introduction: What Is Community Participation?' in S. K. Chauhan, Z. Bihua, K. Gopalakrishnan, L. R. Hussain, A. Yeboah-Afari, and F. Leal (eds.), *Who Puts the Water in the Taps? Community Participation in Third World Drinking Water, Sanitation and Health*. London: Earthscan, International Institute for Environment and Development.

Chauhan, S. K. and K. Gopalakrishnan. 1983. *A Million Villages, a Million Decades? Third World Water and Sanitation from Two South Indian Villages*. London: Earthscan, International Institute for Environment and Development.

Cleaver, F. 1998. 'Incentives and Informal Institutions: Gender and the Management of Water', *Agriculture and Human Values*, 15: 347–360.

Cleaver, F. and D. Elson. 1995. 'Women and Water Resources: Continued Marginalization and New Policies', Gatekeeper Series No. 49, International Institute of Environment and Development (IIED), Sustainable Agriculture and Rural Livelihoods Programme.

Datar, C. and A. Prakash. 1999. *Women Demand Land and Water*. Mumbai: Tata Institute for Social Sciences.

Gavankar, R. 2003. *Paniwalibai (Marathi)*. Mumbai: Sparrow.

Goetz, Anne Marie. 1995. 'Institutionalising Women's Interests and Accountability to Women in Development', *IDS Bulletin*, 26(3): 1–10.

Goetz, A. M. 1997. 'Introduction: Getting Institutions Right for Women in Development', in A. M. Goetz (ed.), *Getting Institutions Right for Women in Development*, pp. 1–28. London: Zed Books.

Government of India (GoI). 1974. *Towards Equality: Report of the Committee on the Status of Women in India*. New Delhi: Indian Council for Social Science Research.

Government of India (GoI). 2002. *National Water Policy*. New Delhi: Ministry of Water Resources.

Government of India (GoI). 2012. *National Water Policy*. New Delhi: Ministry of Water Resources.

Green, C. and S. Baden. 1995. 'Integrated Water Resources Management: A Gender Perspective', *IDS Bulletin*, 26(1): 92–100.

Green, C., S. Joekes and M. Leach. 1998. 'Questionable Links: Approaches to Gender in Environmental Research and Policy', in C. Jackson and R. Pearson (eds.), *Feminist Visions of Development: Gender Analysis and Policy*. London: Routledge Studies in Development Economics.

Harris, L. 2009. 'Gender and Emergent Water Governance', *Gender, Place & Culture*, 16(4): 387–408.

Jackson, C. 1998. 'Gender, Irrigation and Environment: Arguing for Agency', *Agriculture and Human Values*, 15: 313–324.

Jairath, J. 2000. 'By-Passing the Women: The Case of Participatory Irrigation Management Reforms in Andhra Pradesh', Paper Presented at the Indian Association for Women's Studies Conference, Hyderabad, 8 January.

Joshi, Deepa and Ben Fawcett. 2005. 'The Role of Water in an Unequal Social Order in India', in Anne Coles and Tina Wallace (eds.), *Gender, Water and Development*, pp. 38–56. Basingstoke, UK: Berg Publishers.

Joy, K. J. and S. Paranjape. 2005. 'Women and Water: Relationships, Issues and Experiences', in B. Ray (ed.), *Women in India: Post Colonial Period*, pp. 351–391. New York: Oxford University Press.

Kabeer, N. (ed.) 2005. *Inclusive Citizenship: Meanings and Expressions*. New Delhi: Zubaan.

Kabeer, N. and R. Subramanian. 1999. *Institutions, Relations and Outcomes: A Framework and Case Studies for Gender-Aware Planning*. New Delhi: Zubaan.

Krishna, S. 1985. 'Not by Pumps Alone' (Guest Editorial), *Waterlines*, 3(4): 2–4.

Krishna, S. 1996. *Environmental Politics: People's Lives and Development Choices*. New Delhi: Sage.

Krishna, S. 2001. 'Introduction: Towards a Genderscape of Community Rights in Natural Resource Management', *Indian Journal of Gender Studies*, 8(2): 151–174.

Krishna, S. 2004a. 'A Genderscape of Community Rights in Natural Resource Management: Overview', in S. Krishna (ed.), *Livelihood and Gender: Equity in Community Resource Management*, pp. 17–63. New Delhi: Sage.

Krishna, S. (ed.). 2004b. *Livelihood and Gender: Equity in Community Resource Management*. New Delhi: Sage.

Krishna, S. 2007. 'Recasting Citizenship for Women's Livelihood and Development: An Overview', in S. Krishna (ed.), *Women's Livelihood Rights: Recasting Citizenship for Development*, pp. 1–38. New Delhi: Sage.

Krishna, S. 2009. *Genderscapes: Revisioning Natural Resource Management*. New Delhi: Zubaan.

Krishna, S. 2012. 'Gender and Sustainable Livelihoods in India: "Side Stream"/"Mainstream"', in W. Harcourt (ed.), *Women Reclaiming Sustainable Livelihoods: Spaces Lost, Spaces Gained*, pp. 125–141. Houndmills, UK: Palgrave-Macmillan. ISBN: 978-0-230-31648-5.

Krishna, S. 2015. 'Women's Transformative Organizing for Sustainable Livelihoods: Learning from Indian Experiences', in R. Baksh, and W. Harcourt (ed.), *The Oxford Handbook of Transnational Feminist Movements*, pp. 837–854. New York: Oxford University Press.

Krishna, S. and A. De. (eds.) 2013. *Women Water Professionals*. New Delhi: Zubaan.

Krishnan, J. 2009. *Enclosed Waters: Property Rights, Technology and Ecology in the Management of Water Resources in Palakkad, Kerala*. Wageningen University, Water Resources Series. Hyderabad: Orient Blackswan.

Kulkarni, S., S. Ahmed, C. Datar, S. Bhat, Y. Mathur, and D. Makhwana. 2009. 'Water Rights as Women's Rights: Empowering Women Through Decentralized Water Governance in Maharashtra and Gujarat', Final Report of a Study Supported by the International Development Research Centre, Canada.

Kulkarni, S. 2011. 'Women and Decentralised Water Governance: Issues, Challenges and the Way Forward', *Economic and Political Weekly*, XLVI(18): 64–72.

Kulkarni, S. and K. J. Joy. 2012. 'Decentralising or Marginalising Women: Gender Relations and Sector Reforms in India', in M. Zwarteveen, S. Ahmed and S. Gautam (eds.), *Diverting the Flow*, pp. 85–110. New Delhi: Zubaan.

Kulkarni, S. 2013. 'Situational Analysis of Women Water Professionals', in S. Krishna and A. De. (eds.), *Women Water Professionals*, pp. 201–247. New Delhi: Zubaan.

Lahiri-Dutt, K. 2006. 'Nadi O Nari: Representing the River and Women of the Rural Communities in the Bengal Delta', in Lahiri-Dutt (ed.), *Fluid Bonds: Views on Gender and Water*, pp. 387–408. Kolkata: Stree, published in conjunction with the National Institute for Environment (NIE). Canberra: The Australian National University.

Leach, M. 2003. *Gender Myths and Feminist Fables: Repositioning Gender in Development Policy and Practice*. Institute of Development Studies, Sussex, UK: University of Sussex.

Mies, M. 1986. *Patriarchy and Accumulation on a World Scale: Women in the International Division of Labour*. London: Zed Books.

Mies, M. and V. Shiva. 1993. *Ecofeminism*. New Delhi: Kali for Women.

Mukhopadhyay, Carol. 2005. 'The Scientific Gender Gap Should Be Understood Comparatively', *Anthropology News*, 46(3): 4–5.

National Planning Committee. 1948. *Soil Conservation and Afforestation (Report of the Sub-Committee)*. Edited by K. T. Shah. Government of India (GoI), New Delhi, Mumbai: Vora & Co. Publications Ltd.

Nussbaum, M. 1998. 'Capabilities and Human Rights', *Fordham Law Review*, 66(2), http://heinonline.org/HOL/LandingPage?handle=hein.journals/flr66&div=18&id=&page (accessed on 30 April 2015).

Nussbaum, M., A. Basu, Y. Tambiah, and N. G. Jayal. 2003. *Essays on Gender and Governance*. New Delhi: Human Development Resource Centre, UNDP.

Ramamurthy, P. 1991. 'Rural Women and Irrigation: Patriarchy, Class, and the Modernizing State', *South India Society and Natural Resources: An International Journal*, 4(1) (Special Issue: Women and Natural Resources in Developing Countries): 5–22.

Rocheleau, D., B. Thomas-Slayter and E. Wangari. (eds.). 1996. *Feminist Political Ecology: Global Issues and Local Experiences*, 1st ed. Routledge International Studies of Women and Place. New York: Routledge.

Sangari, K. and S. Vaid. (eds.). 1989. *Recasting Women: Essays in Indian Colonial History*. New Delhi: Kali for Women.

Seager, J. 2010. 'Gender and Water: A Good Rhetoric but it Doesn't "Count" ', *Geoforum*, 41: 1–3 (accessed on 21 May 2015).

Shiva, V. 1988. *Staying Alive*. New Delhi: Kali for Women.

Sujaya, C. P 1995. *Women's Rights and Development Policies in India*. The Administrator (Mussoorie: Lal Bahadur Shastri Academy of Administration), pp. 13–26.

Tewari-Jassal, S. 2004. 'Limits of Empowerment: Mallah in Fish Ponds in Madhubani, Bihar', in S. Krishna (ed.), *Livelihood and Gender: Equity in Community Resource Management*, pp. 412–422. New Delhi: Sage.

United Nations. 1992. 'The Dublin Statement on Water and Sustainable Development' (also known as the Dublin Principles', www.un.documents.net/h2o-dub.htm (accessed on 8 January 2018).

UN-Water. 2003. 'Water for People, Water for Life: WWDR 2003' (World Water Development Report), www.unwater.org/publications/water-people-water-life (accessed on 8 January 2018).

Zwarteveen, M. 1997. 'Water: From Basic Need to Commodity. A Discussion on Gender and Water Rights in the Context of Irrigation', *World Development*, 25(8): 1335–1349.

Zwarteveen, M. 1998. 'Identifying Gender Aspects of New Irrigation Management Policies', *Agriculture and Human Values*, 15: 301–312.

Zwarteveen, M. 2008. 'Men Masculinities and Water Powers in Irrigation', *Water Alternatives*, 1(1): 111–130.

# 12 Inter-state water conflicts and linguistic identity in India

## The case of the Cauvery

*Narendar Pani*

### Introduction

The debates over inter-state water disputes in India have tended to focus almost exclusively on the hydrological aspects of the conflict. When non-hydrological aspects like language or ethnicity of the conflicting groups make their presence felt, as they often do, there is a tendency to treat them primarily as matters of detail.[1] The proposed solutions are then essentially hydrological in nature, with the political class expected to implement these solutions. And when the political class fails to implement solutions that have a potentially violent fallout on relations between social groups, it is typically treated as a failure of governance, requiring the intervention of the judiciary (Swain 1998).

Yet, water disputes are also conflicts between two or more social groups. It is quite possible that the conflict between these groups may have dimensions other than water. Indeed, when the groups are defined by elements as volatile as language identity, water may be just one of several triggers that can sharply increase the intensity of the conflict. It then becomes important to ask whether our understanding of inter-state water conflicts, and the solutions that are consequently proposed, would change if we begin with trying to understand the specific social conflict, and then place the dispute over water in the context of the larger conflict.

There are few better cases to explore the relationship between larger social conflicts and water disputes than the one between Karnataka and Tamil Nadu over the Cauvery waters. For over a century, this has been one of the more obvious cases of the interaction between language identity and inter-state water disputes. It has had the unfortunate feature of a decision of a river water tribunal leading to ethnic riots. And in the context of this tribute, it has the additional advantage of being a conflict Prof. Ramaswamy Iyer wrote extensively about.

In choosing to begin with the larger social conflict rather than the specifics of the water dispute, we need to first address some conceptual issues regarding our understanding of conflict. To this end, the chapter begins with a brief discussion contrasting the approach implicit in the conventional wisdom on water disputes in India, with the inclusive approach of M. K. Gandhi. It goes on to interpret the Cauvery dispute using the Gandhian method, leading to the identification of specific non-hydrological dimensions of the dispute. It then explores the implications of these non-hydrological elements, and their expression through language identities, for strategies to resolve the Cauvery dispute.

## Some conceptual issues

The diversity in the approaches to conflict is perhaps best seen in the absence of a consensus on even a seemingly apparent contention that a reduction in the intensity of conflict is desirable. In a position that Naxalites could find common ground with, George Sorel argued that 'proletarian violence, carried on as a pure and simple manifestation of the sentiment of class struggle, appears thus as a very fine and heroic thing; it is at the service of the immemorial interests of civilization' (Sorel 1999: 85). Lewis Coser (1957: 197) extended this argument beyond the realm of class struggle with his claim that 'conflict within and between groups in a society can prevent accommodations and habitual relations from progressively impoverishing creativity'. Situating approaches to river water disputes in India within this wide range of theorization about conflict is constrained by the fact that very little of the literature on these disputes takes an explicit position on what the approach to conflict itself should be. To understand the conceptual base from which the discussion on river water disputes approaches conflict, it is thus necessary to try and capture the theoretical positions that are implicit in the arguments that are usually made on inter-state river water disputes.

The first step in our search for the theorization implicit in the debate on river water disputes would be to recognize what constitutes a theory of conflict. We could go along with Oberschall's set of three requirements of a theory of conflict. First, it must outline 'the structural sources of social conflict, in particular, structures of domination that make struggles over values and scarce resources likely'. Second, it must elaborate the process of 'conflict-group formation and the mobilization for collective action of challenging groups and their targets'. And third, it must explore 'the dynamics of conflict: processes of interaction between conflict groups; the forms of conflict; its magnitude, scope and duration; escalation and de-escalation; conflict regulation and resolution; the consequences of conflict outcomes for the contending groups and the larger society' (Oberschall 1978: 292).

The inter-state river water disputes in India reflect an implicit consensus on the approach towards each of these three requirements. The first requirement – the structural basis for the conflict – is seen to be essentially a matter of sharing river waters. The arguments then extend to the various types of rights a state may claim, ranging from prescriptive rights to the right to equity. While there is a significant body of literature on the relation between water and social relations, they are more often in more decentralized contexts (Baviskar 2005). And when social relations do enter the understanding of inter-state river water disputes, they are, more often than not, given a secondary role.

The second element of a theory of conflict – the formation of the groups in inter-state river water disputes – is understood in terms of a state of the Indian Union or a Union Territory taken as a whole. The relevant group is taken to be all those who belong to the administrative region of a state or Union Territory, treating them as a single entity. It is assumed in much of the debate that the interests of all the smaller groups within the state are uniform. It could be argued that the effective distribution of water within a state could lead to its more efficient usage, and hence a decline in that state's requirement. But the distribution of water within a state is typically ignored in inter-state river water disputes, largely because of issues related to jurisdiction. Indeed, the final order of the Cauvery Tribunal states that 'it is better to allocate water amongst the parties keeping in view the principle of equity for use by the concerned states for any beneficial purposes according to the state's own priority' (IMWR V 2007: 200).

The third element of a theory of conflict – the dynamics of the conflict – is typically seen in three main domains. First, there is the bureaucratic domain where the states outline their interests and raise their demands, with the possibility of a solution being found within the government. Second, there is the political domain, which typically comes into play when the bureaucratic option proves to be ineffective. And third, when political solutions are not available, the dispute enters the judicial domain. The analysis of river water disputes in India often tends to focus entirely on the bureaucratic and judicial domains, with actions in the political domain seen as being disruptive.

In practice, this hydrology-only view of inter-state river water disputes has run into several difficulties. There are cases where the hydrological issues have been overwhelmed by other aspects of the conflict between the two social groups. The ethnic riots between Kannadigas and Tamilians, which broke out in Bengaluru after the Cauvery Tribunal announced its interim award in 1991, are a stark reminder of the influence non-hydrological issues can have on water disputes. The belief that the problem of sharing a river's waters is only relevant at the level of the states, is also not consistent with practice. In 2012, a dispute arose between the farmers of Garlapadu village in Mahabubnagar district and Dudyala village of Kurnool district over the laying of a pipeline (The Hindu 2012). Again, it has proved to be very difficult to resolve inter-state water disputes through the legal process alone.

There is thus a case for using a framework to understand inter-state water disputes that is not confined to the hydrological aspects of the dispute. And one approach that is inclusive in the sense that it provides a role for all interests and issues is an interpretation of the Gandhian method. M. K. Gandhi has himself been subject to varied interpretations, from being a Mahatma who removed untouchability to being an enemy of the castes that were victims of untouchability. Interpreting his ideas, too, is not free of challenges, considering that they are spread over a hundred volumes of his Collected Works. But if we were to lower our sights from targeting *the* interpretation of the Gandhian method to just *an* interpretation of that method, it is possible to distil a method of understanding social processes that may well have contributed to making him arguably the most successful mobilizer of populations in the 20th century. This exercise has been carried out elsewhere (Pani 2001). In this chapter, we only need to apply the approach of that method to the three requirements of a theory of conflict, namely, the sources of conflict, conflict-group formation, and the dynamics of conflict.

A Gandhian method would treat social conflict as an inherent part of all social processes. This method views society as a collection of individuals. Social processes are then the result of the actions of individuals, acting either alone or in groups. When these desired actions are not mutually beneficial, a consensus has to be arrived at through negotiations. These negotiations can take place in a variety of arenas, from those defined in the Constitution to actions on the street. The structural element of a conflict in this method is defined by the fact that a social conflict arises when there is a failure to arrive at a social consensus.

It is in the second element of a theory of conflict – the formation of groups – that Gandhi used an original interpretation of the concept of Swadeshi. As he said in 1916,

> after much thinking, I have arrived at a definition of *swadeshi* that perhaps best illustrates my meaning. *Swadeshi* is that spirit in

> us which restricts us to the use and service of our immediate surroundings to the exclusion of the more remote.
>
> (Gandhi 1998)

This approach to group formation would explain the tendency for local interests to dominate while dealing with water sharing issues. The local would not be seen in terms of the territory of a state alone. While a state would be local when confronting other states, there could be other issues that arise at different levels within a state. There have been river water disputes even between districts in a state. An equally important implication of this definition comes to the fore when we consider the context in which Gandhi made this statement. As this statement was made as a part of Gandhi's address to Christian missionaries, hoping to convince them against conversion, he clearly did not see the immediate surroundings in terms of geographical territory alone. A person's religion, language or ethnicity could also form the basis for her perception of her immediate surroundings.

As someone who believed in the supremacy of actions, it is not entirely surprising that Gandhi focused a great deal on the dynamics of conflict. As social conflict arose from a failure in social negotiations, the elements of negotiations determined the dynamics of social conflict. He saw three elements influencing the strength of a negotiating position. The first element was the degree of empowerment of the social group. This empowerment could arise from economic, social, political and even numerical strength. Gandhi often intervened, as in Champaran, in a way that empowered the impoverished. The second element was the options the individual or social group had. Gandhi believed Khadi provided an alternative occupation to those who had very little bargaining power. To cite a more contemporary example, an information technology professional can enhance her bargaining power for higher wages by having the option of another job. The third element Gandhi emphasized was fairness. While he saw the potential to use moral force that a sense of fairness brought with it, this aspect may have declined over the years. But to the extent that claims of unfairness are an essential part of current disputes, the larger category of fairness remains an essential part of modern conflicts.

## Towards a Gandhian interpretation of the Cauvery dispute

### *Structural basis of the conflict*

When we take a more inclusive view of social conflict, as Gandhi's writing suggests we should, it is quite evident that there is a larger conflict between what were once Mysore and Madras. As is perhaps to be expected between two major neighbouring cultures built around ancient languages, the relations between the Kannada and Tamil communities have been marked by incidents of cooperation, competition and conflict. The territories associated with these two cultures have shifted at various points in history, before gaining an element of permanence in the colonial period. When the British defeated and killed Tipu Sultan, the ruler of Mysore in 1799, they decided to keep Mysore as a princely state. They placed on the throne a young boy belonging to a family that had earlier ruled the state and experimented with a period of indirect rule that lasted till 1831. The failure of that experiment saw the British taking over direct rule for half a century before returning the state to indirect rule in 1881.

Early in the 19th century, the British took several steps that associated the colonial power in the Mysore mind with what was then Madras. Given the fact that colonial rule at the time was still being administered through the East India Company, the British felt the need for a territory that would be directly under the control of the crown: an area to be treated as an 'isolated piece of British territory surrounded by foreign territory'.[2] In order to maintain this isolation, the population of what was to later become Bengaluru Cantonment was brought in from outside Mysore. A significant proportion of this population came from the Madras Presidency. The control of this territory was carried out from Madras, and the culture developed in this territory too was kept different from the rest of Mysore, with Kannada not being used to any great degree in the Cantonment. The local symbol of direct colonial rule was thus Madras.

This identification of colonial influence with Madras was further strengthened when the British returned Mysore to indirect rule in 1881. As a part of the transition, they set up an administrative system in Bengaluru under the Dewans who were initially from the Madras Presidency. These Dewans, especially Sir Seshadri Iyer, contributed immensely to Mysore finding its economic feet and taking its initial steps in science education. But the fact that they were associated with the Madras Presidency, as were several officers who entered the Mysore Civil Service, saw a clear division appearing in the Mysore bureaucracy between Mysoreans and Tamilians.

The greater emphasis on technology and growth after the return to indirect rule resulted in a change in the approach to the Cauvery. The terrain through which the Cauvery flows had its influence on the traditional use of the water. The hilly and the rocky terrain through which the Cauvery flows for much of its route in the old princely state of Mysore made it difficult to use diversionary dams to irrigate land on the banks of the river. In contrast, this elementary technology could be used in the Cauvery delta in the Madras Presidency. And this had been done in the delta for nearly two thousand years. But with technology enabling the building of larger dams, Mysore began to get more conscious of its rights to the Cauvery waters. In 1890, Dewan Seshadri Iyer stated that 'Mysore has a natural right to the full use of all the water in its territory'.[3] But he made it clear that 'in exercising its natural right, Mysore may do anything which does not injuriously affect the enjoyment of its acquired rights by Madras, or materially diminish the supply to Madras works' (IMWR II 2007: 2).

It could be argued that the 1892 agreement between Mysore and Madras on the Cauvery waters did no more than operationalize Mysore's demands. But the agreement was structured in a way that gave Madras control over what Mysore could do. This was reflected in the very title of the agreement: 'Rules defining the limits within which no new irrigation works are to be constructed by the Mysore state without previous reference to the Madras Government'. And the terms of the agreement went further to require the previous consent of the Madras Government. When we recognize that this agreement was signed at a time of emerging suspicions between Tamilians and Mysoreans in the Mysore bureaucracy, it set the basis for a view in Mysore that the agreement was not signed between equal partners. Indeed, the more extreme view in Mysore could even interpret the agreement as evidence of the Dewan of Mysore bowing to the wishes of the Madras Presidency.

By the turn of the century, the dominant Tamil influence on the Mysore bureaucracy was beginning to be challenged. With P. N. Krishnamurthy becoming the Dewan in 1901, the Mysorean voice within the Mysore bureaucracy began to assert itself. There were official moves not to entertain non-Mysoreans in the state's civil service. And with the national movement not having made any great inroads into Mysore at the time, the dominant nationalism was Mysorean rather than Indian. This meant the Tamilians were seen as foreigners. The division that had emerged in the Mysore bureaucracy between Mysoreans and Tamilians is perhaps best captured in this entry made by a Mysore civil servant of Tamil origin, K. R. Srinivasa Iyengar, in his personal diary on 7 August 1904. Noting his conversation that day with a Mysorean officer, he wrote:

> Among other things he made mention of the Government Order prohibiting the entertainment of non-Mysoreans in service and

> tried to draw out my opinion on the matter. I replied cautiously that the Government were right in placing restrictions against the entertainment of foreigners but there should be exceptions and that no hard and fast rule can be accepted. I also said I hoped the prospects of non-Mysoreans already in service will not be affected. As regards Tamilians, I said that we owed our position to nobody's favour, that we don't want any partiality towards us and that we only require a fair field and no favour.
>
> (Pani 1982)

The assertion of Mysorean sentiment was soon reflected in a number of areas of conflict emerging between Mysore and Madras. For instance, in his address to the Dasara session of the Mysore Representative Assembly in 1921, the then Dewan, Kantharaj Urs, spoke of the Government of India appointing an umpire 'to settle the long pending question of the Mysore – South Canara Boundary' (Urs 1953: 266).[4] It was against this backdrop of growing Mysorean resistance to what they perceived as Tamil dominated decisions that the 1892 agreement on Cauvery waters began to fall apart. With Mysore under Sir M. Visvesvarayya going through a period of rapid modernization, there was a demand to build a large dam at Kanambadi. Madras did not consent to the initial proposal. But since it too sought to build a large dam at Mettur, the provisions of the 1892 agreement were no longer useful to either party. As the negotiations began for a new agreement, Mysore began to seek a more equitable distribution of the Cauvery waters. Referring to negotiations between the irrigation experts of Mysore and Madras, Dewan Kantharaj Urs noted in the same 1921 address that 'Their report which embodies the proposals which the technical officers of both the Governments would recommend for adoption as an *equitable* settlement of the dispute is now under consideration' (Urs 1953: 251) [emphasis added]. The agreement, when it was finally reached in 1924, did allow Mysore to build the dam it sought, but there were other clauses that convinced the state of the continued dominance of Madras. The agreement also stated that the

> Madras Government shall be at liberty to construct new irrigation works on the tributaries of the Cauvery in Madras and, should the Madras Government construct . . . any new storage reservoir, the Mysore Government shall be at liberty to construct as an off-set, a storage reservoir . . . on one of the tributaries of the Cauvery in Mysore, of a capacity not exceeding 60 per cent of the new reservoir in Madras.
>
> (IMWR II 2007: 47–48)

The 1924 agreement was due for review after 50 years, but Karnataka and Tamil Nadu have not been able to agree whether that part of the agreement meant that some clauses should be renegotiated, or that the entire agreement was no longer valid. The period soon after 1974 was however one of relative tranquillity in the relations between what was now Karnataka and Tamil Nadu. There were amicable arrangements to exchange water for electric power between the two states. But this situation changed dramatically in the 1980s. As a part of the general trend towards linguistic nationalism across the country, the Kannada movement gathered momentum within Karnataka. The Gokak agitation in the early 1980s sought a more prominent role for Kannada in administration and education. Among the linguistic minorities that had to come to terms with the changing situation were the Tamilians in Bengaluru, especially in the Cantonment with its Tamil-dominated history. By the latter half of that decade, the amicable arrangements on water sharing between Karnataka and Tamil Nadu were no longer politically viable. And when these arrangements did not materialize, Tamil Nadu moved the dispute to the legal domain by seeking a river water tribunal.

It should be clear from this brief account of the dispute that the structural causes for the Cauvery conflict are not in the hydrological dimension alone. The dispute over Cauvery waters is a part of a much more complex relationship between Karnataka and Tamil Nadu. Even as developments in the river water dispute can affect relations between the two states, the attitudes adopted towards water sharing are themselves affected by other elements of the relationship between the larger social groups based on language identities.

### *Group consolidation and mobilization*

When we apply the Gandhian concept of *Swadeshi* to mobilization around the Cauvery issue, the immediate surroundings take on two forms: territory and language identity. The mobilization around territory allows for the entire state to be mobilized behind the demands for the Cauvery waters. Though the major portion of the areas of both Karnataka and Tamil Nadu fall outside the Cauvery basin, the official positions of the two states on the dispute are identified with the respective states as a whole. Indeed, in Karnataka's case, some of the more hard-line decisions, including the one to break from the unwritten code of amicable arrangements in the 1980s and the encouragement of protests that led to ethnic riots in Bengaluru in 1991, were taken by Chief Ministers whose political interests lay outside the Cauvery basin.

There have of course been situations where the focus on territory was not designed to lead to state-wide mobilization, such as when the water dispute was between districts within a state. This was the case in the dispute over the construction of the Varuna canal that was to use the Cauvery waters to irrigate the Mysore district in Karnataka. The canal was opposed by farmers of the Mandya district in the same state as they felt it would be at the cost of water available to them. In 1978, there was a major demonstration of farmers in Mandya against the canal (Jayaram 2002). But the overwhelming popular mood in both Karnataka and Tamil Nadu on the Cauvery issue, especially since the 1980s, has been for the entire state to rally behind the cause of the farmers in their part of the Cauvery valley.

The language identity has taken on a prominent role in both the states, though there are differences in the details of mobilization. In Tamil Nadu, language identity forms an important part of the official positions of the major political parties. The role of film stars in mobilization along language lines is also muted by the fact that the political parties in that state already provide a prominent place for film stars. The mobilization on language identity is thus often identical with party-based political mobilization. The role of language identity in Karnataka's politics is however somewhat less pronounced. While political parties do often take strong positions on language issues, the state's politics has been dominated by national parties with relatively little space for regional parties. Thus, when the Kannada language is to be used for mobilization around the Cauvery dispute, it typically leads to the creation of new organizations. Film stars play an important role in these processes. They usually support the agitation, either through their fan clubs or by directly participating in the protests.

### *Dynamics of the dispute*

The dynamics of the dispute in the Gandhian method is determined by the empowerment of the contending parties, the availability of options and perceptions of fairness. It could be argued that, in the colonial period, Madras being the southern centre of British power had greater influence than the ruler of a native state. But Mysore too was not without its colonial cards. The gold mines in Kolar were run by British companies, and their need for additional power was repeatedly cited as the case for new hydro-electric projects. When the Mysorean section of the bureaucracy came to power, it helped to strengthen Mysore's resolve to get what it believed was its due. After the 50-year period of the 1924 accord ended, the absence of a binding agreement led both sides to depend on show of strength. In the period after 1974, the empowerment was primarily through the demonstrated ability on both sides to mobilize significant numbers onto the streets. This form of mobilization no doubt increased the bargaining power of both sides, with the threat of lawlessness sometimes influencing the course of official decisions.

The heightened tensions generated by threats of mass mobilization in both Karnataka and Tamil Nadu not only reduced the prospects of a compromise but also led the states to focus entirely on the amount of water each of them should be entitled to. The option of reducing the demand for water through more efficient use of this resource was not given too much attention.

The dynamics of the negotiations over the sharing of the Cauvery waters also saw very different claims being made about what would be a fair distribution. Madras and later Tamil Nadu, having had the natural advantage of a terrain that allowed Cauvery waters to be used for irrigation much earlier, built its case for fairness primarily on the need to protect the prescriptive rights of farming communities that had been using the Cauvery waters for irrigation for millennia. Karnataka, having had to wait till technological change allowed it to increase its access to the Cauvery waters, was much keener on projecting an equitable distribution of the water as the only fair way out. But there was no single criterion to be used for equitable distribution, with Sir M. Visvesvarayya even using the length of the river that flowed in each state as the criterion (Visvesvarayya 1951). The Cauvery Water Disputes Tribunal finally decided that it would go by the principle of equity when distributing the water entitlements across Karnataka, Tamil Nadu, Kerala and Pondicherry.

### *Implications for a solution*

The most important lesson to be learnt from taking a more inclusive view of the Cauvery dispute is that the nature of the social conflict is so broad-based that it would be overly optimistic to expect it to be resolved through a solution that deals with its hydrological dimensions alone. Even the weight of a Tribunal's final order has not been sufficient to put an end to the dispute. Well over a decade after the Tribunal's final order, it is still to be fully implemented. And there are at least two ways in which the Tribunal's hydrological solutions come into conflict with the non-hydrological aspects of what is essentially a part of a conflict between social groups.

First, by confining itself to hydrological issues, the Tribunal does not take up the challenge of addressing the need to separate the water dispute from that between linguistic identities. By treating the dispute as one essentially between states, it reinforces the linguistic identities, particularly those of Karnataka and Tamil Nadu. There have been attempts to strengthen the alternative identity of the basin, notably the alliance of farmers of the basin through the 'Cauvery family'. It may be too much to expect the unity of the Cauvery basin identity to overcome the divisions of the linguistic identities at times of crisis. But it at least serves to dilute the intensity of water-turned-linguistic confrontations. Again, the Tribunal could have taken its case for equity further. Having decided to ensure equity on the basis of the in-basin population of the different contenders, it could have gone a step further and determined the shares of individual districts in the basin. By localizing the sharing of the river's waters, it would have once again raised issues that would not necessarily become weapons in the linguistic battle.

Second, the hydrology-only view of the dispute has also ensured a mechanism for the implementation of the order that is open to being continuously challenged by linguistic groups. The implementing agency of the Tribunal's order is to be the Cauvery Management Board, which 'shall be under the control of the Government of India, Ministry of Water Resources' (IMWR V 2007: 224). The distancing of the implementing agency from the contending parties is perhaps an effort to generate prescriptions that will be seen to be objective. In the process, though, the implementation has been left to individuals who have no stake in the distribution of the Cauvery waters. The Board does not find place for a single farmer, let along sufficient farmers, to ensure that the interests of all the sections of the basin are represented in the decision-making. The Board's orders are much more likely to gain acceptance if they are the result of negotiations among stakeholders in the Cauvery basin. Representatives from the basin are also more likely to recognize the opportunities available in the basin to reduce the dependence on the Cauvery waters.

The Cauvery water dispute has repeatedly reminded us that water disputes are also disputes between social groups. A substantial portion of anger the dispute generates has its origins in a variety of socio-political factors, ranging from the deep emotional bonds with the river shared by different groups associated with it to the use of this emotive issue in mass politics. A Gandhian interpretation of the dispute would demand an inclusive view of the conflict, including but going well beyond its hydrological dimensions. By ignoring so many elements of this reality of the Cauvery conflict, we run the risk of actions taken with the objective of easing water conflicts only, serving to make them more intractable.

## Notes

1 See for instance, Richards and Singh (2002).
2 Confidential papers related to the surplus revenue of Civil and Military Station, pol 26, dated 4 March 1880.
3 Notes of discussions at the Conference held in Ootacamund on 10 May 1890, cited in (IMWR II: 2).
4 South Canara was at the time a part of Madras Presidency, and only became a part of Karnataka with the states reorganization in 1956.

## References

Baviskar, A. 2005. *In the Belly of the River: Tribal Conflicts over Development in the Narmada Valley*, 2nd ed. Study in Social Ecology and Environmental History. Oxford: Oxford University Press.

Coser, L. A. 1957. 'Social Conflict and the Theory of Social Change', *The British Journal of Sociology*, 8(3): 197–207.

Gandhi, M. K. 1998. 'Collected Works of Mahatma Gandhi', Volume 1–100. Publications Division, Ministry of Information and Broadcasting, Government of India (GoI), Vol. 13:219, 1958 to 1993, New Delhi.

IMWR II. 2007. 'The Report of the Cauvery Water Disputes Tribunal with the Decision', Volume II, Agreements of 1892 and 1924. New Delhi.

IMWR V. 2007. 'The Report of the Cauvery Water Disputes Tribunal with the Decision', Volume V, Apportionment of the Waters of the Inter-state River Cauvery. New Delhi.

Jayaram, A. 2002. 'Government Cannot Disobey SC Order', *The Hindu*, www.thehindu.com/2002/10/06/stories/2002100601670400.htm (accessed on 28 May 2018).

Oberschall, A. 1978. 'Theories of Social Conflict', *Annual Review of Sociology*, 4: 291–315.

Pani, N. (ed.). 1982. *A Bureaucrat in Princely Mysore: Selections from the Private Diary of K. R. Srinivasa Iyengar, 1904–1941*. Banglore: Indian Institute of Management.

Pani, N. 2001. *Inclusive Economics: Gandhian Method and Contemporary Policy*. New Delhi: Sage.

Richards, Alan and Nirvikar Singh. 2002. 'Inter-state Water Disputes in India: Institutions and Policies', *International Journal of Water Resources Development*, 18(4).

Sorel, G. 1999. *Reflections on Violence*. Edited by J. Jennings. Cambridge: Cambridge University Press, pp. 1–348.

Swain, A. 1998. 'Fight for the Last Drop: Interstate River Disputes in India', *Contemporary South Asia*, 7(2): 167–180, doi:10.1080/09584939808719837.
*The Hindu*. 2012. 'Inter-district River Water Dispute Resolved', www.thehindu.com/todays-paper/tp-national/tp-andhrapradesh/interdistrict-river-water-dispute-resolved/article3382325.ece (accessed on 22 November 2013).
Urs, Kantharaj. 1953. *Addresses of Rajasevadhurina Sirdar Sir M. Kantharaj Urs (Dewan of Mysore 1919–1922) to the Representative Assembly*, Volume II. Mysore: Government Branch Press.
Visvesvarayya, M. 1951. *Memoirs of My Working Life*. 'Uplands', Banglore: Visvesvaraya.

# 13 Dams and environmental clearances

## Learnings and way forward

*Himanshu Thakkar*

## Introduction

Though the need for environmental clearances for dams has been felt in some form or the other since the mid-1970s and the process formally started after the passage of the Environment Protection Act of 1986, we continue to remain on a rather steep learning curve. This chapter gives the status of various aspects involved in environmental clearances of dams in India for the period April 2007 to December 2012 with a few recent updates and provides a sense of a way forward. The essence of what is said here remains relevant for the environment governance of dams and hydropower projects even in April 2018, when this chapter has been updated; if anything, the situation has only deteriorated.

## Evolution of the clearance process

Environmental clearance is issued by the Union Ministry of Environment and Forests (MoEF). The key stages in the evolution of this process have been in 1975, 1980, 1986 and 1994. After the most recent September 2006 Environment Impact Assessment (EIA) notification (MoEF 2006), some of the clearances of B category projects are to be now issued by the state government. The state governments have to set up State Environmental Impact Assessment Authorities (SEIAA) and State Expert Appraisal Committees (SEAC) for this.

### *Various kinds of environmental clearances*

There are several different environmental clearances if we use 'environment' in a generic sense. These include the following:

- what is called 'Environmental Clearance' (EC) under the EIA notification;

- 'Forest Clearance' under the Forest Conservation Act of 1980, which is required when projects involve use of forest land;
- 'Wildlife Clearance' under the Wildlife Protection Act of 1972 when projects involve protected areas or eco-sensitive zones around protected areas (issued by the Standing Committee of the National Board for Wildlife and the State Board for Wildlife);
- Pollution Control Board Clearance (to establish and operate under the Water Pollution Control Act); and
- Clearance from the National Clean Development Mechanism Authority for Clean Development Mechanism (CDM) projects.

However, in this chapter, the term 'Environmental Clearance' is used for clearances obtained under the EIA notification. According to the EIA notification of September 2006 Schedule (now applicable as I update this in April 2018), hydropower projects above 50 MW capacity and irrigation projects with command area above 10,000 hectares are 'A' category projects and require environmental clearance from the MoEF. Hydropower projects of 25–50 MW installed capacity and irrigation projects with command area below 10,000 ha are 'B' category projects and require environmental clearance from the SEIAA. The three-member SEIAA is to be set up by the centre as per the recommendation of the state governments. The state governments also have to set up the SEAC to appraise the projects before they go to the SEIAA. As stated in para 4(iii) of the EIA notification, 'In the absence of a duly constituted SEIAA or SEAC, a Category "B" project shall be treated as a Category "A" project'.

### *Large dams that do not require EC*

The implication of categorization of River Valley Projects (RVP) in the EIA notification of September 2006 is that the following large dam projects *will not* require environmental clearances: hydro projects with capacity below 25 MW, all flood control projects and water supply projects (for drinking water and industrial water needs), irrigation projects with command area below 10,000 ha, river front development projects and river dredging projects. As far as small hydropower projects with capacity below 25 MW are concerned, to assume that they are environmentally benign and do not need environmental clearance is clearly without basis and wrong. Every hydropower project will have adverse impacts and projects above 1 MW would certainly need Environment and Social Impact Assessment (ESIA), public consultation, monitoring and compliance. In fact, under the 1994 EIA notification, all river valley projects required environmental clearance. However, in September 2006, hydropower projects below 25 MW installed capacity were excluded from this process, without any justification.

Similarly, all domestic and industrial water supply dams and flood control dams (as also flood control embankments) were excluded. Again, it shows environmental illiteracy to suggest that these massive projects need not seek environmental clearance or impact assessment just because they rightly or fraudulently claim that the project is for domestic or industrial water supply. Massive dams like the Kalu dam in the Thane district in Maharashtra, the Yettinahole Project in the Western Ghats in Karnataka and even the interlinking of rivers project like the Damanganga Pinjal river link on the Gujarat – Maharashtra border have made such claims and got away with a decision from the EAC and MoEF that they do not need environmental clearance.

In Bihar, the massive embankment projects, affecting lakhs of people adversely, again do not need any environmental scrutiny. We (SANDRP[1] and others) have been writing to the MoEF for a change in this state of affairs for years, but there has been no change so far. A year back, in a meeting with the Joint Secretary, MoEF, when we questioned the environmental justification of such exclusions, we were told that these must have been 'slips of pen'. The MoEF has made several amendments to the EIA notifications since September 2006 but did not bother to correct these so-called slips of pen. Even the then green environment minister of India, Jairam Ramesh, did not change this situation.

### *Run of river projects: myths vs reality*

There is a widespread belief, thanks to some systematic propaganda, that all Run-of-the-River (ROR) projects are environment friendly. Since it is a key issue related to dams and environment, it needs to be highlighted here.

Firstly, the term ROR used in this context is wrong since these projects do not generate power from running water of the river as the term suggests. They all involve huge dams that first kill the river and then divert the river, typically through an underground tunnel several kilometres long, and the head so created is used to turn the turbines and generate power. The dams are all large as per the definition of the Central Water Commission of the Government of India,[2] the World Commission on Dams or the International Commission on Large Dams. These dams have the storage capacity of several million cubic metres. These projects are also not comparable to storage projects since these projects have several additional features like tunnels that traditional storage type dam-based hydropower projects did not have. To cut the long story short, these projects have huge social and environmental impacts and they end up destroying the river over very large stretches, along with biodiversity and habitats of people besides massively increasing the proportions of the disasters as was witnessed in Uttarakhand in June 2013.

### *Stages of clearance*

As per Section 7 (i) of the EIA notification, there are four stages of EC, not all of which are applicable to all projects: Stage (1) Screening (only for Category 'B' projects and activities); Stage (2) Scoping (determination of terms of reference for the EIA, accompanied by preconstruction activities for hydropower projects); Stage (3) Public Consultation; Stage (4) Appraisal by the Expert Appraisal Committee (EAC). In the case of dams, this is done by the EAC on RVP at the central level. At the state level, for category B Projects, the appraisal is done by the general SEAC (MoEF 2006).

Each stage of the EC is crucial and important in its own way. For example, scoping clearance is a signal that the project parameters are finalized and will not be changed or that the project will not be dropped due to environmental considerations. This is not a written law but an unwritten convention that the EAC seems to be following. All such unwritten conventions are generally seen to be pro-project rather than pro-environment, whereas one would expect the EAC to be more pro-environment rather than pro-project. This is apparent from the fact that the EAC has refused to follow its own rather weak norms, just because the project was given scoping clearance several years ago.

To illustrate, in the case of the Luhri Hydro Electric Project (HEP) on the Sutlej River in Himachal Pradesh, when the project came for final appraisal before the EAC for RVP in November 2012, one of the weak norms that the EAC was following was that there should be at least 1 km of flowing river between the projects, both in the upstream and downstream of the project. In the case of the Luhri HEP, there was absolutely no free-flowing river between the Luhri and the under-construction Kol dam in the downstream and between the Luhri and the under-construction Rampur project in the upstream. When we wrote[3] to the EAC about this and demanded that the EAC follow its own norm and ask the project proponent to ensure 1 km flowing river in the upstream and downstream and accordingly change the project parameters, the EAC did not agree, saying that this was not decided at the scoping level and now it was too late to ask the developer to change the parameter, when the construction was yet to start. The Luhri project that the EAC approved did not go through since the World Bank, which was supposed to fund it, declined funding to the project following strong opposition to the project from all concerned. In March 2018, however, the EAC considered the reformulated Luhri Stage I and II and agreed to give Stage I clearance to Luhri II, which Luhri I had already been accorded by an earlier EAC.

Similarly, in the case of the 300 MW Alakananda Badrinath Hydro Project of the GMR group, while appraising for EC, and again at a later date when the project came back to the EAC, in view of the recommendation of the report of the Wildlife Institute of India (WII) to drop the project, the EAC did not even bother to follow its own weak environment flow norms, just on the claim of the project developer, rejecting even the recommendation of the WII. These are just a couple of instances to illustrate the pro-project functioning of the EAC.

### *Expert appraisal committee (EAC)*

#### *Composition*

Appendix VI of the EIA notification[4] provides some description of the kind of professions and experts that may be selected as chairman and members of the EAC. However, this description by itself is seriously problematic since it allows the MoEF to select persons without any background in environment to be the chairperson and members of the EAC. For example, para 4 of Appendix VI says, 'The Chairperson shall be an outstanding and experienced environmental policy expert or expert in management or public administration with wide experience in the relevant development sector'.[5]

This allows the MoEF to appoint any retired bureaucrat without any background in environment or water or dams as the Chairperson of the EAC. Thus, most of the recent chairpersons of the EAC of RVP have had absolutely no background in environment, water, rivers, hydropower or dams. These include the current chairman, Dr. S. K. Jain, previous chairman Alok Perti, Rakesh Nath (he was chairman before Alok Perti) or P. Abraham (who was the chairperson before Rakesh Nath). On 9 September 2013, 58 organizations and individuals from all over India wrote to the MoEF, objecting to the reconstituted EAC on RVP with Alok Perti as the chairperson.

The letter said,

> It is equally disturbing to see that the committee has no woman representation, no sociologist, no one from non-government organisations. All ten members are either from the government, government organisations or government funded academic organisations. This means that none of them would be in a position to take a stand independent of the government. The committee also has no river expert, climate change water expert or disaster management expert, all of which are crucially important issues for a committee like this that decides the fate of India's rivers, even more so after the Uttarakhand disaster.
>
> (SANDRP 2013a)

The Ministry did not reply to the letter.

Appendix VI of the EIA notification also does not define conflict of interest. In fact, P. Abraham, former power secretary, was the chairperson of the EAC while being on the board of several hydropower companies whose projects came up for clearance before the committee he chaired. Neither MoEF nor Abraham saw anything problematic in this even when it was pointed out to them. It was only when Jairam Ramesh became the Environment Minister in 2009 and when we again wrote to him, that Abraham was forced to resign. But even after this episode, there is no mention of 'conflict of interest' as a criterion in the selection of EAC members or in the functioning of the EAC. Dr. S. K. Jain, who was made chairman of the reconstituted EAC in December 2016, soon became Director General of the National Water Development Agency (NWDA), the agency that develops river linking projects and Dr. Jain, as chairman of EAC, cleared the projects of the NWDA.[6] Similarly, there is no code of conduct for the EAC members.

### *Functioning*

There are very serious problems in the functioning of the EAC of RVP. This committee firstly never looks into the details of the issues which have been raised in the public hearing, or the quality of the public hearing, or whether the project developer has adequately responded to the issues raised in the public hearing (that is, whether the public hearing has followed the procedure described in Appendix IV of the EIA notification and so on). Even when serious inadequacies in the conduct of public hearing have been highlighted in submissions to the EAC, the EAC has not responded to these issues.

Secondly, affected people and non-governmental groups have been sending large number of submissions to the EAC, raising issues about projects, their impacts, EIAs, public hearings and so on. In most cases, the EAC does not even acknowledge such submissions or ensure that the issues raised in such submissions are addressed by the developer. In December 2016, the EAC in fact decided the following: 'Thus, in general, the EAC should not take any cognizance of such representations received from any Civil Action Group during final appraisal'.[7]

In some recent instances, where the developer has been asked to respond to the issues raised in submissions, the responses of the developers have been neither shared with the groups who sent the submissions, nor are such responses put out in the public domain. More significantly, the EAC has never invited such groups to the EAC meetings where the projects and issues raised by the groups are discussed, with just one exception where a few of us were invited to meet the EAC in February 2012.

Thirdly, the EAC has never applied its mind to the adequacy of the EIA and has never considered either recommending rejection of problematic EIAs or blacklisting of the EIA consultant. Nor has the EAC looked at the issue of the track record of the developer or that of the EIA consultant. It has also not applied its mind to whether the summary of the EIA made available in English and the local language provides an accurate summary of the project EIA and its impacts and adheres to the requirements for such summary as described in Appendix IIIA of the EIA notification. The EAC has not even responded to any such situations even when these have been brought to the notice of the EAC by submissions citing specific violations.

The EAC has also not ensured that the minutes of the EAC meetings are put out in the public domain within five working days as required by Appendix V of the EIA notification. The quality of the minutes of the EAC meetings have been found to be seriously deficient on several occasions, but even after pointing this out to the EAC, it has not bothered to make amends. The EAC has also not ensured that the necessary documents are available in the public domain at least 10 days before the EAC meeting, as required by the orders of the Central Information Commission.

Most importantly, the functioning of the EAC has shown a strong pro-project bias. The EAC has been seen to adopt rather weak norms on several environmental aspects and does not apply even those in a consistent way. It has consistently refused to agree to any of the recommendations of the expert bodies for rejection of the projects. For example, when the report of the Wildlife Institute of India recommended that 24 projects in Uttarakhand should be dropped for their serious biodiversity impacts, the EAC did not agree to it. When the Madhav Gadgil Committee recommended that the Gundia hydropower project in Karnataka Western Ghats should be dropped, it again did not agree to that recommendation. More disturbing were the standards and reasons that the EAC applied while discussing why the WGEEP (Western Ghats Ecology Expert Panel) rejected the Gundia project, were not applicable to the EAC's own appraisal work.

### *Track record*

Let us see the track record of the EAC of RVP in the period April 2007 to December 2012. SANDRP has done a detailed analysis of the functioning of the EAC of RVP for the said period (SANDRP 2013b, 2013c). The EAC for river valley and hydro-electric projects has had 63 meetings from the date of constitution of the committee in this period.

The EAC has considered a total of 262 hydropower and irrigation projects in close to six years. It has not rejected any project in this period. Even in the case of the two projects that it declined to recommend clearance for the Terms of Reference (TOR) of their EIA, it basically asked the developers to come back with reformulated proposals. It seems the committee is actually an Expert Approval Committee, since it seems to have expertise in approving rather than appraising the projects objectively.

The EAC has shown its strong bias against the people, environment and all those who represent the interests of the local communities and the environment. In February 2012, some of us were invited for a discussion with the EAC, but we saw little impact of our discussions on the functioning of the EAC.

Table 13.1 gives an overview of the situation of TORC (Terms of Reference Clearance) and EC (Environmental Clearance) for the projects cleared by the EAC on RVP between April 2007 and December 2012. The table shows that the EAC has not rejected any of the projects for EC. As against the 210 projects considered by the EAC for TORC, it (only temporarily) rejected TORC for just two projects. Hence, its temporary rejection rate for TORC is less than 1 per cent. The EAC's rejection rate of environmental clearance is nil as it has never rejected any project that has come to it for environmental clearance. It seems the EAC for RVP has been basically rubber-stamping its approval for every project that comes its way.

*Table 13.1* Overview of Clearance Status across India

| *Region* | *Projects for TORC* | | | *Projects for EC* | | | *Total projects considered* |
|---|---|---|---|---|---|---|---|
| | *TORC given* | *TORC rejected* | *Considered for TORC* | *EC given* | *EC rejected* | *Considered for EC* | |
| North | 50 | 1 (300 MW) | 57 | 31 | 0 | 34 | 72 |
| North East | 70 | 1 (420 MW) | 87 | 17 | 0 | 19 | 99 |
| East | 10 | 0 | 13 | 7 | 0 | 8 | 20 |
| West | 28 | 0 | 39 | 14 | 0 | 17 | 49 |
| South | 7 | 0 | 14 | 6 | 0 | 8 | 22 |
| Total | **165** | **2** | **210** | **75** | **0** | **86** | **262** |

Source: SANDRP 2013a, 2013b

## *Temporary rejections for two TORC*

Only two projects were rejected for Terms of Reference Clearance (TORC). Among these, for the 420 MW Kameng Dam, the EAC rejected the proposal from KSK Ltd, since the submergence area was just 350 m from the Pakke Tiger Reserve. The EAC, however, said, 'The Committee suggests that possibilities of locating a suitable site on the Kameng River, upstream of the confluence of the Bichom and Kameng may be explored'.[8] So the project is likely to come back to the EAC. It is surprising, however, that another project in the same basin, namely the 1120 MW Kameng I on the Bhareli/Kameng River in the East Kameng district in Arunachal Pradesh came before the EAC during its first meeting in April 2007. The minutes of the EAC meeting clearly says, 'A part of the submergence area falls under the Pakke Tiger Reserve'.[9] And yet the EAC gave TOR clearance to the project. This is another instance of the inconsistency of the EAC.

Similarly, the 200 MW Bara Bangahal HEP in the Kangra district in Himachal Pradesh was accorded TOR clearance in the 21st meeting of the EAC in December 2008, even as the minutes recorded, 'The project is located within the wildlife sanctuary'.[10] Similarly the 76 MW Rambara project on the Mandakini River in the Rudraprayag district in Uttarakhand, just 6 km from Kedarnath, was given TOR approval in the 19th EAC meeting in October 2008 even as the minutes noted, 'The whole project is located within the Kedarnath Musk Deer Sanctuary'.[11]

Similarly, while rejecting the TORC for the 300 MW Purthi HEP in the Lahaul and Spiti districts in Himachal Pradesh, the EAC said,

'The Committee concluded that the project proponent and the Govt. of Himachal Pradesh may review and revise the proposal in the light of the above observations for reconsideration'.[12] So it is clear in this case too that the rejection is temporary.

### *Massive hydropower capacity cleared*

In less than six years, the EAC has recommended TORC for hydropower projects proposed with installed capacity of 49,458 MW, which is about 25 per cent more than what India has installed in about 66 years since independence.

During the period, the EAC has recommended EC for hydropower capacity of 16084.5 MW, which is about three times the hydro capacity of 5544 MW added during the 11th Five-year Plan. The EAC has recommended all these clearances without giving any consideration to the carrying capacity, cumulative impact assessment, democratic decision-making, sustainable development criteria, full and proper social and environment impact assessment, or desirability of such capacity addition, including that from the climate change perspective.

Also, it has not bothered to look at either the declining generation performance of the existing projects, evidence of which was sent to the EAC, or the poor performance of existing hydro projects, as against the promised generation performance. It also never looked at the issues of compliance of even the environmental and social measures by the projects already cleared.

### *Zero rejection for irrigation projects*

The EAC for RVP considers irrigation projects with Cultivable Command Area (CCA) above 10,000 ha. During the period April 2007 to December 2012, the EAC has given TORC for 3.28 million ha of CCA and EC for 1.59 million ha of CCA. Here we should note that since 1991–1992, there has been no addition to the net area irrigated by major and medium irrigation projects at the all-India level as per Government of India figures (SANDRP 2012: 12). In light of that fact, and considering the over-capacity already built into a number of basins across India, such clearances by the EAC are highly questionable.

## Quality of the EIAs-EMPs and consultants

It is well-known that the quality of the EIAs in India is generally poor and leave a lot to be desired. India's former Environment Minister, Jairam Ramesh, is on record having talked about the poor quality of the EIAs. The Power Minister of Assam has publicly said that the EIAs of the Arunachal hydropower projects get made sitting in the five-star hotels in Guwahati, without going to the affected areas. Even the media has highlighted this issue several times. A large number of submissions have been sent in this regard to the EAC and the MoEF, without any result. The MoEF or the EAC has never recommended rejection of any EIA or blacklisting or any other punitive measure for any EIA consultant for fraudulent or poor quality of EIA even when evidence is given to it. For example, in the case of EIA of the Mohanpura irrigation project in Madhya Pradesh, SANDRP and others have written to the EAC and MoEF highlighting the poor quality of the EIA and plagiarizing in sections of the EIA. However, no action has been taken.

In 2010, as a step to address this issue, the MoEF first initiated and then made it mandatory for all EIA consultants to register with the Quality Council of India (QCI). Numerous environmental groups wrote to the MoEF stating why this is not going to work considering that the QCI essentially represents industrial groups and that no clearly defined criteria for issues of conflict of interest, track record, feedback and quality assurance mechanisms have been put in place. Eight years down the line, the concerns expressed by these groups have been vindicated, as no improvement was seen in the quality of the EIAs since this process started.

### *Public consultation process*

In the entire dam project cycle, today there is just one place where affected and local communities and non-government organizations have some role. This is at the stage of public hearing/public consultation before the project goes for appraisal before the EAC. As mentioned earlier, the quality and adequacy of this public hearing/consultation process is far from the acceptable level. During our meeting with the EAC in February 2012, when we raised this issue, the EAC members told us that they are not looking at the adequacy of the public hearing process and that is left to the MoEF and it is expected that the MoEF will bring only those projects on the agenda of the EAC for which proper public hearing/consultation has happened. However, there is no evidence to suggest that the MoEF is taking care of this issue; they are essentially seeing if the box for public hearing is ticked or not. There have been several cases that were violations of norms at public hearings (e.g., Chamera III HEP in Himachal Pradesh) and have been brought to the notice of the MoEF, instances where affected people have not been allowed to enter or speak at the public hearings (Devsari project or Pancheshwar project in Uttaranchal or Ken Betwa River Link project in Madhya Pradesh). However, in no such case has the MoEF rejected the public hearing or asked for a fresh public hearing.

The EIA notification (para 4.1 Appendix IV) says, 'The District Magistrate or his/her representative, not below the rank of an Additional District Magistrate assisted by a representative of the SPCB [State Pollution Control Board] or UTPCC [Union Territory Pollution Control Committee], shall supervise and preside over the entire public hearing process' (MoEF 2006). This is clearly flawed since the panel should be constituted by independent non-government persons, without any conflict of interest and before whom the local people have no fear in expressing themselves. None of this can be said about the current panel.

Secondly, the main vehicle for the local people to know about the project and its impacts is the EIA. However, the EIA is only available in English and not in the local language. We have been advocating for many years that the full EIA should be available in the local language and there should be a process of facilitating the understanding of the EIA document for the local communities through some credible NGOs. We have shown that all this (translation of full EIA into the local language, facilitation and also conduct of Public Hearing by independent panel etc.) is feasible and useful by ensuring it in the case of the Allain Duhangan HEP in Himachal Pradesh. However, we have a long way to go before this becomes the norm.

Lastly, it is not good enough that the local people have some role only once in the life cycle of a project; instead it should be a continuous process as recommended by the World Commission on Dams.

## *Role of the MoEF*

One agency that should take full responsibility for the state of affairs on environmental clearance for dams is the Union Ministry of Environment and Forests. It has a role in this respect in policy formulation, selection of the EAC chairman and members, selecting projects for the EAC agenda, conduct of the EAC meetings, drafting of minutes, ensuring all documents are available in the public domain in a timely manner, ensuring adequacy of the EIA, public hearing and information availability, to name only a few key areas. Moreover, each EAC has one or two officers from the MoEF, including the member secretary.

The Supreme Court of India, in the case related to the Lafarge Cement Plant in Meghalaya, had directed thus in its judgement of 6

July 2011: 'we are of the view that under Section 3(3) of the Environment (Protection) Act, 1986, the Central Government should appoint a National Regulator for appraising projects, enforcing environmental conditions for approvals and to impose penalties on polluters' (Supreme Court 2011).

However, in a sudden change of stance, the MoEF told the Court on 23 October 2013 that such a regulator is not feasible. The MoEF's affidavit stated:

> Keeping in view the diverse and inter-connected nature of issues involved in grant of environment clearance to various categories of projects, it may not be feasible for a single authority with limited number of experts to appraise proposals seeking environment clearance to projects of various categories.
>
> (Indian Express 2013)

The reason given by the MoEF that such a regulator is not feasible due to the complexities of diverse issues involved is not particularly convincing, since the MoEF itself has not bothered about these complexities when appointing members and chairman of the EAC as we saw earlier. It seems the MoEF does not want to give up the power that it has in providing environmental clearances to the projects all over the country.

### *Right to information and central information commission*

Pursuant to an RTI application followed by an appeal on a petition by the Legal Initiative for Forest and Environment (LIFE) – a non-governmental organization dealing with legal-environmental issues in India – the Central Information Commission directed on 18 January 2012 that under Section 4(1) of RTI Act (2005), the MoEF needs to put on its website all the documents submitted by the project proponents while applying for environmental clearances. When the MoEF was not following these directions, SANDRP filed a complaint with the CIC, following which the CIC issued a notice to the MoEF in May 2012. Subsequently, we saw for some time a gradual improvement in the availability of documents on the MoEF website, though not all the documents as directed by the CIC are available. However, the documents now available have created a greater potential for non-government organizations to participate in the environmental clearance process in a more informed way. Since 2015, the situation in this regard has deteriorated, particularly after December

2016, regarding the availability of key documents and response to civil society submissions by the EAC and the MoEF.

### *Compliance of conditions of clearance and EMPs*

All the environmental clearances are provided with numerous conditions, some project specific and some general. Moreover, the developers are also supposed to implement the Environment Management Plan (EMP) that is part of the EIA report. The implementation of the EMP is supposed to happen *pari passu* with the project. The MoEF is legally responsible for the compliance by the developers with the conditions of the EC and the EMP. However, we have seen over the years that the MoEF has no will, willingness or capacity to ensure compliance. The MoEF officers say this openly to us. Nor has the MoEF shown any interest in improving this state of affairs.

Each project that is appraised under the EIA notification is legally responsible to provide six-monthly compliance reports after the clearances. The MoEF also has regional offices, and scientists from these offices are supposed to visit the project area periodically to check the status of compliance and report back. However, these measures have currently not worked since even when developers do not submit any compliance reports, there are no consequences for them. And even when the reports are submitted, there is no one in the MoEF to check where the project stands with respect to the compliance. In fact, it is doubtful whether there is anyone there to even read the compliance reports. As far as site visits from the MoEF regional offices are concerned, they happen at the most once in five years and then too there are no surprise visits, but visits with sufficient advance notice to the developers so that they can do all the window dressing. In any case, there are no known cases of action by the MoEF where non-compliance has been reported following such visits.

One interesting example as to how compliance can be achieved in a dam project is provided by the legally created mechanism called the Environment Sub Group (ESG) of the Narmada Control Authority (NCA) for the Sardar Sarovar Project (SSP), the body also having a non-government member known to be independent. At each stage of the construction of the SSP, an approval of the ESG of the NCA is necessary and if the SSP goes ahead without such an approval, both the ESG (chaired by Secretary, MoEF) and the developer can be held accountable. While there are many issues related to this mechanism, it has been seen that it worked to an extent and dam work had to be paused on several occasions due to non-compliance mandated by the ESG. A mechanism like the ESG for each dam, with more credible monitoring mechanism than what was available in the case of the SSP, could be a good option.

Any such legally empowered monitoring and compliance mechanism at each project level should comprise at least 50 per cent of the members coming from outside the government, including representatives of the affected communities. But the MoEF has shown no interest in putting together any such credible monitoring and compliance mechanism.

## Cumulative impact assessments, carrying capacity studies, basin studies

Currently, only project-specific EIAs are mandatory. However, in a large number of river basins like the Sutlej, Chenab, Ravi, Beas, Alakananda, Bhagirathi, Mandakini, Chambal, Narmada, Teesta, Krishna and so on, there are bumper-to-bumper hydropower projects and dams with very little flowing river stretches. In such basins, the cumulative impact assessment (CIA) of such large number of projects won't be just equal to the sum of the impacts of individual projects. For example, for biodiversity, too many projects could sound a death knell. It is also important to ascertain the carrying capacity of the basins along with the basin-wide interventions going on. However, today in India, the CIA, carrying capacity or basin studies are not mandatory. Following over a decade-long demands by various groups, in some cases, the MoEF, the Forest Advisory Committee and the judiciary has started asking for the CIA. However, we still do not have what we can call a credible CIA. More CIAs are done by compromised consultants like the Power Developers Association in the case of the Sutlej basin or WAPCOS – formerly Water and Power Consultancy Services, now just WAPCOS Ltd – and the CWC in the case of the North East basins. Since the CWC works more like a lobby for dams and WAPCOS is also under the Union Ministry of Water Resources, none of them have the credibility to do a CIA. We have far to go in this respect as in most others, it seems.

The 28 May 2013 notification from the MoEF says that the assessment of carrying capacity study and cumulative impact assessment study are mandatory for any river basin having more than one hydropower project. But this notification has never been applied by the MoEF; when we raise this issue, they find one escape route or another on how not to follow it.

### *Options assessment*

One of the key components of any EIA is options assessment that will establish that among all the options available to achieve the same objective, the given dam is the best option. However, this is one of the weakest parts of the EIAs. Most EIAs do not do any options assessment and those that do, do not understand its significance and only do it in name. The MoEF manual on the EIA for RVP says that this should be done and so does our National Water Policy and also the R&R Policy. But until this is done in a credible way, we won't be able to take the most optimum decisions about dams. Any such options assessment should also look at the actual performance of existing dam and other water infrastructure and how that is changing and how that can be optimized. Other non-dam options should also be part of this exercise.

### *Performance of dams*

As mentioned previously, while considering any new dam project, the performance of existing dams, how that performance is changing and how that performance compares with the promised performance are crucial. This is particularly relevant for dams.

In the case of dams, over 95 per cent of India's over 5,701 big dams as per the latest version of the CWC's National Register of Large Dams (CWC 2017) are built for irrigation. However, if we look at the area irrigated by Major and Medium Irrigation Projects from official records (SANDRP 2013c), there is no increase in such area since the last two decades.

Similarly, on the hydropower front, the generation performance of operating hydropower projects in India is dismal (when compared to what was promised as 90 per cent dependable generation) and also diminishing, with about 25 per cent reduction in the last two decades in generation per MW installed capacity (Thakkar 2012). While one of the USPs (Unique Selling Proposition) of hydropower projects is peaking power, there is no one in the country even assessing what proportion of current hydropower generation is during peaking hours. Also, neither is any agency doing such performance analyses, nor is such analysis informing our decisions about dams. This is clearly leading to a huge number of unviable dams and unaccountable decisions. Environmental Clearance should be an important decision that needs to be informed by all this.

## Other related clearance processes

There are many other techno-economic decisions that are related to the EC for dams. Some of these include the Technical Advisory

Committee clearance under the CCWC, Concurrence under the Electricity Act by the Central Electricity Authority (which also involves the CWC and the Geological Survey of India), Investment Clearance by the Planning Commission, Public Investment Board and Cabinet Committee on Economic Affairs. These are noted here since all these clearances follow and assume environmental viability. Since our EC does not really ascertain environmental viability, all the subsequent and related decisions are also likely to seriously falter.

### *CCI attempt to bypass MoEF fails, but attempt is on*

There is a constant clamour by the vested interest groups, lobbies and industrial associations that say from time to time that environmental clearances are a hurdle to development, GDP growth and so on. One of the fallouts of this clamour was the creation of the Cabinet Committee on Investments (CCI) in 2013 under the Prime Minister of India (Cabinet Secretariat 2016). This body was earlier proposed as the National Investment Board and, in a rare sign of outspoken courage, the Union Minister of State for Environment and Forests had strongly objected to the creation of the body through her letter dated 8 October 2012 since it seemed designed to bypass the role of the MoEF in giving environmental and forest clearances. The whole mechanism of the CCI, the way it is functioning, seems designed to bypass the environmental clearances (Kohli 2013).

### *National Environmental Appellate Authority (NEAA) and National Green Tribunal (NGT)*

The National Environmental Appellate Authority set up by the MoEF took long time to be set up and was never really fully effective. The National Green Tribunal (MoEF 2010) that was set up through an act of Parliament in 2010 to replace the NEAA seems to provide better hope for relatively quicker redressal of challenges to environmental clearances and also allows questioning of the EC on merit. The issue of the right kind of judicial and non-judicial members on the NGT bench among others is crucial. The MoEF, however, is creating maximum hurdles in the smooth functioning of the NGT and it is only largely due to the regular orders from the Supreme Court of India that the NGT has become a reality.

### *High courts and supreme court*

In the kind of scenario painted here on the issues related to the environmental clearance of dams, one would have thought that the higher judiciary would play a key role in helping improve matters. However, this is generally not the case, leaving aside some exceptions like the NGT-related matters and the Lafarge case mentioned earlier. However, we are yet to see really effective judicial activism on environmental clearances related to dams.

## Emerging issues and way forward

Several issues are still emerging in environmental governance around dams. Besides the ones mentioned previously, some additional issues include the following: the environment flows, fish and fisheries, distance of flowing river between two projects, no dams above a certain height, no dams on certain rivers, percentage of compromised river length by projects, impact of climate change on dams and contribution of dams to climate change, increased glacier melting and its impact on rivers and dams, biodiversity protection, dams and disasters, methane emissions from reservoirs, disaster potential of dams, mining of raw materials for dams, muck disposal, bumper to bumper projects, impact of dams on sediment regimes of rivers, decommissioning of dams, for how many years should the EC be valid and when should the developer be asked to come back for renewal, establishing liability of the developers on downstream areas, impact of peaking operation and so on. These are some of the very crucial issues, but this brief chapter does not provide scope to discuss them in detail.

This chapter is very critical of the state of environmental governance of dams and rivers in India. The way forward is indicated in many of the sections mentioned above and hence is not repeated here. One thing is very clear – we have a long way to go. As stated at the beginning, we continue to remain on a steep learning curve for many years. The fundamental change that we need to bring in is a greater sense of transparency, accountability and participation in the process of our environmental decisions and governance. We have so little faith in democracy and our people. The way forward is to bring in real faith in our democracy and people in environmental governance.

## Notes

1 South Asia Network on Dams, Rivers and People (SANDRP) is an informal network of organizations and individuals who work on issues related to the water sector with major focus on issues associated with large dams.
2 CWC. 2015. 'National Register of Large Dams'. http://cwc.gov.in/main/downloads/NRLD_04012017.pdf (accessed on 10 April 2018).

3 SANDRP. 2013. Letter to MoEF and EAC to Reject Environment Clearance for the proposed 775 MW Luhri hydropower project on Sutlej River in Himachal Pradesh. https://sandrp.files.wordpress.com/2018/03/reject_environment_clearance_for_luhri_hep_letter_from_56_to_moef_and_eac_january2013.pdf (accessed on 10 April 2018)
4 MoEF. 2006. "EIA Notification of September 14, 2006. www.moef.nic.in/legis/eia/so1533.pdf (accessed on 10 April 2018).
5 MoEF. 2006. "EIA Notification of September 14, 2006. www.moef.nic.in/legis/eia/so1533.pdf (accessed on 10 April 2018).
6 See for example: https://sandrp.in/2017/06/05/thanks-dr-sharad-jain-but-plz-step-down-from-eac-let-us-understand-conflict-of-interest/ (accessed on 10 April 2018).
7 MoEF. 2016. "Minutes of the 1st Meeting of the Expert Appraisal Committee for River Valley and Hydroelectric Projects held on 30th December, 2016". http://environmentclearance.nic.in/writereaddata/Form-1A/Minutes/12012017YXHJSW1J1stEACMeetingforRVHEP30thDecember2016.pdf (Accessed on 10 April 2018)
8 MoEF. 2012. "Minutes of the 57th meeting of Expert Appraisal Committee for River Valley and Hydro Power Projects". http://environmentclearance.nic.in/viewminutes.aspx?date1=04/27/2012&code=RIV (accessed on 10 April 2018).
9 Minutes of April 2007 EAC meeting; it is no longer available online.
10 MoEF. 2008. "Summary Record of discussions of the twenty-first (21st) meeting of Expert Appraisal Committee for River Valley and Hydroelectric Projects constituted under the provisions of EIA notification 2006, held on 15th & 16th December, 2008 in New Delhi". http://environmentclearance.nic.in/Report/minutesarchive.aspx (accessed on 10 April 2018), go to the River Valley Projects, click on the date 15 December 2008; specific URL for each older EAC meeting minute is not available.
11 MoEF. 2008. "Summary Record of discussions of the Nineteenth (19th) meeting of Expert Appraisal Committee for River Valley and Hydroelectric Projects constituted under the provisions of EIA notification 2006, held on 15th & 16th October, 2008 in New Delhi". http://environmentclearance.nic.in/Report/minutesarchive.aspx (accessed on 10 April 2018), go to the River Valley Projects, click on the date 15 October 2008; specific URL for each older EAC meeting minute is not available.
12 MoEF. 2012. "Minutes of the 62nd Meeting of the Expert Appraisal Committee (EAC) for River Valley and Hydroelectric Projects constituted under the provisions of EIA Notification 2006, held on 23–24th November, 2012". http://environmentclearance.nic.in/writereaddata/Form-1A/Minutes/18_Final%20Minutes%20%2062nd%20EAC%20-%20Copy.pdf (accessed on 10 April 2018).

## References

Cabinet Secretariat. 2016. 'Functions of Cabinet Committee on Investment', Cabinet Secretariat, Government of India (GoI), https://cabsec.gov.in/writereaddata/cci/english/1_Upload_989.pdf (accessed on 10 April 2018).

CWC (Central Water Commission). 2017. 'National Register of Large Dams', http://cwc.gov.in/main/webpages/Others_%20publications.html (accessed on 10 April 2018).

Indian Express. 2013. 'Govt Tell SC Regulator for Green Nod Not Feasible', Reported by Utkarsh Anand, 24 October, http://archive.indianexpress.com/news/govt-tells-sc-regulator-for-green-nod-not-feasible/1186471/0 (accessed on 10 April 2018).

Kohli, K. 2013. 'Is CCI a Bypass Lane for Laws?' *India Together*, 30 October, http://indiatogether.org/cci-environment (accessed on 10 April 2018).

MoEF. 2006. *Notification*. Published in the Gazette of India, Extraordinary, Part-II, and Section 3, Sub-section (ii). Ministry of Environment and Forests, Government of India (GoI), http://envfor.nic.in/legis/eia/so1533.pdf (accessed on 10 April 2018).

MoEF. 2010. 'The National Green Tribunal Act, 2010', Ministry of Law and Justice, The Gazette of India, www.moef.nic.in/downloads/public-information/NGT-fin.pdf (accessed on 10 April 2018).

SANDRP. 2012. 'Water Governance in India: Problems and Prospects', South Asia Network of Dams, Rivers and People (SANDRP), https://sandrp.files.wordpress.com/2018/03/water_governance_in_india_himanshu_thakkar_iwmi_tata_meet_december2012.pdf (accessed on 10 April 2018).

SANDRP. 2013a. 'Reconstituted Expert Appraisal Committee on River Valley Projects: MoEF Has Neither Environmental Sense, Nor Guts; Unacceptable Committee', South Asia Network of Dams, Rivers and People (SANDRP), https://sandrp.wordpress.com/2013/09/07/reconstituted-expert-appraisal-committee-on-river-valley-projects-moef-has-neither-environment-sense-nor-guts-unacceptable-committee/ (accessed on 10 April 2018).

SANDRP. 2013b. 'The Expert Approval Committee has Zero Rejection in Six Years: April 2007 to December 2012', Analysis of MoEF's EAC on River Valley Projects. South Asia Network on Dams, Rivers and People (SANDRP), February, https://sandrp.files.wordpress.com/2018/03/tor_and_ec_clearance_status_all_india_overview_feb2013.pdf (accessed on 10 April 2018).

SANDRP. 2013c. 'MoEF's Expert Appraisal Committee on River Valley Projects: Stage 1 and 2 Environment Clearance Status, from the Minutes of EAC Meetings', South Asia Network on Dams, Rivers and People (SANDRP), February, https://sandrp.files.wordpress.com/2018/03/eac_meetings_decisions_all_india_apr_2007_to_dec_2012.pdf (accessed on 10 April 2018).

Supreme Court. 2011. 'T. N. Godavarman Thirumulpad vs Union of India & Ors on 6 July 2011', Supreme Court of India, www.lafarge-bd.com/pdf/news/judgment.pdf (accessed on 10 April 2018).

Thakkar, H. 2012. 'Diminishing Return from Large Hydro', South Asia Network on Dams, Rivers and People (SANDRP), https://sandrp.files.wordpress.com/2018/03/diminishing_returns_from_large_hydro_nov_2012.pdf (accessed on 10 April 2018).

# 14 Rationale for independent regulatory agency for water in India

## Reconceptualizing credible commitment

*Sachin Warghade and Subodh Wagle*

### Introduction

In the parliamentary system, an 'Independent Regulatory Agency' (IRA) holds a rather odd place.[1] In the chain of delegation – involving citizens, elected members of parliament, ruling government, ministers and bureaucracy – the establishment of an IRA is seen as the 'ultimate' step of delegation (Gilardi 2001). The IRA, by its very design, enjoys authority and autonomy over the delegated policy matters, without direct political control. Indirect political controls are imposed on the IRA but cannot be so tightened as to take away the autonomy accorded. They are often termed as non-majoritarian institutions of the government that possess specialized public authority and are neither directly elected by the people nor directly managed by elected officials (Thatcher and Stone Sweet 2002). This makes the IRA a very peculiar and complex case of institutional design within the democratic parliamentary system.

Because of its odd place in the parliamentary system, the question of the rationale for IRA becomes highly important. Why delegate powers to an IRA? What is the rationale for the creation of an IRA? What functions can it perform effectively and legitimately within the given democratic system? These are some of the important questions about the institutional design of IRAs. These questions have been adequately addressed in the developed countries, at the practice as well as the theoretical level (Thatcher and Stone Sweet 2002; Gilardi 2001, 2004 and 2008). For example, 'credible commitment' is a well-developed rationale for the creation of IRAs in developed countries (Levy and Spiller 1994). What this rationale is, whether it is relevant for the IRAs in the water sector in developing countries like India, and whether there is any effective role that an IRA can play in the highly complex and life-sustaining sector like water[2] – these are the most important questions that require attention in light of the recent regulatory reforms in India that include the establishment of IRAs in the water sector (Prayas 2007). The IRAs in the water sector have been created in India through legislations in the states of Andhra Pradesh, Arunachal Pradesh, Jammu & Kashmir, Jharkhand, Madhya Pradesh, Maharashtra, Rajasthan and Uttar Pradesh. In this chapter, we focus on the problems and prospects specifically related to the rationale for the creation of these IRAs.

## Credible commitment rationale and institutional design

The 'credible commitment' rationale is the basis for the creation of IRAs, mainly in the privatized infrastructure and utility sector, such as electricity, water and telecom (Levy and Spiller 1994; Thatcher and Stone Sweet 2002; Gilardi 2001, 2004 and 2008). These sectors are often categorized as 'network industry' or 'network utilities' (Phillips 1993). They are characterized by very high economies of scale due to the heavy, sunk and very specific capital expenditure required for laying the network for water or electricity distribution. It is found to be more economical to allow maximum traffic through a single network rather than diverting traffic into multiple networks. This creates a situation of natural monopoly and thereby the high possibility of abuse of monopoly power by the private service provider. This forms a threat to public interest, considering that some of these sectors deliver basic services like water and electricity. Regulation of such network utilities thus becomes the core concern for the government.

Holding these sectors and their service provision within the bounds of public ownership is an important policy requirement to overcome the problem of natural monopoly. Public ownership itself becomes an important mode of regulation in this situation. However, as the fiscal constraints build up, there are pressures to attract private investments in the sector, and then back it up with strong regulatory measures to protect public interest. The establishment of an IRA to regulate this situation is an important measure in this regard. But the pertinent question is this: why is it an 'independent' regulatory authority, and not some other form of government authority controlled by politically elected members, that is required to regulate? One of the important rationales put forth in this regard is that the IRA can provide a 'credible commitment' to private investors on behalf of the political decision makers (Levy and Spiller 1994). To enter into a regulated network utility business, private investors need a credible commitment from the government towards protection of their investment and returns. Because the government will regulate these businesses for protecting public interest, the private investors fear that their financial interests will not always be protected, even if the government promises protection. It is argued that only an independent regulatory agency, being autonomous of any direct political control, can provide credibility to the commitment made by elected policy makers for ensuring a fair return on investment for private investors. This particular rationale, using the credible commitment argument, is hereafter referred to as the 'privatization-centric' credible commitment rationale.

The design of the IRA largely follows this particular privatization-centric rationale of credible commitment[3] (Brown *et al.* 2006). This model of IRA is considered conceptually and practically feasible and achieves a certain amount of coherence in policy and institutional design. The issues of overall institutional design have been largely settled so as to consider this as a standard model of economic regulation through the IRA. For example, the composition of the IRA, its selection process and its functions are all geared towards providing a credible commitment to the private investors. Towards this end, the IRA is comprised of independent expert members. They cannot be serving government officials. Selection is done through an independent selection committee. The members of the regulatory agency are protected by law from random removals by their political counterparts. The IRA is empowered to take autonomous decisions on aspects such as tariff that directly affect the financial returns expected by private investors. All these features of the institutional design of the IRA are tailored towards the rationale of 'credible commitment' required by private investors.

As mentioned earlier, there is a need to protect public interest due to the natural monopoly that exists in network utilities. So, the protection of interest of the private investor has to be balanced with that of the public. Public interest protection through the IRA involves aspects such as ensuring minimum service standards and cross-subsidization to protect those who cannot afford basic services. Grievance redressal is also an important role of the IRA for protecting the consumers. However, all these functions of protecting public interest are within the bounds of ensuring a fair return on investment for private investors. Anything beyond this boundary is seen as the responsibility of the government, as part of its 'redistributive' role. For example, any concession on tariff set by the IRA can be given only if the government treats this as a subsidy and guarantees upfront payment to the private service provider. Hence, the core social rationale of 'redistribution' is largely not the mandate of the IRA. The social rationale of regulation remains within the purview of the government departments headed by politically elected members of parliament. This is how the IRA is designed as per the privatization-centric 'credible commitment' rationale.

## Design rationale of water IRAs in India

The Maharashtra Water Resources Regulatory Authority (MWRRA) Act of 2005 was the first legislation enacted for the creation of an IRA in the water sector in India. Many of the other states that have enacted such laws have used the MWRRA as the model for understanding the regulatory framework and have replicated some of its aspects. There are state-specific variations but the influence of the MWRRA is evident from the way the authority is structured (Wagle *et al.* 2015). Hence, the MWRRA can be used as a representative case of an IRA in the water sector in India. The MWRRA is not only the first but also the only IRA in the water sector that has been functioning for more than a decade. This allows analysis of the design as well as the implementation of an IRA. This is important because the rationale for an IRA should be assessed based on not only the articulated design (as given in the law) but also on the actual implementation. This section of the chapter focuses on the assessment of the rationale based on the design of the law, while the section subsequent to this will assess the same based on the implementation of the law.

### *Organizational structure of the IRA*

The organizational features of the IRA in the water sector in India, as seen from the MWRRA, largely resemble the design features of an IRA driven by the privatization-centric credible commitment rationale. As discussed in the previous section, such IRAs provide credibility to the commitment given by the policy makers for protecting private investments. This is because of the autonomous, expert-oriented and apolitical decision-making process of an IRA. The features of such decision-making also exist in the case of the design of the IRAs for the water sector in India. This is evident from the organizational structure of the MWRRA. For example, as per the MWRRA Act 2005, the members of the regulatory agency include experts in water engineering and water economy.[4] They cannot be serving government officers. The members cannot be removed by their political counterparts without due process and reason. Members have powers equivalent to a civil court and are accorded powers to make decisions autonomously in crucial areas such as water tariff. Thus, the members are isolated from their political counterparts for decision-making or for other daily routine matters. The IRA law in the state of Uttar Pradesh also provides for payment of salaries to the members of the IRA from the consolidated funds of the state, earmarked permanently in the state budget, thus removing the financial dependency on political functionaries. The members are selected for their expertise in economics and engineering. This shows the importance given to techno-economic rationality in decision-making, which is required for regulating a utility based on commercial business principles. Thus, the organizational structure for the IRAs in the water sector matches very closely with the requirements of providing a credible commitment to private investors.

### *Absence of privatization agenda in IRAs*

The laws for the establishment of IRAs in other sectors in India have been justified largely on the basis of the credible commitment rationale in the context of the privatization of the utilities. For example, the Electricity Act of 2003 in India came with a package of reforms that included provision for privatization along with a provision for creation of an IRA. Thus, a private sector investor is allowed to operate within the regulatory purview of an IRA. This can be seen as the perfect example of justifying the IRA through the credible commitment rationale.

Unlike the Electricity Act, the MWRRA Act does not provide for privatization of water infrastructure and services. Effectively, the IRA in the water sector will end up regulating the publicly held water utilities and departments. This is a paradoxical situation, given the conventional privatization-centric rationale of the IRA model discussed earlier.

This does not mean that the privatization of water services is not undertaken. Several reforms and pilot projects are already underway as far as the privatization of water services in India is concerned (Dwivedi, Rehmat and Dharmadhikary 2007). The point is that policy makers have dissociated the IRA laws from these privatization initiatives. This is puzzling as far as the question of the rationale for an IRA is concerned.

### *Cost recovery negates the possibility of privatization*

The cost-recovery principle is important in the tariff determination process conducted by an IRA. It allows determination of tariff for recovering all costs associated with service provision. This creates conditions conducive for future possible entry of private investors because it guarantees recovery of their investments through tariff. So, this can actually be considered part of the design that follows the privatization-centric credible commitment rationale.

A detailed look at the cost-recovery principle provided in the MWRRA Act shows that the costs to be recovered are limited to just the operations and maintenance (O&M) cost. Hence, it negates the possibility of the recovery of capital cost as well as return on investment, which are necessary components of the cost-recovery principle for private investors. In the absence of this form of 'full cost-recovery' in the water IRA laws in India, privatization cannot be seen as the formal agenda behind the creation of the IRA.

### *Implausibility of market-based allocations*

Analysis shows that the water IRA laws make concrete provision for 'resource' privatization, if not 'service' privatization. This is because of the provision in the law for water entitlements that can be traded in a market system. The creation of a water market is certainly the formal agenda articulated in the MWRRA Act. Traders in such a market would be ready to trade only if there is a credible commitment from the government that their transactions and proceeds from the trade will be protected through regulators like the IRA. This sounds like a logical way to define the rationale for the water IRA, but it has remained irrelevant due to the implausibility of its implementation.

Water distribution and allocation is deeply ingrained as a political function in India. Attempts to bring even the water distribution function under the purview of an IRA have been opposed by the political functionaries in Maharashtra (Wagle *et al.* 2015). If a simple regulatory purview on water allocation is unacceptable to the policy makers, then it will be implausible to bring in market as a mechanism to allocate water. Adding to this implausibility is the fact that various social activists and organizations have strongly opposed any move towards the creation of water markets.[5] This is evident from the fact that the MWRRA could not pursue this agenda even when it tried to come up with an approach paper for the same in 2011 (MWRRA 2011). So, the rationale of privatization-centric credible commitment, based on the argument of the water market, exists but remains practically irrelevant.

### *Social and environmental rationale*

It is interesting to note that the laws for the establishment of the IRAs in India emphasize equity and sustainability as the key principles to be followed in regulating water. The preamble of the MWRRA Act specifies these principles and also provides some operational provisions in this regard. For example, equity is applied as a principle in determination of water entitlements, in sharing of water among upstream and downstream water users, and in prioritizing fund allocation and project implementation in regions affected by drought and developmental backlog. The MWRRA is entrusted with special powers to monitor the eradication of the irrigation backlog, which is one of the causes of the developmental backlog in the Vidarbha and the Marathwada regions of the state. For application of the principle of equitable sharing of distress during scarcity among upstream and downstream users, the Act provides for the release of water from upstream reservoirs to downstream reservoirs in such a manner that the percentage of utilizable water in these reservoirs is approximately equal. This is a unique and radical provision with regard to basin-level equity. Canal-level equity is also brought under the regulatory purview by making the IRA ensure implementation of tail-to-head irrigation.

Sustainability is operationalized in the form of the 'polluter pays' principle. Also, 'environment' is considered one of the water-user categories, thus paving the way for ensuring minimum environmental flow. Control on over-extraction of groundwater is also considered an important function of the IRA.[6] Overall, the MWRRA Act presents a model where social and environmental regulation is also brought under the purview of an IRA.

### *Towards institutional dissonance*

It can be concluded from the analysis of the design of the IRA that the conventional privatization-centric credible commitment rationale is not the relevant rationale in the laws enacted for the establishment of IRAs in the water sector in India. In fact, what emerges from the substantive principles accepted in the law is the emphasis on social and environmental objectives for regulation. But, at the same time, the organizational form of the IRA resembles the requirement of the privatization-centric rationale. Thus, a form of organization (i.e., IRA) designed originally for some specific purpose (i.e., providing credible commitment for private investors) is accepted in the Indian context for some other purpose (i.e., a mix of social and economic purposes). There is, hence, an apparent dissonance in the institutional design.

This raises an important question on the relevance and conception of the credible commitment rationale for IRAs. Is the credibility of policy commitment, which is a serious concern for protecting private investment in the water sector, also an equally serious concern for protecting the social and environmental values in the water sector? Is there a need for developing a broader conception of the said rationale to encompass commitment problems around social and environmental values? Answering these questions will help in assessing whether there is any relevant rationale for the kind of IRA accepted in the local context by policy makers in Indian states. It will help in analysing the paradoxical situation of creating an IRA in the absence of privatization of water services. More insights into these questions can be gained through an analysis of the implementation phase of the IRA, discussed in the subsequent section.

## Rationale emerging from implementation

Apart from the legal statutes related to the IRA design, a deeper understanding of the design can be gained through insights from implementation. After closely analysing the implementation of the MWRRA Act, it becomes clear that the role of IRA-like institutions in the water sector in India cannot be judged based on the conventional privatization-centric credible commitment rationale. This is exemplified here through the cases of regulatory actions related to the IRA.

### *Social criteria for tariff determination*

As per the law, MWRRA is mandated to determine tariffs, based on the principle of the recovery of O&M cost. Public consultation is mandatory in the process. MWRRA conducted such a process and issued the first tariff order (including tariff criteria) for the control period 2010–2013.[7] The public pressure and concerted advocacy efforts of senior activists and NGOs, during the tariff consultation process, led to the inclusion of important social criteria in tariff structuring (Warghade and Sathe 2013).[8] These criteria include the following: free water to tribal farmers (limited to the tribal sub-plan), concessions to project-affected people (like dam oustees rehabilitated in the command area), concessions to small and marginal landholders and concessions to backlog-affected farmers. The results on tariff criteria clearly suggest the shift from the standard economic regulation model of the IRA. It challenges the conventional privatization-centric rationale of credible commitment. It has opened avenues for ensuring commitment to equity and other social considerations in tariff determination. An argument against such an IRA-driven process for bringing in social criteria is that the awarding of concessions to the disadvantaged section is a redistributive function of tariff policy and the same should technically fall in the realm of political decision-making. If the IRA takes on the role of determining such redistributive policies, though creditable, it technically leads to inconsistency with the logic of the institutional design of the IRA. But this line of argument does not hold after analysing the basis on which the stakeholders argued for social criteria in tariff determination. Its basis was the fact that the MWRRA law clearly provides 'equitable' management and regulation of water resources. Hence, the principle of 'equity', accepted by the legislators in the MWRRA law, is also applicable for tariff criteria. The stakeholders were, in a way, reiterating that the legislators had already committed to equity and that the MWRRA should respect that commitment in determining the criteria for water tariff. Eventually, this points towards a situation where the stakeholders are demanding credible commitment from the government on its policy of equitable water management and regulation. Here, an IRA which is originally designed to provide credible commitment for protecting private investment is seen to be a medium of providing credibility to the government's commitment to social policy considerations in water regulation. This hints at the potential role of the IRA, irrespective of the privatization rationale.

The process also throws light on the future prospects and potential of the regulatory implementation through a participatory mechanism, done under the purview of an IRA (Warghade 2015). For the first time, the determination of water tariff became an issue discussed and debated in the public domain. Farmers, water user associations, experts, activists, NGOs, media and other stakeholders got an opportunity to raise demands and present analysis and viewpoints on water tariff. The important feature of this participatory process was that it was conducted under the purview of an independent regulatory body. This certainly provided the much-needed non-partisan political space for the participants to engage with policy issues and influence the same.

### *Equitable water allocation and entitlements*

The preamble of the MWRRA Act emphasizes the role of the regulator in equitable distribution of water. The potential role of an IRA to provide credibility to the expressed commitment of the political functionaries towards equity is found relevant from the analysis of the case of water reallocation in the state of Maharashtra (Wagle, Warghade and Sathe 2012). The analysis of the inter-sectoral allocation of water, between 2005 and 2010, showed that the political functionaries bypassed the powers of the MWRRA, as well as the principle of equity, while granting permission to reallocate 1,645 million cubic metres of water (available in reservoirs) from agriculture to urban-industrial use (Warghade, Sathe and Wagle 2013). A campaign was launched by civil society actors against the huge amount of water diverted from agriculture use to industrial use. Legal petitions related to these were filed before the High Court as well as before the MWRRA. Interestingly, one of the arguments used to showcase the illegality of these water reallocation decisions was the ground that it was the MWRRA, and not the political functionaries, which was empowered to decide water allocations. The argument further emphasized invoking the principle of equity, accepted in the MWRRA law, in the case of inter-sectoral water allocation and reallocation. Beyond the regulatory action, the campaign also focused on mass protest through street demonstrations, legislative campaigns and media campaigns.

The objective of placing this issue on the political agenda was successfully achieved by the civil society actors. It was interesting to observe how political functionaries reacted to this complex situation which demanded credibility of their own commitment towards the equity principle. It was assumed that they would initiate a policy debate around inter-sectoral water allocation to evolve criteria which would then be enforced by the MWRRA. Instead, the political functionaries decided and managed to counter the campaign by amending the MWRRA law in favour of their past decisions of water reallocation.[9] All past water reallocation decisions made by the political functionaries were rendered legally valid by inserting a provision to that effect in the MWRRA law. The powers of the MWRRA to determine allocations based on the principle of equity were also withdrawn. Hence, the political functionaries not only failed to provide credibility to their commitment towards equity but also eventually rolled back the commitment itself. Thus, the political functionaries failed to provide credibility to their commitment. This highlights the relevance and utility of credible commitment as a rationale for social criteria.

### *Project review and clearance*

As per the MWRRA Act, every new proposal for a water project requires review and clearance from the MWRRA. These are projects, such as dam or canal construction, undertaken by government agencies. This is not the same as the conventional model where the IRA is the licencing authority for private developers or service providers. Regulation of publicly owned and operated projects is a new dimension of the IRA model introduced in the MWRRA law. The review criteria include not only economic criteria, such as benefit-cost analysis, but also other socially relevant criteria like adherence to the Governor's directives on the removal of the irrigation backlog in backward regions. These policy criteria, with their own distributive implications, are given in the law in the form of policy commitment. Similar to the case of water allocation, the role of ensuring adherence to social and economic criteria is envisaged for the MWRAA in the case of publicly owned projects. The political functionaries have expressed commitment to the social criteria in the form of legal provisions, while the credibility of these commitments is achieved by allowing the independent regulator to ensure adherence to the criteria.

Water projects, being capital-intensive, bear the risk of financial irregularities and corruption (Wade 1982). Over the years, serious allegations of corruption in the irrigation sector in Maharashtra have been made (Kamdar 2007; Jog 2012; Khetan 2012). A special investigation team was appointed by the state government and criminal prosecution is underway in some of the cases (Government of Maharashtra 2014). Hence, to keep a check on this and other such crucial public-interest matters, a regulator may be warranted, even if the projects are government-owned. This represents one of the prospects for the IRA model in the water sector. Unfortunately, it remains unexploited in the case of the MWRRA. Many projects have been reviewed and approved by the MWRRA but the regulator has abstained from enhancing the scope of the review to keep a check on various irregularities in project finances and capital expenditure. The review is currently limited to ensuring compliance of mainly the documents required as per the existing guidelines of other government agencies. However, such compliance checking is also important considering that projects often begin execution without complying with the criteria laid down by the various agencies.[10]

### *Privatization of a dam project*

The conventional privatization-centric credible commitment rationale rests on the function of the IRA to regulate private sector investment and operations in the sector. As mentioned earlier, the MWRRA law dissociates itself from this core functioning of the IRA. The paradox of dissociating an IRA from ongoing privatization initiatives was exposed through a petition filed before the MWRRA against the process of privatization of a dam project called Nira-Deoghar.[11] The government department that coordinated the process of the MWRRA law formulation itself ignored the role of the regulator when it initiated the process of selection of a private investor for a dam project. The MWRRA Act does not provide for any direct regulatory purview on privatization but based on the other powers of the MWRRA, such as to determine tariff, the petitioners argued that the process of inviting expressions of interest from private developers needs to be brought under the purview of the regulator. It was argued that because the role of the regulator was ignored, the privatization process should be deemed unwarranted and illegal. After four hearings and very detailed analytical arguments by the petitioners, the MWRRA issued a strong order in favour of the petitioners. The regulator directed the concerned government department to withdraw the ongoing tendering process. The order further stated that if the government wanted to pursue privatization in the future, the proposal would have to be vetted by the IRA, especially the revenue model. This order forms the basis of bringing within the regulatory purview the otherwise non-transparent and unregulated privatization process initiated by the government department. This case indicates the prospects of ensuring a counter check through the IRA on government decisions in different processes where private parties are involved in infrastructure development, maintenance and service delivery.

### *Adjudicatory role through petitions*

As per the law, the MWRRA has been accorded powers equivalent to the civil court. The various petitions that the MWRRA has heard and disposed of, indicate another area of future prospect.[12]

In the case of the petition against reallocation of irrigation water for industries from the Hetavane dam, the IRA provided relief to the farmers in the region by cancelling the reallocation. This was possible because the petitioners argued that industry was not able to use the water in the stipulated time. Similarly, the petition against the privatization of the Nira-Deoghar dam project (discussed in the previous section) highlights the important outcome of ensuring that the privatization process comes within the regulatory purview. The outcome was achieved by the use of the adjudicatory role of an IRA. In another case, during a drought in the state between 2013 and 2015, the MWRRA played an important adjudicatory role in giving effect to the provision of equitable sharing of distress by the release of water from the upstream reservoir to the downstream reservoir.[13] This was the most challenging role for the IRA, where a progressive and radical policy commitment towards equity got implemented through the power exercised by a regulatory agency. Considering the political fallout of such a radical provision of releasing water from an upstream dam to a downstream dam, it was not easy for the MWRRA to undertake *suo moto* actions. It could proceed on this matter only after judicial activism (through a public-interest litigation) led to directions from the High Court to file the petition before the MWRRA. This empowered the MWRRA to overcome political pressures and utilize the opportunity to assert regulatory power over the crucial issue of the equitable distribution of water among the reservoirs. The High Court also relied on the technical expertise and adjudicatory role of the MWRRA, and the final execution happened within the joint purview of the MWRRA and the High Court.

All these petitions and the hearings within an IRA set up provided an opportunity for going beyond adversarial proceedings, by allowing the parties to engage in a discussion and negotiation mode.

## Conclusions: alternative rationale and institutional design for IRA

The question of independent regulatory authorities (IRAs) in the water sector in India is turning into a maze of complexity and diverse interpretations. The question of their role and place in the overall parliamentary system has been settled in the case of developed countries, based on the well-developed rationale of providing credible commitment to private investors, i.e., the privatization-centric credible commitment rationale. This privatization-centric conventional IRA model has been institutionalized in India in several commercial sectors, like electricity and telecom. However, the attempt to transplant this model into India's water sector points towards the need to think beyond the conventional IRA model. The design of the water IRA in some of the states in India clearly shows that the credible commitment rationale associated with privatization of utilities is not the relevant rationale. The cases of implementation of the water IRA in Maharashtra highlight the possible role of the IRA in India, especially pertaining to the social rationale. The lessons from design as well as implementation of the water IRA are summarized in the following sub-section. It is followed by a discussion on the rationale for the IRA and a proposal of an alternative institutional design.

### *Limitation of the privatization-centric credible commitment rationale*

The laws enacted for the establishment of the IRAs in the water sector in India do not include privatization as the main articulated focus of the legal framework. Instead, the laws emphasize socially relevant objectives such as equity and sustainability. If this emphasis in law is accepted as the societal preference, reflecting the currently pressing problems of the water sector in India, then the question is whether the IRA is an appropriate institutional form to achieve these objectives. Since this institutional form rests on the rationale of credible commitment, the question further needs to be narrowed down to asking whether credible commitment is the core problem in achieving these social objectives.

The experience around the implementation of the MWRRA law provides adequate evidence to suggest that though the political functionaries have articulated their commitment to the social objectives in the legal statutes, there is still a lack of credibility towards this commitment. The case of water reallocations in Maharashtra shows how the lack of credibility is the core problem in execution of the social objectives to which the political functionaries had committed. The case of water tariff determination further shows how this credible commitment was achieved in the case of the application of the principle of equity in water tariff regulations. Similar findings are seen in the case of the privatization of dam projects, equitable sharing of distress at the basin level, review and clearance of projects and in the case of various petitions heard and disposed of by the MWRRA. These cases of the actual functioning of the IRA in the water sector in India show the prospects of the role of the credible commitment rationale and the related institutional form of the IRA. But here the credible commitment rationale is not the same as the conventional privatization-centric rationale. Hence, there is a need to evolve an alternative conception of this rationale and of the related institutional form of the IRA.

### *Prospects of equity-centric credible commitment rationale*

The alternative conception of the credible commitment rationale can only be done by exploring the roots of this rationale. This will help in going beyond the privatization-centric conception of the said rationale. At the root of the credible commitment rationale are two important problems of public policy implementation, viz., time inconsistency and political uncertainty (Miller 2011; Gilardi 2008). Time inconsistency arises due to the problem of making choice over time. Policy decisions have to be made for implementation that spans a future period of time. But when the time for implementation occurs, there might be various forms of temptations to change the decision. This leads to inconsistency in decisions over the period of implementation. The inconsistency may arise due to opportunistic behaviour of the decision makers or due to external factors related to the change in the context.

One major source of inconsistency is political uncertainty which is connected to the electoral process in which the election results might lead to a change in the ruling government. The new government might not follow the policies of its predecessor. This creates the problem of inconsistent policy framework, which is a concern for policy areas where long-term vision and consistency is paramount. For example, sustainable and equitable water resource management can be achieved through a long-term vision and consistency in policy making and its implementation.

Time inconsistency and political uncertainty threaten the credibility of the policy promises or commitments made by the political functionaries. Ensuring credible commitment requires that the choices of the decision makers are constrained after the policy decision is made. Constraining such choices once the commitment is made is called 'credible commitment' (Miller 2011). This broader conception of credible commitment widens the scope of its application beyond the conventional privatization context.

The commitment towards the protection of private investments and the fair return on such investments are not the only situations in which credible commitment is relevant. The root problem of political uncertainty and time inconsistency occurs in several other situations. Examples of different situations where credible commitment is needed are property rights and contract enforcement, minority protection, equity promotion, poverty reduction, environmental protection and resource conservation (Miller 2011). Schlager (2005) points out that credible commitment is one of the important features of institutional design in several situations of water management, other than privatization. For example, credibility of commitment is crucial in decentralization of powers from higher government authorities to water user associations.

How to achieve credible commitment for the policies determined by political functionaries is a classic problem in public administration and institutional design. This is achieved by the separation of powers between the political functionaries and the regulators (Miller 2011). It creates barriers to opportunistic behaviour, constrains choice of policy makers once they commit to a particular policy, thereby ensuring credibility of the commitment through consistency and continuity in the policy. This separation is ensured through delegation of regulatory functions to an IRA. The conventional bureaucracy is controlled by the elected members, and hence the conventional bureaucratic delegation does not provide credibility to the commitment. Delegation to an autonomous agency, which is not controlled by the politically elected members, is seen as the appropriate institutional mechanism to resolve the commitment problem.

Considering the design of the water IRA laws in India and the actual functioning of one such IRA (MWRRA), it is clear that the conventional rationale of credible commitment for protecting private investors in the water sector is less relevant than alternative applications of the rationale. These alternative conceptions revolve around the commitment over substantive principles of social equity. It can be termed as the 'equity-centric credible commitment rationale'. For example, the case of water allocation in Maharashtra clearly highlights the importance of credible commitment towards designing and enforcing an equitable water distribution system. The IRA can be seen as a mechanism for ensuring that the commitment of equity given by the legislators, is credibly operationalized and enforced by overcoming the problem of political uncertainty and time inconsistency.

### *Alternative institutional design*

Designing an appropriate institutional form for an independent regulator on the basis of the equity-centric credible commitment rationale would be a challenging task. Several elements of the conventional privatization-centric IRA model would need rethinking and reform. For example, the conventional IRA is composed of members with expertise only in the engineering and economic aspects of water. If equity is the core concern, then the members should have expertise in the social and political aspects of water too.

But, beyond these apparent changes, there is a need to rethink the core assumptions of the conventional IRA model. For example, one of the assumptions of the privatization-centric IRA model is that the IRA should be the sole apex-level regulator in the sector. Thus, it is expected that the IRA would single-handedly regulate the economic and other aspects of regulation in the sector. The equity-centric credible commitment rationale would require the systems approach rather than the unitary approach to regulation. The systems approach is appropriate considering the distributed and decentralized nature of water resources. The emphasis will have to be on developing a complete regulatory system rather than just an apex-level IRA. This conforms to the decentred nature of regulation, which is required in sectors where the regulatory power is not concentrated in single apex institutions but is distributed among multiple stakeholders (Black 2002; Scott 2001).

In such an approach, the political functionaries (from the state to the local level), the water users (from the project to the canal level), the IRA and other stakeholders will have to undertake collectively the necessary regulatory functions in ensuring an equity-centric credible commitment. For example, the political functionaries from the state to the local level will have to evolve a political consensus on the equity principle and then articulate the same as a political commitment in an appropriate legal and policy instrument. This type of consensus and commitment building will be a dynamic process of capturing the changing preferences of the citizens towards various aspects of equity. The IRA will have to provide the necessary credibility to this political commitment by ensuring implementation of and adherence to the committed principles. The regulation of implementation and enforcement cannot be achieved without adequate involvement of community-level systems of regulation. Hence, the focus of institutional design will have to be on the complete regulatory system and not just on a single IRA.

An exercise to address some of these aspects of regulatory design was conducted by the working group constituted by the erstwhile Planning Commission of India for developing a model bill for the water regulatory authority.[14] After deliberations among the government as well as non-government members, the 15-member sub-group actually developed a model bill for the water regulatory 'system' instead of 'authority'. This shows the importance of the systems approach in the design of regulatory institutions in the Indian water sector. One of the main design imperatives used in this exercise was to match the authority and autonomy of an institution with the type and source of legitimacy of that institution. Hence, the role of the independent regulator has been limited to those functions where expertise and independence play an important role. Here the role can be seen in the form of providing credibility through ensuring implementation and enforcement as per the policy commitments made by the political functionaries. The power to decide the substantive social policy principle and criteria (including equity) are retained with institutions having due political legitimacy. This means that the political functionaries, from the state to the local level, are responsible for deciding the level of commitment on social policy considerations. Thus, instead of a single apex-level IRA, the model bill has come out with a complete set of authorities at different levels, representing an entire regulatory system. On substantive or functional areas of regulation, the bill proposes a modular approach, where state-specific problems can be identified and context-specific objectives can be set. Based on these objectives, there is also a possibility of selection of an institutional structure that logically fits within the given purpose of the regulation. There is also a provision for a transition from one level of institutional structure to a more advanced level, within a timeframe. This modular and transitional approach will provide the flexibility to learn and evolve effective regulatory systems around the rationale of the equity-centric credible commitment.

Considering the current confusion around the design of an IRA in the water sector in India, there is a need to develop this approach further, to arrive at state-specific models. This will enable identification of logically and conceptually appropriate functions, and the rationale for an IRA in the overall regulatory system. For example, the Maharashtra experience points towards some concrete ideas in this direction. This experience points towards the following role that the IRAs could effectively play (as discussed in an earlier section of the chapter): determining tariff-based appropriate combination of social and economic criteria, conducting an independent deliberative process for tariff and other regulatory measures, administrating and regulating inter-sectoral water allocations based on the equity principles decided through political processes, regulating project proposals to keep a check on possible financial and other irregularities, ensuring equitable allocation during scarcity, acting as a quasi-judicial authority for effective resolution of disputes and regulating private-sector investments and operations. The water sector is plagued by widespread technical and financial inefficiencies. This is also a big issue for the independent regulators to address.

The ultimate step of delegation to an IRA, in the chain of delegation that starts from citizens, will be completed only by establishing accountability of the IRA towards the citizens. This accountability is in terms of robust procedures (Dubash 2008; Nakhooda, Dixit and Dubash 2007). Hence, procedural accountability through effective provisions for transparency, accountability, participation and capacity building (TAP-C) should be considered as the keystone on which the regulatory framework of the IRA can stand.

## Notes

1 Independent regulatory authority (IRA) is a statutory body comprising of members who are experts in the particular sector. It is often a quasi-judicial body. The various State Electricity Regulatory Commissions in India or the Telecom Regulatory Authority of India are typical examples of an IRA.

2 These pertinent questions were raised by Ramaswamy R. Iyer in his contribution titled '*A Regulatory Authority for Water?*', in a conference organized by Prayas on regulation in 2007 (Prayas 2007).
3 There are other rationales behind the delegation of powers to an IRA, such as information asymmetry, blame shifting and political uncertainty. But the rationale of credible commitment for private investors is the more prominent and dominates the regulatory practice.
4 The organizational structure of the Act was amended in 2016 through the Maharashtra Water Resources Regulatory Authority (Amendment) Act, 2016. Two more members were added to accommodate an expert in the field of law and in the field of groundwater.
5 The collective of civil society organizations in the state of Maharashtra opposed the process initiated by the MWRRA for trading in water entitlements vide letter dated 30 January 2010.
6 The MWRRA is entrusted with the responsibility of an apex regulatory agency for groundwater, as per the Maharashtra Groundwater (Development and Management) Act, 2009.
7 Tariff order available at: www.mwrra.org/current_tariffs.php (accessed on 28 May 2018).
8 The coalition of civil society organizations, named as *Lokabhimukh Pani Dhoran Sangharsh Manch* (Struggle Forum for Pro-people Water Policy), played an important role in advocacy.
9 Refer to the Maharashtra Water Resources Regulatory Authority (Amendment and Continuance) Act, 2011.
10 For example, refer to the controversy over the Kalu Dam in Maharashtra. The construction of the dam began without the mandated clearance required as per the Forest (Conservation) Act 1980 (see http://sandrp.wordpress.com/2013/04/25/kalu-dam-in-western-ghats-fac-goes-back-on-its-word-without-any-justification/, accessed on 28 May 2018).
11 Refer Case 1 of 2008 before MWRRA. For details of the petition refer to Wagle and Warghade 2009.
12 Orders on various petitions available at: www.mwrra.org/petitions_order.php (accessed on 28 May 2018).
13 Refer to the orders given by the MWRRA (www.mwrra.org/petitions_order.php) related to projects named Ujani (Case 1 of 2013), Jayakwadi (Case 1 of 2014) and Kukadi (Case 7 of 2015).
14 The sub-group submitted the Model Bill for State Water Regulatory System Act, 2011. This has been included as part of the 12th Five Year Plan. The bill can be accessed at: http://planningcommission.nic.in/aboutus/committee/wrkgrp12/wr/mb_wtrgrnd_181011.pdf (accessed on 28 May 2018).

## References

Black, Julia. 2002. 'Critical Reflections on Regulation. LSE Centre for the Analysis of Risk and Regulation', Discussion Paper 4. London: LSE.

Brown, A. C., Stern, J., Tenenbaum, B., and Gencer, D. 2006. *Handbook for Evaluating Infrastructure Regulatory Systems*. Washington, DC: World Bank.

Dubash, Navroz. 2008. 'Independent Regulatory Agencies: A Theoretical Review with Reference to Electricity and Water in India', *Economics and Political Weekly*, 43(40): 43, 46–54.

Dwivedi, Gaurav Rehmat and Shripad Dharmadhikary. 2007. *Water: Private, Limited – Issues in Privatisation, Corporatisation and Commercialisation of Water Sector in India*. Badwani: Manthan Adhyayan Kendra.

Gilardi, F. 2001. 'Principal-Agent Models Go to Europe: Independent Regulatory Agencies as Ultimate Step of Delegation', Paper Presented at the ECPR General Conference, Canterbury (UK), 6–8 September.

Gilardi, F. 2004. 'Institutional Change in Regulatory Policies: Regulation Through Independent Agencies and the Three New Institutionalisms', in J. Jordana and D. Levi-Faur (eds.), *The Politics of Regulation: Institutions and Regulatory Reforms for the Age of Governance*. Cheltenham: Edward Elgar.

Gilardi, F. 2008. *Delegation in the Regulatory State: Independent Regulatory Agencies in Western Europe*. Cheltenham: Edward Elgar.

Government of Maharashtra. 2014. *Sinchan Vishayi Vishesh Chaukashi Samiteecha Ahwal* (Report of the Special Investigation Team). Report published in March 2014. Mumbai.

Jog, Sanjay. 2012. 'What Is Maharashtra Irrigation Scam', www.business-standard.com/article/economy-policy/what-is-maharashtra-irrigation-scam-112092503026_1.html (accessed on 16 October 2017).

Kamdar, Seema. 2007. 'Irrigation Scheme Opens Floodgates of Money for Few', www.dnaindia.com/mumbai/report-irrigation-scheme-opens-floodgates-of-money-for-few-1100407 (accessed on 16 October 2017).

Khetan, Ashish. 2012. 'Greed: The Inside Story of 70,000 Crore Irrigation Scam', www.tehelka.com/2012/10/greed/ (accessed on 16 October 2017).

Levy, B. and P. T. Spiller. 1994. 'The Institutional Foundations of Regulatory Commitment: A Comparative Analysis of Telecommunication Regulation', *Journal of Law, Economics & Organization*, 10(2): 201–246.

Miller, Gary J. 2011. 'Credible Commitment', in B. Badie, D. Berg-Schlosser and L. Morlino (eds.), *International Encyclopedia of Political Science*. Thousand Oaks, CA: Sage.

MWRRA. 2011. *Draft Approach Paper on Trading in Water Entitlement*. Mumbai: MWRRA.

Nakhooda, S., S. Dixit and N. Dubash. 2007. *Empowering People: A Governance Analysis of Electricity*. Washington, DC: World Resources Institute and Prayas.

Phillips, C. F. 1993.*The Regulation of Public Utilities: Theory and Practice*. Arlington, VA: Public Utilities Reports, Inc.

Prayas. 2007. 'Regulation and the Poor in Electricity & Water Sectors', Proceedings of the National Conference, New Delhi, 12–13 July, www.prayaspune.org/peg/publications/item/68-report-on-the-national-consultation-on-regulation-and-the-poor-in-electricity-and-water-sectors.html (accessed on 28 May 2018).

Schlager, E. 2005. 'Getting the Relationships Right in Water Property Rights', in B. R. Bruns, C. Ringler and R. Meinzen-Dick (eds.), *Water Rights Reform: Lessons for Institutional Design*. Washington, DC: International Food Policy Research Institute.

Scott, C. 2001. 'Analysing Regulatory Space: Fragmented Resources and Institutional Design', *Public Law*: 282–305.

Thatcher, M. and A. Stone Sweet. 2002. 'Theory and Practice of Delegation to Non-Majoritarian Institutions', *West European Politics*, 25(1): 1–22.

Wade, Robert. 1982. 'The System of Administrative and Political Corruption: Canal Irrigation in South India', *The Journal of Development Studies*, 18(3): 287–328.

Wagle, S., S. Warghade, T. Pol, and M. Sathe. 2015. 'Water Security: Assessing the Role of Reforms Related to Independent Regulatory Authorities in India', in A. Gurtoo and C. Williams (eds.), *Developing Country Perspectives on Public Services Delivery*. New Delhi: Springer.

Wagle, S., S. Warghade and M. Sathe. 2012. 'Exploiting Policy Obscurity for Legalizing Water Grabbing in the Era of Economic Reform: The Case of Maharashtra, India', *Water Alternatives*, 5(2): 412–430.

Wagle, S. and S. Warghade. 2009. *Independent Water Regulatory Authorities in India: Analysis and Interventions*. Pune: Prayas.

Warghade, S. and M. Sathe. 2013. 'Maharashtra Water Tariff Story: The First Independent Regulatory Process on Water Tariff in India', Report Published by Prayas, Pune.

Warghade, S., M. Sathe and S. Wagle. 2013. *Water Grabbing in Maharashtra: Analysis of Water Reallocation Decisions and Amendments in MWRRA Law*. Pune: Prayas.

Warghade, S. 2015. Policy formulation tool use in emerging policy spheres: a developing country perspective. In: Jordan, A. J. and Turnpenny (Eds.). *The Tools of Policy Formulation: Actors, Capacities, Venues and Effects*. UK: Edward Elgar Publishing.

# 15 Reforming India's water sector

## Which way forward?

*Mihir Shah*

### Introduction: the new meaning of 'reform'

Over the last 30 years, not just in India but all over the globe, reform has acquired a very specific meaning. It is generally used to connote a policy shift in the direction of privatization and reducing the role of the state in the economy. In many respects, this has been a welcome move as the state has handed over sectors of the economy to the private sector and greater competition has led to increases in efficiency and cheaper availability of many goods and services to the consumer, at higher quality.

At the same time, however, the tragic fallout of this blind and dogmatic change in policy has been to further worsen access to basic services for a large mass of the population. Whether it is access to quality health and education, water, sanitation, nutrition or credit etc., a massive reform deficit has afflicted these sectors, for the reform required here was not the one being proposed under the 'Washington Consensus'. Indeed, it is not the private sector that is the panacea for these sectors, which suffer from massive market failure. What is required in each of these cases is reform of government, which would make state systems more efficient and accountable to the people.

It is clear, for example, that falling ill is perhaps the single biggest cause of people slipping below the poverty line. Health care in India remains predominantly private, with India's spending on public health provision being among the lowest percentage of GDP globally. Unprecedented farmer suicides and recent farmer agitations point to the continued failure of state intervention in a situation of humongous market failure. We need to expand procurement operations to a much wider array of crops such as millets and pulses to incentivize farmers to diversify their cropping patterns. The functioning of the ICDS (Integrated Child Development Services) and MDMS (Mid-Day

Meal Scheme), the flagship nutrition programmes, remains highly unsatisfactory in the north Indian Hindi heartland, where malnutrition levels remain among the highest in the world. Adopting more participatory approaches to their implementation is the key reform required. Learning outcomes in government schools remain abysmally poor as revealed by the ASERs (Annual Status of Education Reports). Overall, one can say that depending on the specific challenges of each sector, the desired direction of reform could be collectivization (as in agri-marketing), nationalization (as in banking) or reform of functioning of government programmes (such as MGNREGA). Reform can, of course, include a greater role for the private sector and liberalization, but this must be examined and decided upon on a case-by-case basis.

A focus on the question of governance reform in the water sector helps illustrate how critical it is for us to understand precisely the kinds of reforms we need in key sectors of the Indian economy, and not to be blinded by a dogmatic adherence to the Washington Consensus. There is no simple quick-fix that this conception of reforms can offer. What we need to recognize is that the role of the state is critical but this role itself needs profound reform. What we also need to understand urgently is that each sector of the economy has some very specific features, and reforms need to be defined with reference to these *differentia specifica* of each sector. To put it in a nutshell, it is not a question of larger or smaller government: the way forward lies in the maxim 'better government is better'. When it comes to the question of a natural resource like water, a key specific element of the reforms needed is the recognition that the economy is but a small part of the larger ecosystem, and that proceeding with a narrow notion of economic development without an adequate recognition of this huge fact can only lead to disastrous outcomes, as evidenced by the fate of the planet currently in this age of the Anthropocene.[1]

Why has it become necessary to focus on reforming water governance in India today? What is it about the nature of the water crisis facing the country that necessitates such an emphasis? What are the dimensions that water governance reform needs to cover? And in which broad direction must this change occur?

## Water crisis of unprecedented proportions

India faces a major crisis of water as we move into the 21st century. This crisis threatens the basic right to drinking water of our people; it also puts the livelihoods of millions at risk (Shah 2013).

The demands of a rapidly industrializing economy and urbanizing society come at a time when the potential for augmenting supply is limited, water tables are falling and water quality issues have increasingly come to the fore. As we drill deeper for water, our groundwater gets contaminated with fluoride, arsenic, mercury and even uranium. Our rivers and our groundwater are polluted by untreated effluents and sewage. Many urban stretches of rivers and lakes are overstrained and overburdened by industrial waste, sewage and agricultural runoff. These wastewaters are overloading rivers and lakes with toxic chemicals and wastes, consequently poisoning water resources and supplies. These toxins are finding their way into plants and animals, causing severe ecological toxicity at various trophic levels.

In India, cities produce nearly 40,000 million litres of sewage every day and barely 20 per cent of it is treated. The Central Pollution Control Board's 2011 survey states that only 2 per cent of our towns have both sewerage systems and sewage treatment plants (Shah and Kulkarni 2015).

Climate change poses fresh challenges with its impacts on the hydrologic cycle. More extreme rates of precipitation and evapo-transpiration will exacerbate impacts of floods and droughts. More intense, extreme and variable rainfall, combined with a lack of proper drainage, will mean that every spell of rain becomes an urban nightmare, as roads flood and dirty water enters homes and adds to filth and disease. Our flood management strategies no longer seem to provide an adequate answer to growing flood frequency and intensity. It is no wonder then that conflicts across competing uses and users of water are growing by the day.

Water use efficiency in agriculture, which consumes around 80 per cent of our water resources, continues to be among the lowest in the world. At 25–35 per cent, this compares poorly to 40–45 per cent in Malaysia and Morocco and 50–60 per cent in Israel, Japan, China and Taiwan (Shah 2013).

The two main sources of irrigation are canals and groundwater. The relative contribution of canal irrigation has been steadily declining over time while groundwater, especially that extracted through tubewells, has rapidly grown in significance over the last 30 years. But the alarming fact is that both these sources of water are now beginning to hit an upper limit.

India has, in recent years, been suffering successive droughts, causing great misery to millions of people, even resulting in suicides by farmers. At the epicentre of the present drought is Maharashtra, the state with the highest number of dams in India. Intervening in a debate in the

State Assembly on 21 July 2015, the Chief Minister of Maharashtra remarked that the state has 40 per cent of the country's large dams,

> but 82 per cent area of the state is rainfed. Till the time you don't give water to a farmer's fields, you can't save him from suicide. We have moved away from our vision of watershed and conservation. We did not think about hydrology, geology and topography of a region before pushing large dams everywhere. We pushed large dams, not irrigation. But this has to change.
>
> (Shah 2015)

## Governance reform at the heart of change needed

It is our contention that this crisis that we have just briefly summarized has a very close link with the prevailing paradigm of governance of water in India. Before explicating these links and also suggesting the changes required, let us first summarize the key *features, dimensions* and *principles* that characterize the existing paradigm, each of which need to undergo urgent transformation:

1. **Command-and-control:** Whether it be rivers or groundwater, the dominant paradigm is of command-and-control. There is no understanding of river systems or their interconnections with the health of catchment areas or groundwater.
2. **Bureaucratic Governance:** Large, centralized, decaying bureaucracies are charged with administering water throughout the length and breadth of India.
3. **No Reference to Hydrological Entities such as Aquifers or River Systems:** When I joined the Planning Commission in 2009, the word 'aquifer' could hardly be found within the government discourse, and the integrity of river systems is still not understood.
4. **Uni-disciplinarity:** Since the goal is command-and-control through dam construction and groundwater extraction, the only disciplines invoked are engineering and hydrogeology, that too in their narrowest versions. Water cannot be understood with this narrow disciplinary focus.
5. **Uni-dimensionality:** Since the focus is extraction and development, all dimensions of water, other than economic resource use, are ignored. These various other dimensions are however of critical importance to the primary stakeholders of water in India.
6. **Water in Silos:** We have divided water into silos of groundwater and surface water, as also irrigation and domestic use, with little

dialogue across silos, leading to 'hydroschizophrenia' (Jarvis *et al.* 2005), where the left hand of drinking water does not know what the right hand of irrigation is doing; and the left foot of surface water does not know what the right foot of groundwater is doing.

7 **Instrumental View of Water, Especially Rivers:** The way we look at our rivers is as water resources to be exploited, ignoring completely the numerous ecosystem services provided by living river systems, as also the intrinsic value of rivers for our people and other forms of life.
8 **Supply-side Focus:** The entire focus has been on augmenting supplies, with little attention being paid to the demand management of water.
9 **No Reference to Sustainability:** In the preoccupation with extraction and development, there has generally been an absence of considerations of sustainability, endangering the future of both groundwater and river flows.
10 **Discrimination and Lack of Equity in Access to Water:** Historical forms of discrimination combine with the impact of growing economic inequalities in the country to create severe discrimination in access to water on grounds of caste, class, gender, location and community.
11 **Lack of Transparency and Access to Water Information:** Over the years, there has been needless secrecy in access to water data and information for researchers and stakeholders, which, in turn, has only meant that the quality of water management has suffered, and conflicts have gotten exacerbated.
12 **British Common Law:** The legal framework governing water belongs to the 19th-century British common law, which legitimizes and perpetuates inequity in access to water by giving unlimited powers of the withdrawal of water to owners of land.

Our central argument is that the present crisis of water in India is a direct consequence of this 12-fold paradigm of governance that needs urgent reform, if we are to find effective solutions to India's multiple water problems.

## CWC: engineering command-and-control over rivers

The biggest example of centralized command-and- control is the construction of large dams on our rivers. Even if we put aside the humongous human and environmental costs of these structures, the benefits of this kind of engineering supply-centred effort have been underwhelming.

Huge public investments over the last 60 years have meant that the irrigation potential created through major and medium irrigation projects has increased nearly five-fold from 9.72 Mha in the pre-Plan period to around 46 Mha by the 11th Plan. But how much of this water has actually benefitted the farmers for whom it was meant, is not clear. At the same time, there is incontrovertible evidence that these projects have suffered from massive time and cost overruns.[2]

The worst offenders are the major irrigation projects where the average cost overrun is as high as 1382 per cent. Twenty-eight out of the 151 major projects analysed witnessed cost overruns of over 1000 per cent. Of these, nine had cost overruns of over 5000 per cent. The cost overruns were relatively lower for medium projects but still unacceptably high, the average being 325 per cent. Twenty-three out of 132 medium projects had cost overruns of over 500 per cent and 10 had cost overruns of over 1000 per cent.

The number of projects awaiting completion peaked in 1980 to 600; then there was decline till 1992 (460), after which it has again risen to 571, almost touching the 1980 figure. Major irrigation projects are expected to have a gestation period of 15–20 years while medium projects should take 5–10 years for completion. Against these norms, a large number of major as well as medium projects are continuing for 30–40 years or even more. This reflects poor project preparation and implementation as well as thin spreading of available resources.

Recent scholarship points to definite limits to the role new large dam projects can play in providing economically viable additional water storage (Ackerman 2011). A World Bank study shows that 'there is little value to additional storage in most of the peninsular river basins (the Cauvery, Krishna and Godavari) and in the Narmada and Tapti' (Briscoe and Malik 2006: 32). Similarly, a study by the International Water Management Institute (IWMI) (Amarasinghe *et al.* 2007) suggests that the Krishna and the Cauvery have reached full or partial closure. Another IWMI study shows that in the Krishna river basin, the storage capacity of major and medium reservoirs has reached total water yield (Venot *et al.* 2007), with virtually no water reaching the sea in low rainfall years. Concern has also been expressed that

> the capture of so much water within the basin and the evaporation of an additional 36 BCM of water has changed the regional climate, increasing humidity and changing temperature regimes, aggravating saline ground water intrusion, and putting at risk the delicate wetland and estuarine ecology, which is important not

> only for aquatic habitats and fisheries but also for preventing shore erosion.
>
> (Ackerman 2011: 6)

Given these constraints, the trend, increasingly, is to locate new projects in relatively flat topography that multiplies disproportionately the areas to be flooded and the people to be evicted. It also tends to aggravate already contentious relations between states, as witnessed in the Polavaram dam in Andhra Pradesh, strongly opposed by both Odisha and Chhattisgarh.

Water flow in the Himalayan rivers, particularly the Ganga, is, of course, far greater than in Peninsular rivers, but here there are other constraints. In the Ganga Plains, the topography is completely flat, and storages cannot be located here. In a study for the Asian Development Bank, Blackmore (2010) has argued that surface irrigation through dams in the Ganga river basin is of low value since water tables are already high. Similarly, for the Indus, Blackmore shows that 'the next major dam (at a cost of USD 12 billion) will yield less than 1.5 per cent increase in regulated flow' (ibid.).

There is also the problem that further up in the Himalayas we confront one of the most fragile ecosystems in the world. The Himalayas are comparatively young mountains with high rates of erosion. Their upper catchments have little vegetation to bind soil. Deforestation has aggravated the problem. Rivers descending from the Himalayas, therefore, tend to have high sediment loads. A 1986 study found that 40 per cent of hydro-dams built in Tibet in the 1940s had become unusable due to siltation of reservoirs (Pomeranz 2009). Studies by engineering geologists with the Geological Survey of India record many cases of power turbines becoming dysfunctional following massive siltation in run-of-the-river schemes.

Climate change is making predictability of river flows extremely uncertain. This will rise exponentially as more and more dams are built in the region. Diverting rivers will also create large dry regions with adverse impact on local livelihoods (fisheries and agriculture).

Dam-building enthusiasts also often overlook the fact that the rapid rise of the Himalayas (from 500 to 8000 metres) gives rise to an unmatched range of ecosystems, a biodiversity that is as enormous as it is fragile. The northeast of India is one of just 25 bio-diversity hotspots in the world (Myers *et al.* 2000).

According to Valdiya (1999), as also Goswami and Das (2002), the neo-tectonism of the Brahmaputra valley and its surrounding highlands in the eastern Himalayas means that modifying topography by excavation or creating water and sediment loads in river impoundments can be dangerous. Quake-induced changes in the river system can adversely impact the viability of dams as several basic parameters of the regime of rivers and the morphology and behaviour of channels may change. 'The last two major earthquakes in the region (1897 and 1950) caused landslides on the hill slopes and led to the blockage of river courses, flash floods due to sudden bursting of landslide-induced temporary dams, raising of riverbeds due to heavy siltation, fissuring and sand venting, subsidence or elevation of existing river and lake bottoms and margins, and the creation of new water bodies and waterfalls due to faulting' (Menon *et al.* 2003). Even more recent research published in *Science* (Kerr and Stone 2009) on Zipingpu reservoir-induced seismicity as a trigger for the massive Sichuan earthquake in 2008, raises doubts about the wisdom of extensive dam-building in a seismically active region.

The ambitious scheme for interlinking of rivers also presents major problems. The comprehensive proposal to link the Himalayan with the Peninsular rivers for inter-basin transfer of water was estimated to cost around Rs 5,60,000 crore in 2001 (the cost is officially stated to have risen to Rs 11 lakh crore today). Land submergence and R&R packages would be additional to this cost. There are no firm estimates available for running costs of the scheme, such as the cost of power required to lift water. There is also the problem that because of our dependence on the monsoons, the periods when rivers have 'surplus' water are generally synchronous across the sub-continent. A recent study further indicates that deficit rainfall years are growing in river basins with surplus water and falling in those with shortages (Ghosh *et al.*, 2016). A major problem in planning inter-basin transfers is how to take into account the reasonable needs of the basin states, which will grow over time. Further, given the topography of India and the way links are envisaged, they might totally bypass the core dry land areas of Central and Western India, which are located on elevations of 300+ metres above MSL. It is also feared that linking rivers could affect the natural supply of nutrients, through the curtailment of flooding of the downstream areas. Along the east coast of India, all major peninsular rivers have extensive deltas. Damming the rivers for linking will cut down the sediment supply and cause coastal and delta erosion, destroying the fragile coastal ecosystems.

It has also been pointed out that the scheme could affect the monsoon system significantly (Rajamani *et al.* 2006). The presence of a low salinity layer of water with low density is a reason for maintenance of high sea-surface temperatures (greater than 28 degrees Celsius) in the

Bay of Bengal, creating low pressure areas and intensification of monsoon activity. Rainfall over much of the sub-continent is controlled by this layer of low saline water. A disruption in this layer could have serious long-term consequences for climate and rainfall in the subcontinent, endangering the livelihoods of a vast population.

Given the emerging limits to further development in the major and medium irrigation sector, we urgently need to move away from a narrowly engineering-construction-centric approach to a more multidisciplinary, participatory management perspective, with central emphasis on command area development and a sustained effort at improving water use efficiency, which continues to languish at a very low level. Given that nearly 80 per cent of our water resources are consumed by irrigation, an increase in water use efficiency of irrigation projects by 20 per cent will have a major impact on the overall availability of water not only for agriculture but also for other sectors of the economy.

## Need for irrigation management transfer

The Government of India needs to both incentivize and facilitate states to ensure that they undertake the reforms required so that the trillions of litres of water stored in our large dam command areas actually reach the farmers for whom it is meant. India's irrigation potential created is 113 Mha and the potential utilized is 89 Mha. This gap is growing by the year. This gap of 24 Mha is massive low hanging fruit. By focusing our efforts on bridging this gap, we could add millions of hectares to irrigation at half the cost involved in irrigating through new dams.[3]

The way to do this is to move towards Participatory Irrigation Management (PIM), which has been successfully adopted in countries across the globe. This includes advanced nations such as the United States, France, Germany, Japan and Australia; East and South Asian countries like China, Sri Lanka, Pakistan, Philippines, Indonesia, Vietnam and Malaysia; Uzbekistan and Kyrgyzstan in Central Asia; Turkey and Iran in the Middle East; African nations such as Mali, Niger, Tanzania and Egypt, as also Mexico, Peru, Colombia and Chile in Latin America.

But even more significant are the successful examples of PIM pioneered by states in India such as Dharoi and Hathuka in Gujarat; Waghad in Maharashtra; Satak, Man and Jobat in Madhya Pradesh; Paliganj in Bihar; and Shri Ram Sagar in Andhra Pradesh. PIM implies that the states only concentrate on technically and financially complex structures, such as main systems up to secondary canals and structures at that level. Tertiary level canals and below, minor structures and field channels are handed over to Water Users Associations (WUAs) of farmers, which enables the transformation of last-mile connectivity through innovative command area development.

What the centre needs to do is to set up a non-lapsable fund that reimburses the state irrigation departments a matching contribution of their Irrigation Service Feed (ISF) collection from farmers on a 1:1 ratio. In order to generate competition among Major and Medium Irrigation (MMI) staff across commands, states would be allocated the central grant to MMI systems in proportion to their respective ISF collection. To encourage PIM, the centre should provide a bonus on that portion of each state's ISF collection, which has been collected through WUAs. And this will be on condition that WUAs and their federations are allowed to retain definite proportions of the ISF, which would not only enable them to undertake repair and maintenance of distribution systems but also increase their stakes in water management.

It has been estimated that even without building a single new large dam project, by simply completing the ongoing projects, we could create new MMI irrigation potential of 7.9 Mha. Again, by simply closing the gap between Irrigation Potential Created (IPC) and Irrigation Potential Utilised (IPU) we could add 10 Mha by prioritizing investments in Command Area Development and Management (CAD&M) projects. And we could also restore an additional 2.2 Mha of lost irrigated potential through Extension, Renovation and Modernization (ERM) works in old MMI projects.[4]

Sadly, in its current state, the Central Water Commission (CWC) is ill-equipped to undertake these kinds of radical reforms. More on that a little later.

## CGWB: unlimited extraction of groundwater

The relative ease and convenience of its decentralized access has meant that groundwater is the backbone of India's agriculture and drinking water security. Groundwater is used by millions of farmers across the country. Over the last four decades, around 84 per cent of the total addition to the net irrigated area has come from groundwater. India is by far the largest and fastest growing consumer of groundwater in the world. But groundwater is being exploited beyond sustainable levels, and with an estimated 30 million groundwater structures in play, India may be hurtling towards a serious crisis of groundwater over-extraction and quality deterioration (Rodell, Velicogna and Famiglietti 2009).

Recent work based on data from NASA's Gravity Recovery and Climate Experiment (GRACE) satellites reveals significant rates of non-renewable depletion of groundwater levels over large areas. The declines were at an alarming rate of as much as one foot per year over the past decade. The study concludes that unsustainable consumption of groundwater for irrigation and other anthropogenic uses is likely to be the cause.

A major contributor to this rapid depletion in water tables is the overwhelming dependence on deep drilling of groundwater through tubewells, which, at over 40 per cent, is the single largest source of irrigation today. Indeed, we are close to entering a vicious infinite regress scenario where an attempt to solve a problem re-introduces the same problem in the proposed solution. If one continues along the same lines, the initial problem will recur infinitely and will never be solved. This regress appears as a natural corollary of what has been termed 'hydroschizophrenia' (Llamas and Martinez-Santos 2005; Jarvis *et al.* 2005), which entails taking a schizophrenic view of an indivisible resource like water, failing to recognize the unity and integrity of the hydrologic cycle. The most striking example of this in India is the increased reliance on tubewells, both for irrigation and drinking water, not recognizing that one can potentially jeopardize the other.

Indeed, the problem of 'slippage' in rural drinking water has become a recurrent and serious one. The portents have been visible for some time now. Issues related to water quality have also emerged as a major new concern over the last decade or so. Till the 1970s, quality issues were to do with biological contamination of the main surface water sources due to poor sanitation and waste disposal, leading to repeated incidence of waterborne diseases. But, today, this has been supplemented by the serious issue of chemical pollution of groundwater, with arsenic, fluoride, iron, nitrate and salinity as the major contaminants. This is directly connected with falling water tables and extraction of water from deeper levels. States continually report an increasing number of habitations affected with quality problems.

According to the Ministry of Drinking Water Supply and Sanitation, out of 593 districts for which data is available, we have problems of high fluoride in 203 districts, iron in 206 districts, salinity in 137 districts, nitrate in 109 districts and arsenic in 35 districts. Biological contamination problems causing enteric disorders are present throughout the country and are a major concern, being linked with infant mortality, maternal health and related issues. Estimates made for some of these water quality related health problems suggest a massive endemic nature – Fluorosis (65 million (Susheela 2001)) and Arsenicosis (5 million in West Bengal (WHO 2002) and several magnitudes more, though unestimated, from Assam and Bihar). Fluorosis caused by high fluoride in groundwater leads to crippling, skeletal problems and severe bone deformities. On the other hand, Arsenicosis leads to skin lesions and develops into cancer of the lung and bladder (Krishnan 2009).

The result is that nearly 60 per cent of all districts in India have problems related to either the quantity or quality of groundwater or both.

## Sustainable and equitable management of groundwater, the CPR, based on partnerships

While its decentralized character enables easier last-mile connectivity of groundwater, the problem arises in the inequitable distribution and unsustainable extraction of this common pool resource (CPR). As the work of Nobel Laureate Elinor Ostrom shows, the first design principle in the management of a CPR is the clear delineation and demarcation of its boundaries, plus an understanding of its essential features, which in the case of groundwater includes its storage and transmission characteristics. About 54 per cent of India (comprising mainly the continental shield) is underlain by formations usually referred to as 'hard rocks'.[5] Groundwater in hard rocks is characterized by limited productivity of individual wells, unpredictable variations in productivity of wells over relatively short distances and poor water quality in some areas.

Initially, the expansion of tubewells following the Green Revolution was restricted to 30 per cent of the alluvial areas of India, which are generally characterized by relatively more pervious geological strata. From the late 1980s, tubewell drilling was extended to hard rock regions where the groundwater flow regimes are extremely complex. Deeper seated aquifers often have good initial yields, but a tubewell drilled here may be tapping groundwater accumulated over hundreds or even thousands of years. Once groundwater has been extracted from a deeper aquifer, its replenishment depends upon the inflow from the shallow system or from the surface several hundred metres above it. In general, the rate of groundwater recharge is much lower. This presents a severe limit to the expansion of tubewell technology in areas underlain by these strata.

However, even in the alluvial heartlands of the Green Revolution, for which tubewell technology is relatively more appropriate, we are moving into a crisis zone. Three states – Punjab, Rajasthan and Haryana – have reached a stage where even their current level of groundwater extraction exceeds recharge and is therefore unsustainable. Three other states – Tamil Nadu, Gujarat and UP – seem to be fast approaching that stage.

Participatory, sustainable groundwater management, recognizing its CPR character, is the need of the hour, where management strategies are duly attuned to the specific requirements of each hydrogeological setting, which need to be carefully mapped at a scale that makes possible such participatory management by the primary stakeholders. It is not possible to police 30 million groundwater structures through a licence-quota-permit raj. The challenge of groundwater management arises from the fact that a fugitive, common pool resource is currently being extracted by individuals, millions of farmers in particular, with no effective mechanism to ensure that the rate of extraction is sustainable.

It is this understanding that underpins the National Aquifer Management Programme (NAQUIM) initiated recently by the Government of India in the 12th Plan with a budgetary allocation of Rs 3,539 crore. This is the largest such programme ever initiated in human history. Nothing of this scale has been attempted before: the term 'scale' is used in two senses – one, the *extensiveness* of the scale and, two, the *fineness* of the scale (resolution of the maps). The aquifer mapping programme is not an academic exercise and must seamlessly flow into a participatory groundwater management endeavour. This demands strong partnerships among government departments, research institutes, gram panchayats/urban local bodies, industrial units, civil society organizations and the local community.

Tragically, so far, the programme has failed to take off with the requisite momentum. The major reason for this is the huge lack of capacities in the CGWB and the state groundwater boards. The institutional mandate of CGWB should be strengthened to enable it to perform its role as the manager of groundwater resource, including hiring from the fields of community institutions, participatory management of resource, political economy and economics, water markets, regulatory systems, alternative uses, opportunity cost of groundwater extraction, energy management and so on.

## River basins as focus of water governance

For some time now, policy makers and scholars alike have emphasized the need to integrate our interventions on surface and groundwater, given that the ultimate source of all water on land is precipitation as rain, snow or hail. The need to focus on river basins as the appropriate unit of intervention is evident in the watershed programmes initiated by the government over the last 40 years. River Basin Organizations have also been set up.

However, it remains true that progress on integrating surface and groundwater has been slow in terms of actual work done on the ground. In recognition of this fact, the recent National Water Framework Law (NWFL) drafted by the Ministry of Water Resources, River Development and Ganga Rejuvenation has placed special emphasis on integrated river basin development and management, as also on river rejuvenation, as the central pillars of national policy.

The draft bill emphasizes the integral relationship between surface and groundwater. The NWFL recognizes that 'water in all its forms constitutes a hydrological unity, so that human intervention in any one form is likely to have effects on others'; and that 'ground water and surface water interact throughout all landscapes from the mountains to the oceans'. This is evident in the fact that

> over-extraction of groundwater in the immediate vicinity of a river, destruction of catchment areas and river flood-plains have very negatively impacted river flows in India; such a decrease in river flows, in turn, negatively impacts groundwater recharge in riparian aquifers in the vicinity of the river.
>
> (MoWR 2016)

And because 'the fall in water tables and water quality, as also the drying up of rivers, has serious negative impacts on drinking water and livelihood security of the people of India, as also the prospects for economic growth and human development in the country', it is vitally important that 'each river basin, including associated aquifers, needs to be considered as the basic hydrological unit for planning, development and management of water, empowered with adequate authority to do the same' (MoWR 2016).

The NWFL places central emphasis on river rejuvenation and enjoins the appropriate government to 'strive towards rejuvenating river systems with community participation, ensuring:

1 "Aviral Dhara": continuous flow in time and space including maintenance of connectivity of flow in each river system;
2 "Nirmal Dhara": unpolluted flow so that the quality of river waters is not adversely affected by human activities; and
3 "Swachh Kinara": clean and aesthetic river banks' (MoWR 2016).

## Need of the hour: national water commission[6]

The CWC and CGWB were created in a very different era, with a mandate appropriate for that era. The challenge today is for us to restructure these agencies so that they can

1 work on the new mandate that the nation has placed before them,
2 work in a manner that overcomes the schism between groundwater and surface water, and
3 work with greater presence on the ground at the river basin level.

The Committee on Restructuring CWC and CGWB has proposed that a National Water Commission be created that unifies these two apex bodies. Both the CWC and the CGWB have useful and formidable capabilities for water resource exploration, assessment and monitoring, and planning of infrastructure projects; these must be preserved, nurtured and built upon. These capabilities are no doubt important even today and will remain so in future too. However, technologies available today are so advanced that these tasks can be performed better and in a more cost-effective manner than is being done now. The need of the hour is to enhance significantly the effectiveness of assessment, monitoring and planning capabilities and their effective deployment.

The CGWB grew out of a small organization with a narrow, specific purpose, viz., drill exploration wells to assess groundwater resource. The CWC even today views itself as 'an apex *technical* organisation in the field of water resources development'. Neither agency ever viewed itself as a water governance organization.

In the new water resource governance scenario facing the country, we need to envisage a high level central organization that is forward looking, strategic, agile and transdisciplinary in its skill set. This has to be conceived of as an action organization rather than merely an assessment and monitoring organization, although these too will remain aspects of its mandate.

It is true that all the action in the water sector lies with the state governments. Yet a well-designed central organization can deploy and use funds as well as scientific and knowledge resources to influence and support what states do in water governance. This organization should have a compact leadership with a broad range of expertise related to water. Moreover, it has to have a culture of cross-disciplinary teamwork rather than different disciplines operating in silos. The need of the hour is a new organizational culture, new skill-mix and new operating style.

Both the CWC and the CGWB are weighed down by their highly specialized but narrow-based skill-structure. These are massive organizations using up huge resources and energies in managing themselves. Their functioning is also mired in a highly dysfunctional organization culture. There is literally a quagmire of hundreds of different designations, which has nightmarish consequences for framing recruitment rules, career progression ladder, promotions, seniority, pay scales etc.[7] All these limitations constrain the capacity of these agencies to rise to meet major new challenges facing India's water economy. The larger water governance challenge requires a new-age, modern, agile and compact apex organization that is untrammelled by the burden of the irksome internal management complexities of these unwieldy bureaucracies.

What is more, the organization needs to view both groundwater and surface water in an integrated, holistic manner. The CWC and the CGWB cannot continue to work in their current independent, isolated fashion. The one issue that brings out the need to unify the two bodies more than any other is the drying up of India's rivers. The single most important factor explaining the drying up of post-monsoon flows in India's peninsular rivers is the over-extraction of groundwater. The drying up of base flows of groundwater has converted so many of our 'gaining' rivers into 'losing' rivers. If river rejuvenation is indeed the key national mandate assigned to the Ministry of Water Resources, then this cannot be done without hydrologists and hydrogeologists working together, along with social scientists, agronomists and other stakeholders.

Both the CWC and the CGWB are lacking in the capacities essential for them to respond to the needs of the water sector in 21st-century India. Civil engineers (the main discipline overwhelmingly present in the CWC) and hydrogeologists (the main discipline in the CGWB) are crucial for effective water management. But they cannot be expected to shoulder the entire burden of the new mandate alone. There is an acute lack of professionals from a large number of disciplines, without which these bodies will continue to under-perform. These disciplines include, most importantly, the social sciences and management, without which we cannot expect programmes such as Participatory Irrigation Management and Participatory Groundwater Management to succeed; Agronomy, without which crop water budgeting cannot happen and water use efficiency will not improve; Ecological Economics, without which we will not gain an accurate understanding of the value of ecosystem services, which need to be protected in river systems; and River Ecology, which is essential to the central mandate of river rejuvenation.

It is therefore imperative that:

1 a brand new National Water Commission (NWC) be established as the nation's apex facilitation organization dealing with water policy, data and governance;
2 the NWC be an adjunct office of the Ministry of Water Resources, River Development and Ganga Rejuvenation, functioning with both full autonomy and requisite accountability;
3 the NWC be headed by a Chief National Water Commissioner, a senior administrator with a stable tenure and a strong background in public and development administration, and it should have full-time Commissioners representing Hydrology (present Chair, CWC), Hydrogeology (present Chair, CGWB), Hydrometeorology, River Ecology, Ecological Economics, Agronomy (with focus on soil and water), and Participatory Resource Planning & Management;
4 the NWC have strong regional presence in all the major river basins of India; and
5 the NWC build, institutionalize and appropriately manage an architecture of partnerships with knowledge institutions and practitioners in the water space, in areas where in-house expertise may be lacking.

The key mandate and functions that the National Water Commission needs to pursue has the following building blocks:

1 enable and incentivize state governments to implement all irrigation projects in reform mode, with an over-arching goal of *har khet ko paani* (water for every field), and improved water resource management and water use efficiency, not just construction of large-scale reservoirs, as the main objective;
2 lead the national aquifer mapping and groundwater management programme;
3 insulate the agrarian economy and livelihood system from pernicious impacts of drought, flood and climate change, and move towards sustainable water security;
4 develop a nation-wide, location-specific programme for rejuvenation of India's rivers to effectively implement the triple mandate of *nirmal dhara*, *aviral dhara*, *swachh kinara*;
5 create an effective promotional and regulatory mechanism that finds the right balance between the needs of development and environment, protecting ecological integrity of the nation's rivers, lakes, wetlands and aquifers, as well as coastal systems;

6 promote cost-effective programmes for appropriate treatment, recycling and reuse of urban and industrial wastewater;
7 develop and implement practical programmes for controlling point and non-point pollution of water bodies, the wetlands and aquifer systems;
8 create a transparent, accessible and user-friendly system of data management on water that citizens can fruitfully use while devising solutions to their water problems;
9 operate as a world-class knowledge institution available, on demand, for advice to the state governments and other stakeholders, including appraisal of projects, dam safety, inter-state and international issues relating to water; and
10 create world-class institutions for broad-based capacity building of water professionals and knowledge management in water.

## New paradigm of water governance in India: features, principles, dimensions

From the above discussion, we get a clear idea of the fundamental change we need to effect in the paradigm of water governance in India, if we are to meet the challenge of sustainable and equitable access to water and livelihood security for the Indian people. The new paradigm would need to have the following features, principles and dimensions:

1 **Weaving our Interventions into the Contours of Nature:** Rather than command-and-control, our attempt needs to be to fully appreciated and apprehend the enormous diversity that characterizes this nation and plan our interventions in full cognizance and understanding of this diversity, making them as location-specific as possible, to avoid the pitfalls of indiscriminate centralized planning. Watersheds, aquifers and river systems would be the cornerstones of such planning.
2 **Governance Based on Partnerships:** Rather than making governance the sole responsibility of governments, we need to craft a carefully designed architecture of partnerships, where all primary stakeholders get deeply involved in the collective endeavour of participatory water governance.
3 **Multi-disciplinarity:** We must acknowledge that we cannot understand water other than in a deeply multi-disciplinary perspective. This involves not just engineering and hydrogeology but also river ecology, agronomy, soil science, the various social sciences and management, among others.

4 **Multi-dimensionality**: We must adopt the perspective proposed in the current draft of the National Water Framework Law, which states that:

> water is the common heritage of the people of India; is essential for the sustenance of life in all its forms; an integral part of the ecological system, sustaining and being sustained by it; a basic requirement for livelihoods; a cleaning agent; a necessary input for economic activity such as agriculture, industry and commerce; a means of transportation; a means of recreation; an inseparable part of a people's landscape, society, history and culture; and in many cultures, a sacred substance, being venerated in some as a divinity (MoWR 2016).

5 **Breaking the Silos**: The proposed NWC will hopefully help in our being able to take an integrated view of water, so that the current hydroschizophrenia can be overcome, ensuring protection of watersheds, river systems and endangered aquifers.
6 **Demand Management and Sustainability as a Central Focus**: Rather than seeking to endlessly augment supplies of water, the focus must shift to effectively managing demand so that we recognize the finite nature of the resource and that sustainable use will be impossible without this shift. The supply-side thrust is a vicious infinite regress with no end in sight other than depletion of quantity and quality.
7 **Emphasis on Equity in Access to Water**: We need to centrally emphasize the imperative to end discrimination in access to water on grounds of caste, class, gender, location and community, as underlined in the National Water Framework Law.
8 **Transparency and Easy Access to Water Information**: The issue here is not just transparent access to information but also availability of information in a manner and form that is useful to and useable by primary stakeholders. The aim must be to proactively proffer water solutions to problems people face.
9 **National Water Framework Law**: The Draft NWFL provides an essential corrective to British Common law by building upon the Public Trust Doctrine enunciated by the Supreme Court, whereby the state at all levels holds natural resources in trust for the community. This would ensure that no one's use of water would be able to deprive anyone of their right to water for life as defined under the NWFL.

## Concluding remarks

It is our considered view that only through this comprehensive shift in the paradigm of water governance in India can we come to grips with and find sustainable and equitable solutions to the grave crisis of water facing the country. This is the kind of reform, reflecting the specificities of the water sector, that we require, rather than a blind adherence to the agenda embodied in the Washington Consensus. Only through this kind of detailed and comprehensive exercise in each sectoral context, can we begin to get a grip on the real reforms India needs, to solve the emerging challenges of the 21st century. It is, therefore, not simply a matter of privatization, liberalization and globalization. That is a lazy dogma that we must decisively reject, while carefully considering the requirements of change in each sector of the economy.

## Notes

1 See *Beyond the Anthropocene,* a talk by one of the world's leading climate scientists, Johan Rockström (www.stockholmresilience.org/research/research-news/2017-02-16-wef-2017-beyond-the-anthropocene.html, accessed on 28 May 2018).
2 This section is heavily drawn from the Twelfth Plan chapter on Water (Planning Commission 2012).
3 *Report of the Committee on Restructuring* CWC *and* CGWB that I handed over to the Government of India in July 2016 (Shah *et al.* 2016).
4 *Report of the Committee on Restructuring* CWC *and* CGWB that I handed over to the Government of India in July 2016 (Shah *et al.* 2016).
5 'Hard rock' is a generic term applied to igneous and metamorphic rocks with aquifers of low primary inter-granular porosity (e.g., granites, basalts, gneisses and schists).
6 This section draws upon the *Report of the Committee on Restructuring CWC and CGWB* that I handed over to the Government of India in July 2016 (Shah *et al.* 2016).
7 For example, the CGWB has as many as 125 different designations (Scientific: 71, Engineering: 20, Ministerial/Administrative: 34). Rampant increase in court cases and representations related to seniority, promotions, etc. bear testimony to the fact that there is a link between number of designations and court cases/representations.

## References

Ackerman, R. 2011. 'New Directions for Water Management in Indian Agriculture', *Global Journal of Market Economics*, 4(2): 227–288. https://doi.org/10.1177/097491011200400205 (accessed on 28 May 2018).

Amarasinghe, U. A., Tushaar Shah, Hugh Turral, and B. K. Anand. 2007. 'India's Water Future to 2025–2050: Business-as-usual Scenario and Deviations', IWMI.

Blackmore, D. 2010. *River Basin Management: Opportunities and Risks.* Manila, Philippines: Asian Development Bank.

Briscoe, J. and R. P. S. Malik. 2006. *India's Water Economy: Bracing for a Turbulent Future*. Washington, DC: The World Bank.

Ghosh, Subimal, H. Vittal, Tarul Sharma, Subhankar Karmakar, K. S. Kasiviswanathan, Y. Dhanesh, K. P. Sudheer, and S. S. Gunthe. 2016. 'Indian Summer Monsoon Rainfall: Implications of Contrasting Trends in the Spatial Variability of Means and Extremes', *PLOS*. https://doi.org/10.1371/journal.pone.0158670

Goswami, D. C. and P. J. Das. 2002. 'Hydrological Impact of Earthquakes on the Brahmaputra River Regime', Proceedings of the 18th National Convention of Civil Engineers, Guwahati.

Jarvis, Todd, Mark Giordano, Shammy Puri, Kyoko Matsumoto, and Aaron Wol. 2005. 'International Borders, Ground Water Flow and Hydroschizophrenia', *Ground Water*, 43(5).

Llamas, R. and P. Martinez-Santos. 2005. 'Intensive Groundwater Use: Silent Revolution and Potential Source of Water Conflicts', *American Society of Civil Engineers Journal of Water Resources Planning and Management*, 131(4).

Kerr, R. A. and R. Stone. 2009. 'A Human Trigger for the Great Quake of Sichuan?' *Science*, 323(5912), 16 January.

Krishnan, S. 2009. 'The Silently Accepted Menace of Disease Burden from Drinking Water Quality Problems', Submission to the Planning Commission.

Menon, M., Neeraj Vagholikar, Kanchi Kohli, and Ashish Fernandes. 2003. 'Large Dams in the Northeast: A Bright Future?' *The Ecologist Asia*, 11(1).

Ministry of Water Resources (MoWR). 2016. *National Water Framework Law*. Government of India (GoI).

Myers, N., Russell A. Mittermeier, Cristina G. Mittermeier, Gustavo A. B. da Fonseca, and Jennifer Kent. 2000. 'Biodiversity Hotspots for Conservation Priorities', *Nature*, 403.

Rajamani, V., U. C. Mohanty, R. Ramesh, G. S. Bhat, P. N. Vinayachandran, D. Sengupta, Prasanna Kumar, and R. K. Kolli. 2006. 'Linking Indian Rivers vs Bay of Bengal Monsoon Activity', *Current Science*, 90: 12–13.

Rodell, M., I. Velicogna and J. S. Famiglietti. 2009. 'Satellite-based Estimates of Groundwater Depletion in India', *Nature*, doi:10.1038/nature08238.

Planning Commission. 2012. *Twelfth Five Year Plan*. Government of India (GoI).

Pomeranz, K. 2009. 'The Great Himalayan Watershed: Agrarian Crisis, Mega-Dams and the Environment', *New Left Review*, 58: 5–39, July–August 2009.

Shah, Mihir. 2013. 'Water: Towards a Paradigm Shift in the 12th Plan', *Economic and Political Weekly*, 19 January.

Shah, Mihir. 2015. 'Push Irrigation, Not Dams', *Indian Express*, 14 August.

Shah, Mihir and Himanshu Kulkarni. 2015. 'Urban Water Systems in India', *Economic and Political Weekly*, 25 July.

Shah, Mihir et al. 2016. 'Report of the Committee on Restructuring CWC and CGWB', Submitted to the Ministry of Water Resources, Government of India (GoI).

Susheela, A. K. 2001. *A Treatise on Fluorosis*. New Delhi: Fluorosis Research and Rural Development Foundation.

Valdiya, K. S. 1999. 'A Geodynamic Perspective of Arunachal Pradesh', Keynote Address at Workshop organised by the GB Pant Institute of Himalayan Environment and Development.

Venot, J. P., Hugh Turral, Madar Samad, and François Molle. 2007. 'Shifting Waterscapes: Explaining Basin Closure in the Lower Krishna Basin', IWMI.

WHO. 2002. 'An Overview: Gaps in Health Research on Arsenic Poisoning', 27th Session of WHO South-East Asia Advisory Committee on Health Research, 15–18 April, Dhaka, Bangladesh.

# Contributors

**Late Latha Anantha,** was the Founder Director of River Research Centre based in Kerala. She held a Doctorate in Agriculture. She started her involvement in environmental conservation in the early 1990s through nature education activities in Kerala, which later evolved into research and information-based campaigns amongst communities, community driven river basin management and environmental flows of rivers. She played a key role in policy formulation and legal enactments related to river basin management, water and sand mining in Kerala. She was selected as an Ashoka Fellow in 2012. She was the South Asia Advisory Board Member of International Rivers, and contributed many papers and articles on environmental flows, rivers and river basin management and Western Ghats conservation.

**Neha Bhadbhade** is working as a research associate at SOPPECOM, Pune. She completed her PhD degree in Biosytems and Agricultural Engineering from the Oklahoma State University, USA in 2014. Her research interests include hydrology, environmental flows, river basin management and low impact development.

**Biksham Gujja** was head of Freshwater program of WWF-International (1993–2010). He also worked with ICRISAT and Deccan development society. He has established AgSri to promote productivity of water. AgSri is working with farmers in India and Africa. Gujja has a PhD from Jawaharlal Nehru University, Delhi.

**S. Janakarajan,** Former Professor at Madras Institute of Development Studies (MIDS), is currently the President of South Asia Consortium for Interdisciplinary Water Resources Studies, Hyderabad. Professor Janakarajan, basically an economist, obtained his Master's degree from Madras Christian College and PhD from MIDS

(Madras University). Janakarajan has been working on water, ecology and environment-related issues for over three decades. His current interests are urban water, climate change, delta vulnerability and food security and transboundary water disputes.

**K. J. Joy** is a founder member of Society for Promoting Participative Ecosystem Management (SOPPECOM) and also coordinates the activities of Forum for Policy Dialogue on Water Conflicts in India. He has been an activist-researcher for more than 30 years and his areas of interest include drought, institutions, participatory irrigation management, river-basin management, multi-stakeholder processes, water conflicts, water ethics and people's movements. He has published extensively on water-environment-development issues including the two co-edited books: *Water Conflicts in India: A Million Revolts in the Making* (2008) and *Alternative Futures: India Unshackled* (2017).

**Sumi Krishna** is an independent feminist scholar and former President of the Indian Association for Women's Studies. She has over 40 years of experience in gender, environment and development encompassing biodiversity, natural resource management, people's movements and livelihood issues; and has advised universities and institutions on integrating science and social science curricula and methodologies. She is a widely published author and is based in Bengaluru.

**Himanshu Kulkarni** leads ACWADAM, a not-for-profit knowledge institution and think-tank on India's groundwater. He is a hydrogeologist by qualification and has been working on aquifers and groundwater across India's diverse groundwater typology for more than 30 years. ACWADAM has partnered with a variety of organizations on piloting and mainstreaming the ideas of participatory groundwater management and springshed development across India, neighbouring Nepal and Bhutan. It has just begun work in North Africa.

**Seema Kulkarni** is one of the founding members of Society for Promoting Participative Ecosystem Management, Pune (SOPPECOM). She is presently in SOPPECOM, Pune and coordinating the gender and rural livelihoods activities within the organization. She has coordinated various studies and programmes around decentralization, gender and land, water and sanitation. She is currently the National Facilitation Team member of Mahila Kisan Adhikar Manch (MAKAAM).

**Kuntala Lahiri-Dutt** is Professor of The Australian National University (ANU). In ANU, she is based at the Crawford School of Public Policy. Kuntala has led research on precarious livelihoods in environmental resource dependent communities. On water/rivers, her publications include *Dancing with the River: People and Lives on the Chars in South Asia* (co-authored, 2013); *Water First: Issues and Challenges for Nations and Communities* (co-edited, 2008) and *Fluid Bonds: Views on Gender and Water* (edited, Stree, 2006). More about Kuntala's work is on her staff page: https://crawford.anu.edu.au/people/academic/kuntala-lahiri-dutt.

**Sharachchandra Lele** is Distinguished Fellow in Environmental Policy and Governance at the Centre for Environment and Development in ATREE, Bengaluru. He is an interdisciplinary environmental researcher, bridging the natural sciences, economics and political science to understand the concepts of and pathways to environmentally sustainable and socially just development. He works on sustainable forest management and forest governance, urban water management, water governance and pollution regulation.

**Sunita Narain** is an environmentalist and writer, and presently serves as the Director General of Centre for Science and Environment (CSE) and Editor of the fortnightly magazine, *Down To Earth*. She plays an active role in policy formulation on issues of environment and development in India and globally. She has co-authored influential publications on India's environment, conducted in-depth research on the governance and management of the country's environment and directed campaigns on air pollution control, community water management, sustainable industrialization and food and toxins, among others. In 2016, she was featured in *Time magazine*'s list of 100 Most Influential People in the World.

**N. C. Narayanan** is Professor at the Centre for Technology Alternatives for Rural Areas (CTARA), IIT Bombay. He has a PhD in Development Studies from the International Institute of Social Studies, Netherlands. In the past he was the Executive Director at SaciWATERs, Hyderabad and his research was mostly on the issues of water policy, governance and conflicts. His research interest lies in water policy and governance, development theory, transdisciplinary research, scaling up decentralized PV solutions and political ecology.

**Narendar Pani** is Professor at the National Institute of Advanced Studies, Bengaluru. He is also Adjunct Faculty at the Indian Institute of

Science. An economist by training, he has worked in both academic and media institutions, including Indian Institute of Management, Bengaluru and The Economic Times. He has, over the last three and a half decades, written extensively, in both academia and the media, on a variety of subjects including water issues. His books include 'Inclusive Economics: Gandhian Method and Contemporary Policy'.

**Neelam Rana** is a doctoral candidate at Indian Institute of Technology-Bombay (Mumbai, India). Her research interests include governance and public policy processes. As part of her PhD work she is attempting to understand stability of centralized wastewater management approach, a socio-technical regime, in the Indian context. Prior to IIT Bombay, she was working for a reputed NGO in New Delhi on issues pertaining to state of the environment reporting, green economy, climate change vulnerability and resilience assessment and public policy.

**Abraham Samuel** has completed his M. Phil in Sociology from JNU and is associated with the water sector for the last two decades. He worked with a large number of organizations and people's movements engaged with water sector issues. Currently he is a freelance researcher and consultant especially on watershed-based development and rural livelihoods. He is also closely associated with SOPPECOM, Pune and Forum for Policy Dialogue on Water conflicts in India. He has to his credit a number of publications in Journals and books. Currently he is based in Pune, Maharashtra.

**Mihir Shah** has spent three decades living and working in central tribal India as part of Samaj Pragati Sahayog, which is one of India's largest grass-roots initiatives for water and livelihood security. From 2009 to 2014, he was a member of the Planning Commission, and was chiefly responsible for the paradigm shift in water enunciated in the 12th Plan. He is Distinguished Visiting Professor, Shiv Nadar University and Visiting Professor of Political Economy at Ashoka University.

**Tushaar Shah**, an economist and public policy specialist, is a former director of the Institute of Rural Management at Anand, India. Since 2000, Shah has been working with Colombo-based International Water Management Institute (IWMI) and has been leading IWMI-Tata Water Policy Program (ITP) which applies design thinking approaches to water-energy problems. Shah has served on several high level committees of Ministry of Water Resources, Government of India and the erstwhile Planning Commission.

**Hajara Shaik** is a trained Sociologist and an Independent Consultant on water technology and issues of socio-economic development. She has written articles on water and social issues and she is a resident of Switzerland.

**Veena Srinivasan** is a fellow at the Ashoka Trust for Research in Ecology and the Environment (ATREE), Bangalore, where she leads the Water, Land and Society Programme. Veena's research interests include water allocation, conflict transformation, impacts of multiple stressors on water security, ground and surface water linkages, low-cost sensing and citizen science, and sustainable water management policy and practice.

**Himanshu Thakkar**, graduate engineer from Indian Institute of Technology (Mumbai), is coordinator of South Asia Network on Dams, Rivers and People (https://sandrp.in/). He has been involved in water-related issues of India for over 25 years and has in the past been associated with the work of the World Commission on Dams, Narmada Bachao Andolan and Centre for Science and Environment.

**A. Vaidyanathan** is a well-known scholar and has contributed significantly to the discourse on the water sector in India. A former member of the Planning Commission of India, he has also headed various governmental committees including the Irrigation Pricing Committee set up by the Government of India in early 1990s.

**P. S. Vijayshankar** is a founder member of Samaj Pragati Sahayog (SPS), an NGO based in Dewas district of Madhya Pradesh. He received his M. Phil from Jawaharlal Nehru University, New Delhi. He has lived and worked among the tribal communities of the Narmada valley for over 25 years. He has co-authored the book, *India's Drylands: Tribal Societies and Development through Environmental Regeneration* (OUP, 1998) and edited the book, *Water: Growing Understanding, Emerging Perspectives* (Orient Blackswan, 2016). He has been a Visiting Scholar at the Centre for Advanced Study of India (CASI), University of Pennsylvania, Philadelphia, USA, in February–March 2011.

**Subodh Wagle** is Professor at Centre for Technology Alternative for Rural Areas at Indian Institute of Technology Bombay, India. He has helped establish PRAYAS, an independent policy analysis and advocacy group working in the energy, electricity, water, development and environment sectors. He discharged various responsibilities at PRAYAS between 1997 and 2006, including as a 'Core Team Member' of the 'Energy Group' and the 'Group Coordinator' of the 'Resources and Livelihoods Group' of PRAYAS. He has been a Trustee of PRAYAS since 1995. Between 2006 and 2014, he was an Adjunct Professor in CTARA (IIT Bombay), where he helped design and initiate the Master's program in Technology and Development. Dr. Wagle was a Professor at Tata Institute of Social Science (TISS) between 2007 and 2014. At TISS, as the Founding Dean, he established the School of Habitat Studies and headed the Center for Water Policy, Governance and Regulation. From June 2015 to November 2016, he was a Visiting Faculty at the Center for Energy and Environmental Policy, University of Delaware, USA. He has served on various government committees and institutions and has led many international research collaborations.

**Sachin Warghade,** Assistant Professor, Tata Institute of Social Sciences (Mumbai), teaches courses related to regulatory policy and instruments. He is a visiting faculty for the Masters programme on Public Policy at the National Law School of India University, Bangalore. He specializes in regulatory policy with focus on public utility regulation. He contributed as a member in the Planning Commission's XIIth Plan sub-group for development of 'Model Bill for State Water Regulatory System'. He was awarded a Doctoral Fulbright Fellowship at the Washington University in St. Louis in 2011–2012.

# Index

For Product Safety Concerns and Information please contact our EU representative GPSR@taylorandfrancis.com Taylor & Francis Verlag GmbH, Kaufingerstraße 24, 80331 München, Germany